MW00605373

HERE I AM
An Unconventional Life

By Jeff Podgurski

Edited by Pauline Adamek
Published by Jeff Podgurski

Copyright Page "Here I Am: An Unconventional Life."

Copyright © 2013 Jeff Podgurski
All rights reserved. This book or any portion thereof may not be
reproduced or used in any manner whatsoever without the express
written permission from the publisher except for the use of brief quo-
tations in a book review.

Story by Jeff Podgurski

Cover and Layout by Ashley Revell
Printed in the United States of America
First Printing, 2013

ISBN 978-0-9893444-2-5

Contents

For more photographs, visit Jeff's flickr gallery.

Prologue

They entered the house with a vengeance, barreling through the windows, tearing down the sheets that were hanging as curtains. They barged into the kitchen and wiped out the kitchen table with everything on it. They slammed me against the wall, and then Mush-Melon took the pistol and pressed the barrel into my forehead so hard and so suddenly, it made my neck snap backwards. It felt like whiplash.

With the gun's hammer jacked back, I had this swamp rat telling me to get out. "Get the fuck out of the house, I mean *now*, cocksucker, or I'll dump your brains all over the floor!"

I backed out through the screen door, tripped and fell down the front steps of the porch. I remember thinking on the way down: this could be it, they might stomp me to death if I stay on the ground. By the time I hit the dirt, I bounced to my feet. But I'd barely got up when the beating continued, blows raining down on my head. I got struck from behind and when I fell forward, it was straight into the guy with the revolver, who hauled off and pistol-whipped me. CRACK.

This may not be the best place to start my story, so let me take you back to the beginning...

I was born a poor Polish child...

PART ONE

Chapter One
A Poor Start

Bam! *Here I am*: November 5, 1954, 11:20 p.m., eight pounds and eleven ounces, nineteen and three-quarters inches long… *Ouch!* (Sorry Mom. Like trying to push a tennis ball through a garden hose.)

"Jeffery Podgurski," no middle name. Mom thought the name was long enough. The son of Edward Joseph and Shirley Anne Podgurski, I was coming into this world with all the hope, potential and optimism of any new child, well, at least speaking on my behalf. But then again, what the hell did I know? I had just gotten here, and the lights just came on.

It was a typical freezing November night in Baltimore, raining ice and sleet outside. That should've been an omen. It would be the first and last time my father would ever lay eyes on me. Hey—*I'm kidding!* I didn't have a clue what the weather was like outside, and it felt like I'd just come out of a drug-induced coma. It would take at least a year before I was alert enough to have some type of conscious memory, and by that time my mother was dating a man by the name of Jim Ward who would turn out to be my stepfather. Within two swift years I would have a half sister, born in September of '56. She'd turn out to be… well… if you've got nothing to good to say about someone, don't say anything. When my mother first started seeing my stepfather, he wasn't a bad guy at all. But as time went on and their family grew, he had nothing but a negative influence on my brother and I. More on *that* moron later…

Ah, my brother Frank Podgurski. A year-and-a-half older than me, born in 1952, he was an old soul, and more responsible. He would turn out to be one of my best friends. One of my fondest memories as a toddler was of my mother's parents, Veronica and Ed Strauss, who rented a home on an island in the Chesapeake Bay. To get to their home you had to cross a single-lane wooden bridge where you would arrive at a two-story house. My grandparents rented the second floor, and the people who owned the home, as well as the island, lived on the first. Searching back, in a two-and-a-half year old's mind, I esti-mate the property being one acre. It felt vast and spacious. There was a wooden dock down at the front of the property, with rowboats tied to it. Behind the home was a two-foot sea wall, with a sandy beach beyond that.

I remember my grandfather, who we called "Pop," rowing out into the icy water one fall, ice hatchet in hand, to rescue a swan that had be-come stuck in the ice. I remember in the summer, when we weren't be-ing chased by Pop's new dog—a boxer—that we were allowed to play in the water off the golden sandy beach out back, but we were constantly warned to keep away from the front because "The Devil lurked in the lake under the dock." Of course, realizing now, there was a steep drop off in the lake in front of the house, so this was a necessary deterrent for two little rambunctious kids. Hey, we were only two or three years old; we couldn't swim.

At this point, if my brother or I could've read, we might've seen the writing on the wall. My new half-sister was the star of the family. Not just because she was a newborn and a pretty little girl with dimples, but also because she was the first born child of Jim Ward, who was the youngest in the Ward family.

Speaking of my stepfather's family, the Wards were Southerners from Virginia. Grandma Ward was warm and wonderful and the best southern cook in the world. Her chicken and dumplings were second to none. But on the other hand, Grandpa Ward could've given Stephen King a run for his money. This guy was into psychological torture.

He derived great pleasure from luring my brother and I over to his lap. Whereas we were infants, we forgot what happened the last time we sat on Grandpa Ward's lap. He'd set Frank and I up like bowling pins and proceed to knock us down. Once we were in his lap, his favorite torture would ensue. With a lightning move, he would attach clothes-pins to our earlobes, our nose, our lips, and our eyelids. Before we could scramble away, these elements of torture would be attached to

10

our tiny little fingers, and clamped to our hair. Anywhere that caused great irritation, and borderline pain.

Then, about the time the sheer terror of that experience would wear off, he would call us over again, and tell us he wanted to show us something. But we weren't dumb enough to get back in his lap. But what he had was a foot-long stick with a clothespin attached to it, and a notch at the end of it. At about the time your infant mind thought, "Gee, what is that?" you'd find out real quick it was a homemade rubber-band gun. So now you would spend the next twenty minutes in Hell being chased around by this old geezer having the bejeezus stung out of you by Dr. Frankenstein's homemade hick contraption.

I don't believe for a second that my brother and I were his only two targets. He was way too good a shot. He could beam in and hit you from across the room, right behind your tender two-year-old ear. And as if this house of horror wasn't enough, about an hour later when your infant mind had forgotten that you shouldn't be around this sadistic senior without a bodyguard, he would invite Frank and I out into the backyard where he kept livestock, mainly chickens.

He would leave us for fifteen minutes to get comfortable with the animals. Then he would then go into chicken coop and grab one unsuspecting bird off of death row, bring it outside for us to pet and then abruptly cut its head off with an axe. Immediately he would let it go, so it would race around the yard minus its head and squirting blood everywhere. (Hence the saying, 'running around like a chicken with its head cut off.') Hell, I didn't know where chicken and dumplings came from, but this was a horrific way to find out.

Once the chicken finally collapsed, it was up to Grandma Ward to pluck it, clean it and throw it in a pot. But he wasn't done with us yet. No sooner had we had stopped shrieking in terror at the bloody pantomime and death throes, there was more fun to come. He would go back into the chicken coop, coming out with the rooster held upside-down by its legs, flapping and squawking in fury, and deliberately pissing off the alpha-male of the coop. He would then leisurely stroll back up onto the porch, turn around and toss the tormented bird at us, only to step inside the back door of the home and lock us out.

Fleeing the irate and vicious rooster as fast as our little legs could go, Frank and I would finally figure out, after a couple hundred laps around the back yard, that the safest place to be was on top of the chicken coop. There we sat for what seemed to be hours, with a bird's eye view of the back door, where we could see 'Edgar Allan' Ward and his son, Jim, laughing at us. So *here I am*, aged three, stuck on top of a chicken coop, with one pissed off rooster parading menacingly beneath us, while 'Edgar Allan' and his offspring have a good laugh sipping tea and whiskey. Well there you have it, medieval torture games at 'Edgar Allan' Ward's.

Then one evening, my mother's parents, Veronica and Ed Strauss, stopped by to tell us they had made the decision to relocate from Baltimore to Florida. What did I know? This didn't sound like a good idea. For me, my grandparents move to Florida sounded like they were moving to a faraway foreign country. Next thing I knew they were gone, and I had broken heart. I loved my grandparents, so I must have pestered my mother every day, "When is Gram and Pop coming back?" And I got the same response every day: "Go play with your brother, you sound like a broken record."

A short time later, something occurred that seemed to be a miracle. I got up in the middle of the night to use the bathroom and overheard my mother and stepfather in the kitchen discussing the possibility of moving to Florida. *Hallelujah!* I shook my brother Frank awake and excitedly informed him, Gram and Pop weren't coming back, but we were moving south to be close to them. I don't really remember all the effort and organization it took to move, but I do remember standing on the station platform, waiting to board the train with my brother, each of us wearing matching Perry Como shirts that my mother's parents had bought us to wear on the trip. I remember how excited I was looking out the window watching the countryside passing us by over a couple of days. In retrospect, I think that long train ride is what hooked me on adventure. And to this day, when I hear faint whistle of a train, it seems to soothe me of all pain.

That train ride left a lasting impression on me. I was not only going to see the two people I cherished most, but I would also celebrate a birthday. I turned five on our journey to Florida. I have a vivid memory as a toddler of looking out the train window at the Florida countryside—also known as the swampland—and spotting a flamingo. Pink birds—who in the hell thought *that* up? When we got to the West Palm Beach train station, my grandparents were waiting for us. Stepping off the train, we were all dressed for thirty-seven degree weather, which it had been back in Baltimore. *But we weren't in Baltimore anymore, Dorothy!*

Florida in November—eighty-three degrees with 100% humidity. *Welcome to the Sunshine State!* I remember my stepfather standing on the train platform, looking around and seeing all the sand and making a wisecrack; he thought we'd arrived in the Sahara Desert. As soon as all the hugs and kisses were over, we all crammed into Pop's car, an early fifties convertible Cadillac, and headed south to Lake Worth. For our first residency, Gram and Pop got us a small apartment on the south end of Lake Worth bordering Lantana, right off the Dixie highway.

So, *here I am* in Florida, my home for the next twenty years. My brother would begin the first grade here, and I would have to wait another year for that turbulent experience. By the time I get to the sixth grade, my brother and I will have attended five or six different grade schools. In the future, people will find it hard to believe that I was once a professional fighter. But my destiny was set before I even knew it. Little boys, unlike little girls, are tested from the first day they enter a new school. Being involved in a variety of different schools, that same scenario would constantly be played out. The first couple of days I would befriend some nice kids, who would be considered nerds or geeks by today's standards. And as if entering a new neighborhood and school wasn't hard enough, we had a last name that more than stood out. "Podgurski." No one could pronounce it, and even I could barely spell it until I got into the fourth grade. Being burdened with this embarrassing last name—plus sporting a buzz cut hairstyle that my stepfather insisted on during the days of Elvis, The Beatles and mop tops—was more than enough to earn ridicule. And oh yeah, did I mention my poor brother had to grow into his enormous ears? Of course, all these quirks provided legitimate reasons for any red-blooded redneck kids to have issues with. At each new school, it only took one or two kids to have a bad encounter of the worst kind with me for the whole school to figure out I wasn't gonna be their whipping-boy. Oh, quite the contrary. On the other hand, my poor brother was a far mellower soul. Frank was just a sweet kid who couldn't bring himself to hurt anybody. But I had more of my mother's fiery temperament and personality. Once assaulted, I was someone to be reckoned with. With the temperament of a Scots-Irishman and the determination of a German Jew, topped off with the stubbornness of a Pollack, I refused to yield.

At first I just defended my brother and I, but once those boundaries

13

were established I couldn't stand to see my friends brutalized either. So I would stand up for them as well. So *here I am* in the principal's office, getting my ass paddled for about the tenth time that month. Did I mention it was the 60s, and they still embraced corporal punishment? They sent me home with a note to my mother, whereupon she would promptly hand me my ass, delivering a tirade throughout the beating of why I shouldn't fight in school. My brother would come home a few days later with a bloody nose and a torn shirt, after being picked on by the other kids. When Mom demanded to know if Frank had defended himself and he replied, "No," she beat his ass for not fighting back. *Houston, we have a problem!*

At this point, as if school isn't hard enough, after I get home, I have to decipher this shit? At six, seven, and eight, this is more than your little cranium can calculate. My conclusion? *The hell with it!* Why take three beatings? Defend yourself furiously, take your whacks at school, then take the beating at home? This was obviously a situation where more was *not* better. But I have to admit, I got pretty good at picking and choosing my battles, and I developed some pretty thick skin when it came to name-calling, and boy did we get it. It consisted of a major diet of being called 'stupid,' 'ugly,' 'Pollack' and 'dummy.' Then there was that one descriptive term back in the 60s no little boy wanted to be affiliated with: 'queer.' I could never figure out if they really thought we were homosexuals or if they just thought we were odd, but all that was pretty irrelevant.

Passing down the school hallway, if I heard someone say 'dumbo' I would look back just in time to see someone flick my brother behind the ear. That's all it took for me to go berserk. In the spirit of a kamikaze pilot, it didn't seem to matter how many bullies there were. Two, three, or four—I would still tear into them like a tornado. Looking back on my grade school years, there were two specific fights that stand out in my mind.

A couple of blocks away from my grandparents' 10th Avenue and K Street home was North Grade Elementary school, where my brother and I spent our first school years. This was because my grandparents, Gram and Pop, were gracious enough to take in Frank and me. My parents simply couldn't afford to keep us all; Frank and I had three other half-sisters by now. One Saturday while I was in the fourth grade, we went down to the schoolyard to play. We were playing baseball with some junior high kids on the elementary school baseball diamond.

14

One of the older kids offended me—what it was exactly, I don't remember—but on that day and time, I had to draw the line. Well, you don't win every battle. This older kid threw me around like a rag-doll; he knocked the snot out of me. And, although it probably wouldn't have done any good, I wish someone would've pointed out the size difference between that junior high schooler and me. But I wasn't going to quit; I just kept coming at him. After he had punched me and thrown me down three different times, for whatever reason he suddenly stopped punching me, but continued to throw me around.

Eventually, I found myself on my hands and knees trying to catch my breath. When I looked to my left I saw my grandparent's paperboy, Eddie, who lived across the street from North Grade approaching. Eddie evidently knew junior jerk-off here, so Eddie explained to my newfound foe that he delivered papers to my grandparent's house, and he knew me. Eddie explained to this jerk-off that if he didn't expect to be here all day, he'd better apologize. By this time, I was on my feet, huffing and puffing, and junior stared me up and down then demanded to know if I was ready to fight some more. When I nodded yes, he began to laugh. Then he stuck his hand out, and said, "Let's call it a draw." Because I wasn't winning, I was okay with that. God bless Eddie, he was a great guy. But I honestly think junior jerk-off was more afraid of Eddie taking up my cause than he was worried about throwing me around for the rest of the day. Eddie was cool. He was polite to my grandparents, he delivered their papers on time, and he saved my ass. *Thanks, Eddie!*

The other fight that I vividly recall happened two years earlier on a school day. Once again, I had just transferred from another elementary school. I had befriended a kid named Leslie, whose red hair and freckles made him an easy target. I watched some kid walk up to my friend Leslie, who was standing in the shade under a banyan tree. He spoke to Leslie for a moment, and then he knocked his books out his hands. Little did I know, but this was the school bully, and everyone was petrified of him. When Leslie bent over to pickup his books, this kid slapped him on the back of his head. Once Leslie gathered his things, he walked over to me choking back the tears. I tried to comfort my friend, but I wanted to know why would he take that kind of abuse? Right then, Leslie broke down and bawled. It turns out this belligerent bully had failed a grade or two and, like everyone else, Leslie was afraid of the older boy. Then I told Leslie something my mother had told me,

"The big dog might get the meal, but at least get a bite." You might get beat up, but if you get a good lick in, they might leave you alone. Pain is a great deterrent, because if you don't ever put up that struggle, there's no reason for Mr. Belligerent ever to leave you alone. This, I could tell, did not resonate in Leslie's head, because when he went back over to stand in the shade, Mr. Belligerent started to shove him around. At this point my mind was screaming, *push him back, strike him, do something, don't take it!*

At that point I couldn't take it. I went over there and I shoved him myself. He turned around wide-eyed with dismay, demanding, "Who the hell are you?" Straight out of an eight-year-old's mouth, from the 60s, I retorted, "Pick on someone your own size." I claimed, "He's my friend." He remarked that I was his size, and I was eager to agree, "So pick on me," I suggested. This was probably exactly what he wanted to hear, but I swarmed him like angry bees spewing from a beehive. He never landed a punch, but by now we had drawn the attention of the crossing guard, the principal, and the teachers. It seemed like everyone in school was watching me light this guy up. By the time the teachers had cleared the schoolhouse, every kid in the schoolyard had gotten between me and our belligerent bully, who now was lying on the ground crying his eyes out. I had inadvertently been pushed behind the banyan tree, and all the kids in the schoolyard were now trying to conceal me. When the teachers picked up our belligerent crybaby, they wanted to know whom he'd been fighting with. Since I was new to the school, he didn't have a clue, and no one was ratting me out. When they took him into the schoolhouse, I was watching from behind the banyan tree. All of a sudden I was weightless and going up into the air. At first it startled me, and then I realized where I was. Some of the kids had lifted me up on their shoulders and started prancing me around the banyan tree, while they cheered me on. Evidently, Leslie wasn't the only one being picked on. This episode would have a lasting and profound effect on me. This would be my first brush with popularity and being accepted, and even thought I didn't know it, I would spend the rest of my life trying to achieve this high once again. Even though it was just a small group of kids, I had a taste of fame. I believe that everyone and everything that breathes life on this Earth has a purpose. It's funny how destiny can give you a nudge or possibly a kick to get you started in the right direction. Even though I got away with this fight, I would be sent home dozens of time for scrapping, only to get

16

my ass handed to me by my mother when I got there. But I had experienced glory.

What I haven't confessed is that I was also something of a daredevil, and once my friends figured this out, they were constantly daring me to do what seemed impossible. Let me assure you—I was never malicious. I never tried to set the schoolhouse on fire or took a can of spray paint to a car, but when it came to my own safety I had no regards. So *here I am* standing on the roof of a two-story schoolhouse ready to jump, and not one kid is trying to talk me out of it. Quite the contrary, they are cheering me on. So with a leap of faith, I landed with a thud, and instantly a sharp pain shot through my leg. I thought I'd broken my ankle. I couldn't limp away fast enough. A teacher grabbed me by my ear, and hobbled me into the principal's office, where they promptly bent me over and paddled me for my efforts. As luck would have it my grandmother (better known as Gram) worked in the school cafeteria serving food. So it wasn't long before my latest exploit reached her ears. By the time I got home, my mother was well informed. Then it was MAHTM (my ass handed to me). At dinner that evening with Pop and Gram, my grandmother got me ice for my ankle and asked me what I was thinking. Then she demanded to know who the hell did I think I was, "Superman?" I paused for a moment, then looked her dead in the eye, and with a juvenile grin, I answered, "YEP!"

At this point I was in a vicarious position, already headed down a dangerous path. Between wanting to stick up for my friends with a sense of fairness that my grandparents had instilled in me, and trying to perform feats that no mortal or sane person can achieve, I was teetering on the edge of doom. This is where I would find acceptance from my peers, so to me it was worth the risk.

Chapter Two

As I mentioned earlier, my brother and I had attended a variety of grade schools. Jim Ward, our stepfather, always thought he had a better angle, so he was constantly uprooting his family and planting us somewhere else. I guess I can't blame him. By the early 60s, he was the sole breadwinner for two adults, five children and one on the way. Although, at this point he did have a decent trade; he was a short order cook for a famous prestigious restaurant in Miami, Wolfy's, that had just expanded to Palm Beach County. After the new baby was born he had eight mouths to feed, and with the promise of being promoted to chef, Jim Ward packed us up, and we all moved to St. Petersburg for yet another Wolfy's location. This move broke my grandparents' hearts, as well as killed my brother and my spirits. But we packed up nonetheless and moved to the west coast of Florida, to the St. Petersburg area. This was where I entered the sixth grade, and my brother Frank started junior high.

For the first time in our lives, we were now going to different schools. Now I would be a prime candidate for ridicule. At my new school, I could tell I was going to be ridiculed; I had been placed in special needs class because I was behind and lost. Imagine that! Frank and I would no longer have each other for support, which only made things more chaotic. After switching school five or six times in as many years, it was a miracle that either one of us could spell our own name. Despite the fact that I tried to keep my head low, a kid from an upper-middle class family singled me out that first week. He would stop by my desk at the beginning of class with the same insults that by now had begun to sound like a broken record. I was ugly, Polish, and stupid. He'd berate me again at the end of class, like I didn't hear him the first time. By week's end, I had decided to tell my mother what was going on at school. I wanted her point of view.

Let's just stop here for a moment, so I can give you a little insight into my mother. Shirley Anne grew up in coal mining country in a little town called West Newton, just outside of Pittsburgh. Every other day on the way home from school, Mom would get into a fist fight with the little black girls, because she had to pass through their neighborhood. She swore to my grandmother that it was those girls who start-
18

ed the fight; she was trying to finish it. Nevertheless, she would come home with skinned knees and a torn dress. And the consequences for being in a fight? My Gram would beat the tar out of her. Can you see a pattern here? Mom was also somewhat of a daredevil herself and an excellent athlete. She had been selected to be an alternate on the Olympic swim team, but because of a heart murmur she was blacklisted. She also had great form diving from a springboard. Which brings us to the story of her friends dragging her out of a river, unconscious…

My grandmother had forbidden her to go swimming in the Allegheny River, let alone dive off the local bridge. But of course she did, in spectacular fashion. And once she got home, and Gram found out, well, *can you say shellacking?* Now you'd think, all the time that Frank and I had spent around our grandparents, my mother would've figured out we might have heard some of these stories. More than once, while sitting at the kitchen table, I overheard my grandparents reminisce with my mother about some of her antics, and then laughing until tears came down their faces. Though Frank and I would laugh at the stories, I didn't get it. I was just like my mother. It confused me that she didn't understand what I was going through.

But back to Mom's response to my current dilemma. She told me to stand up, look the kid straight in the eye and tell him; if he bothered me one more time I was going to knock his teeth out. I couldn't believe my ears. You could've dropped a cantaloupe down my throat without a brush of my lips. This was the same woman who beat me unmercifully for five-and-a-half years every time I got sent home from school for fighting. I was stunned, but I did feel validated. So I went to school the next day and played it cool. I went to my special ed class, and hoped—no, I prayed—that Richie Rich would come my way, and he didn't disappoint me. He approached me right before the bell rang to start class. He pushed my paper and pencil off my desk and let it hit the floor. As he began to laugh I jumped up nose to nose and stared him dead in the eye. I told him, "This isn't a threat, it's a promise. If you mess with me one more time, I'm knocking your teeth out." Then, our teacher entered the room, the bell rang, and we were told to take our seats. While class was being conducted, I had a hard time focusing. I was hoping—no, I was praying—that this rich reject would roll up on me. Besides, if I was so stupid, what was *his* excuse for being in this class?

When the bell rang, here he came. He barely got a syllable out of his mouth when I jumped up grabbed him by the shirt, and pulled him

19

into my right fist, which caught him square in the mouth. You guessed it, tooth extraction 101. Both his front teeth sheared off, and bounced on the floor. He let out a wail, and every dog in the neighborhood chimed in on his howling. This got our teachers' undivided attention, which got me a one-way ticket to the principal's office.

So, *here I am*, once again sitting in the waiting room of a grade school's principal's office. Staring at a door, I hear a muffled conversation coming from within. A heated discussion was going on between my teacher, the principal, and the kid with the new million-dollar smile. I sat there wondering what my fate might be. Although I realized I was in a lot of trouble, I was relatively calm, because I had a plan.

The door opened, and I was told to come in. And there they stood, my teacher who was almost in tears, a bewildered principal and, oh yeah, toothless. My teacher graciously bowed out; she had to get back to a class that was stirred up like a hornet's nest, no thanks to me. The principal told me to have a seat, and then asked what would possess me to do such a thing. After I explained myself, I went on by saying my mother had actually green-lit the assault, and was, in fact, the mastermind behind the plan. And then two things happen, toothless started wailing again, and my principal almost fell out her chair. I'm sure this was the first time she had to wrap her mind around the fact that a mother would send her child to school equipped with premeditated violence on the agenda. But my principal didn't know Mom, and since Mom *had* validated my actions, I was enjoying this just a little bit. I was hoping that my mother was beginning to understand the hell my brother and I have been going through for the past six years. But back to toothless, whining and wailing like the pansy he was. He kept repeating to anyone that would listen that his smile didn't cost a penny. At first I didn't understand what he meant, and then I realized what he was trying to say. His parents had just paid to have his teeth capped, and they weren't going to be too excited about the new jack-o-lantern smile he'd just acquired.

Right then, the principal came around from her desk to calm this Richie-reject down. That's when I stood up, and told this new retainer recipient that if he came any closer, I was going to break his nose. My principal was in a state of shock; she couldn't believe her ears. This was the 60s, and children were supposed to be seen and not heard. Trust me, I had heard that line from my mother a million times. But I was serious. Why not a nose job to enhance his new dental work? My principal was brokenhearted—she was really a nice lady—but I had left her no alternative; she was going to have to give me a paddling, which I declined. Now, this was unheard of in this day and time. Again, this was the 60s and children didn't question authority. It was a perplexing situation, and so she phoned my mother.

I couldn't hear the conversation, but the way my principal turned with her back facing me, it left me with no imagination as to what was being said. By the time this poor woman hung up the phone, she seemed dizzy and looked nauseated. But one thing was sure; she didn't understand my mother's thinking. So I was sent back to class, with the stipulation that I would have detention after school. *Detention my ass!* I knew what I was doing and for the first time in my life, my mother seemed to be on my side, so I was taking full advantage of this opportunity. I strolled down the hall, with the confident air of a Fortune 500 millionaire. When I passed the cafeteria, I took a hard left, and walked right off the school campus.

Right around this time, my stepfather was starting to have an affair, although it would take a month before it came to my mom's attention. Pinellas County in St. Petersburg was a beautiful place, and my brother and I had discovered a pond about a mile and a half from where we lived. There was an island in the middle of it, which we discovered was a bird refuge. Frank and I would collect stale bread from the grocer, and then go down to feed the ducks. Then I had a bright idea. We would lure the ducks far from the water enough where I could chase down the little ducklings. Then, the next day, I would show up at school with a paper grocery bag full of little downy ducklings. The little girls at school would go ape manure. So *here I am* trading little down-covered ducklings to future debutantes in exchange for their lunch dollars. It didn't take long for this little enterprise to go bankrupt. A couple of days later, two little girls showed up and demanded their money back; it seemed their ducklings had died. But I couldn't see how this was my fault. This was a cash-with-no-money-back exchange. So guess what they did next? Yep, *here I am*, sitting in the principal's office again trying to explain my side of the deal. It would seem as though they had rules against selling pets at school. You would at least think they would have had that rule printed on a bulletin board somewhere on campus. Next thing you know I'm standing in front of my mother with yet another note from school. And from the look on her face I could tell she was beginning to not understand me at all. There was no

21

disappointment here, only a whipping with the coffee pot cord. That evening in bed, I heard my mother explaining my capitalistic endeavor to my stepfather, who started laughing hysterically until my mom joined in. *Anyone here confused? I know I am.*

For comic relief I used to take my dog, Rusty the wonder dog (a cross between Terrier and Cocker Spaniel or possibly a long-haired Dachshund), put a bonnet on him and put him in a baby stroller I had found and wheel him around the neighborhood, just to get a reaction. Some people would slow their cars down and others actually stopped to do a double take. One gentleman who was watering his lawn stopped and asked me if I was walking the dog or was the dog walking me.

At this point, it had come to my mother's attention that my stepfather was having an affair. I was young and almost oblivious to the seriousness of what was going on. Besides, I was on to my next moneymaking scheme.

I had figured out it only took one thin dime to open the newspaper vending machines, whereupon I would grab every newspaper in stock, then promptly stand in front of the automatic doors at the grocer hawking newspapers to everyone exiting the store. But like all my get rich quick schemes, not to mention my amateur criminal endeavors, it was flawed. Going into the second week, the grocery store manager had figured out what I was up to. When the manager stepped outside to question me about what I thought was a pretty lucrative career, I denied it, and swiftly walked off. It might've fallen between the cracks, except for the fact that I lived behind the grocer. And just a few short days later, when the manager was leaving the store, he saw me standing in my front yard and pulled over and then he asked me if that was where I lived. I played it stupid, "Huh—who me?" Just on cue, my mother stepped outside. The first thing out her mouth: "What the hell did you do now?" Our friendly grocer explained what he suspected. *Busted!* My mother instantly confirmed I didn't have a paper route, and sent me into the house.

Looking out the window in anticipation, I observed dialogue I could not hear. Whether it was instinct or intellect, I knew there was something to fear. I witnessed Mom do an about-face, and storm the front door, like General Grant when he took Richmond. And I think we all know what's about to happen here, well sort of. When mom stormed through the front door, she backhanded me with her wedding ring hand, which cut my lip. Then she grabbed me by my hair with her left hand and started pumping right uppercuts into my chin, all the while lecturing me about the evils of stealing. *For Christ's sake, where did she learn this stuff?* And then the unthinkable happened—she hurt her right hand. Being a decent-sized kid at ten, using her hand on me was more likely to sustain injuries to herself before she could inflict enough pain on me to get the message across. Now in a fit of rage because she had hurt herself (and of course, somehow that was my fault) she went to the old stand-by: the coffee pot cord. At the age of ten, I was just big enough to try and get away, well almost... Now she would swing at me with uncontrolled fury. When I was little, I would take the whipping on my ass and the back of my legs, but by this stage I was taking the beatings on my back and around my face. Of course running only made her angrier. But there's something about enduring pain that would make us all look for a safe place.

Ah, but life wasn't all bad living in the Sunshine State. Summer rolled around, and my grandparents sprang for two round trip Greyhound bus tickets to Lake Worth, so that Frank and I could visit them there. So *here I am*, with my brother, on a southbound Greyhound headed back to West Palm Beach, Florida. We were gone for little more than a week when my mother called my grandparents with the news that my stepfather, Jim Ward, had abandoned his family. My mother and four half-sisters were left alone to fend on their own. He hadn't been home for over a week, the rent was due, and there was nothing to eat. That weekend came and Pop packed my Gram, my brother and yours truly into his car and headed to 'St. Pete.' Mr. Sloan, the owner of Wolfy's Restaurant, had called; Jim Ward hadn't reported to work in a week. When my mother spoke of her suspicions to Mr. Sloan, he was appalled. He couldn't believe that Jim Ward would abandon his wife and six children, as well as his job after he had paid to relocate us to the west coast. There are a lot of unflattering things said about the Jewish people, but when Mr. Sloan inquired how she was getting by and my mother confessed she wasn't—that there was no food in the house and we were two weeks behind on the rent—the very next day two catering trucks pulled up in front of our house with enough food in them to feed half of Pinellas County. We had never seen so much food in our lives, and it was all pre-prepared. There were turkeys, chickens, steaks and ribs, casseroles, cakes and pies. Mr. Sloan even showed up personally to oversee the whole operation. He had the caterers, as well

23

as my brother and I, running back and forth across the lawn with food to stock the cupboards and refrigerator. Then I overheard him speak to one of the caterers; he said that he wouldn't have been able to sleep at night knowing that the little kids that lived in this house might be going hungry. I would like to thank Mr. Sloan and the Sloan family. We might've gotten by, but we would've been whole hell of a lot hungrier. Now Mom's got a new problem—something she's never faced before. She was on the verge of pulling her own hair out because she didn't know what to do with all this food. God bless the Sloan family.

Gram and Pop stayed 'till Sunday morning as Pop had to be back to work on Monday. We spent the week trying to organize our move back to West Palm Beach, and I spent part of it dodging projectiles flung at me by my stressed-out Mother. By midweek, we had most of our stuff packed up in boxes ready to ship out.

We had just sat down at the dinner table to have something to eat. What I did or said I don't remember, but I do know this: my mother jumped up and flung the whole table and everything we were going to eat on top of me, catching my fellow siblings as well. We all knew my mother's rage, but this was a top ten-er, I fell backwards out my chair and quickly rolled to my feet. Mom extracted the carving knife from the turkey, and I was already on the move through the hallway, which led to the bedroom. Just as I'd gained passage into the hall, I heard the flung carving knife whistle past my ears and stick into the wall heater next to that doorframe. That woman was hot on my heels as I bolted down the hallway. My brother grabbed me and shoved both of us into the bedroom, pushed the door shut and put his back up against it. He looked at me and said, "You've done it now Jeff," and called me a dumb ass. I wondered out loud, "What did I do?" Mom was already pounding at the door yelling, "I'll kill you, you little bastard!" I looked at my brother in bewilderment. Frank told me to go out the window and that I'd better hurry. I couldn't agree with him more. So out I went, and I stayed out 'till well after dark. By that time, she was no longer interested in mayhem, just torture. The toll to come back into the house was—you guessed it—the coffee pot cord. And the message that ensued? One I'd heard many times before: if I ever ran from her again, she'd break both my fucking legs.

The weekend came, *thank GOD*, with Gram and Pop with it. We packed up everything we owned, and moved back to West Palm Beach. We landed in Lake Worth, and spent the night with Gram and Pop.

The next morning Mom went straight to work on finding us a place to live. My poor Mother was on the verge of a nervous breakdown. She was in charge of six kids she had to clothe, house, and feed. And God bless her, she was tough. She was working on raw nervous energy. And God bless my brother Frank, too; he was there for support. And me? Well, I did what I could by supplying stress relief. Mom found us a place to live, in a low-income community called Hypoluxo. This wouldn't be my first visit to 'Hell Peluxo.'

Chapter Three

Back in the early sixties, during my second and third grade, we spent more than a year in Hypoluxo. That was when my life (and my brother's) changed dramatically. My mother had met a fellow Pennsylvanian, Joanne Cornell, who lived a couple blocks over and behind us. Ms. Joanne had seven kids of her own, and she ran her family like a military boot camp. She would sit and drink coffee with my mother while her kids did all the chores. My mother took to this, like a duck takes to water. So now you have a six and a seven-year-old babysitting and responsible for a four and two-year-old. We also got moved into the workforce. Which wouldn't be too bad, but Frank and I *were* the workforce, tasked with mowing the lawn, doing the dishes, mopping the floor, taking the garbage out, and laundry detail. Unlike today, there were no clothes dryers and even if there had been, we couldn't have afforded one. So it was clothespins and clotheslines for the dynamic duo.

Before you make a snap decision about children babysitting infants and having domestic duties, it gets better. My mom also adopted Mrs. Joanne's renaissance torture tactics. First on the punishment list was standing with your face in the corner of a room for hours, but it didn't take me long to figure out how to beat this cruel and unusual punishment. I would stand on one leg, and lean into the corner and actually fall asleep. Number two was a pretty slick way to ration food; I would be sent to bed without being fed. But by far, the worst instrument in this Pandora's Box was the dreaded electric coffee pot cord. One day over at Mrs. Cornell's, my mother was drinking coffee with her and she witnessed Mrs. Cornell pull the plug out of the percolator and out of the wall socket and then use it as a weapon of discipline. This would be a new and valuable weapon in the house of corrections or, should I say, the house of horrors. This seemingly innocent domestic item would draw blood from me thousands of times. She started off on my rump and on the back of my legs as a grade schooler, but eventually she escalated to whichever target she could see at the time. On more than one occasion, she would hit me on my back, the cord would wrap around my neck and face. Trust me, I had an idea of what the slaves went through earlier in this country's history.

26

Back to babysitting. Frank and I had to alternate babysitting days. More than once Frank would enter the house on my day to check on my sisters. One of my sisters would be crying, and Frank would rush into the bedroom to determine why. Frank would holler for me, and I would sprint in thinking that something dreadful had happened, only to find that baby Jamie had pulled off her diaper and, taking some of that mustard colored manure only infants produce, had used it as finger paint on the wall. This kid was a regular Picasso. She'd have her face painted, the crib, and her hair. There'd be crap everywhere, and guess whose job it was to clean it up? *Yours truly!* By luck of the draw it was my day to watch my sisters. My brother told me I had to clean it up and I had to do it fast, because Mom was on her way home. Okay, time out. What you don't know about me is I had a phobia about 'kaka'. I could barely wipe my own ass by the time I was six. When they were potty training me, they would leave me on the toilet for hours, and I would just sit there whining for someone to come wipe my ass. I'd sit there until my poor brother would come in tell me to shut up and bend over. That's not something you want to hear, unless of course you trust someone. Well enough of that, the issue is: who was going to clean up this mustard-colored masterpiece of manure? My poor brother Frank pleaded with me—no, he begged me—saying "Jeff you better clean that up" countless times. "Mom's coming home, you better clean that up," he urged in an attempt for motivation. "You better get in there, I'm telling you, she's on her way. I don't want to see you get a whooping," he said one last time. With absolutely no regard for my well-being, I replied, "Screw it." Frank went into a state of panic; he couldn't believe it. I was more willing to suffer the wrath of my mother than scrub the shit off the walls and clean up this masterpiece of manure. Just like that with perfect timing, my mother came in the back door, the last words out my brother's mouth before the fun began was, "You done it now Jeff!" Go ahead take a guess what happened next. I got batted around like a tetherball. You'd have thought *I* took a shit on the wall. And that was how I started the second grade.

Another thing from that time that is significant, and damaging, was that one morning I rolled out of the top bunk bed and fell and hit the terrazzo tile floor face first. I could've been killed. My stepfather came into the bedroom, because he heard the thud and, without a whole lot of regard for my well-being, he picked me up and put me in bed with my mother. I had a goose egg on my forehead the size of a softball and

I threw up green puke for almost three days. For some reason, I could hear symphony music playing in my head and I couldn't get the music to stop. That was concussion number one (there were more to come). In my household you either had to be missing a limb or almost dead before you got to see a doctor. And let's face it; mine was probably one of the least tragic stories of 'Hell Peluxo'.

The whole neighborhood consisted of over-populated families crammed in two bedroom homes. Besides, I didn't have to look far to see how bad it could get. Gary Cornell, Ms. Joanne's oldest son, became best friends with Frank and me. He was a bit lanky, a good kid with more of his mother's disposition, thank God, because his father Reggie, was a red-haired, womanizing redneck who always seemed to be pissed off. On more than one occasion, I witnessed Reggie bat his young son around the yard with his fist. *Why?* Can you tell me why any father would knock his grade school son around with his bare fist, because I would like to know.

Our remedy? Like any poor kid's antidote for a bad home life, we would get preoccupied with life's little adventures. From riding our bicycles into neighborhoods where we didn't belong, to exploring the cemetery off of Seacrest Boulevard and jumping off the 20-foot high sand dunes that we found near our house. The idea was to stay as far away from home for as long as possible.

Chapter Four

So *here I am*, back in 'Hell Peluxo' again, better known as Hypoluxo, and can you believe it? We're only three doors down from where we originally lived. Mom got a job as a waitress, something she did well, and she enrolled my brother and me into Boynton Beach Junior High. The family seemed to be doing fine, but guess who showed up three or four weeks later? If you guessed Jim Ward, you win the booby prize. Now take him, *please*. He was camping out in our carport. It would seem as though he got dumped, and he wanted back into Mom's good graces in the worst way. Almost from the moment he showed up, his daughters started crying and whining to my mother to let him back in. Their father sure knew how to work them. Hell, he was whining and belly aching to get back in himself. It seemed like a daily routine that when my brother and I got home from school, we would find Jim sitting at the kitchen table crying to my mother. He tried to work me, and I'm sure he was in my brother's ear as well. But neither one of us were willing to take the bait. It was a no-win proposition, if we voted him in, we were signing up for more of the same horrible treatment, and if we voted him out, and he got in anyway, there would be hell to pay.

He was the same old drunken hillbilly that beat on me like he was trying to tenderize meat. Not only that, but how do you trust a guy who takes his daughters to the Winn Dixie grocery store and then has them steal the lawn chairs that are on sale out in front of the store? He had them load the chairs into the trunk of the car as if he'd paid for them, only to come home to brag about his accomplices, boasting about how slick they were. *Slick my ass!* This was the 60s, and it took doorknobs like him to screw up the honor system for the rest of the decent world. Unfortunately for us, Mom eventually relented, and he was back into the house.

Frank and I were in shock. Someone must have performed a secret lobotomy on my mother in the middle of the night. How could she so easily forget everything this clown had done? But then again, she had six kids. She probably thought if she bit the bullet and took him back, she could protect the family. Sometimes you should just be thankful for the things you don't have and move on. So now, we have eight people in a two-bedroom house. Mom had been sleeping on the couch, and so guess who lost their room? You guessed it; we did. Jim's little princesses weren't going to sleep on the terrazzo floor. In retrospect, Frank and I should be thankful he never had a son. Mom got Jim a job at the diner she worked at and he was a good short order cook. She could keep a good eye on him this way, as well. My mother also had to apply for welfare. *Gee, thanks Mom!* I know my mother meant well and was trying to keep us all fed, but it took me all but one trip to the school cafeteria to realize I didn't need to draw more criticism from kids at school for having a welfare voucher. I really didn't need this kind of attention; I would rather starve then give some hero another shot at this zero.

Despite all this trials and tribulations, I always felt inside like someone special. Not in an egotistical kind of way, but somewhat like the thrill of knowing that someday something's going to happen. Just like when you're a kid on Christmas Eve. Well, we didn't quite make it to a year when Jim Ward decided to move us out of 'Hell Peluxo'—which by the way was squeezed between the borders of Lantana to the north and Boynton Beach to the south. And oh yeah, my biggest claim to fame at Boynton Beach Junior High was that I'd had more whacks (that's paddling) than the whole seventh and eighth grade school body combined. As you might have guessed, I was rebellious and constantly told I was a problem. Being a person who takes great pride in who he is, and what he does, I thought the hell with it, I'll go for broke, and be the biggest problem they ever had. One such trip to the Dean's office began from a dare. One particular week, it seemed as though every time I was in the hall on my way to my next class, someone would stick me with a pin. After a few days, I was beginning to feel like a pincushion. Towards the end of one week of this, I stepped out into the hall to change classes, and got stuck from behind. When I turned around, I saw it was my friend Ward Yourdy, who was doing it out of good fun. I decided I needed a weapon of my own, and he gave me the solution. Ward mentioned that at the end of the Home Economics class, they sweep the floor, so he told me to look at the edge of sidewalk in front of the 'Home Ec' class and I could find a weapon of my choice. *Eureka!* There it was. When the rest of my classmates would show up to a gunfight, they would have a BB Gun. I, on the other hand, would have a .44 Magnum: a three-inch sewing needle; a heavy-duty one for leather no less! I jammed the needle into the eraser of my pencil, constructing a bayonet. Now I was feeling the intoxication of power. I was armed

30

and dangerous; well, actually more dangerous to myself. But I wouldn't find that out 'till later.

One day they called a fire drill, and within minutes the whole student body was standing outside in the parking lot. Vicky, a girl I liked, was standing in the line next to me, and when she turned around, pardon the pun, I gave her a prick. She spun around and looked at me, and began to laugh. And then she double dared me to stick my teacher. Yep, you can see where this is going. When they called us back into school, my teacher was standing at the bottom of the stairs. I turned right, jabbed him square in the ass, dropped my weapon, and tried to make a run for it up the steps. Too late! He grabbed me by the neck and jerked me out of my shoes. He was gritting his teeth so hard, I thought they were going to snap off. Then he bent down and picked up the weapon. I could see it in his eyes; he wanted to give it back to me, if you know what I mean? Instead, he marched me down to the Dean's office, kicked the door open, and slung me into a chair. He pointed at me, displayed my penetrating pencil to the Dean, and declared, "I think you know what to do with him." Then the two of them stepped outside the office to discuss my immediate future. Once the two of them stepped back in, they had decided to call my mother. *Uh oh.* After the Dean had hung up the phone, I could tell by his grin that I was in big trouble again. Mom had green-lit any punishment he deemed fit. Then the Dean pulled open the drawer to extract his special paddle. I say 'special', because he had his initials drilled into the contact end of it. Then I was instructed to stand up behind my chair, bend over and grab the arm rests on it. Now *here I am* this twelve-year-old boy is bent over in his underwear, sweating bullets in anticipation. Did I forget to mention the fact that they'd made me drop my drawers? Now the two of them debate who's up first at the plate. First up was my teacher, who flailed away until he got winded. Next up was the Dean. For Christ's sake, I thought this guy was trying out for a pinch hitter spot with the New York Yankees. When he got winded, he got sloppy, and caught me with the edge of the paddle a couple of times. My ass wasn't sore; they had spanked me past numb. They had actually broken the skin and I was bleeding. But I wouldn't shed one tear. Now I had to stand up on the school bus for the ride home. When I got home, Mom was waiting with the coffee pot cord. And once again, it was MAHTM (my ass handed to me). She actually gave me stripes on my back to go with my busted ass. That evening, I had to draw bathwater with Epsom salts

31

and soak in it before I could peel the underwear off my body.

And then we moved again. Needless to say, it didn't break my heart to leave 'Hell Peluxo.' So, *here I am*, on 40th Street and Greenville Avenue in West Palm Beach. Things seemed to be looking up. Although the house had been built somewhere in the 20s or 30s, Frank and I finally had our own room. Well, sort of… Someone had closed in the patio in front of the house and turned it into a room. There were railroad tracks running right through our backyard, which would prove to be a source of entertainment for me later. Diagonally across the tracks behind our house was a recreation center. Hey, I thought, this might not be too bad. Frank and I started attending a brand new junior/senior high school called Northshore. It was now the late 60s and JFK, RFK, and the Reverend King had all been assassinated. The Civil Rights movement and 'busing' was in its infancy, and although there were mild racial tensions, my brother and I didn't fit into either group. Even though my brother and I had grown up in a bigoted household, Frank and I had very few problems with black kids. But, as with patterns of the past, I got into a couple of scrapes at Northshore.

Chapter Five

So, *here I am*, repeating the seventh grade, but this time, I'm determined to do it with more than just one pair of pants. Pop now worked for a laundry and had a truck route with accounts on Singer Island, which consisted of hotels along the beach, a few motels on the island, as well as Lost Tree Village. On alternate weekends Frank and I would work with my grandfather. Although I was repeating the seventh grade, I was determined that no one would make fun of me because of the way I dressed. I had made enough money to buy some new shoes, some white jeans, and a gold and black striped pullover. I thought I was the man, I was so proud of my new threads. Of course, on the first day of school, I was running down the hall so I wouldn't be late for my next class, and some kid reached out and kicked me in my brand new white pants. I hesitated for a second, because I was late for class, but after a few steps, I decided I couldn't let this pass. I turned around and followed the kid into a hallway with lockers. As he opened his locker, I approached him. When I called him out on his offense, he went Muhammad Ali on me. He began dancing around and told me he would kick my white ass. I grabbed him, slammed him into his locker, which got the attention of some of his friends. This wouldn't be the first time I had to fight more than one guy; I just never seemed to win any of those fights. I was unaware that my brother, on his way to his next class on the second floor, had looked over the railing, and seen the predicament I was about to face. I had Mr. Bojangles, the white pants offender, pinned against the locker when I got jumped from behind. I turned around just in time to witness what looked like the caped crusader pounce on Mr. Bojangles' two friends. My brother, sensing the urgency of the situation, had climbed over the second floor railing and dropped down on my two would-be assailants (who at this point were more than dazed and confused). Well, that was the end of that, so we thought. A couple days later, we ran into two of the same kids and had words with them. At the end of that day, they got on our school bus to follow us home. Frank and I looked at each other, and wondered the same thing. *What were these guys up to?*

Back in those days, you lived in a neighborhood that was predominately made up of whatever your race was. When we arrived at our bus stop and got off, they followed. Once the bus took off, they pulled off their belts, wrapped them around their hands a couple of times and advanced, swinging their belt buckles. I ducked back and forth and did pretty well; I hadn't been hit. Frank decided to charge his man. He threw his left arm up in the air, and when his assailant's belt wrapped around it, he pulled him in, and cracked him with his right hand. Our bus stop happened to be in front of a grade school. One of the grade school teachers came running out yelling at Frank and I to stop fighting. She actually said, "Stop picking on those boys. Leave those kids alone!" Frank and I were stunned. Little did she know... That was just the way it always seemed to go for me and my bro. These clowns were smarter than they looked. As soon as they saw the teacher, they jumped behind her like we were the ones that were assaulting them. Frank and I tried to plead our case, but it fell on deaf ears. She just wouldn't hear it. She was convinced that since they were out of their neighborhood, we must have been picking on them. And that's even though they were the ones with the weapons, and Frank had a welt on his arm and a knot on his head. Mortally defeated, we decided to go home.

The next morning at school, Frank insisted on walking me to my class. I think he was suspicious, and with good reason. Once I was safe at my class, Frank was on his way to his when our two black, belt-buckle toting buffoons jumped him. Later that morning in P.E. class, one of my black buddies told me I should watch out for myself, and then he told me what happened. I beelined straight to the Dean's office, but Frank had already been sent home—he'd needed stitches. It would turn out, our two black, belt-buckle-toting buffoons had snuck up behind my brother and swung for the fences. A home run. They would now be suspended for their efforts, as if that was some type of punishment for a couple of clowns who didn't want to be in school anyway.

Around this time I met a kid by the name of Johnny Jones who would become a great friend. Johnny was cool—not because he acted like it, but because he was. He seemed to have all the friendship and respect one could want, which was kind of strange because he was a loner, a James Dean type of character who marched to his own beat. Kind of a cross between a beatnik and a hippie... Johnny loved playing drums and he took it seriously, taking lessons a few days a week after school. My suspicions were that his old man was a jerk, although I never met him. I always had to leave before he got home from work, and

34

the vibe was had I been there when he got home, Johnny would have got his ass handed to him. John had his drums set up in a practice area up in the attic. He'd turned it into a kind of clubhouse, installing a great sound system, black lights, and fluorescent posters. It was a great place to hang out. We would go up in his attic after school and crank up the volume full throttle. Johnny introduced me to some great music. His favorite group was Blood Sweat & Tears, a jazz-rock fusion band who were way ahead of their time. And how strange is life? Years later, in my late 30s, I was introduced to a man through a mutual friend who I would privately teach Karate to and strike up a friendship of my own. That man was none other than Johnny's idol, Bobby Colomby, the founder and drummer of Blood Sweat & Tears.

But in the day, I don't think anyone understood the friendship I shared with John. What I realize now is that John was cool because he never judged anyone. Man, I dug the cat. He respected me for who I was, and he respected everyone for who they were. I never heard a derogatory word come out his mouth. He didn't make judgments; he made observations. Johnny was an old soul and wise beyond his years. A few years after I moved from 40th and Greenville, I ran into John. He was studying to become a chef. After his girlfriend had become pregnant, he gave up on his dream of becoming a drummer, to do the right thing. God bless you John, I hope life has worked out for you.

But while we were still living on 40th Street, Pop went to work one weekend without my brother or me. He stopped by the Port of Palm Beach to pick up the laundry from a fresh dock freighter. Pop knew the ship's captain, so he went up to the bridge to speak with him. The freighter had just been unloaded. On his way down, Pop slipped on the metal stairs and fell over forty feet down into the belly of the ship, feet first. He should have been killed, but instead he crushed the heels and ankles on both his legs. This would be the writing on the wall for Pop. It seemed to take all the fire right out of him. He was stuck in a wheelchair with cast up to his knees on both legs for over a year. After that, they fitted him with casts that had rubber stops on the bottom, and handed him a walker. It was time for my brother and I to give back, and we wished we could have done more. Pop was our best friend. Every other day my brother and I would alternate slowly walking Pop around the block. This would kill us as much as it hurt him. He could hardly bear the humiliation and the pain.

In grade school, back when we lived with my grandparents off of

10th Avenue in Lake Worth, I always thought my grandfather was Irish. Every St. Patrick's Day, Pop would show up with plenty of noise makers and those plastic green Derby hats that had gold four leaf clovers on them. We would have a blast. For Christ's sake, you would have thought *he'd* driven all of the snakes out of Ireland. Then on New Year's Eve, Pop would pull all the pots and pans out of the cupboard and give us something to beat on them with. We beat them 'till they had dents in them. Then Grandma would get pissed off because every New Year's Day, she would have to go out and buy new pots and pans so she could cook. But that wouldn't stop Pop; he was having fun with the boys, and we were following the bandleader. Most nights when Pop came home from work, he didn't just come in the house—he made an entrance. My grandfather was an absolute blast. Whenever you got in the car to run errands with him, you didn't know what was going to happen. It could be anything from drag racing with teenagers, to getting into a fistfight at a red stoplight…

The day they took the casts off Pop's feet, I accompanied him to the hospital, along with my mom and grandma. On the way home, we had to stop at the grocery store. As soon as Mom and Gram got out of the car and out of sight, Pop moved to the driver's seat and looked at me, and said, "Let's get the HELL out of here!" I couldn't help but rejoice from within—this was the Pop I knew, but immediately I was concerned. I didn't realize how liberating that escapade must have been for him. It wasn't long after that ride, that my brother and I both realized how great a toll that accident had taken on his spirit.

But prior to all this, Frank and I heard they were selling all the old rowboats off over at Latent's Boat Yard. Latent's sat right there on the Intracoastal Waterway on the north side of the Port of Palm Beach, right across from Peanut Island (which was at the mouth of the Palm Beach inlet). Latent's wanted $12 a boat. Frank and I had $8, Pop made up the rest. So we bought a boat, which was water logged, and had more holes in it than a block of Swiss cheese. But we owned our own vessel. Frank and I would take turns; one would row, and the other would bail the water out with a coffee can. When one of us got tired we would switch off. It was a tossup as to who was going to wear out first. This piece of junk was an accident waiting to happen. We would dock our Titanic at the marina at the end of 40th Street, well, if you could call it that… Actually we found a cinder block that we tied up with an old rope and used as an anchor. Then we would tie the stern to an old pier post so we could keep track of it. *Why?* Because every time we went down to use the boat, it was submerged. Every time we wanted to use the Titanic, we had to drag it onto shore and bail all the water out of it. But that didn't deter us from having our fun. Soon as it was afloat, we would set sail, and neither one of us could swim a stroke. We'd paddle that boat out into the Intracoastal and head north to the Palm Beach inlet, which was easily two miles away. We'd sit at the mouth of the inlet, and stare at the breakers out in the ocean, then look at each other and swear that one calm day we were going to paddle out to sea. But of course—and thank God—we never did. We'd just turn around and paddle back towards the marina.

We had to have been a sight, sitting in the middle of the Intracoastal Waterway, with a fishing rod in one hand and bailing with the other. One day we saw a pod of manatee, better known as "Sea Cows" in South Florida. Frank had a brilliant idea. The manatee were headed south, so we paddled over to them, cast out a line, and snagged an adult for a free ride home. Well, almost… This lasted for about 100 yards, but it never dawned on us that the adult might take us as a threat to the younger ones. All of a sudden we got rammed. Not a capsizing jolt, but it got our attention nonetheless. While we thought we had leaks before, now we had a couple of holes the size of Indian Head nickels. Suddenly we felt we were sitting in the middle of Caesars Palace's fountain. Now we're headed for shore, rowing and bailing like hell. When the water level inside the boat matched the level of water outside, we had to abandon ship. Thank God we got close enough to shore, by the time we exited our Titanic we were in chest-deep water. We waded into shore. We turned around and realized we had lost the fish we caught, our fishing rods, and were now watching our tackle box sail out through the inlet. We, of course, lost our boat, but we did have one hell of a story. In the history of the manatee coming to Florida via South America to clear vegetation out the canal, there is no record of anyone ever losing their boat to one. Ah, to be Polish… But for a short six weeks, we had a lot of adventures in that boat.

Once while rowing the Intracoastal, we came upon a floating milk jug with a rope tied to it. When we pulled it up to see what it was anchored to, *jackpot!* It was a crab trap full of blue crabs. *Finder's keepers, loser's weepers.* We promptly declared it 'our' crab trap and marked it by ditching their milk jug for our bleach jug and tied it to the trap. When we got home, we were the heroes. We had two buckets of fresh

37

blue crabs. For the next couple of weeks, we had fresh crab every other night. Pop schooled us on throwing the females back, who carried their eggs on their underbelly. Then someone did to us what we'd done to them. *Easy come, easy go.*

Ah, but winter is here. Normally it doesn't get cold in Southern Florida, but because of the humidity it can be annoying. The old stucco home that we rented had a fireplace and we decided to use it. One night I was sitting, staring at the fireplace (because the television didn't work) when I noticed a little smoke escaping from a crack in the fireplace's mantle. Mom demanded to know what I was staring at. She probably thought, "GREAT, now the kid is plotting a career as a pyromaniac." I went over to investigate and saw there was a crack right where the wall met the mantle. I could see hints of flickering flames. I placed my hand on the wall above the mantle, and snatched it away; you could have fried an egg on it. I called my mother over to check it out. The next thing I knew, the whole family was standing on the lawn with the West Palm Beach Fire Department watching the house burn down. As it turned out, no one had used that chimney in years and it was missing a few bricks on the inside. With the house having been built during the late 20s, someone was missing a few marbles even to use the fireplace. The fire had crept up inside the wall and into the attic. You can connect the dots. The half destroyed house was then condemned. But what was my reward for being alert and displaying heroism? Humiliation. We had to live there regardless, and the landlord refused to fix the place. One of the local TV stations had just started airing a consumer report show. So they sent out one of their trouble-seeking reporters to do a segment on us. Great, *here I am* with my mug plastered on the television set with the rest of my loser family while my mother describes to the reporter what dire straits we're in because the rat fucker of a landlord won't fix the house. Excuse me if I sound a little bitter here! This was just what I needed; more ridicule when I got back to school.

As it turns out, I got mixed reviews. Some of the kids thought it was kind of cool that I was on TV, and the other half, of course, made fun of me. The house was in pretty bad shape. Frank and I entered the attic and the roof looked like it might cave in at any moment. All the trusses were charred, and the wall that the fireplace was in was done. Well-done. But we had nowhere else to go, so we had no alternative except to mop up the mess that the fire department had made and pray that it didn't rain. But with the house having been condemned, a few months later the authorities made us move.

Chapter Six
Minor Delinquency

So, *here I am* on Whispering Pines Road and Military Trail, preparing to enroll in yet another school, which will be the last school I attend. Jefferson Davis Junior High—*Welcome to Hillbilly Haven!* We now lived off a dirt road, across from a dairy farm. The house itself wasn't too bad. It was big enough, but it was oddly laid out because it had been built onto a few times. The yard was two feet lower than the roadway, so when it rained we had a lakefront property. This would turn out to be the last house I lived in with my parents, and as it turned out the most fun and the most tragic.

After a few days in my new school I met a kid named Kenny. His nickname was Bubba, and he lived in my neighborhood. He lived three blocks down my dirt road where you had to take a left. One block in, you took another left to circle back. Kenny lived on that bend. Continue two more blocks and take another left and that put you out on Whispering Pine's Road, right in front of my neighbor's house. Just beyond the tall pine trees in our backyard was a canal, or should I say a ditch. A few homes past ours sat a vacant lot, which we'd cut through and cross the ditch into the next neighborhood, which had paved streets. Our new friends Timmy and Johnny Morris, as well as Danny Glick and Chuck Mock, lived in that neighborhood. Years later my brother would marry Timmy and Johnny's younger sister Patsy, a disaster I'm sure he would like to forget. Traveling south through that neighborhood, which only consisted of a few blocks, the road ended at the Polo Grounds.

The Polo Grounds was an equestrian center that was equipped with horse stables and training arenas. And oh yeah, they had a big-top tent stadium where they held professional wrestling matches. *Holy jackpot! Can you say fun trifecta?* The Polo Grounds was just east of Military Trail and sat just off Summit Boulevard. Also on that same corner was a Winn Dixie shopping plaza. Right at this time I met a girl from school who stabled her horse at the Polo Grounds, and lived in that very neighborhood. To me, this was a dream come true. Finally I could ride a horse just like all the cowboys on my favorite westerns. I use to plead with her—no, beg her—to let me ride her horse. She warned me her horse didn't like men, and I should've listened. Every time I got on that ornery horse it tried to kill me. It would take off like a shot through the bushes, bucking wildly, and then try to rub me off on a barbed wire fence. Then it would spring through the woods and try to decapitate me with a low-lying limb. Once it cantered through the Winn-Dixie parking lot and decided to hurdle the trunks and hoods of parked cars. Thank God I cleared the asphalt before it threw me. That horse hated me, and the feeling became mutual. But that didn't deter me; I thought I was Hop-Along Cassidy, although I resembled Limp-Along Larry. I should have been killed more than once, and I know that horse damn sure tried.

One night I had a flash of brilliance and stole my stepfather's car in the middle of the night. The ensuing joyride would prove so much fun that it turned into an addiction. I would crack open my parents bedroom door, slither in on my belly like a commando, purloin the car keys from my stepfather's pockets, and slither out the same way. Now the problem was getting the car out of the driveway. For starters, there was that three percent downward grade from the road to our house. I couldn't start the car in our driveway, for fear of the obvious. I'd open the car door, put my back against the doorframe, grab the steering wheel and push like hell backwards and up the slope until I got the car out on Whispering Pines Road.

Then I would start the car, take a left on Military Trail for one block, and turn east into Danny Glick's neighborhood. I would coast up in front of Danny's house, get out, and go around to the back of the home and tap on Danny's bedroom window. The next thing you know, Danny and I were cruising. Neither one of us looked old enough to drive, so we avoided Military Trail like the plague. We went straight to the Polo Grounds, which had acres of horse pastures. This provided us with a location for our fun, but after a few hours of spinning donuts,

41

we became bored. So we had to step it up with a game we'll call "Kill the Cowboy." This would rev the fun meter up way past the redline. We'd sneak into the stables and find a tack room, grab a halter, and then look for a horse that was suitable. So *here I am* in the Polo Grounds' pasture, flipping a coin with my buddy Danny. The winner rides the horse, and the loser drives the car (as if that makes any sense). The guy on the horse takes off like a bat out of Hell, with the guy in the car in hot pursuit. Two simple goals: the guy on the horse would try to get the guy in the car to spin out, while the guy in the car was trying to get the guy on the horse thrown. How neither one of us was killed was an act of God. With the grass in the pasture being knee high and full of dew, the guy on the horse had sure footing. The car, however, would go into a power slide for sixty or seventy feet before either of us could get it under control. This unique equestrian event would start at midnight, and by dawn there would be twelve to fifteen deranged horses running free in the pasture. Just after dawn, I would get Danny back to his house, then I coasted the car back in our driveway, snuck back into my parent's room to slip the keys back in my stepfather's pockets, slithered back out the room, and climbed back in bed for one hour of sleep before I got up to go to school. The first few times we participated in our newly invented equestrian event, we tried to put the horses back in the stables. But these horses were scared—scared out their minds (and we were just out of our minds). But the baffling thing about this new non-Olympic equestrian event we had created was that no one seemed to catch on. So this became a mandatory, once-a-week competition. On the day after these death-by-suicide rodeos, Danny and I would stop by the Polo Grounds after school, and not once did we hear someone complain that their horses had been hijacked and set free in the pasture. So what can I say? With no deterrent in the way—you guessed it—we rodeoed away.

Then one night, almost by accident, we took the thrills and spills and turned it up one notch to chills. After I got Danny to spin out, naturally I was thrown from my horse. Just as I bounced up, the car had spun to a stop and was pointing straight at me. Although I was blinded by headlights, I could sense a smile creep up on Danny's face. I could hear the engine revving, and then it came: two tons of Ford Fairlane. I dodged one way, and then dove the other. Danny went into a power slide and mowed down ten yards of grass. This would bring a whole new urgency to our game of "Kill the Cowboy." After one full night of this nerve racking, horse bucking, car dodging and power sliding, even two moron-thinking idiots like us decided—we better give it a break.

But we weren't through with the Polo Grounds just yet; there was still a lot of fun to be had. With a little creative thinking we came up with a new game we'll call, "Stampede." Danny and I would sneak out of our homes and rendezvous at the Polo Grounds at midnight. Then we would proceed to a paddock where there were unkept horses that no one wanted anymore. It also had weeds higher than we were tall. Oh, did I forget to mention, we had our pellet pistols and BB guns with us? Now these horses had been abandoned, so no one was riding them, brushing them, or stabling them. They were, however, being fed and watered. We crossed over the barbed wire fencing into a field that was smaller than a pasture. We would split off, and head out to opposite ends. We couldn't see each other because of the thick brush. One would holler 'Ready!' and once the other answered, *let the stampede begin.*

Anyone who's grown up around horses knows they can be spooked pretty easily. Danny and I would sneak through the weeds and bushes to get as close as we could to these unsuspecting beasts. Once we were upon them, we would aim for their hindquarters and open up, rapid firing our pellet pistols and screaming like banshees with only the moonlight to see by. Now at this point I know what you are probably thinking, and you'd be right! But stampeding those horses over the top of each other just seemed like a lot of crazy fun at the time. It was eerie and exhilarating, much like a horror movie come to life. This would turn out to be a great source of entertainment. So much so that we drafted some troops. The first recruit up: my brother Frank. Then we enlisted Johnny, then Larry, and then Bubba, and then our new pal Mike, the black kid who'd just moved in across the street from us. *Welcome to the neighborhood!* But Mike only lasted one night. Some of the guys thought he was chicken, but he just wasn't up for this lunar lunacy. He was more of an inner-city kid and hadn't gotten the hang of hillbilly haven just yet. Actually, he was showing more signs of intelligence than the rest of us. But you already knew that, right? Besides, we had one man too many anyway.

So we split up into three-man teams, and with that much firepower, you could actually turn a stampede around and head them back the other way. Now we had a war, and as these horses hadn't been ridden in a while, they were close to being wild. And like I mentioned, horses are skittish anyway. So you take a moonlit night along with a handful of lunatics with BB guns and what at best feels like multiple bee stings to a horse, and you have a recipe for disaster. After a few of us had been slammed into the barbed wire fence, all had been knocked down, and I had been trampled, I decided it was time to put the BB guns away. Looking back on it now, I'm surprised we didn't try to mount these broken-down horses and take potshots at each other. Ah, something for another day...

Well as you should've guessed, thanks to this nocturnal vampire life I was living I had pretty much given up on school. I didn't have a clue what was going on there anyway. But this would present me with a big problem; there was a large period between midnight and dawn and I was wide-awake. *What to do?* And then I remembered that some months previously, Danny and I had borrowed some mini dirt bikes from some rich kids down there near Bubba's house without their permission. Uh, okay, well... we stole them. But we brought them back; we just went joy riding. Okay, in reality, it was probably only a few weeks earlier, but you know how time drags by when you're a kid. Down near Bubba's house there was a private driveway with a gate, which traveled from his dirt road through a couple acres to Gun Club Road. Halfway through that property was a beautiful two-story home, and these kids had toys the rest of us could only dream about owning. On one restless night Danny and I decided to sneak up on their house and borrow their dirt bikes once again without permission.

We were heading to the Polo Grounds to do some joyriding, and we meant to bring them back. But halfway to the Polo Grounds one of the dirt bikes broke down. So we hid it in some bushes, went back to Danny's house, and grabbed his older brother's mini-bike. At this time, the mini-bike was Honda's latest invention, while Danny's brother's mini-bike had a lawnmower motor with a centrifugal clutch. Now we had three vehicles and only two riders. Danny and I were buzzing around deep in the Polo Grounds in one of the pastures, easily one hundred yards away from the main road. A Sheriff's car pulled over on Summit Boulevard and the cop started scanning the field with his spotlight. I dumped the mini bike I was riding in some bushes, and Danny took off on his brother's mini-bike, with the spotlight trained on him, and rode all the way to the Sheriff's car on Summit Boulevard. As I watched nervously, standing in the pasture, I heard a car creep up behind me. It was another Sheriff, who'd entered from a maintenance path that the tractors use. The deputy got out of his car, and leisurely strolled up to me. I had a lit cigarette in my hand I gotten from Danny, and I didn't even smoke. I was so nervous; I had to do something as I watched Danny ride over to Sheriff Number One. Sheriff Number Two had closed the distance between us, and I hadn't budged when he suddenly then pounced on me.

So *here I am*, in the back of Palm Beach County Sheriff's police car, and deservedly handcuffed. In the presence of a man, about 45 years of age, burning a hole through me with his hostile stare. It became abundantly clear that the mini bikes we borrowed (stole) belonged to *him*.

The deputy who nabbed me started off with, "We've got one, you might as well tell us where the other dirt bike is!" It blasted through my mind: did they find the one that broke down that we hid in the bushes? Or do they think Danny's mini-bike is theirs? I decided to keep my mouth shut. But heading across that pasture to Sheriff Number One, I get an earful. I learned that two weeks earlier, someone had broken into their garage and stole their mini-bikes, and they had just gotten them back. Evidently hoodlums with larceny on their minds think alike. Now that I have the 411, I'm hoping Danny sticks to the code of the criminal and invokes his Fifth Amendment rights. In other words, keeps his mouth shut. Danno was already a step ahead of me; he had convinced Deputy Number One that there was only one mini-bike, it belonged to his brother, and he was on it. So he didn't know what they were talking about and what's more, he worked for Colonel Collins, the man who owned the Polo Grounds, and the good Colonel had granted us permission to use the pasture (*and get this!*) as long as we didn't scare the horses. Naturally, the best time to use the pasture was in the middle of the night. Danny can sling shit a mile high—I think he eventually ran for political office. *Slam dunk!* Our planets (and stories) had aligned without us knowing it. After hearing the name of the original thief—now Florida's most wanted—one of the Sheriffs realized he knew him well and now they were considering the possibility of that bandit striking again. I guess he was a… troubled kid. Now the two deputies are trying to convince Daddy Determined (the Sheriff) of our innocence, against his protests might I add. He was convinced he'd heard his son's mini dirt bikes out in that field, but he finally relented and accompanied the deputies back to the original thief's house. Danny and I didn't celebrate until the tail lights of the sheriff's cruiser ceased to exist in the abyss.

Now we have another problem, what do we do with the two bikes? It was too risky to take them back. Our conclusion—dump them in a canal, which would turn out to be an all night endeavor. We didn't consider ourselves thieves; we'd borrowed from the rich (them) to give to the poor (us) only to return them to the rightful owners (them). This whole scenario wore me out, and left me feeling kind of dirty.

So *here I am* at twilight, which was when they turned the street lights on. We were at the baseball diamond just off the corner of Gun Club Rd and Military Trail, just down the street from Larry Clark's place and the whole crew was there. My brother Frank, brothers Johnny and Tim Morris, Danny Glick and Mike Flanagan, Larry Clark, and Bubba. We were all watching the once-a-week baseball game. When I looked across the field and my instigator light bulb flashed on. On the corner of Military Trail and Southern Boulevard, sat MacArthur Dairy. Actually it was their refrigerator house building; a storage unit with a whole fleet of milk trucks parked behind cinder block walls. Back in the day, instead of going to the grocery store, people relied on milk trucks to deliver fresh dairy goods straight to their homes. Things like milk, cheese, bread, eggs, and... ice cream. I leaned over and told the guys I had a brilliant scheme for when the game was over. Once the game ended, we did our usual walk of one block to the Little General Store (which is like a 7-Eleven in the South). Over Pepsis and apple turnovers I laid out my plan.

First, we needed the ballpark to extinguish its lights. The sky was illuminated all the way to the dairy and we needed darkness to operate. My plan was to sneak up on the dairy, scale the 10-foot wall, and once on the other side, raid the milk trucks. Tim Morris was out, which didn't surprise me, but what shocked me was Danny bailed on me, and what was equally shocking was my brother was in—he wasn't usually up for this sort of thing. Johnny was in, too; he usually instigated this type of delinquency. Johnny never ceased to crack me up, with some of his crackpot ideas. But fifty percent of the time I'd find myself following through on his hair-brained schemes. Larry was in, as long as he didn't get hurt, and Bubba was always up for an adventure as long as he didn't think he would get caught. And Mike Flanagan, who was older than all of us, he knew we were on a roll and said he wouldn't miss it.

So *here I am* with the raiders of MacArthur Dairy, pushing our way through the weeds and bushes, up to the bank of Southern Boulevard canal. We had decided a frontal assault wasn't in our best interests. The canal ran east and west along Southern Boulevard, and across the Boulevard: West Palm Beach's International airport. We would enter the canal a quarter of a mile east of the dairy for our stealth approach. We stripped down to our underwear, placed our clothes into a plastic trash bag, and started dog paddling towards the dairy. Let's stop here for a moment of reflection. When you think of Florida you have to think of swamps, and when you think of swamps, you think of poisonous snakes and… ALLIGATORS. Now, I truly can't remember which one of us mental midgets came up with the canal scenario, but it wasn't me, and I can only pray they made better choices as the years passed by.

But we made it, and were now staring at the southeast wall of the dairy. Frank wasn't too keen about actually going into the dairy yard, so he became our lift to help each of us to the top of the wall. Johnny, Bubba, Mike and I would do the actual raiding. Larry would lay flat at the top of the wall as a lookout, leaving his leg dangling on the inside so we would have something to grab and use to climb back up over the wall.

Once inside we split up in four different directions. It felt like we were in a James Bond movie or an episode of Mission Impossible. We zigzagged and darted from truck to truck. After ransacking each one, we ran back to Larry with all the loot we could carry. Each one of us had no less than four or five half-gallon cartons of ice cream, not to mention, all the eggs and bread we could carry. We methodically took our time and lobbed every brick of ice cream over the wall to my brother Frank. Then each one of us, one by one, climbed up Larry's leg and over the wall, for a clean get away.

We couldn't believe how easy it was to pull this off. So, like any illogically thinking buffoons, we repeated our caper many times, but we changed our angle of attack. Then we got brazen. We skipped the whole canal scenario. We simply waited for the ballpark to turn out its lights, and then we casually strolled across the field, hugging close to the woods along the way.

Now we were entering from the south side of the dairy, and either that wall got easier and easier to scale, or we got so darn good at it. After a few weeks, though, it got down to slim pickings; they had to have caught on, because the trucks were all but empty. I felt as if I was being challenged; I took this setback personally. I wasn't through with the dairy just yet. Always one to escalate the thrills, I decided to bump it up a notch. I was now going to enter the main building and raid the freezers of the dairy. I dove from milk truck to milk truck to cloak my assault on the main building.

So *here I am* on the loading dock, with my hand on the freezer door handle. The door is five feet wide, seven feet tall and one foot thick. I popped the door and stepped inside, there's no backing out now. If the door slams behind me, it's like a vault and I'm stuck in here 'till the cows come home. I'd told my brother and friends, I would rather go to the "pokey" than become a popsicle. But all of that would evaporate from my mind the moment I see pallets stacked with heavenly ice cream. I pulled it off, or should I say we pulled it off as smooth as the product we were pilfering. I returned triumphantly to my waiting buddies, with arms full of ice cream cartons. Then it was back over the wall, along the woods, and across the baseball diamond to the corner of Whispering Pines and Military Trail we went. This would be the first time we experienced the notion that there truly is too much of a good thing. We peeled the cartons back and, like ravenous mice on cheese, started to devour those bricks of heavenly cream.

We had slabs of vanilla, strawberry, chocolate, coconut, and peaches and cream, with a little neapolitan. And I don't know how many half-gallon bricks of ice cream *you* can eat, but this 14-year-old was good for maybe two and a half. Ice cream was a delicacy never before seen at my house, and I'm sure seldom (if ever) seen at the rest of these hooligans' homes. Our score consisted of bread and a few cartons of eggs as well, something we could split up evenly and give to our moms, but we still had an overflowing quantity of ice cream and none of us could risk filling our freezers with half-gallon bricks. The bread and eggs could possibly be explained away, but the ice cream, well, that would be the pig that flew.

Well, like they say, necessity is the mother of invention. So we came up with a creative way to get rid of the incriminating ice cream: a new game we'll call "launched depth charges." We took an old bicycle inner tube, laid one of us down on the ground, and looped it around his feet. That person put his legs straight up in the air, spread-eagle style, then we stretched the inner tube back like a rubber band, grabbed a brick of ice cream, and well, I think you get the picture. Oh, did I forget to mention? Our human slingshots were pointed directly at traffic on Military Trail. One of us would be a spotter, and tried to time the traffic as it approached. This was more excitement that juvenile primates are supposed to have. Just the possibility of us nailing a motorist as they passed by had us worked up into a beta-endorphin frenzy. Even the misses were great. Launching a half-gallon brick of ice cream through the air and watching it hit the hot asphalt and explode kept our endorphins just shy of urination. But we were determined to nail somebody. We kept adjusting our projectile; getting closer and closer and then *BULLSEYE!* Someone was passing by driving a pickup truck with their passenger window down. Our flying ice cream brick shot right through that window, skipped across his dash and windshield, and ended up in his lap. The truck pitched sideways and almost crashed. GEE, CAN YOU IMAGINE THAT? It scared the bejeezus out of us, so what's a poor boy to do? We bolted down Whispering Pines and disappeared in a humid mist.

We darted through the empty lot, through the ditch, and into the safety of Timmy, Johnny, and Danny's neighborhood. We were laughing like hyenas and barely containing our mirth, as well as our curiosity. We just had to know what had happened. So we passed though their neighborhood, and headed over to Military Trail, coming out a couple hundred feet south of our launch site, right in front of the Carnival Bar. I crossed Military Trail (dodging four lanes of traffic) so I could approach our launch site from the opposite side of the highway. By myself, I might add. The good news: the driver didn't crash. The truck was sitting in the parking lane on the east side of Military Trail heading north. The bad news: there was a Palm Beach County Sheriff's squad car sitting right behind him.

The deputy was investigating what would turn out to be forensic evidence we left behind. He found a couple empty boxes of ice cream, and our inner tube. I don't think anyone of us realized how lucky we were. We could have targeted the deputy's car, or even worse, caused an accident. Nevertheless, my friends thought I was completely out of my mind when I decided to cross Military Trail just to find out what was going on. Everyone else had wisely decided to disappear back into the neighborhood, but not me. In my mind, this would just add to the adrenaline rush.

Once I passed Whispering Pines, I ran back across Military Trail, just so I could walk by our bullseye and ice cream recipient, as well as the sheriff. I could almost hear my brother's voice echoing in my head from somewhere back in the neighborhood: "Are you crazy?! Get back over here! Jeff, damn you, *get over here!*" Then I forced an actor's grin on my face and innocently asked the deputy what happened.

The Sheriff said it looked like some punks were using a bicycle inner tube to launch half-gallon cartons of ice cream at unsuspecting motorists. I threw my hands in the air, exclaiming, "Unbelievable!" Then I brazenly pointed to my house and said, "I live right there," and told him I would keep a watchful eye out for those hooligans. When Frank finally got home, he shook his head and told me I was crazy, and that may well be, but I came close to dying from hysterical laughter a thousand times telling this story. When you think of all the people you know, how many of them have robbed a dairy? This little stunt scared the hell out of us—but what do you think it did to the driver? Imagine driving down the highway at 45 miles an hour, when all of sudden you get unexpected drive-through service with a half-gallon of ice cream dumped in your lap. For Christ's sake, what's next? *Nuts with sprinkles?* We didn't set out to be thieves. We just wanted to have some fun. So, I took a break, you know, some time off from a life of delinquency.

Chapter Seven

Well, winter came and went, and Gram and Pop bought Frank and me an eight-man tent for Christmas. So we planned a camping trip as soon as it got warmer, and all our friends were in. Everyone chipped in to get canned goods and supplies. We had a perfect spot picked out at Haverhill dam, which really wasn't a dam; it was more the Haverhill locks. On one side were eighteen to twenty feet of crystal clear water. You could see every fish, water snake, and turtle swim by. On the other side were turbulent rapids. *PERFECT.* With less than two hours away from blast off, we had all our camping gear packed away on the side yard by the road. Bubba's dad was going to give us a ride out there in his pickup. After the weekend, we planned for him to rendezvous with us to give us a ride back home. Bubba's dad was a great guy who was a Native American Indian. He grew up on an Indian reservation and was a hard working plastering contractor. Whenever we were invited to a barbecue at one of his friend's cattle farms, he would throw Bubba the keys to his truck, and we would drive every acre of the ranch. If he hadn't seen us in a while he would come looking for us in a tractor, only to find us stuck in a ditch. And instead of being mad, he would laugh and pull us out, and let us be on our way.

Here's a good story: When Bubba's dad and his brother (Bubba's uncle) found out their favorite watering hole was up for sale—a little dive bar named the Port Hole Lounge—they pooled their money and bought it themselves, which is like having the mice guard the cheese. We loved it, and on the weekends we would go in the backdoor, raid the beer coolers and then we would go out in the woods and cop a buzz, try on condoms, and talk about the girls we'd like to nail at school, like any of us would know what to do if we scored. Bubba's dad had his demons too, but more about that later.

So *here I am* with my brother Frank patiently waiting for our canal camping cohorts to arrive. Frank and I were so excited. For the first time in our life we had something cooler than anyone else in our peer group, and we couldn't wait to share it with them, thanks to Gram and Pop. We must've told anyone that would listen for weeks our plans and expectations for that weekend. And then it happened, the unforeseen, the unthinkable, the unfair—the phone rang. Mom stuck her head out the side door of the house and hollered out that our stepfather was on the phone, and he wanted to talk to us. This didn't sound good.

Once inside the house, Frank got the phone first, after a few minutes of dialog he declined, then it was my turn. Evidently—and these was his words, not mine—his "lazy nigger dishwasher" didn't show up for work that day. *GREAT.* Now all of the sudden either my brother or I would have to inherit this responsibility. Ah, there is nothing quite like free labor, is there, but this wasn't the first time this had happened. But this time I wasn't going to go along with it, so he told me give the phone back to my mother. Frank and I looked at each other and just shook our heads. After a few moments of conversation, mom looked at us, and hung up the phone. Then she dropped the bomb; we were grounded. This would be our punishment for not wanting to help out our stepfather.

I have to admit, normally, my brother would reluctantly accept the burden of this responsibility, but he was just as excited as I was about this trip. We went back outside with our long faces, and sat down by our gear and stared at each other. Frank was so pissed off he was on the verge of tears. Right then, as always, I came up with one of my bright ideas. I suggested that when everyone got here, we should quietly pack up and go anyway. We were going to be camping for four whole days and, as usual, our parents didn't know where. So what were they going to do, track us down and, when they eventually found us, beat us up? It took all but sixty seconds to talk Frank into this. *What the hell!* It would be worth the ass whooping when we got back. So when our friends showed up, we packed up and jumped into the truck. Mom had caught wind of what we were doing, she hollered out the side window, "You boys better get back in this yard." In the back of that pickup with all our friends, we drove away and stared at the house as her shrieking voice finally faded away. With all the excitement of the forthcoming weekend, compounded with the fear of the return, we all began to laugh. Ah, there's nothing like rebellion when you're a teenager.

Bubba's dad dropped us off at the woods alongside the canal. Once we got our campsite setup next to the dam, we had a blast. First thing in the morning, after we ate, we went exploring in the woods and collected firewood. Then, we would swim all day and fish in the evening. We had Spam and eggs for breakfast and we had plenty of canned goods to carry us through. We had green beans, baked beans and corn, hot dogs and buns, and fresh fish. We lit a bonfire every night where we sat and told stories. One of mine was hopping the train when it passed through our yard on 40th and Greenville, only to bail out about a mile later. But by far, the center of our entertainment for that weekend was swimming in that canal. We'd play water tag and jump off the dam, swim in the canal only to get swept into the locks and get spat out downstream in all the rapids. *What a blast!* After a few days Frank and I had completely forgotten about our dilemma at home.

It had been a fantastic escape, but sitting in the back of Bubba's dad's pickup truck, on the way home, there was kind of a weird nervousness. Frank and I knew we were going to have to face the executioner. *Tick tock, tick tock...*

So, *here I am*, watching the sun go down, as my stepfather pulls into the driveway. And the first person he sees when he enters the house: yours truly. He started to bat me around and when I'd had enough, I bolted out the front door while I was calling him some filthy name. He was in hot pursuit, so I made him chase me around his car a few times. Once he ran out of breath, he was on the opposite side of his car from me. I started taunting him, saying I was going to kick his ass when I turned 18. I had been telling him that since we lived in St. Petersburg. Back when we were living there, one evening after I had showered, I stepped out of the bathroom with a towel wrapped around me. One of my sisters had her friend from next door over visiting, a girl who I happened to have a crush on. Jim Ward thought it would be funny to pull the towel from around me. At the ripe old age of 11, as you might imagine, I found this more humiliating than humorous. Standing there, fuming, with my onion cupped in my hand and with not one weed sprouted in the garden, this had been the first time I promised him that when I turned 18 I was going to kick his ass.

Back to the story. It was at this point I grabbed my sister's tricycle by the gooseneck, and winged it across the top of the car at him with all my might. Thank God he ducked, or it could have killed him. By now he had caught his breath, so he chased me up the dirt road and, just like in a Warner Bros. cartoon, I played Pepe Le Pew and stayed just a few steps ahead of him, taunting him along the way. I was egging him on and laughing at him with jeering comments like, "What's the matter fat boy, can't you keep up?" as I ran backwards. I heard him start wheezing and coughing as he slowed down, and then he dropped dead... *Aw I'm kidding!* I couldn't have been so lucky, but I did have to spend the night over Danny Glick's. A few days later I started sneaking back into the house at night, after my parents had gone to bed. Eventually things blew over.

Well you didn't have to work at NASA to figure out there was no love lost between me and that half-drunken hillbilly I had to call my stepfather. One night, out of restlessness, I decided it was time for some recon. I snuck into my parent's room, snagged the car keys and shook my brother awake. I had a flash of brilliance or should I say ignorance. I wanted to take the 20-25 mile drive down to 'Hell Peluxo' to see our old friend Gary Cornell. At first my brother Frank resisted. He wanted to know why I just didn't take the car and just drive down there myself. But I had a baby face, and knew I would get pulled over by the cops. Frank looked older and more mature; I needed him to pull this caper off. My poor brother, what could he have ever done to deserve me? But he fell for it and gave in, plus it was a whole lot easier pushing that car out the driveway with two of us. As soon as we cleared the driveway we hit Military Trail and pointed the car south and headed towards Hypoluxo.

Everything was moving smooth as a baby's behind until we got to Lantana Road where we had to make a left and head east. There was a canal that ran parallel to Lantana Road that ran from Lake Osborne and it was twenty feet deep. The stoplight at Military Trail and Lantana Road turned amber just as we approached it. In the excitement, Frank took the left turn a little wide, and we barely escaped taking the car for a swim. Instead, we were spun out on the side of the road with Frank pissed off and freaking out. Even with the car now pointing west, and Frank cussing me out, I somehow convinced him we had made this far, let's just continue with our journey. I had only been on this Earth for a total of fifteen years, but I'm sure Frank thought for fourteen of them I was trying to get him maimed, killed or locked up in prison. My brother. He had to have loved me dearly. If the shoe had been on any other foot, they would've put it straight up my ass and they would've had nothing to do with me.

So, *here I am* in front of Gary Cornell's house. We hadn't spoken to him in years, and we weren't sure which room he was sleeping in, but as luck would have it, we tapped on the right window. When Gary cracked it open, he couldn't believe what he saw; the two of us standing there, grinning like delinquent idiots. He asked us what the hell we were up to. I told him we missed him, and we'd come down to take him for a little joy ride... He grabbed his shirt and snuck out of the house.

54

When we got to Seacrest Blvd, we turned south to head towards Boynton Beach. Just as we made our turn, a Palm Beach County Sheriff's deputy pulled up behind us. Frank freaked out, and as well he should have. It was two o'clock in the morning with three teenagers driving aimlessly around in a stolen car. Frank called me every name in the book, but I knew I had to keep him calm, because if we blew it here, phase one—spending the night in jail—would be the easy part. Phase two, I'd rather not think about… So, with a reassuring and steady voice I told Frank to put his turn signal on to turn left at the next street, and of course the deputy followed us. The next street we came to was Gary's, so we made another left and headed towards his house. The deputy turned left, and pulled behind us, but he hadn't lit us up. I told the fellas we were going to pull in to Gary's house, park in the driveway calmly get out, and walk towards the front door like we were going enter the home. It was a beautiful plan, and it worked. The Sheriff had slowed down until we stepped up on Gary's porch and then he drove off. I thought I was a genius, but Frank was pissed off, and Gary had had enough. He was afraid his old man was going to catch us standing on the front porch. So he made us swear we would never come by and pick him up with a stolen car again. *Party Pooper!*

Years later I would realize there was a bigger force watching out for me. Thankfully that was as far as we went on that ride. Now Frank and I had a 20-25 mile ride to get back home, and I think he cussed me out for 19-24 of it.

The next day, I had to share the story with some of our friends, which only angered Frank because he had to live through it all over again. But then he laughed it off. If I had a buck for every time Frank said he was going to kill me for getting him involved in one of my escapades, I would have more than Howard Hughes' fortune, and I would be able to trump Donald Trump. I can speak from experience, and I'm sure you can see, a teenage mind is a horrible thing to waste. But as the saying goes, all good things must come to an end.

On one of my days to babysit one evening, right before my parents got home, the two middle girls, Jamie and Louann, had gotten into a fight. So I separated them and had them sit on opposite sides of the living room. When I turned to look out the living room window, I saw Jim Ward's headlights entering the driveway. I spun around and looked at the two girls and said, "Good, mom and your old man are here. Now *they* can deal with you."

My parents entered the home and, unsurprisingly, they were drunk. They had made their usual pit stop at the local tavern on their way home from work. As soon as my step-dad stepped into the home, my sister Jamie let out a shriek. He looked at me and said, "What the hell is wrong with her?" When I asked her, she just bawled, when he asked, she blurted out that I had hit her. That's when he backhanded me and asked if I thought I was a tough guy. I told him I didn't touch her, so he shoved me again, and then, like a thunderbolt, an idea struck me (and this is usually where I get in trouble). I was now over six feet tall and, although thin, the promise of kicking his ass when I turned 18 was getting closer to reality. Right then he pushed me one too many times. Looking in his eyes I knew I could take him, so I let him have it with a right-handed sucker punch, and he dropped like the sack of fertilizer he was. I immediately followed up by jumping on top of him and pinning him with my left hand by the throat. At that same moment I pulled my right hand back to deliver the *coup-de-grâce*, when all of a sudden I heard the "tap tap tap" of feet moving rapidly across the living room floor, and then "shhwack!" A flash of lightning and I saw stars, like in a Bugs Bunny cartoon. I staggered to my feet and stood up. My mother, in a drunken stupor, had run across the living room and kicked me in my face, snapping my head back. I stared at her, paused for a heartbeat, and then I sped through the makeshift room I had at the front of our house. I dashed through my bedroom like my ass was on fire. Grabbing what I could, I dove right through the window taking the glass and the screen out along the way. This wouldn't be the first time I left home, but it would be the last. I headed for China's house—that was my girlfriend at the time.

About six months earlier Frank and I both had left home along with our good friend Mike Flanagan, who was having problems with his dad. The three of us found refuge camping out at the Polo Grounds. We were living in the locker room in the main arena that the wrestlers would use. We collected empty boxes from behind the Winn Dixie grocery store, flattened them out and stacked them about an inch high to provide insulation from the cold concrete floor where we slept. The good news was we had running water and showers, a whole stall of them. The bad news? No hot water. Did I forget to mention it was at the end of winter?

My brother Frank, and Mike, both had jobs at gas stations. This was back when gas stations actually had garages with mechanics on duty and you didn't have to pump your own gas. Because of the hydraulic lifts in the garage area, I was too young to be insured, so I couldn't work with them. So my responsibility at dawn was to watch for the bread and produce trucks, which left pallets of fresh vegetables and bread behind the grocer, and raid those pallets before the store opened. And then, off and on throughout the day, I would enter the Winn-Dixie and steal packets of baloney, cheese and potato chips for sandwiches. Oh, and just when you think there is nothing lower than being a thief, leave it to me to find a way to top it.

I found work with a septic tank company, digging out clogged septic tank systems. So, *here I am*, standing in human waste up to my scrotum with a shovel. Can you believe that they had no age restriction for this crappy job? Within a couple weeks, Pop had caught wind that we'd left home, and he was pretty resourceful. It took him all of one day to track us down to the Polo Grounds and find us. He walked in on us one evening, in the middle of a baloney and potato chip sandwich dinner. Evidently, Pop had a little conversation with our step-dad. Although there were no blows thrown, he gave the hillbilly a little tune-up. He told Jim Ward in no uncertain terms that if we weren't back in the house immediately there might be a problem.

That was then. But this time... This time would be the last time I left home.

So *here I am*, aged fifteen, on my own at the beginning of what would turn out to be a brutal yet amazing journey.

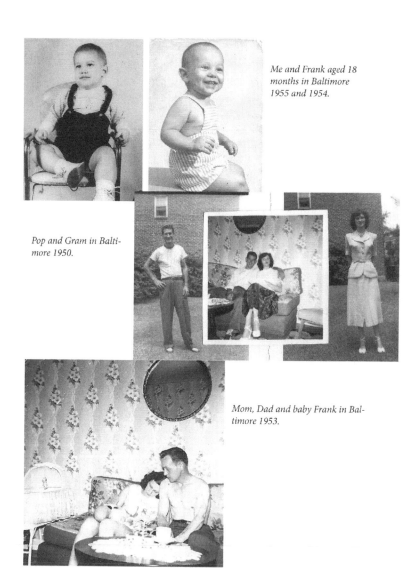

Me and Frank aged 18
months in Baltimore
1955 and 1954.

Pop and Gram in Balti-
more 1950.

Mom, Dad and baby Frank in Baltimore 1953.

58

*Pop ready to feed
the squirrels in Lake
Worth, FL 1961.*

Mom in 1947.

*"Pop" - Edward Strauss in Philidelphia
around 1942.*

Frank aged 7 & 1/2 in Hypoluxo, FL.   *Me aged 6 in Hypoluxo, FL.*

*Frank, Shirley Ward
(Mom) holding Jaime,
Brenda and me - the odd
man out.*

Me aged 8 Lake Worth, FL.

Me with Rusty the Wonder Dog.

Me aged 10 Lantana, FL.

Gram and Pop Lake Worth, FL.

Frank, Gary Cornell and me. Boynton Beach, FL.

PART TWO

Chapter Eight
Rough Road

First things first, I had to pick up my car which I'd left parked down the street. Oh yeah, I had bought Larry's mom's old car after someone had rear-ended her. I'd given her $150 for her wreck, which had to have the trunk tied shut with clothes hanger wire. My parent's never had a clue I owned a vehicle, and although I didn't have a driver's license that was hardly a deterrent for me. A license, insurance, registration—all that sounded like a lot of unnecessary rhetoric to me. I had places to go, things to do, and people to meet. I was a man on the move... And I had a car!

The second thing on my agenda was to go to my girlfriend's house, China. China was one of the sexiest women in Palm Beach County at the time, which is not easily achieved when you're only 15-years-old. She had sun-kissed, honey-blonde hair, big Bambi-brown eyes, and a body that could rival any Playboy centerfold. She was a slam-dunk (one hot chick). Oh and did I mention she could dance like Tina Turner? China's mother was French, right off the boat, with a beautiful French accent, and a very liberal European attitude, and thank God it was never a problem for me to spend the night. And right now, I needed a place to stay. China got the okay for me to stay over, and the first thing on my agenda tomorrow was to find a job, but tonight, my luck was holding up. I'm having dinner with a beautiful French woman and her equally stunning offspring. The first thing in the morning I had breakfast with China then she was off to school. And for me? I had to formulate a life. While China got on the school bus, I turned and kissed her mom on the forehead, and thanked her. I left that morning with every intention on finding a job. As soon as I drove out of their mobile home park, I was in a daze. I had a thousand different plans and ideas racing through my mind; they were all fragmented and going in a thousand different directions.

I couldn't seem to focus on any game plan, now that I had the burden of being solely responsible for myself. But I knew I had a lot of responsibilities and had to formulate a life, and it was giving me a headache, so I chucked the whole idea and went over to my friend Bob Wood's house. I pulled up to Bob's with a 'damn-the-torpedoes' attitude, and then the realization hit me - oh yeah, Bob's in school just like everyone else. So now it was time to implement Plan B. I did what any self-respecting South Floridian teen would do; I had enough gas so I headed for the beach. Once I had parked, I found exactly what I was looking for; friends who had skipped school to surf. I found myself repeating this pattern for the next few days. The ocean is a Zen-like zone. Once in the water, I would lose myself and it was easy to forget about the dilemma I was facing. I was self-medicating, that is until I got to my car and then the rush of reality would set in once again.

By now, I told China and her mom I'd found a place to stay. In reality, I had not, but I didn't want to be a burden to them. I simply waited until late at night, then parked my car over by the Polo Grounds and slept in it. When it got too cramped I snuck into a stable. Then Friday evening came, and I decided to go see my friend Danny Glick. Danny and his family had moved out west of town, off Lake Worth Road. Just as I pulled up in front of Danny's, a Palm Beach County deputy lit me up. This would be detrimental to my plan, even though I didn't have one. Thank God back in 1970 law enforcement didn't have computers in their cars yet. So I lied, and it wasn't the first time. "Yes sir, that's *Frank* P-O-D-G-U-R-S-K-I."

Thank God for my brother—he was the responsible one. The one with a driver's license, that is... When the deputy got to the part where he needed my address, I began to stutter. I told him I didn't have one, that I was "between residences." Danny had come out of the house to see what was going on. I was explaining I had been kicked out of the house by my step-dad. Right between the Deputy putting his citation book on the hood of his car, with him reaching for his handcuffs, Danny intervened. He told the officer to use his address because I would be staying with him. I had gone out to see Dan because he knew of a job I might be interested in. But in the middle of my shit storm, the thunder roared. Having this run in with the law, compounded by the rest of my situation (meaning daily survival) had my adrenaline pumping so hard that I was borderline-dizzy and on the edge of nausea. I took a deep breath and watched the deputy drive off and thought *it can't get any worse than this!* That is, until I got in my car and tried to start it.

Bam! Lightning had struck; the car wouldn't start. Now I was homeless, jobless and carless. Just my luck—the unfortunate trifecta! But I wasn't dead yet. I left my car more stranded than parked on the side of the road in front of Danny's place. I hitchhiked back to China's. I couldn't think another thought; my head was pounding so hard I thought it was going to explode. So I checked out. Instead, I crashed at China's and thank God, when I woke up the next morning it was the weekend. One week down, and I hadn't drowned.

I had breakfast with two lovely ladies, and then hitchhiked to Bob's house. Once at Bob's, the two of us jumped into his car and set out to Mark Turner's house. I'd met Mark and Bob at the same place I'd met China: at a place called Music Casters. As well as meeting them, I also joined a group of other new acquaintances. Music Casters was a teenage nightclub and dancehall. It had a great dance floor, a terrific lightshow, and an amazing sound system. It had a counter that sold cinema-type concessions, snacks and drinks, and an outdoor patio that sat facing a small lake where kids rented two-person paddleboats that you peddled like a bicycle. It attracted a 14-20 year old crowd, which meant there was no booze, but that was no problem because we supplied our own. Another nightspot next to Whispering Pines, off of Military Trail, was the Carnival Bar: a country and western dance hall with a packing store. We found out these hillbillies seldom checked anyone's IDs, so it was a liquor store tailor-made for juvenile delinquency. From there it was a 12-15 minute ride, so we would pound a couple Colt 45s, (you know, malt liquor), and hit the dance floor with a slide. Once we worked up a sweat, we'd head to the patio deck. Once we danced ourselves straight, it was time to get out on the lake.

One by one we would find ourselves in a flotilla on the lake where no one could see what we were doing, or smell what we were smoking. By the time we came back in, we not only were half drunk but we were half-baked. We were lucky no one drowned. By this time we thought we were getting pretty creative with our dance moves. But by far, China was the best dancer in the whole place. I remember the first time I saw her she was dancing by herself and I couldn't stop staring. I was

65

mesmerized, as were all the other guys. She looked like the star pupil of the James Brown or Tina Turner dance studios. Don't ask me how, but after a couple of weeks, I worked up the nerve to talk to her, and I managed to make her laugh. The next thing I know we were dating. I didn't dance yet, but there was never a problem with her dancing with other guys; I just loved to watch her move. Then one night she talked me into going out on the dance floor. Once my feet hit the floor, it was like throwing a duck into a bucket of water, I splashed around for a few moments, and then you couldn't get me to sit down. The Music Casters didn't close 'till around midnight, but we didn't care because by then we were just getting started. We were boozed up, smoked up, and well... *fucked* up. Now with our teenage hormones heated up, we were ready to tear it up.

On that rare occasion when someone's parents were out of town, we'd head straight over to their place. More often than not, we'd end up out in the woods at a bonfire party, and sometimes party until dawn. We had plenty of dope to smoke, and cases of beer and Boones Farm wine to chug once we got to the woods; no one was eager to leave there (at least, until the sun came up). It was just deep enough in the woods that the authorities couldn't find us, not to mention we would use a different location every weekend. Back at this time in South Florida there was no shortage of canals, ponds or lakes we could party next to. Which would inspire some skinny-dipping. It was a lot of fun but there was an occasional fight, and as always, my brother and I would find our share of trouble. But as a group, we pretty much policed ourselves.

So *here I am* with Bob Woods, watching Mark Turner pack a bag to go to Boston with our pal Al LaFortune. Mark had grown up in Lowe, Massachusetts—a suburb of Boston—before moving to Florida to attend high school. Al was also a Bostonian and had to make a court appearance in 'Beantown' the following week. Al would turn out to be a good guy. Well, after he sucker-punched me over China, I had to beat his ass. But once Al was your friend, he was an honorable guy. But he did have delinquency in his blood. He was that guy—and everybody knows one—who just couldn't seem to stay out of trouble. Mark hadn't been to Beantown in a couple of years, so the two of them had put their heads together come up with a whole new plan. Al would turn in his plane ticket for cash, and the two of them would hitchhike to Boston. So Al took off to cash in his plane ticket.

The possibility of this adventure intrigued Bob and me. Bob had spent all his grade school years in New York, outside of the city. I could see the excitement in Turner's eyes; Bob and I were in. Now the four of us would start off on this odyssey, hitchhiking up the eastern seaboard. Our first stop: New York, to catch up with some of Bob's old friends, and then on to Boston for the tea party. And after that we'd hitchhike back, well that was the plan anyway. Ah, what a 15-year-old mind would deem reasonable.

The next thing I knew we were back at Bob's and he was trying to put things together. Then all of a sudden he stops packing and decides to call his mom, just so he could fill her in on our hair-brained hysteria. He explained he was hitchhiking to New York to see some old friends, bumming a ride to Boston to meet some new friends, and then flagging a ride to Florida with stories to tell all of our friends. I thought she was gonna come through the phone after him. I could hear Mrs. Woods' voice shrieking down the phone line, and I was on the other side of the room. I'd warned him not to call her. Parents don't see the advantages of a trip like this; they've been blinded by wisdom.

Bob hung up, and I don't wanna say he sat on the edge of his bed like a pouting schoolgirl, but he did mumble something along the lines that his mom said he couldn't go. Well *duh*, did you think she was going to tell you about the spare cash she kept in the cookie jar and that she'd see you when you got back? As for me I was liberated. I had nothing to lose, and I needed to tempt fate to make something happen. I decided to use a technique that always worked on my brother. All I had to do was convince Bob that the penalty was outweighed by the profit. What's the worst that could happen? They gonna spank you? They gonna ground you? They gonna send you to bed without any pudding? I knew they weren't going to beat him up. In all fairness, Bob had some of the coolest parents on the planet. They used to let us throw get-togethers at their place, although they didn't condone liquor and drug use. They let you socialize with the adults, and they respected your opinion, which was the exact opposite of what I'd grown up with. As soon as Bob snapped out of it and committed, I had to high tail it back to China's place and grab what few belongings that I had. It all fit in a brown, paper grocery bag. Oh, and I didn't have any ID, not even a piece of paper that had my name on it.

So *here I am* at the entrance of the Florida turnpike, off of Okeechobee Boulevard, where Bob and I agreed to meet Mark and Al, who were nowhere in sight. Our snap conclusion? They must've taken off without us, thinking that we would back out. But we would surprise them; we'd catch up to them on the road. Oh, the delusional mind of a 15-year-old...

Incidentally, one dramatic thing had happened just before I left home for good. The first time Frank and I had run away, Pop had come to our rescue. But this wasn't an option now; Pop was gone. A few months earlier, he had suddenly passed away. He died in a Miami veteran's hospital from a rare disease they thought he might have contracted overseas while fighting in the Second World War. I was at my good friends Chuck's house when I got the shocking news. It almost dropped me; it was as if the air had been sucked out my body.

One of the last films my grandfather took my brother and I to see when we were kids was "Cool Hand Luke." I distinctly remember coming out of that cinema, looking at my brother and thinking, *I get it.* It was as if someone flipped the light switch on. Suddenly I clearly understood every lesson my grandfather tried to teach us; every value, virtue, moral, and standard of being a man. I think my brother Frank would profess to this as well. Those lessons were something we both try to carry with us to this day. If you've ever seen the movie, you'd know my grandfather: A character in life with profound principles.

Anyway, God bless my pal Chuck. Why he befriended me is a mystery. I was one confused 14-year-old when we met, and he was nineteen years old. He was a passionate guy who composed great music and poetry and possessed wisdom beyond his years. I owe Chuck a great deal of gratitude. He was aware that he was young enough to relate to me, yet old enough to help keep me grounded. Chuck had a great, fun-loving mom who was always kind to me, and his two gorgeous sisters, Sue and Dee Dee, were always sweet to me. I could always count on Chuck to try and steer me in the right direction. But on the day I got the devastating news of my grandfather's passing, standing in Chuck's front yard with his cousin Frosty Garrett and his best friend Timmy Case, who were both quite a bit older than me, there was nothing to be said or done. They all tried to comfort me, because they were great guys, but Chuck knew I needed to be alone. A short while later after I got home, I went in to use the restroom. I'd just sat down when my stepfather entered the bathroom drunk. For Christ's sake, does anyone believe in knocking? What would take place next defies description. This Virginian hillbilly was going to give me his take on my grandfather passing.

So *here I am* thinking, *is this guy for real?* As I sat on the commode, thinking of dropping a load, watching this hick flap his lips, not hearing a word he was saying, just wishing I could just take my shit in peace. Was his brain so polluted that he thought nothing of having this discussion with me at this place and time? It was like being on a bad acid trip, but it was surreal enough to make you swear off the pink lemonade. This missing member from the cast from the movie "Deliverance" couldn't stand on an extension ladder and kiss the bottom of my grandfather's ass.

When he was growing up, Pop and his little sister were abandoned and circled between relatives until they ended up in an orphanage. After ten years, at 17, they released Pops. He went straight down to the harbor and signed up as a Merchant Marine. Then he turned around and went straight back to the orphanage to sign out his sister, acting as her guardian. He got her a place to live with the advance salary they had given him and then went straight out to sea. And as if that wasn't a test to his character, as soon as his time was up in the Merchant Marines, the Second World War broke out. Pop was assigned to the infantry in the European campaign. One day a handful of soldiers, including him, had unwittingly broken through enemy lines. When they took a break, Pop saw a big rock and sat down behind it, leaning up against it to have a cigarette. Just as he lit up, he happened to glance over and see a German officer strolling through the countryside, just like he was on a Sunday walk with his hands clasped behind his back.

Pop grabbed his rifle, got up and aimed it, gaining the officer's attention, and then quietly motioned for him to come over to him. His reward for capturing a Captain in the Nazi regime? He was sent to the front lines where he and his solider friends were instructed to hold a hill. While chaos was exploding around him, a hand grenade found its way into his foxhole, which would explain his shrapnel scars in his leg, as well as his Purple Heart medal.

The other significant thing that happened between Pop dying and me leaving home was that my brother and I had a showdown. Up until I was 10, I could always beat my brother up. But once he turned 12, he all of a sudden gained some adolescent strength, and I was still a kid. As fate would have it, for the past four or five years he'd maintained the upper hand. My answer to this? Sibling terrorism. When my brother challenged me, I would back down. Then, when he turned around, I would punch him square between the shoulder blades as hard as I

69

could, and then I would run like hell. Then came the day to pay the piper. One day he challenged me to go out in the front yard, I thought screw it, let's do it. My brother Frank had always been stronger than me, and despite my subsequent professional athletic career, to this day he probably still is. I knew if he got me on the ground, it would be all over except for the slow walking and the sad talking. So I chose to stand up and fight like a boxer – not that I knew anything about boxing at the time, mind you. I simply emulated what I had seen on TV, and it worked. Every time he tried to wrestle me to the ground, I got away from him, and went back to punching him. Before this ended, the neighbors in the surrounding homes had come out in their front yards and cheered us on, not much caring who won. When Frank decided he'd had enough, he stood up, beaten and bloodied, raised my hand and announced to the neighbors: "My little brother can kick my ass." I would never be half the man my brother Frank is.

But back to my cross-country journey. It didn't take Bob and I very long to hitch our first ride all the way to Orlando. Not bad for our first ride. But, in Orlando we would be stuck for a couple of hours by the side of the road before a car full of rednecks pulled up and started harassing us. They told us they wanted our money and our drugs. We told them we had no drugs, and the only money I had was the 10 dollars I'd borrowed off of my friend Mike Flanagan right before I got back to Bob's. They didn't want to hear it; they thought there was no way we were traveling and hitchhiking without speed, an upper, to keep us awake.

But before they tumbled out of their car to attempt to fight us, an FHP (Florida Highway Patrolman) car pulled up right behind their car, and they exited our lives as quickly as they had entered it. But the officer was as big of a southern redneck as well, only legalized. He chased us to the other side of the street and told us in no uncertain terms: when he circled back around in twenty minutes, we better not be standing there trying to hitchhike north-bound traffic on the Florida Turnpike, or he would make it his personal crusade to make sure we spent the weekend in jail.

So with that, Bob and I picked up our stuff and started walking north into Orlando. But not before we had carved our initials into a telephone pole to mark that we had been there. Neither one of us knew anything about Orlando, but it turned out to be a stroke of luck. We managed to catch a ride, and they put us off at the entrance to

70

I-95. This brief encounter with rednecks in the city that would later be known as the happiest place on Earth should've been an omen. In a couple of years Orlando would turn out to be my Achilles heel, and then twenty-five years later my city of triumph. But more about that later... If you know anything about the state of Florida, then you know that the I-95 will take you straight up the eastern seaboard right to our destination. The Florida Turnpike would put us in Atlanta!

After an hour passed by and no one picked us up, Bob and I got bored. So Bob pulled his pocketknife out again and we carved our initials and the date into a telephone pole next to the on-ramp of the interstate. Once we'd finished, we turned around and looked across the street at the mega gas station. You know the kind with the convenient store and its own gas pumps? Right then, a late model Firebird pulled into the station driven by a young blonde about 19 or 20, who got out and started pumping her own gas. Being the typical, hormonally-charged teenage boys we were, we started discussing our fantasies of her picking us up. When she was done pumping, she whipped across the street and pulled in about twenty-five feet away from us, rolled down her passenger window, and then asked if we were rapists. Bob and I snapped a look at each other, shrugged, looked back at her and said, "NO!" The door opened and we had a ride.

Bob called shotgun, which gave him the rights to the front seat. Once we were in the car, I could see the advantages of having the backseat. It turned out she was a college student on break, heading home to see her family in Washington D.C. But before we would reach our nation's capital, we stopped for beer. After tossing a couple back, Bob made a pass at her, and it worked. And why shouldn't it? Bob had thick blond hair, a model's look, and a high school track star's physique; women swarmed all over him. She went for him, and next thing I knew they are macking over the center console of the car. It must have worn her out, because she was trying to focus on her driving while leaning over the center of the car making out with Bob at the same time. It proved to be too much for her. The next thing out her mouth—after Bob removed his tongue, that is—was that she wanted to know if they could switch places so Bob could drive. Bob jumped at the opportunity; you name me one 15-year-old male who's not more than excited to drive a late-model muscle car while molesting a college co-ed at the same time. Okay, they're out there, but they're gay. With Bob driving with one hand, and trying to fondle her with the other, he was in a

71

tight spot. There was no room to pursue this activity any further. I'm sure they both had a great time, no harm no foul. But like I said before, all good things come to an end.

So *here we are*, exiting I-95 in Washington DC, and it was a kind of sad affair. After all the hours we spent driving, the three of us had bonded (especially her and Bob). But with tears in her eyes, she kissed us both goodbye, and left us standing on the side of I-95. This would prove to be a wakeup call; a lesson never to mistake your world for the way the world is. My world—South Florida—was always 83 degrees and sunny. D.C.'s world was 37 degrees and raining ice. Oh and did I forget to mention the wind was blowing it at a 45 degree angle? I thought I was going to freeze. I didn't have a coat, a jacket – not even a long sleeved flannel shirt. All I had grabbed was a t-shirt, a tank top and polo shirt and thrown them into the paper bag; I was now wearing all three. You know that feeling of freezing when you don't wanna move because you're afraid you'll disturb any heat you might have generated? When I finally look at Bob, he was wearing every single stitch of clothing he had brought with him. Every time a semi-truck came by we ducked for cover; it was like a mini-blizzard.

So, *here I am* with my good friend, in a non-homoerotic bear hug, jumping up and down at the side of the interstate, stopping just long enough to stick our thumb out when a vehicle passed us by. If any of our Floridian friends had witnessed us doing the iceberg waltz, while holding each other tight, we would've never heard the end of it. But you let all that shit fly when you think you're about to die, and thank God, we just got a ride. And none too soon, either; we're fried. I climbed straight into the back seat where I could get some sleep. It took thirty seconds for our good Samaritan to convey to Bob that he had to pick us up; because he was afraid he was falling asleep. Bob's head snapped back to look at me; he had the same glassy-eyed stare you would find in an Alzheimer's ward. I looked him dead in the eye and mouthed "Shotgun."

We finally made it to New York. We called our friend Debbie, who Bob had gone to high school with, and who I knew from the dance club Music Casters. Debbie never really fit in with our crowd. It wasn't that we all didn't love her; she just stood out like a diamond in a black man's ear. She was beautiful and she dressed very cosmopolitan with an air of sophistication that was far beyond any of us. After settling her father in Florida, and she was very nurturing in that way, she had decided to move back to Jersey City and live with her mother and step-father. So at the end of the school year, we threw her a great big going away party, and she made each one of us promise if we ever were in the New York area, we would stop by or at least call her. *SURPRISE!*

When we first called her, she was in total shock and then she became excited. As soon as she calmed down, she gave us specific directions on how to make it to a street corner in Jersey City where she'd met us. Debbie's parents were great; they had no problem in putting Bob and I up for a couple of days. And the following day, Debbie's mom took the day off so the two of them could take Bob and me on a grand tour of sightseeing in New York City. They took us downtown to check out all the major department stores, not that we had any money to buy anything. Then it was off to the top of the Empire State Building where we flung pennies off the roof and acted like the tourist-dopes we were. And then it was off to lunch at a real New York City deli, where they didn't slice the meat until you ordered the sandwich. Then later, for an afternoon snack, Bob screwed the pooch. He bought a hot dog off a street vendor's cart—*bad move!* Bob was sick all night. After a neces-sary day of recuperation, it was time for us to hit the road. We had a journey to complete, but we found it tough to say goodbye. These were warm and caring people, and not once did they ask us, "*What the hell are you doing?*" I know I thanked them then, but I would like to thank them again, for putting up with Bob and me on our juvenile jaunt.

Well it was on to our next stop on this hobo adventure of hopscotch. So, *here I am*, on the subway train headed back over the New York state line to meet Bob's uncle, his mom's brother. By this point, and you've probably guessed, we had given up all hope of meeting up with Mark and Al on the open road. After our hillbilly harassment in Orlando, and our non-homoerotic icecapades in D.C., we were feeling slightly abandoned. And they say misery loves company, so here's hoping they were just as miserable as us, because up until we got to Debbie's place we had been living off vending machine peanut butter crackers and Pepsis. We had only budgeted ten dollars for the whole trip, mainly because that was as high as my credit line went, but we really had no idea when the trip would end. But after our little pit stop at Debbie's, we not only had full bellies, but a renewed confidence in our mission.

Now standing on Bob's Uncle's porch, when his uncle came to the door, it answered the questions that had been looming in the back of our minds. At Music Casters back over the summer we'd got into two pretty big brawls with Puerto Rican kids. One of these Latin lovers had asked Bob's girlfriend to dance, all of sudden Bob is throwing punches. Once Bob threw a punch, Jeff Farrington was in and started throwing punches, and once Jeff was in, Mark Turner started throwing punches. Once Turner was in, Herbert Wells started throwing punches, and, well I think you can see where this is going. When Bob got home, he started bragging about how we beat up the Puerto Rican kids, his mom always defended them. She'd tell us we shouldn't try to beat them up; we should try to get along with them. Bob's answer? He flat out couldn't stand them. Bob was a blue-eyed blond haired cracker; at least he was until we got to his uncle's house...

With his Uncle standing in the door it couldn't be denied, Bob was half Puerto Rican. The greatest thing about it was that he didn't even know it. He was so young when he seen his Uncle last in New York, he didn't comprehend such things. *Oh, to see the world through the eyes of a child!* That night, when Bob's Uncle stepped out of the room that we would be sleeping in, we both erupted into laughter that would rival hyenas. I had to say I was somewhat relived, I didn't want to have to fight with someone simply because of their nationality. Bob's mom knew something that I was acutely aware of: how ignorant that is. But the weekend came and Bob's uncle was a great host. He took us, along with his family, up to a beautiful mountain view lake where we set up camp and barbecues.

But when we got back into town, Bob's uncle got a call from his sister, Bob's mom. She had called out of desperation. Bob had ran away with yours truly, she was lamenting, and that's when he interrupted her and told her we were sitting right in front of him. She got so excited we could hear her voice over the phone from where we were sitting. She instructed her brother to grab a hold of us, and told him he was not to let us leave. This is where Bob's uncle blew our minds. He laughed and told her we were on the adventure of our lifetimes and that he would do no such thing. He really meant it too, because the next morning when he saw us off, he handed both of us a twenty-dollar bill. We looked at each other stunned. So now we had a green light. Our next targeted stop—Bob's old grade school buddy Ernie's house.

We hitched a quick ride to Bob's old neighborhood and we got there before the sun went down. Bob wasn't exactly sure which house was Ernie's, so we knocked on a door, and when the door opened: *BIN-GO*—it was Ernie's mom. She was more than surprised, but happy to see Bob and how he had grown up. I don't know what she thought about me. So *here I am* sitting at Ernie's dining room table with his mom serving Bob and me a huge meal, which I ploughed into while Bob and Ernie's mom reminisced and caught up on how their families were doing. Funny how things played out, because Ernie wasn't even home, he was on an adventure of his own and he wouldn't be back until the next day, so she insisted that we stayed, and we gladly said, "Okay!" She offered us his room.

The very next morning we had breakfast with Ernie's family, and around midday Ernie showed up. Of all the people that were shocked, stunned and overwhelmed by our sudden appearance, Ernie took the cake. He had the most enormous smile and hugged Bob and they started jumping up and down. They looked like a couple of preschoolers in the playground. As soon as they were done, Ernie got down to business. Where'd we wanna go, what did we wanna do, and who did we wanna meet? Also, what was our plan? God I love East Coast people. Our plan? Our plan was to see Ernie. Mission accomplished. But now we no longer had a goal. So in roars Ernie, like a cattle stampede. Ernie wasn't a guy who lacked ideas; I loved him! So Ernie came up with a new destination, but it involved a MG (a small, two-seater sports car). This would work for Bob and Ernie, but I was already 6 foot 4—hardly trunk size. But Ernie's friend just so happened to show up with a car the same size as Ernie's—a Triumph Spitfire, another two-seater. So here we go on the second half of our North Eastern tour, two British sports cars trailing each other. Our next stop: Atlantic City. I love the way Ernie thinks.

As it turned out, Atlantic City wasn't the jewel of the gaming world it is today. This was 1970, and so it was pretty run down. Oh sure, they had the Boardwalk and the carnival out on the pier, but all those grand hotels from the 40s and 50s had simply disappeared. But for two wide-eyed Florida boys like us, it was still a rush. We immediately dug in underneath the boardwalk so we could sleep beneath it—that is, before the cops ran us off and told us if they caught us beneath the boardwalk trying to sleep they would take us in for vagrancy. We got caught up in the Carnival-like atmosphere. Watching the roller coaster and Ferris wheel running at full speed, Ernie came up with one of his ideas. One of his high school buddies had just entered college and was working the night shift at one of the hotels. *Lucky us!*

He tracked his pal down to the hotel where he worked and, as it turned out, at midnight they shut down half the lobby by turning out the lights. It was blacked out at 12:01 when we cruised in and there were plenty of couches in the dark to choose from. When our collegiate colleague's shift was up, he would rouse us, which put us out on the street right at dawn. The next stop: the diner for our breakfast and our trusty 'dine & dash' scheme. As soon as we were done eating, one by one we would go to the men's room, but instead of coming back to the table, you guessed it, we each headed out the front door. Every day we would rotate the last guy out just to be fair. We never got caught, but we did get chased. And next it was on to collecting coke bottles for their deposit.

And then came the discovery of an interesting phenomenon. When the beach filled up, we headed back over to the carnival rides. This is where we discovered if you stood underneath the rides that turned people upside-down—*jackpot!* Money fell straight out of their pockets. After our fun-filled weekend in Atlantic City it was time for us to get down to the nitty-gritty. Ernie and his buddy had to get back, and Bob and I didn't know jack about our next plan of attack. Then the light bulb went off in Bob's head. Why not go up to Yonkers and see his grandparents? I knew that was the beginning of the end. I was having a ball. What an assortment of experiences! But I think the whole seat-of-your-britches adventure was beginning to wear on Bob. Bob had a perfect upper-middle class upbringing, with great parents, a two-car garage and a swimming pool in the backyard. It was something to look forward to returning to. And me? I was just hoping my car hadn't been towed and I wouldn't have to sleep in the rain.

I was already drawn to the adventure of life, and the possibilities it might bring. I didn't want to look back. I wanted nothing to do with the trailer trash existence I seemed to be destined for. I was willing to roll the dice and I'd be damned if that was going to be my life. I was determined to break the chain of poverty. I remember our first Christmas in Florida, I was five years old and my grandparents bought my brother and I both bicycles, and mine had training wheels. We were allowed to ride in the alley between the two streets that made our block. Every time my brother had made a stop, I rammed him. He finally had to rat me out, because I dented his fender. My parents warned me: ram him one more time, and they would remove the training wheels from my bike. The next day, the second time down the alley I couldn't help myself. I don't know what came over me, but I rammed him. My stepfather stripped the training wheels off my bike, stepped back and chuckled and said, "Let's see what you can do now, tough guy." It took all of sixty seconds to learn how to peddle that bike by myself. I was rolling down the alley laughing my head off. With my newfound confidence, I reached the end of the alley, looked both ways, and peddled right out of my neighborhood. I guess I've never really stopped moving since.

So, *here I am*, knocking on Bob's grandparent's door. He had called them first, so when they opened the door they were expecting us. But their faces lit up. And the first thing they did? Of course, they called his parents. They were Bob's father's parents and they were warm gracious people as well. Next thing you know, Bob's uncle is present—his dad's brother—and everyone is relieved (including Bob). That is, everyone but me, and for good reason. After some discussion, they had all decided that if everyone pitched in, they could fly us both back home. I would come to find out later Bob's uncle was against it. He was up for flying Bob home, but me? Screw it, I could find my own way. But thank God for Bob's parents; his mom wouldn't hear of that. One of us was not going home without the other one. So, *here I am*, on a jet airliner flying to South Florida. This was pretty exciting stuff as I had never been on a plane. When we landed, Bob's parents were there to pick us up. His mother smothered him with hugs and kisses. Me? His dad just smiled and patted me on the back. To his folks' credit, they were past being angry; they were just tickled to death that nothing had happened to either one of us. That night Mrs. Wood cooked a meal for us. While we were eating, Mr. Wood leaned over and whispered to me I'd have to assume responsibility for the price of the flight back home, which was only fair. Only $125 and I was back in South Florida? I assured him soon as I found a job, I would take care of it.

First things up: I headed out to Danny's to retrieve my car, but it was gone. Danny told me that the sheriff's department had been watching it, but since I was gone a month they'd red tagged it and towed it. Honestly, I never found out what happened to that car. Danny and I discussed my options, and then I was off to the Polo Grounds where I knew I could find a place to sleep. After a couple days I was hungry. I wasn't starving because my friend Chuck only lived two blocks away and his family was good for one meal a day. I knew I needed to make something happen, so I decided to track down my brother, who was living in a mobile home in Riviera Beach that he was renting from my uncle. Evidently my brother left home just after I did. And though I'm sure he thought I was out of my mind, he was still happy to see me.

Frank couldn't wait to hear about my journey. His mobile home was a three-bedroom one. *Bingo!* My new residency. My brother agreed to let me move in with my meager possessions, under one stipulation: I had a job at the end of the following week. I had no wheels so that made it tough, but I did notice they were hiring at the tomato fields, about a mile north of Blue Heron Boulevard off Military Trail. So guess what I did? Meanwhile, my brother was working as a carpenter, off 45th Street, building footers for new town homes. Once the carpenters started rolling, they had to hire laborers to dig the trenches for those footers. I would dig out five shovels worth of earth and three would fall right back in. At 98 degrees in 100% humidity this was a job for the young and dumb. *Podgurski, reporting for duty sir!* But I was thankful as it paid a lot more than picking tomatoes, and the temperature was the same.

Chapter Nine
The Beating

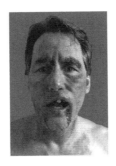

But before my intellectual sabbatical, where I left sunny South Florida for a winter vacation in Yonkers, I'd somehow saved enough money to put a down payment on a cheap 450 Honda, over at the local Harley shop where I knew the owner. I didn't get to play until it was completely paid off, that is. I was forbidden to have a motorcycle when I lived at home but now I was out on my own. And with no parents for a loan, it took me a few weeks before I paid the bike off, and then I had wheels. Forget the fact that I still didn't have a driver's license; that was rhetoric. I knew how to drive. Now that I had my bike, I was able to get to and from construction sites and make two-fifty to three hundred dollars a week. Not bad for a kid with no education in the early 70s. Then I got hooked up with the Shriner brothers, who were giants: Charley, Leonard, Clifford, Wayne and Walter. Ranging in height from 6 foot to 6'7, they each weighed from 200-245. And me, standing at 6'4 at 170 pounds—I was hardly a beanstalk. I mostly worked with Leonard, who had bulging, muscular forearms like Popeye and a grip to match a gorilla's. All the Shriner boys loved cars, especially Leonard who had five vehicles and professionally drag raced two, which is an expensive habit if you have a wife and family. And Leonard had no problem busting his ass at work to fuel his racing addiction.

At this point I hadn't seen Kenny "Bubba" Duncan in some time. There were hints of Disney buying property up in Orlando. Bubba had moved in with his father to work construction at the future site of the Magic Kingdom. But now he was back, and he needed a job. So I told him I'd see what I could do, but I warned him, the Shriner brothers were working my ass off and he could expect the same treatment. Well, I scored him a job, and a day later at lunch he told me he needed to head back up north to Orlando to collect his stuff. At this point I owned a car, and naturally he asked if I could do him a favor and drive him. Unfortunately, I said, "Yes." This one act of friendship and buddy loyalty would have a catastrophic effect on the rest of my life.

So when the weekend rolled around, I wrangled my old traveling partner Bob Woods to join us for this road trip. We iced a cooler of beer and the three of us headed north for Orlando, which was about a two-and-a-half hour drive. About the time we popped the top of our third beer, Kenny stared telling us about some guy who owes him $200, and he wanted to stop and collect his debt while we were in Orlando. This sounded fair enough, especially after mixing alcohol with seventeen-year-old testosterone. When Kenny and I first met each other some years earlier we both discovered we shared a love for comic book heroes. His favorites were Spider-Man and Thor, and mine were Captain America and Batman. The whole romantic notion of good versus evil, and our chosen comic book characters disarming numerous bad guys with their martial arts moves absolutely intrigued us. Kenny as a kid had his crosses to bear, being half Native American, and his dad and his uncles had all grown up on an Indian reservation. Although I don't think he was tested near as frequently as I was (mainly because he grew up around the same kids and didn't switch schools like we had), I'm sure he had to prove himself more than once.

So, *here I am* in a rural neighborhood, where the threadbare lawns are lower than the dirt road we're driving on, when Kenny yells, "Stop!" As we all piled out of the car, I noticed the home had no screens in the windows and had bed sheets for curtains. At this point Bob and I had no idea where we were. As we stepped down into the yard, I noticed that off to my left was an old, rundown wooden frame house sitting on cinder blocks, which had a porch with a screen door and a small, half-damaged deck to the side that faced a small ugly swamp. There was another building about ten to fifteen yards away from us, not quite a garage but more than a shed. When we pulled up, I noticed a handful of kids entering the shed. As we approached my instincts were telling me to use caution, but Kenny was moving with intent. As I got to the shed, I could hear voices. I also got a whiff of pungent chemical fumes. I hesitated for a moment and then peeked around the corner, looking through the open door. I saw six or seven teenagers, two of which have their faces sealed inside a plastic bag, inhaling some type of paint thinner, glue or solvent. It was anyone's guess.

I threw my arm out at chest height to stop Kenny, but he said, "Fuck 'em" and immediately blasted through the door. Bob and I followed suit and, as you might imagine, we more than startled these mush-brained morons. Before any negotiations commenced to settle this $200 debt, a yelling match had begun. Before we knew it we were in the side yard, and Kenny was fixing to yoke the kid with the running nose. Now mind you, the good guys (us), had no idea how long the bad guys (them) had been in that shed committing mass murder on their brain cells. So it was anyone's guess. Was that mucus coming out of that kid's nose or was that his brains running out of his melon? Now Kenny was in his pseudo Spider-Man Karate stance, and the kid charged him. Kenny threw what looked like a front kick but missed. They both fell to the ground. *So much for Karate.* But Kenny had wrestled in high school, so he flipped the kid over and ended up on top. Then he drove three straight hard rights into the kid's mush-melon. Just what this kid needs—*more* brain damage. He was out cold. Right at that moment the screen door to the porch flew open. One of the other kid's leaves the porch without even touching a step; he had a 32-ounce coke bottle in his hand, and whacked it upside Kenny's head. I'm talking old school here—the thick glass bottles that people used to collect and return for their deposit. Kenny is knocked forward out cold—not cucumber cold, but incoherent nonetheless.

I had been watching the whole event transpire while leaning against my car with my arms folded. When I came off the car to leap to Kenny's aid, a kid about six-feet away spun around and stuck a revolver in my face.

So, *here I am* with Gonzo the glue sniffer telling me he's about to blow my fucking brains out. He's got the gun pointed at my head, he is so close that I'm not looking at the barrel but literally counting the bullets in the chamber. I glance up at his eyes, his pupils are dilated and the size of pinheads. My brain shifts into overdrive. I've got a sixteen year old standing in front of me, who's had his face in a paper bag inhaling God-knows-what, for God knows how long, pointing a gun at my head. This was a sobering experience. I immediately started convincing old Gonzo here that shooting me and going to jail for the rest of his life for killing someone he didn't even know wasn't his best option. Again he threatened to "blow my fucking head off." I told him to think about it, reasoning, "Why kill someone you don't even know, and then waste your life away in prison?" I stated my case a few more times, not sure if I was getting through to Einstein. I assured him I meant him no harm; I just wanted to grab my buddy and get the hell out of there. And then I witnessed something strange and uncommon in his dilated eyes, coherency. So I urgently stated my case once again with jackhammer repetitiveness. I think he started to realize the current was taking him down shit creek and he didn't have a paddle. So he took a step back from the hydroplane to hell. He told me to get my friend and get the hell out of here. Bob and I rushed on over to Kenny, who was groggy but already pulling himself up off the ground. We got him in the car, and you guessed it, we shot out of there like a bat out of hell. Now, within the safety of the car and a mile away, I had some questions.

What the hell did we just walk into? And why? Kenny came clean. It turns out, he and mush-brain back there had gone in together on a pound of pot, which they had planned to bag up into ounces and sell for profit. But mush-brain got greedy and snagged the whole pound and headed off to Orlando. Kenny felt that he was owed at least his share of the investment back. So much for this amateur drug cartel. Kenny was hell-bent on getting his money or a pound of ass! So what did we learn today, children? Drugs are for dopes, and only dopes do drugs. But it gets better! This wasn't the first time I'd had a gun pointed at me, but it only seemed to happen when Kenny was around...

For instance, back when I lived off of Whispering Pine, Kenny's dad and uncle would turn down our street in an old pickup truck on a Saturday, after a long day of plastering. And what do plasterers do when they get off? They get plastered! More times than I could count, Kenny's dad went by our house hanging out the passenger's side window of the truck, red-eyed drunk, waving a large-caliber revolver around and pointing it at anything that moved. My dog, a cat, the squirrels, a bird... We learned to stand still. And that's not to mention any given time you might pull up to Johnny and Timmy's house on a motorcycle. Their old man might pull a shotgun out from behind the seat of his pickup truck and take pot shots at you. Ah hillbilly haven, nothing quite beats the smell of corn bread in the oven and scent of discharged gunpowder.

But enough reminiscing. Now that we'd taken care of this first piece of business that was really none of my business (and which almost ended my business), it was time to get something to eat and shake off this unreal sensation that you would normally experience when watching a big screen from the safety of plush seat in an air-conditioned movie theater while cradling a bag of popcorn. Being adolescent, we couldn't have dreamed what was about to happen to us in the next hour. Even as an adult, we couldn't have predicted this shit.

So, *here I am*, on yet another dirt road pulling into a house that Kenny and the men in his family had been staying in while they worked in Orlando. Kenny's cousin Timmy was there to greet us and happy to see us. After all the backslapping and hellos, we started a conveyor line to pass all of Bubba's belongings from the house to the trunk of my car, a '68 Buick Riviera. It was plum in color with black interior—a beautiful car that was only four years old when I had acquired it from one of the Shiner brothers. It had a spacious trunk and it was all we needed. The sun was shining, at least for the moment. Bubba had house duties, because he knew what belonged to him. He'd hand things off to Timmy on the porch, Timmy would pass them along to Bob, and Bob would give them to me, because I was organizing the packing of the trunk. That was our conveyor system. I had my head buried deep inside my truck when I had a question. I backed out and lowered my trunk lid. Kenny had just stepped out of the house carrying two suitcases. Before I could utter a word, his face turned white as a sheet, and he dropped both cases.

At that moment, someone tapped me on my shoulder. Instinctively, I turned to my left to see who it was. All of a sudden, it was like a powerful bolt of lightning had struck me. I fell face first on the trunk of my car. My mouth had been shattered, and what felt like gravel and sand filling my mouth would turned out to be my pulverized teeth. I saw a flash of light, as if staring at the sun, I had a deafening ringing in my ears, and I was dizzy and disorientated. When the high-pitched ringing in my ears began to fade, I heard a voice with a back woods southern drawl utter, "I knocked this mother-fucker's teeth out." In my short seventeen years on this planet, I had been sucker-punched and kicked in the head more than once. Shit—I'd even wrecked a motorcycle without wearing a helmet. But the only thing that compared to this almighty blow to my head was when I took that swan dive off the top bunk as a kid, falling face first on the floor. Yet this was much, much worse!

My head was still spinning when I tried to push myself off the trunk of my car, attempting to shake my head to clear it. Leaning forward with both hands resting on the rear of my car, I looked under my left armpit and saw the feet of my assailant. As I tried to gain focus, I remembered thinking *this has got to be one big son of a bitch to hit me this hard.* I had just started to spin to my left to search for a target to land my right-hand haymaker when the barrel of a shotgun was jammed down into my neck, slamming my head onto the trunk of the car. That's when I heard the same voice from the cast member of "Deliverance" tell me if I moved he'd blow my fucking head off.

My eyes darted around, I picked out fifteen to twenty people. There was Mush-Melon and his band of mongoloids. But the most frightening player must've been the lead cast member of "Deliverance" here, who has my head pinned to the trunk of my car and who's got his finger on the trigger of a shotgun which is jammed into my neck. The rest of them were all men. Bubba (meaning Kenny), Bob and myself were only around 17 and Timmy was 15. But in contrast, on the other side of the Mason-Dixon line, stood Einstein and his pal Mush-Melon, along with their chemical-inhaling gang who were all about our age. If you do the math, that made ten to twelve men on their side ranging in age up to 45.

From what I could gather, our bio-chemical lab rat pal Mush-Melon's old man must have come home right after we left and, in true Hatfield and McCoy fashion, well I guess you get the picture! Mush-Melon's father wanted Bubba to fight 'Dain-bamage' again. And though I don't remember Good Ol' Dad being too tall, he had thick fingers the size of most people's thumbs. He slapped Kenny around and egged him on. But Kenny declined; he was as scared as a goat at satanic ritual. And who could blame him? Poor Bob, in the middle of all this, got clocked and he went down for the count and then some. Right about then the bitch slapping ceremony was over, and they were ready for the main event.

Despite the fact that they drew first blood, *mine*, they looked at me and said, "Get the tall guy, get the Pollack," and I immediately knew then that the warm ups were over. At the very least, this was a wardrobe malfunction. I couldn't have picked a worse garment to wear that day; a football jersey with my last name plastered across the shoulders. "Jeff Podgurski," spelled P-O-D-G-U-R-S-K-I am having a bad day. *Let the beating commence!* I got punched from the left, punched from the right and took a pipe blow on the top of the head. Plus, I copped a crack from a 32-ounce coke bottle that shattered on my cheek. I got kicked between the legs, but I was fighting with everything I had to keep from going down. Somehow I got spun around and got back-pedaled up onto the front porch where I fell through the screen door.

They entered the house with a vengeance, barreling through the windows, tearing down the sheets that were hanging as curtains. They barged into the kitchen and wiped out the kitchen table with everything on it. They slammed me against the wall, and then Mush-Melon took the pistol and pressed the barrel into my forehead so hard and so suddenly, it made my neck snap backwards. It felt like whiplash.

With the gun's hammer jacked back, I had this swamp rat telling me to get back out of the house. Of course, the conclusion later was they wanted me outside because they were afraid I knew where there was a weapon inside. This was surreal; it took me some time to realize what they wanted me to do. "Get the fuck out of the house, I mean *now* cocksucker or I'll dump your brains all over the floor!"

So now I am back out on the front porch, but unfortunately I tripped and fell right off of it. I remember thinking on the way down: this could be it, they might stomp me to death if I stay on the ground. The instant I hit the dirt I bounced to my feet. Once I got up, the beating continued. I got struck from behind and when I fell forward, it was straight into the guy with the revolver, so he pistol-whipped me.

I was warding off the strikes when I got backed into my car. I looked down and saw Bob coming to. At this point he wasn't knocked out, but he did the right thing, he gave them the fake-out. There was so much violence and hostility directed towards me. Even in the middle of my shit storm, it flashed through my mind that Bob was awake and doing well, but getting him hurt wasn't going to lessen my suffering. At that minute one of them reached across the hood from behind, grabbed my hair and pulled my head back. And with that, they grabbed me by my arms and legs and spread me eagle across the front left fender of my car. Then four or five of them formed a conga line for field goal practice, where they took turns trying to put my balls through the uprights. At this point, it should be abundantly clear—I wasn't going to win this, but I was wearing them down. I was taking the severe beating, but they were doing all the huffing and puffing. With my adrenaline maxed out, my instinct for survival kicked in; I was past the point of feeling pain.

The closest home was 60 to 70 yards away. These were huge properties, and we were practically out in the swamp. I was acutely aware of people standing in their yards staring while others wandered down the dirt road to watch me take my beating. This was much better value than watching wrestling on TV. At this point I had worked a hand loose and was striking at anything that came in range. Then, like a parting of the Red Sea, these rejects from Hee Haw stepped away from me. And the reason for that became abundantly clear; one of their heroes stepped into that void in a boxer's stance and started shadow boxing. With his fans rooting him on from the front row, I pieced together his record. No, I mean his criminal record. Evidently twinkle toes here had spent a few years in prison and picked up the fine art of pugilism. Being fresh out of the joint, he was eager to display his newfound skills on fresh meat: *me!*

So, *here I am*, after being battered with guns, beaten with pipes and pummeled with fists (not to mention being trashed by more than a few bottles), I'm expected to stand in the middle of a makeshift circle and now abide by the Queensberry rules? I was already bleeding profusely from my mouth, my nose, and one ear. Every molar on the top left side of my mouth had been sheared off to the gum except for one. Not to mention a few other miscellaneous teeth were dislodged. My nose was broken and I couldn't hear out of my busted left ear, but out of my right ear I heard a voice that seemed to have come from an angel in heaven. Four words, *"The Sheriff is coming!"* And these cockroaches scuttled off into the woods faster than they'd appeared. I was lurching and clinging to the side of my car just to stay on my feet. I glanced around and they were all gone. When I looked at Bubba and Timmy, their faces were white as sheets. I quietly slid down the side of my car to the driver's door. Poor Bob, he struggled to get to his feet. I fumbled with the door and finally managed to slide into the driver's seat. Sitting there, my heart was beating so hard it sounded like a bass drum pounding in my head. Then I mumbled, "Let's get the hell out of here." I could feel my face swelling with every heartbeat until the darkness crept in. By the time everyone got into the car, I couldn't see. I clenched the steering wheel and fumbled with the keys. I hesitated for a moment, then muttered, "Someone else has to drive."

Bubba jumped from the back seat into the front seat of the vehicle and came around the car to help me. I struggled for a moment to get out, but once I was on my feet Bubba, Timmy, and Bob walked me slowly around my car and tried to get me comfortably seated. Then Bubba jumped in the driver seat and drove us out of there. Not a word was spoken for over an hour. My mind was reeling after what had just taken place. I'm sure we were all sharing the same dazed state of mind. Over the years I've related this story over a hundred times, and more than a few men have told me "what they would have done." But you can trust me on this; you don't have a clue what you'd do until you're forced to wear those shoes. I've never blamed Bubba, Bob, or Timmy for holding their ground. God bless them. If they had tried to do more, the fight would have escalated, and we might all be dead. Besides, any one of them getting hurt wasn't going to ease my pain.

Over thirty years later Mel Gibson would make a film, "The Passion of the Christ," which I would go see by myself because I knew what I was in for. It was Tuesday night, the last showing at 10:30 p.m. I was one of three people in the theater. There was a couple that sat in the very back, up against the wall. I intentionally sat in the middle of the Cineplex. Although you might not find anything about me that's Christ-like, unfortunately, we share one thing in common; we can both take a beating. When it got to the part where the Romans caught and flayed Jesus, I wept, as quietly as I could. How people can inflict such pain on someone they don't know, or who has done them no wrong, is beyond the comprehension of the civilized and humane.

After more than an hour in the car in shocked silence, believe it or not, I broke out with an infection. No, not the type you need antibiotics for, but the type that makes it impossible to catch your breath: laughter. I blurted out, *"What the hell was that?"* and started laughing uncontrollably, which became contagious. Now the three of us were laughing like idiots for a solid ten minutes. Don't ask me why, I guess it was the release of all that tension, and the relief we were all alive. After traveling a few miles and sorting through all the fog, it just seemed funny.

The *battle royale* took place on a Saturday, so I spent the weekend lying on ice. Monday came, and I couldn't go to work. Tuesday—no work. Wednesday, also no work. Thursday—well, I think you get the picture. But that Thursday evening, I dragged myself down to enroll in one of the two Karate schools in my hometown. I was determined never to let this happen again. Luckily, the one I selected was the right one, Mark Herman and Carl Stone's "The Dojo."

Carl, one of the school's two owners, took me around their studios and told me that once I healed up, they would be happy to sign me up. I would find out years later that after I left, everyone cracked up and took bets on whether I'd played chicken with a Mack truck and lost. The next morning I drove myself to work to hang sheet rock. That evening when I got off, I went straight to the Karate school and laid down my money, and told them I'd be there on Monday for training.

I'm a man of my word. Monday came and, after hanging sheet-rock all day, just as I promised, at 6 p.m., I was at the Karate school for training. I had two black eyes, a broken nose and was busted up with missing teeth. I was black and blue all over and had a painfully swollen face, but I'd decided I was ready. This was never going to happen to me again. Kenny and I started training on the same day, but after six or so weeks, 'Bubba' seemed to lose interest. Then he tried to convince me I was going to burn out. I couldn't believe my ears; I loved this stuff. This was my new mission in life. If I could have, I would have gone to bed at the Dojo and woken up at the Dojo. I would breathe, eat, drink and sleep Karate for the next five years. I was aiming for my black belt, but I had no idea, what else I had signed up for when I joined that Karate school.

This odyssey that I'd set forth on known as The Dojo would make the film *Pulp Fiction* look like a Disney fairytale classic, but more on that later. Most people realize when you sign up at a Karate school you start off as a white belt. With a white belt at the Dojo, you weren't allowed to spar; hell, you didn't have any skills. So I'd take my one-hour (basics) class, and then take the following white belt class for one hour. After hanging sheet-rock for 8-10 hours a day, Monday through Friday, I would go in and take these two one-hour classes back to back. I wanted to know this stuff, and I wanted to know it well. Then, on Saturday mornings after my workout, I would stick around and watch the advanced belts spar. By the time I would test for blue belt—our first color belt—I needed to know a variety of blocks, strikes, punches, and kicks as well as twenty self-defense techniques—ten from the front and ten from the rear. These techniques were designed to enable you to break out of holds such as headlocks, wrist grabs, arm bars, chokes and bear hugs. You were required to know all these techniques before testing for blue belt, and only then could you spar.

This was a blessing. Standing up straight at almost 6' 4, and weighing 169 pounds, I was hardly a beefcake. I couldn't afford for anyone to grab a hold of me. Besides all of that, the advanced belts were looking for someone like me to prey on. I was somewhat gangly and a little slow; perfect for them to practice their new techniques on. So yours truly ended up being the "Official Dojo Punching Bag"—namely, fresh meat for the advanced class to practice on. And since I didn't know any of their techniques I had to push the rules and boundaries of the Karate school. I weaseled my way in to the advanced class. I was so determined and dedicated, not to mention tough, that I think they turned a blind eye when I showed up for the advanced class.

I always seemed to be the last student to leave the Dojo. One night when Carl Stone was locking up, he casually strolled through the bag room where I was kicking a heavy bag and said, "Podgurski, you want to go over Chuck Watkins' house, shoot some pool, and drink some beer?" I reeled back; I couldn't believe my ears. Mark Herman and Carl Stone were two of the toughest street fighters on the face of the planet, and now one of them just asked me to go party with him.

"Who me? Sure!" This would be the beginning of a long buddy-mentor friendship. Then he compounded my shock by telling the other guys he'd catch a ride with me, and we'd see them over at Chuck's house. This was a strange and sometimes bizarre world that I was stepping into.

My newly adopted lifestyle would take a strain on anyone, but I became obsessed with Karate training. Thank God for my resilience during my late teens and early twenties, because that's what got me through the grueling regimen. My daily schedule: up at 6:30, at work by 7:30, hang sheet rock for eight or nine hours, drive straight home, inhale my dinner, shower off the construction dust, then make a beeline to the Karate school where I would spend the next four hours working out, including three one-hour classes back-to-back. Then I'd go into the heavy bag room and practice the moves I had just learned and kick the heavy bag for the next hour. I consistently made it a habit to be the last student to leave the Dojo every night.

I found myself participating in the beginning, intermediate, and eventually the advance classes Monday through Thursday. I didn't think it was any big deal; I just wanted to know this stuff. But it didn't take long for my instructors to make use of my enthusiasm. By the end of the year, I was in front of the class teaching warm up exercises and calisthenics prior to one black belt putting a foot on the mat. By the time I got to green belt, which is half way to black belt, I was teaching one-third of the classes. Then Carl put me in charge of warming up the advance class.

So, *here I am*, the lowest ranking member in the class, warming up the black belts. But you have to keep this in mind: everybody that was in Mark and Carl's inner circle had their accelerator foot pinned to the floor. We were partying every night and every night was a party. In September 1972, when I first started studying Karate, there were only two people with national recognition that were associated with the martial arts and both were cinema idols: Billy Jack and James Bond. There was a quiet mystique about martial arts. Then, by 1974, Bruce Lee exploded on the scene with the film *Enter the Dragon*. It would seem as though I got started in prime time.

By this stage I had advanced to a yellow belt, and had already been tested in a street fight. I had gotten into it with a biker bouncer one night when I was out with Bob Woods. Bob and I had stopped by a nightclub called, Bacchus House. I was standing out front talking with some friends when, out of the corner of my eye, I saw a doorman giving Bob some grief. Soon as I turned around to see why he was yelling at Bob, the doorman let Bob have it. Bob's feet went straight up in the air; he flat backed it. This guy weighed about 210-230, Bob was 150-155, and I might have been around 170 pounds.

I leaped into action, starting off in a classic front stance, and threw out my first weapon in a combat situation: a front thrust kick, which stopped just shy of its target. *So much for my depth perception!* But now the bouncer has grabbed me by my hair, which was fashionably long, hanging down to my shoulders. Now he's throwing wild right hand punches at my head, but I'm ducking so all he seems to do is punch through my hair. But each time I'd bob back up, I'd zero in and punch him square in the nose. When you find something that works, stick with it. I kept ducking, he kept missing, and I kept hitting him (in the nose, that is). After multiple reverse-punches to his head, he was bleeding so badly that the other doorman intervened. I never took a shot, but he did rip out a handful of my hair. When the word got around through the Karate school that I had been victorious, I'd earned a new sense of respect. Oh sure, I could execute Karate moves at the studio in a controlled situation, but now I had been street tested.

Now no one had doubts that I wouldn't throw down, and by 1974 we were being treated like rock stars. We had Karate groupies for Christ's sake! At this point Mark Herman and Carl Stone were known throughout the county, if not the state; even the local police held them in sincere respect out of fear. It was as if we could do no wrong. Unknown to me, and I'm sure some of the other fellas, Mark Herman al-

90

legedly had ties to the underworld and black market businesses. If you needed protection, or debt collection, or drugs, or guns, or fencing of stolen goods—it would seem as though anything you could need from a darker-than-gray area, Mark would provide.

Right after that episode, Carl invited me to Chuck's house to shoot pool. I had befriended a fellow classmate, Skeeter, who just so happened to be Mark's younger brother. Although Skeeter and I were the same rank, he knew some pretty slick moves. He had additional insight that I didn't have access to; he was Mark's younger brother. Then, one night he invited me to a party that he said his brother and some other cool people would be at. *"What the hell, I'm in."*

I picked him up in my car, and we drove to Rivera Beach. We parked in front of Acme Fish Company, which sat on the Intracoastal Waterway. It was 9 o'clock at night, the fish house was closed, and it smelled… well, like fish. But Skeeter jumped out and said, "Come on." He headed towards a two-story cinder block building with a rusted out wrought iron fire escape leading up to the second floor. We're at the fish house. *I got dressed up for this?* Besides, it stank. Once we had ascended to the top of the rusted out wrought iron fire escape on the north side of the building, we were now looking at a wooden door. That is, a solid door with a 6-inch by 4-inch miniature door set within it at head-height, covered by a wrought iron grill through which to peer through. After pounding on the door for more than a few moments, someone eventually answered it. Well, sort of. That little door with the wrought iron grill opened, and I could see half a cheek, an eyeball, and part of a mustache. Then that one eye and part of a mustache announced, "It's only Skeeter," and the big door opened.

Chapter Ten
The Awakening

And with that, the world as I knew it changed. Anyone who's ever stood on an East Coast fishing dock on a calm summer's night can testify to this. The air is heavy and humidly thick, musty and pungent, and in South Florida, it's *always* summertime. I didn't realize it then, but by stepping inside, my life would no longer be the same.

The contrast was as powerful as standing outside on those wrought iron steps in 90-degree weather, to stepping into a heavily air conditioned townhome. It looked as if Hugh Hefner's personal interior designer had decorated it. Once inside this private club the party was raging. There were 30-35 people dancing to a sound system that would rival any nightclub. With strobes and black lights flashing, Skeeter introduced me to the eyeball and mustache—the owner, Danny Lanes. I'd come to find out later why you couldn't detect any partying going on from outside. Danny had added on the second floor to the fish house and the whole thing was soundproof. Plus, the three-inch thick wooden door that we had entered through had a lead core, you know—so as not to be bothered by the Rivera Beach police.

But back to the party. Skeeter and I were playing catch up. We'd had a few drinks, but everyone else at the party seemed to be high on drugs. There were lines of coke, mint bowls brimming with Quaaludes and ashtrays filled with joints. But the drugs of choice for that evening were hallucinogenics. With booze flowing like water, Danny offered me a drink, and then he checked me out for a moment. And why shouldn't he? He had a lot to lose. Acme Fish House supplied a lot of seafood restaurants along the East Coast. They made a fortune.

92

Just then the party got turned up a notch. They turned on a strobe light. I wasn't even high yet, and the flickering light was messing with my head. Danny had a fish net hammock that was anchored to the wall that he would stretch across the living room and then anchor it to a post at the end of his bar. This is how he would initiate any new girls that came to his parties. Mark Herman would climb into the hammock. And with Steve Masciello on one end and Danny Lanes on the other, they'd begin to twirl it around like a jump rope. *Fun, right?* Then they'd con some rookie girl into climbing into the hammock. You have to understand; these guys were doing this all the time, old hat right? But now they've conned some rookie girl into her first trip around the world. I did mention the hallucinogenics, didn't I?

Now caught in the spider's web, they wouldn't let her out until they were ready, which was usually when she fell silent. After twenty to thirty revolutions, they'd finally release her from the hammock and then chaperone her over to a beanbag chair where she would sit quietly for the rest of the night. And now, in a show of masculinity, and not to be upstaged, all the guys from the Dojo would take their spin in the hammock. Just when you think being high on hallucinogenics and being spun in a hammock is bizarre, it's not half as weird as its about to get.

Danny was a knife guy; he had been cleaning fish for his old man since he was a little kid. He could toss a knife with either hand with the same accuracy. With the music pounding and the white strobe lights flashing, and everyone moving robotically, the samurai swords came out. With 40% of the party high on mescaline (which is only a mild hallucinogenic), and 40% high on acid (namely, LSD), with the other 20% smoked up and doped up on Quaaludes, Danny and Mark would take center floor. Mark, wearing a traditional rising-sun bandana, and Danny, with his fisherman's ball cap on backwards, would bow to each other and then launch into a samurai sword fight. To this day, I can't believe someone wasn't killed or physically maimed. This was a cherry popper, as in virgin-no-more. This would be the first of many nights I would spend on top of Acme Fish House witnessing bizarre and impossible feats.

Moments after the strobe light was turned off and the dueling sword fight was over, it was time for act three, the circus knife thrower. Mark would play the assistant, and stand with his back pressed against Danny's bedroom door, which was every bit as thick as the entry door and also had a lead core. Danny was more than aware of the criminal element that possessed his neighborhood. With Mark's back to the door, his feet shoulder's-width apart, his arms elevated to shoulder's-height and parallel to the floor, Act III would begin. Danny would take his seat in a chair directly across from Mark in the living room, easily 10-15 feet away, and would begin to throw knives with each hand that would outline Mark's body. He'd put knives between his legs, along his side, and next to his ears, never once standing up out of the chair or hitting him. Pretty impressive when you remember they were, uh, high on hallucinogenics.

After I got to know Danny a bit better, I questioned his equal accuracy with either hand, and what he told me made sense. In a split moment if you had to defend yourself, you might not have time to reach for a weapon with your favorite hand. So you should train your body to be equally effective from either side. The light in my head went on, so I applied these words of wisdom to my Karate training.

So by now, it's approaching 11 p.m., and we're wound up, cranked up, and well, *fucked* up. Someone suggests we all head over to their favorite nightspot; Neil's Night Club. So, *here I am*, behind the wheel of my vehicle waiting to follow my hair-brained, hallucinogenic heroes on a procession through town to Neil's Night Club. *Gentlemen start your engines!* It was obvious to me this was a freight train that couldn't be stopped and, being 18, I wasn't going to miss a thing. *What next?*

Chapter Eleven

Not long after this eye-opening odyssey night, I was at the Dojo working out, when one of the advance students—Curtis Lucas—came walking in. He had a friend in tow that he introduced to all of us: George McClease. Curtis would become one of my closest friends and George? Well, he turned out to be my brother from another mother. Curtis was Hawaiian; about 5 foot 7, 180 pounds, tough as nails and quick as lightning. He also had a bit of an attitude. I would turn out to be the only tall guy he really liked, but at first, I kept my distance. He would say the most outlandish things, and I would crack up, which caused him to snap a glare at me. But through that glare, he appreciated my sense of humor and we became close friends.

Curtis was constantly telling people I was a waste of height. By the time Bruce Lee's films "Chinese Connection" and "Fists of Fury" had hit the screen, I had been studying Karate for over a year, and members of our Karate school, better known as "The Dojo," had *carte blanche* throughout Palm Beach County. It was as if we could do no wrong; we had access to every hot spot, restaurant and nightclub in town. We had groupies and a sincere respect out of fear from the local law enforcement. I know this sounds a little far fetched now, but at the time, Palm Beach County was barely on the map. This was 1973 and the martial arts world still had a mystique swirling around it. Besides, Mark Herman had already made his mark on Palm Beach County. Back when he and Carl decided to open up the Dojo, they came up with an unorthodox way to advertise.

Mark took a job at one of the toughest country-western nightclubs in town as a doorman. The patrons were the blue-collar workers of the South. From big rig truckers to construction workers, from 'Conch's' to dairy farm workers, to boat builders and cowboys—what a mix. 'Conch's' were commercial fishermen who stayed out for days laying nets. When the nets were full, they would reel them in and then proceed to Acme Fish House. Their catch would get weighed, and then they would get paid. After that, they'd spend days getting drunk and trying to get laid.

If you rounded up this group of hard-working men and put them in one bar together, *boom*—spontaneous combustion. And you can almost feel sorry for them, aside from the fact that most of them were narrow-minded rednecks. Men that work hard like to play hard. So they show up at the door of their favorite night spot watering hole only to be confronted by a 5-foot-six, 145-pound man wearing a purple jumpsuit. Oh, did I forget to mention the matching purple hat with an ostrich plume? Mark might've been conducting himself as a doorman, but he looked like a pimp. Years later I would come to realize what Sensei was doing: he was waving a red cape in front of a bull. One look at Mark, and potential troublemakers couldn't wait to get inside. He'd end up filtering them out on the sidewalk before they even entered the establishment. Those poor hicks; they never knew what hit them. They had never really witnessed anyone quite like Mark before and Karate was something James Bond occasionally did in the movies. Weekend after weekend, fight after fight, knockout after knockout—anyone who witnessed a throw down was sure to sign up for Karate lessons. And then, of course, there was Mark, with his sense of courtesy or his sense of humor, it's your call: he'd leave his business card in the front shirt pocket of his knockout victims.

It was right around this time that the senior element at the Karate school reached out and put its collective arm around me. I had been put through a discipline of torture, physical as well as mental. After being the advance class' punching bag for over a year, I had finally gained their respect. I realized this when Curt Lucas and David Bunning, two of the advanced belts, approached me one day. In conversation, the Orlando incident came up and then they dropped the bomb: what did I think about some of the advanced belts going up to Orlando and paying the guys that jumped me a little visit?

This caught me totally off guard. But I did think about it for a few moments, and then I declined their offer. I liked what I was doing and the direction I was headed. My instincts told me that this was generating negative energy. But to this day, close to forty years later, I can still hear that old woman's voice call out in my head: "The Sheriff is coming!" as if she was standing behind me. And then there was no Sheriff. I've wrestled with this mystery thousands of times, and my conclusion? She must've thought I'd had enough and if someone didn't do something and do it quick, she might bear witness to the killing of this kid. But I often did contemplate revenge.

But I was now on a roll and committed to a solid routine. I'd breathe, sleep, eat and drink Karate. It would seem as though I finally found a place to fit in. So *here I am* at my first Karate tournament in Daytona Beach, Florida. The tournament promoter is Master Pi, a kung fu practitioner. This was before they developed and introduced safety equipment to the martial arts world, so you fought with bare fist and bare feet. Safety protection was your option: a mouthpiece and a groin guard. We were supposed to pull our punches, strikes and kicks within inches of our target without making contact. Then the three judges within the ring would halt your assault and then determine if you would've caused injury.

There were different categories: white belt through black belt, as well as divisions: lightweight all the way to super heavyweight. I was constantly matched up with heavyweights because of my height, but in reality I was closer to a middleweight. And the categories were beginner white belt, advanced white belt, green belt, brown belt, and of course black belt. The most brutal of all categories, hands-down, was beginner white belt. You could be fighting with someone who'd been training for six months and had some basic skills, or someone who'd signed up six days earlier and now thought they were in a bar room brawl, which could leave you bruised, battered and sprained, and with contusions. And although I'd trained and sparred with more advanced belts back at the Dojo, I'd already experienced a couple of street fights, and so I knew how this stuff worked. But I had never sparred in a tournament atmosphere with someone I didn't know.

I was called to the center of the ring with my opponent. We bowed to the judges and then bowed to each other. We assumed our fighting stances and then we were told to *kumate*, which means "fight" in Japanese. I made one move forward and froze. A thousand techniques rushed through my mind as to what I should do, but then I got kicked in the kisser. They stopped the match. I was bleeding profusely through the nose and mouth. The judges' conclusion? They disqualified us both. Him for kicking me in the face and me for not blocking the kick, although the rules stated clearly there was to be no contact to the head area. You were allowed to make contact to the body, however, which meant that everyone was trying to bury one another. After over 40 years of experience, I've never heard of nor witnessed this decision being made since. But this disqualification only made me more determined to go back to the Dojo to train even harder.

To pick up the speed of my kicks, I started wearing 2.5-pound ankle weights on my legs and doing 250 kicks a day, five days a week. In all the years I fought in Karate tournaments, I took first place only a handful of times. Usually after making it to the finals, I would get disqualified for striking someone. But I seldom placed lower than the top three. Then, in the mid seventies, I fought my way all the way to first place and won the US Grand Nationals. Prior to this victory, in 1973, I was lucky enough to participate in one of the biggest and best Karate tournaments in all of America, Joe Corley's "Battle of Atlanta."

I hadn't planned on attending, but the excitement drew me down to the Dojo to see some of our fighters off. I was talking to Sensei Mark Herman when Steve and Ed Shepherd came through the front door with a friend of theirs, all gung-ho and ready to go to the Karate tournament. But they'd missed the bus. So now they turned to me in hopes that I would get caught up in all the hysteria and drive them to the tournament. But I needed new tires for my car, and I wasn't financially fit and couldn't afford to replace them. That's when Sensei Mark said maybe he could help me out.

The next thing I know, I'm at Sensei Mark's home standing in front of his garage. When he opens the garage door, *bam!* From the concrete floor to the rafters in the ceiling, four rows across and as far back as I could see: brand new tires still on their rims. He told me they were Pontiac rims and asked me if they would fit. I had a Buick Riviera, which was a GM product. I told him, "Perfectly."

So I did what any overly excited 18-year-old would do, I jacked up my car and started changing my tires. Later I would come to find out how Sensei Mark came by all these tires. A few miles north of his home, on US-1 was a Pontiac dealership. An acquaintance of Sensei Stone's would go down to the dealership by night and rob it. He'd park a block away after midnight, and then walk to the dealership where he'd find himself in a sea of Pontiacs. Once in the middle of this ocean of Pontiacs, he would submerge himself and then jack the cars up and steal the tires and rims right off of the hubs.

You know when you drive by a car dealership and a section of the lot has the same make and model with every color you could want? You ever notice the roof and hood heights are all the same and the only variation is in their color? Can you imagine the salesperson's face when they showed up for work the following day only to note that three rows back, every car on the lot is two feet shorter than the front row? Is it an optical illusion, or is that car sitting on its brake hubs? This is one of those situations where you would pay money to be a fly on the wall so you could listen in and see how they explained this to their fleet manager.

Fortunately for me, all GM cars had the same lug pattern at the time. Unfortunately for our thief, he tried the same ritual more than once; this mental midget got busted somewhere around his third or fourth outing. I think it was at a Chevy dealership. But for me right now, ignorance is bliss. I'm on my way to Atlanta with a future World Champion, his brother and a friend, and I've got brand new tires and rims. But unfortunately for our thief, he's put in all that hard work and sweat (stealing tires is not easy), gotten dimes on the dollar and some deserved time off.

One observation I've made about criminals: I reckon if they put as much time and effort into a legitimate job as they do their criminal activities, they might go somewhere. (Somewhere besides jail, I mean.)

So *here I am* on my way to one of the biggest Karate tournaments in the country. But after we had gotten packed up, boozed up and gassed up, it's already 11:00 p.m. You can do the math; it's an eight or nine hour drive from West Palm Beach to Atlanta. The first few hours were a blast. We were amped up, we were smoking joints and drinking screwdrivers... Then everybody fell asleep, and I drove the whole way.

We cracked the city limits of Atlanta at 8:30 a.m. and the tournament started at 9:00. Steve had woken up just as we hit the city limits. He was pretty amped up and insisted on driving... *Thanks, pal!* I tried to sleep for about twenty minutes, but we pulled up to Georgia Tech University at 8:55. Like I said, the tournament started at 9:00 a.m., so we ran up the stairs to the registration table. As soon as I was done filling out my form, I ran to the locker room. I stripped down and then punished myself for drinking and driving all night: I entered the shower and turned the cold water on full blast. I stood under it until I was more than awake.

I jumped into my *gi* and ran out on the main floor with my hair still wet. I made it. I got there just in time for them to split up the weight divisions. I ended up fighting thirteen times that day, winning twelve matches and taking fourth place. By the time we got a hotel room after the main tournament, it was six o'clock. Everyone ran in to take a shower; we had to be back at the University by seven if we wanted to watch some of the top black belts in the nation fight. And then, of course, after that there was a huge party with the best of the entire Karate world. But I was fried and went to bed.

At 2:00 a.m., the fellas busted into the room like a herd of buffalo and gave me a blow-by-blow description of what had taken place. Boy, did I miss it! The next morning, while we were at breakfast, I had to hear it all over again. I can't explain how unappreciated I felt. After all, we took *my* car, we used *my* gas, we smoked *my* grass, and I felt like an ass because I got stuck driving all night. But that's the way my luck goes… I made a mental note: the next time I go to the Battle of Atlanta, I'm gonna kick some ass *and* have a blast.

And that's exactly what I did. I swore off partying before tournaments. I competed four different times at the Battle of Atlanta and although I never placed first, I punched and kicked the hell out of a lot of guys. I gained a lot of respect, and they damn sure knew I was there.

But back in West Palm Beach, if you can believe it, the insanity got turned up just a little. I bumped into Kenny Duncan ("Bubba") who I hadn't seen in a while. We got laughing and telling stories and reminiscing. Then he said something that I couldn't believe and which stunned me; he starts talking about the time in Orlando when we got jumped by the Ku Klux Klan. *The Ku Klux Klan?!* He was insistent; surely I must remember? It was when I got all my teeth knocked out. I assured him that I hadn't forgot—nor would I ever—but what the hell did the Klan have to do with me and that beating? And that's when he explained to me for the first time that the father of the kid he beat up for owing him money was the Grand Wizard of the Klan in the Orlando area. *You can't make this shit up!* You think you might wanna clue your friends in on this important information before you put them in harm's way? Like they say, no good deed goes unpunished. Out of friendship, I drive this guy a few hundred miles so he can pick up all of his worldly possessions only to run into a hillbilly's reenactment of the slaughter at the Little Big Horn (with me in the title role). And you still call yourself my friend?

Ah, but what the hell. By now I'd surrounded myself with a whole new group of friends, all from the Dojo. These guys were loyal, dedicated and committed. There was an unspoken rule, our loyalty to each other was paralleled by the U.S. Marine Corps Recon or the Navy SEALs code: No man left behind.

At this point, I was getting pretty cocky. With each fight, I was gaining more confidence. Competing in tournaments? That was for fun. Beating people up? That's just what we did. I can honestly say I never went out of my way to start any fights, but I can't make that testament for some of my friends. Hey, in for a penny in for a pound. Whenever someone from the Dojo got in a fight, there must've been a reason, so their friends were guilty by association. You kicked ass and took names later. Besides, with these newfound skills, why take any crap?

I'd go out to a popular club called Shady Side, which was owned by a fellow named Ted. Ted was as wide as a refrigerator, and just about as thick. The story went that he had been a bodyguard for an alleged Irish mobster who owned a chain of nightclubs, as well a sister chain. One night, things went bad. The guns came out, and Ted did his job in aces. He stepped in front of his man and took a bullet that was meant for the mobster. His man, as you can imagine, was greatly appreciative. So what did he do to say thanks? The rumor was he gave Ted a nightclub.

I stepped into Ted's nightclub one evening and my usual band of hooligans was hosting a good time. I'm in the club fifteen, twenty minutes tops, when some guy walks over to me at the bar and knocks my drink out of my hand. Like I said, I didn't go out and start fights, but assholes like this is what I'd trained for. I gave Mr. Finesse a moment to apologize, but he wanted to debate whose fault he thought it was. I assured him it was his, because I hadn't moved from the bar. That's when it got ugly.

He told me to go fuck myself, so I questioned him on what he thought about Bugs Bunny cartoons. He looked at me in puzzlement and then asked what I meant. "I mean, you're getting ready to spend some time at the largest overnight sleep facility in the world. Maybe you've heard of it, it's called 'the hospital.' They'll be happy to arrange transportation, and although you'll be comfortable, it won't be a limo." That's when this bar room buffoon tried to push me, so I trapped his hand with my right and blasted him on the chin with the heel of my left hand. I knocked him out cold at the bar. Just as I struck him, my friends rallied around me as an onslaught of doormen headed my way. My friends got between the bouncers and me as they approached, slowing their progression. One of my friends shoved me out the side door. I found myself at the fire exit on the west side of the building. I ran towards the alley in the back. I looped the building and started walking towards the east end of the nightclub. Just as I got to the front, Danny Lanes had pulled up and gotten out of his car. He greeted me enthusiastically with, "What's happening?" *What's happening?!* I'm trying to get away from a bar fight! I explain what had just happened and Danny chuckled with laughter, put his arm around me and said,

"You're with *me* kid, and we're going back in."

So we did. I walked past the door guys like I had just gotten there with Danny. And now the funny part: they walked the bar room buffoon right past me. He was in such a daze, he didn't know what or who hit him. There were so many people in the club that they never got a clear look at who dropped the bomb on the buffoon. My friends were now embracing me like they hadn't seen me in years and laughing their asses off. They couldn't believe what I'd just pulled off.

Right about the time our laughter died down, Mark and Carl entered the club. When the fellas explain what had just happened, Carl began laughing so hard that tears were running down his face. When he caught his breath, he gasped, "Only the Pollack!" and that started the laughter all over again. I just shrugged my shoulder and stated, "Everyone's trying to outsmart the other guy. I try to out-dumb them."

That night, we hit a few more clubs before we ended up at Mark Herman's house at 5:30 in the morning where the debauchery continued. We were drinking, we had drugs, and the girls were now doing strip teases for us. We were all having a good time. I was sitting on the far side of Mark's living room on a chair facing the hallway that went to his bedroom.

Trust me, no one saw what happened next coming. They were too preoccupied with watching the girls run around in their bras and panties. That was when Mark entered the hallway and ran to the living room, in his Fruit of the Looms underwear, waving an automatic rifle. He leapt onto a footstool in the middle of the living room where someone had pushed it to get it out of the way. With the footstool spinning, he proceeded to unload a full clip into the ceiling of his own home. Wood chips, drywall dust and smoke were everywhere. All the women were running around screaming bloody murder, all the fellas dove underneath things for cover. I was laughing so hard I almost coughed up a lung. I didn't budge—I'd seen it coming. But now it was raining smoke, splinters and shells. For all of you who haven't experienced machine gun fire in a 12 by 14 room, it's deafening. While our ears were still ringing, everyone started laughing like hyenas. I'm sure the girls were relieved nothing bad had happened and the guys totally got the joke. If you think this is bizarre, what's about to happen is equally puzzling.

When the ringing in our ears died down the doorbell rang. COPS. When Mark answered the door, he tried to step outside but the cops were definitely trying to look in. Mark finally got the door shut and stepped out on his porch to talk to the police. Now eleven adults, and some in their underwear are holding their noses, their breath and laughing at the same time. Mark eventually stepped back in with a grin and told us the story he had concocted.

He told the police he was watching an old John Wayne western with some friends and must've had the volume up too loud. I don't know how he explained away the smoke, the splinters and the smell of gunpowder, but it worked. The officers said to turn the TV down, and tell all of us to go home and get some sleep. But I don't think they believed him.

But *here I am* in Miami Beach at another Karate tournament, in traditional posture on my knees with my back to my opponent, waiting for the inevitable: disqualification. Back in the day, you would get one warning for making contact to your opponent's head or face. There was no second warning. And I had a habit of kicking my opponents in the head, so I was out. But my good friend Leon Nubin, who was like a brother to me, had taken the one-hour drive south to Miami to watch the tournament. Now he's amped up, and had decided he wants to compete, but he didn't bring his *gi* or his gear. So I did what any good sibling would do, I loaned him mine.

There were more than a few eyebrows raised when Leon stepped to the center of the ring wearing my *gi* with my last name plastered across the shoulder blades—PODGURSKI—and his black face. It was as if they had witnessed the sighting of an albatross. Let's face it, there aren't a lot of black Pollacks in the world. And to compound the confusion, as luck would have it, Leon won the tournament! He took first place in his division, which gave us an excuse to party! Not that we needed one...

Our Karate school, The Dojo, had close to forty contestants competing in that tournament on that Saturday. The result: close to twenty trophies. As you might imagine, everyone was fired up, especially Sensei Carl. It was a drag race to get back to Palm Beach County where we could get our groove on. But not before a little detour into Fort Lauderdale.

Back in the 70s, Fort Lauderdale was the spot. With nightclub upon nightclub lining the beach, it was the party Mecca of South Florida. Miami's South Beach, on the other hand, was still twenty years from conception. Now 90% of the regular students at the Dojo had regular

103

lives, 9-to-5 jobs. They went to work on Monday, they paid their parking tickets and they paid their taxes. But not the advanced belts; we were living double lives. So about twelve of us broke off and headed into Fort Lauderdale, still wearing our *gis* (yes this wasn't the first time, nor would it be the last that we went out partying in our Karate uniforms). You can't even imagine what the doorman, let alone the bartender's faces looked like—or the patrons—when twelve fully-grown men stepped into a nightclub in full Karate attire, belts and all, and approached the bar for drinks. Easy to say, we pretty much had it all our way.

Now we were loose in Fort Lauderdale. I think it was about 12:30 a.m. when we were asked to leave for dancing on the bar. We had already killed a few hours in Fort Lauderdale so we agreed it was time for us to leave. So we're headed north to West Palm Beach with our merry band of misfits, with Leon and me in the lead. We had exited I-95, on our way to a nightclub, when we get pulled over by the West Palm Beach Police.

Now Leon wasn't your average young black man of the 70s. He didn't gravitate towards that "Supa Fly," pimp look; he didn't have a 'fro and wasn't drawn towards Cadillacs or Lincolns. He drove a MG. He was articulate, well-groomed and well-spoken. He was his own man and had his own dress code. You were more likely to see him out in a corduroy and denim outfit than some super fly hat and matching suit. Together we were quite the dynamic duo (and we fared pretty well with the ladies). But right now, we're getting blue lit by a police officer. Leon hit the emergency brake and jumped out the driver's door. I couldn't help but notice on his way out he had reached under the seat and grabbed a pair of nunchucks. *What's gonna happen here?*

When Leon hits the asphalt, it's just like a Broadway show: the spotlight is on him. He goes through a series of moves called a *kata*; a weapons demonstration. He's twirling the sticks around and under his arms, behind his back and around his neck. Terror strikes me; I'm beginning to think he might get shot. Thank God the police officers were stunned. They had never seen anything like this before. They hadn't gone for their guns. We were barely approaching the mid seventies and, at that time, no one outside of the Karate world knew what nunchucks were yet.

When we got lit up, Carl had pulled over as well. He approached the police officers and—just our luck—he knew one of them. So Leon got

104

a stern lecturing and his nunchucks confiscated. Two days later, he had to go to the police station to fill out some paperwork to get his sticks back. It was a minor inconvenience when you consider what could've happened. Besides, this was a great story as we continued our night on the town. From that moment on, Leon was christened with a new nickname: Leon Lee!

Not long after this demonstration of martial arts and Asian weaponry for the West Palm Beach police, it was Easter. Most of the advanced class, including myself, made a living in the construction industry, which gave us Good Fridays off if we wanted them, and boy did we want them. It wasn't that we were righteous, well you've probably guessed that, but it gave us a whole extra day to party. And this was an Easter that would go in the record books.

My good friend, Curt Lucas, lived in the same mobile home park as I did (right at the corner of Military Trail and Blue Heron Boulevard). Curt, being married with a son at least a year old, had devised a weekend escape plan (that I assisted him with). Curt lived three blocks east and one block north of my and my brother Frank's mobile home. I would leave my house and pull within a block of the corner that I had to turn left at to go to Curt's. I would get out of my car and cut through the yards to the back of Curt's trailer. Now standing outside of his bedroom window, Curtis would toss a bag full of his dress clothes out to me. Once I had everything he needed, I'd cut back through the yards and stash his clothes in my trunk. This wouldn't be the first time we pulled this maneuver, nor would it be the last.

Now I'd jump back in my car, take the left-hand turn, pull into his driveway and there would be Curt standing on his porch in his *gi* and with his workout bag. He would turn and give his wife a kiss goodbye, I would wave "hi," he'd jump in the car and it was *bye-bye.*

We were off to the Karate school, where we *would* work out; but what she didn't know is it was the last she would see him for the weekend. Just to set the record straight, Curtis loved his wife. He talked about her all the time. And he adored his little boy; he had him doing splits and kicks from the time he could barely walk. His wife Lou and his son Chris were his life, but he was a young man barely in his mid-twenties. After weeks of listening to our weekend stories, he'd have to sneak out and get involved in one himself every once in a while.

Now Curtis was Hawaiian-America, and if he stuck to drinking beer he'd be fine; but if he drank anything else, it was showtime. He could

105

be a handful and, like the rest of us, he enjoyed good-looking women around him. But I don't recall him hitting on any girls or leaving the party to go be with one. Also, the guy used to crack me up. He'd make me laugh so hard that I could barely stand up. Like the night we were at Big Daddy's... A handful of us were on the dance floor with some girls and we were having a great time. Here comes Curt and he hits the dance floor. He doesn't have a chick in tow; he's just dancing with any-one he knows. Now Curtis could dance. He'd come shuffling across the floor on one foot, spin around, drop down in a split, then jump back up and shuffle off the other way. Much like James Brown, he had some moves. The funny part started when he came up from one of those split moves with a pair of nunchucks in his hands—where he got them, I don't have a clue. Then he gave me a little prelude of what was to come: he reached over and tapped me on the shin, which caused me to grab my shin and hop up and down on one leg, but I was laughing. And then Curtis went ballistic. He went around the dance floor and started whacking every male in the shin with his pair of nunchucks. Now half the floor was pogo sticking, holding the shin of their assaulted leg in their hand. Every guy from the Dojo on the dance floor jumped right in like we'd invented a new dance. Everyone grabbed their shin and started pogoing around. Now this one incident was not enough to get us thrown out of Big Daddy's, but the doorman insisted that if Curtis continued, we'd have to take him home.

But back to our epic Easter weekend. We had a two-hour workout at the Dojo, which was Plan A. Plan B? Hit every pool bar in town. First stop: a little dive bar where Curtis' brother tended bar. At first his brother was happy to see us. At 6'2 and 250 lbs, he was hard to miss. We had a good time; we threw some darts and shot some pool. Then we headed off to another place.

After we had hit a couple of other places, we went back to see the big Hawaiian. When we walked in, we noticed a guy we had seen ear-lier, he was all but passed out. But the place was livelier and the pool table was backed up about six deep. So Curtis and I started cutting up. We weren't going to wait six games to play one. Our attention quickly turned to our semi-comatose victim who was sitting at the bar with his head propped up in his hand with his elbow on the bar, his mouth wide open and his head slightly cocked back. This presented the pos-sibility of a new game.

Curtis and I quickly ordered a basket of peanuts each. Trying not to be obvious, we'd crack peanuts open and throw them in the air to try and catch them in our mouth. One for us, and one for our new game of 'dunking the drunk.' We were beaming this guy. Peanuts were bouncing off of his forehead, his eyelids, and into his beer mug. And then Curt took steady aim and launched one, bullseye! It must've went straight down his windpipe, he snapped awake and to attention. He started flailing his arms like he was drowning, wiped out every drink on the bar in front of him and started gagging. That punched our ticket.

Curtis' brother came from around the bar without even checking to see what happened and started chasing us. I guessed he'd witnessed Curtis' juvenile behavior before and he didn't approve. So *here I am* being chased from this dive bar where you can buy a draft beer for fifteen cents, trying to make it to the car before my best friend's brother kills me. We lit out of the parking lot sideways, laughing like a couple of mongoloids at a self-molestation convention.

The next stop was the closest honky tonk where we ran into two of our closest friends, David Bunning and Mark Turner (who we proceeded to convince they should ride with us). You remember Turner, from the Mark and Al Boston Road Show? The trouble was their show never got on the road, which lead Bob Woods and me on our own Eastern seaboard odyssey that ended in upstate New York. Turner was now studying Karate at the Dojo. He had studied once before with Warner Siciliano. It was rumored that Siciliano was President Kennedy's bodyguard at one time, but it seemed as though his students spent more time doing *katas* than fighting.

So once Mark got released from the Palm Beach county stockade, I had convinced him to start training with us at the Dojo. Poor Turner... He wouldn't have any luck at all if it wasn't for bad luck. He'd had to spend time at a minimum-security prison with some other fellas we knew for something he didn't do. Eighteen months earlier, a group of guys that we hung out with went out gay bashing, although at the time it was called "rolling a queer." These "friends" of ours had come up with what they thought was a brilliant idea to make some money. These knuckleheads would go down to the three-square blocks known as the gay part of town. I gathered they flipped a coin to see who would be bait, and then the loser would enter a bar and try to solicit a date. This is where they would convince their newfound love they shouldn't wait and lure this future emergency room visitor to the alley, where he got more of a surprise than he had counted on.

They had executed this get-rich-quick scheme more than once and had profited from it, but now they were looking for recruits. This wasn't my thing. I wasn't into hurting people (unless, of course, they were trying to hurt me), but like the saying goes, "curiosity killed the cat." Mark tagged along out of boredom just to see what they were doing. Big mistake. They got pinched. Not in the act, but in a dragnet a few weeks later. Mark was sitting in one of our homophobic heroes' homes when the cops raided it. At the police station when they did a lineup, one of the victims recognized Mark. Poor Turner, he'd never punched, kicked, or struck anyone on those jaunts. Hell, I don't think his hands left his pockets, but being there was all it took; he was guilty by association. I think he got six months in the Palm Beach County stockade. Occasionally, at different social gatherings, I'd run into Mark's girlfriend, Kathy Jones. Kathy, and her younger sister Carole, were probably the best-looking sister act in the whole state of Florida. Nevertheless, whenever I ran into Kathy, I'd give her whatever money I had on me to take out to Mark and put it in his canteen, which is like a prison bank. What else could I do? He was my friend. Besides, by nature, Mark was really a good guy; he was just a victim of circumstances. Consistently.

But now he was taking Karate at the Dojo with the rest of us, and I had gotten him a job with Curtis. Curtis was a plumbing foreman on the First Marine Bank being built in Riviera Beach. Curtis was pretty sharp; he was the first apprentice foreman in the whole state. One day he mentioned he needed help so I suggested Mark.

But *here I am*, it's about 8:00 p.m. and I'm entering Big Daddy's on Okeechobee Boulevard with my merry band of misfits, which is way too early in the evening by Florida standards since the bars don't close until four. We had entered through the back parking lot via an access road that was a little wider than an alley that ran parallel to Okeechobee Boulevard. Although you could enter from Okeechobee Road by a one-way driveway on the east side of the building, and the exit *onto* Okeechobee was a one-way driveway on the west side of the building, this one-way exit on the west side of the building leading to Okeechobee Boulevard would prove to be our Achilles' heel.

We entered Big Daddy's in good spirits, and why shouldn't we? We had the whole weekend ahead of us, and we had just convinced two of our closest friends to ride in our car. Curtis and I had a head start from hitting a chain of beer bars. We were on a roll, although that never presented a problem. But what became an issue was the surprise that Big Daddy's had for us: they had fired the whole door crew and the club was under new management.

Now we were all at the bar ordering drinks, but the surprise was yet to come. Oh sure, we saw all of the same familiar faces behind the bar, but once they had served us our drinks they didn't stick around to talk. We had paid for our drinks and started to knock them back when someone mentioned that the place didn't seem right. That being said, it didn't slow Curtis and I down from describing our childlike antics that day.

We were in the middle of a belly buster from explaining the last four hours of our day to our friends when two guys rolled up on us like Starsky and Hutch. The tallest (and the leader of this dynamic duo) told us we had to leave. Curtis' response: "Why?" And it was explained in these blunt terms: "You're those Dojo fuckers and your ticket has been punched." This is where we found out that the management and the door crew had been let go simply because they used to let us have our way.

That's when Starsky announces that all us "Dojo fuckers" have been banned, and he's throwing us out. If Starsky here thought we were going to leave peacefully, he took the wrong approach. This had the equivalency of a schoolyard bully bitch-slapping you in the face. We couldn't let that stand.

Curtis was the master of the quick comeback, which was something I always found hilarious. He told this future recipient of rhinoplasty that he didn't think he was big enough. You know, as in sarcastically calling him "Big Boy." Facing Curtis, with the bar to his right, Starsky leaned over his shoulder and told Hutch to go call the cops. With that, Hutch takes off running, Curtis tells me to get him. Just as my weight goes onto my front leg to go into a sprint, I hear a crack. I don't even look; I know exactly what just took place. I catch up to the second part of this dynamic duo two-thirds of the way down the bar. Just as ol' Hutchy-boy looks over his right shoulder to see if I'm gaining on him, I let him have it. I hit him hard enough that his momentum took him up onto the bar, which wiped out all the drinks that had been resting on it. This little sprint put me deep in the midst of a bar room brawl of John Wayne proportions. All of the sudden, I was surrounded by doormen; it was as if they were lying in wait. And oh yeah, there was more than one person pissed off at me for issuing them a cocktail bath.

My adrenaline was pumping and the next thought that pierced my brain had all the subtlety of stepping barefooted on a thumbtack. I had been in these fights before. With my friends more than thirty feet away, I wasn't exactly alone but I did feel isolated. The worrisome thought of collateral damage wasn't my concern. In fact, I would come to realize as the years passed by that I actually fought better when there was more than one opponent. There's something about accepting the fact that I am about to get hurt that causes me to get loose and relaxed and actually fight better.

Anyone who approaches you while in a brawl is fair game (except, of course, women and children), but after all, Wild Bill *did* shoot his best friend. I'm in up to my earlobes. The brawl is on and I drop the first few guys that came at me––a punch, a kick and another punch take out the first three. All of a sudden, I'm being grabbed from behind. I can sense I'm being put into a full nelson; I push off and run backwards as hard as I can until we crashed into the wall, which loosens his grip. I slam my head back into his face in a reverse head butt and he lets go of me. But because of all the time I had to spend there, now I'm being charged head-on. I try to do a skip side-kick, but I'm over amped and almost jump over the guy's head. I land on his shoulders, cocked and ready to kick, and we both go to the ground. I roll and scramble to my left and when I look up, a guy has picked up a chair from a cocktail table. He's lifted it over his head in a threatening gesture, but then—finally—the cavalry arrive. I dodge for cover under a table when I see a foot come straight up between the guy's legs from behind. He curls up and grabs his groin instantaneously and falls to the ground face first. When he goes down, Curtis is standing directly behind him.

Curt grabbed me by the shirt and helped pull me to my feet, now we were back-to-back like Newman and Redford in "Butch Cassidy and the Sundance Kid." Squared off. At this point, so many guys have been dropped that at least ten or twelve were lying on the floor holding various body parts and moaning.

No one was willing to remount an assault, so things calmed down for a moment. Curt and I maintained a ready posture, but worked our way over to the bar where Mark and David were. There was still commotion and tension in the air, and for some reason I focus in on Mark and some doorman arguing over who started the brawl. My next move was not necessary, but this was where my sense of humor came

110

out. Besides, their macho stance was the wrong approach. No one offered to reimburse us for our drinks, nor did they ask us politely to leave. They'd tried to bully us, and we wouldn't be bullied. So I politely walked up to Mark and the doorman he was arguing with. I said, "Excuse me," and looked Mark dead in the eye and told him never to interrupt me in the middle of a bar room brawl. I then turned towards the doorman and *bang*, punched him square between the eyes, which started the whole brawl up again.

We fought our way back to the door we had entered through. Once in the parking lot, Curtis and David ran for the car. They pulled up to the west side of the club in the one-way driveway that led to Okeechobee Boulevard. David got into the passenger's side of the car where there was a four foot high chain link fence separating the Big Daddy's parking lot from a Datsun dealership, which would eventually be known as Nissan. I headed to the driver's side where Curtis could only get the door partially opened because the club's brick wall was in the way. Right then I noticed a couple of doormen leaving the bar, one of them with a whiskey bottle in hand, holding it by the neck as if to use it as a weapon.

Without warning, I felt an elevated surge of rage come up through my body from the balls of my feet to my scalp. I must've been having an Orlando flashback, because when I turned towards the kid brandishing the whiskey bottle, he saw something in my face that caused him to backpedal faster than he had been moving forward. Now I had turned back to the car, but it was too late; the police had boxed us in. I didn't waste a moment, with three quick steps I hurdled the four-foot chain link fence to the Datsun dealership. We scattered just like cockroaches do when you first get home and hit the lights. I ducked and wove my way through the brand new cars until I got to the far side of the lot, where once again I hurled myself over the chain link fence. I didn't stop running until I got to Palm Beach Lakes Boulevard.

Once there, I remember bending over and grabbing my knees to catch my breath. When it all suddenly dawned on me: *What are you going to do now, Socrates?* Oh sure, I'd escaped, but my friends were probably all being arrested, and I didn't have a ride home. I threw my hands up in the air and turned around. I went back to the Datsun dealership, hopped the fence and hit the ground belly-down. I crawled on my hands and knees across the dealership car lot until I got within 20-25 yards of the first chain link fence I'd hurdled. On the other side

111

of that fence was Curtis' car. Doors wide open, motor still running and Led Zeppelin blaring. Crouching down and hiding behind a car, I looked around. I dropped to my belly and I slithered underneath a car that was parked right next to the fence, and that was when I very clearly heard, "Who the hell do you think *you* are? G.I. Joe?" I glanced from underneath the car to my left and saw the shoes and pant legs of a police officer. I scampered from underneath the car like a frightened rat. I popped up and started laughing, then took off running once again, serpentining through the lot where I cleared the fence on the far side.

So *here I am*, at Palm Beach Lakes Boulevard, out of breath and in the same predicament I was fifteen minutes ago. I walked over to the access road that ran behind Big Daddy's, trying to think of a good vantage point where I could see what was going on. Right then, a car exited the Big Daddy's parking lot, and the headlights were headed my way. I gradually started banking a 45-degree angle off of the access road just to give myself a buffer between the car, and whoever might be in it that wanted to chase me.

The car slowed, my heart is racing, my brain is pounding. When the car got to me, I heard a phrase all too familiar: "Hey Pollack, where you goin'?" It was Curtis and our band of merry men. They flipped the passenger door open, so I ran around the car and hopped inside. Once inside the car, we started laughing like the idiots we were. As it turned out, they all got tickets and then they were released. Sure, they had court dates that they had to appear for, but our party continued.

The following Tuesday rolled around, and I saw Curtis at the Dojo. His first comment when he sees me? "Hey where's your buddy Turner? I gave him a job and he didn't show up Monday or today." I had no idea where Mark was. After a few days passed and I hadn't heard from Mark, I decided to call his parents' house. I talked to his mom, but she hadn't seen him either. I wasn't worried, but I was slightly concerned. But after three weeks, I was more than worried. Then we found out that the Monday morning following our Big Daddy's bar room bash, Mark had gotten up to go to work. As soon as he stepped outside, the cops were waiting with a warrant for his arrest. It turns out that he had violated his probation for that little misunderstanding he'd had with the gay community a little more than a year earlier. So that got him free room and board for the next nine months at a state institution: the Palm Beach County stockade. I never felt any animosity come from Mark, but I did feel like his parents had blamed me for his second trip

112

to jail.

But the truth is, curiosity had killed the cat again. He had basically gotten away, but then he'd decided to turn around and mingle in with the crowd. He pushed his way to the front where he could hear the story the doorman was telling the cops. He said for a moment it was funny, a whole crew of doormen with icepacks on their necks, their heads, and faces trying to describe the whole scenario blow-by-blow. That's when one of these doorknobs—better known as doormen—happened to glance up and, you guessed it, he fingered Mark.

In the meantime, Curtis and David sprinted across Okeechobee Boulevard and entered a neighborhood called Westgate. I don't know what Curt was thinking; as he was dashing and dodging through the yards of Westgate, the police were going through his car. If you remember, it was boxed in on the side of Big Daddy's with the engine still running and the doors wide open, with Robert Plant screaming something we weren't getting much of: *a whole lotta love.*

Now I would've paid money to see Curt and David's faces when the Sheriff leisurely cruised through Westgate announcing over his speaker: "CURTIS LUCAS. Come out with your hands up."

So once again, I'm giving money to Kathy, Mark's girlfriend, for her to take out and put in his canteen so he has money to draw on. And on occasion I would see Mark on the side of the road with numerous other prisoners. Florida was one of the last states to abolish the chain gang. Prisoners actually had to work. They would pick up litter from the side of the road, and at times were given sickles to go down into the canals and clear out the vegetation. Forget about the 90-plus-degree weather, the 100% humidity, the water moccasins and other poisonous snakes, how about a face-to-face encounter with an alligator? It's time for a little reality check. Picture yourself trying to get away from a twelve-foot, prehistoric lizard that can snap 2-by-4's in half with one bite while you're chained to two other men, one on either side of you!

But despite all of that, whenever we saw Mark on the side of the road, we'd make a couple of passes until we were sure he saw us. Once eye contact was made, we'd take an empty cigarette pack we had put money and a couple of joints in, and toss it out the window. And then we'd make one more pass by just to see Mark's smiling face. I had never gone out to visit Mark at the stockade, although I probably should have. But as a young fella in my late teens, it seemed like I had a thousand things going on. Besides, I had a stack of bench warrants out for my own arrest, so I couldn't risk it. I had twelve to fifteen warrants for my arrest for not appearing in court for various traffic violations. Knowing that they would take a look at any visitors who went to see the inmates, I couldn't afford to sign the guest registrar. Besides, who had the time? Between hanging drywall for eight or nine hours a day, taking three or four one-hour Karate classes in a night, and spending the evening and the early morning hours drinking, smoking pot, and ingesting God knows what with a few of my friends and my instructors, I couldn't squeeze anything else in. My agenda was booked. I was maintaining a pace that would kill the average man. It almost *did* kill me.

Chapter Twelve
The "Top Ten" Journey

After ten to twelve weeks of this high-powered routine, I'd go to get out of bed on a Monday morning and realize I couldn't move. I would find myself completely depleted of energy. There was no way I could hang drywall that day, so I would lay in bed all day without eating. But God bless youth and its enthusiasm because by 6:30 p.m., my motor was running. I couldn't stand to miss a Karate class.

Somehow, I'd convince myself I had the energy to go to the Dojo and train, which would start this cycle all over again. It was around this time that the serious competitors at the Dojo were getting amped up. The "Top Ten" Grand National, which was being held in St. Louis, Missouri, was approaching fast and we were determined to be there. Carl had rented the first motor home that hit the market, a Winnebago, as well as a van that converted into a camper. We had ten guys going and two vehicles; six would drive in the motor home, and four in the camper. By this time, I was Carl's unofficial gopher for anything he couldn't do, or any shit bag task he didn't *want* to do.

So *here I am* with David at the motor home rental office with a check from the Dojo trying to pick up the motor home and the van, but the guy behind the counter isn't buying any of it. And hell, who could blame him? My name isn't on anything (and I don't even possess a driver's license), so why am I standing here? No dice. Now I get to take this wonderful news back to Carl. Here's what nobody quite understands: just because you're the go-to guy and/or the gopher, everyone thinks you're under your man's wing and therefore gaining a lot of perks. What they don't understand is, 90% of the time when this guy's getting bad news, it's coming out of *your* mouth.

Upon receiving this news, Carl goes ballistic. He's madder than a junkyard dog because now he's gotta go down and deal with this issue on his own. Unfortunately, this would set the climate and the pace for our long journey to St. Louis and back. But you have to understand—I loved these guys. For the first time in my life I felt like I belonged to something. I had never felt like I belonged with my family, but for some reason, among my fellow martial artists, I never felt like I was the odd man out; I just seemed to fit. Besides, I loved Carl and probably would've died for him. Mark and Carl had the key to the knowledge I sought. Looking back on it now, with 20/20 vision, I realize we were all misfits, weirdos and oddballs that Karate had drawn together and now the fighting had bonded us.

But now, *here I am* on the launch pad to St. Louis, T-minus nothing, ready to blast off on yet another insanely bizarre but fun mission. The van and the motor home were well stocked and loaded, as were most of us. We had enough booze on board to drown a clinic full of binge drinkers, and enough drugs on stock to make Timothy Leary break out in a cold sweat.

I don't want to point fingers or name names; I was certainly as guilty as the rest of this madcap militia for drinking libations, ingesting drugs, and smoking dope. But for some reason, I was starting to take this competition thing a little more seriously, so I had sworn off smoking weed, drinking, and drugging until after the tournament. Of course, this was only a 72-hour vow. Hell, just a few nights earlier, I was blasted out of my mind and having more fun than the Polish are allowed to. I had managed to get myself thrown out of three nightclubs in a single evening.

Driving from South Florida to the Georgia state line is a long haul, so I opted for the Winnebago. I had never been in one before, and I needed some space. I was kind of an antsy kid, and to make matters worse, Carl was on the warpath and criticizing every little thing I did. The very first thing on the agenda for this killer Karate clan was, well, if you guessed anything besides self-medication, then you just haven't been paying attention. The booze came out, plus enough grass to choke a weed whacker.

Anyone who's ever traveled in a motor home knows how cramped it can become, especially when traveling with a handful of adult males. Some of the fellas decided to play a game of poker at the kitchen table, which was located at the rear of the mobile home. Just above the kitchen table was a bed that could be pulled down. Once locked in the down position, it would only leave two to three inches of head clearance for anyone sitting at the table. At the opposite end of the motor home was another twin bed that sat over the cab, just above the driver and passenger seat of the vehicle.

I was stuck. I didn't play poker, I had nothing to read, and you couldn't operate the TV while the vehicle was moving, which left me pondering what to do, so I came up with a brainstorm... At least I though it was. I could walk through some of my moves right there in the aisle way of the motor home. This was not received well by Carl.

Christ, you would've thought I'd just pissed in his beer, and may I quote here: "If you don't knock it the fuck off, I'm gonna come fucking back there and break both your fucking legs." So much for on-the-road training... But it was just as well. By now there was so much smoke built up in the motor home, it looked like a foggy day in San Francisco. That was thanks to a non-stop pass around. As soon as a joint went out, a pipe had been packed and it made its rounds.

The smoke was so thick in our rolling travel lodge that the contact high would've put Cheech and Chong in a coma. One thing can definitely be said for the Dojo's inner circle: they had an extremely high tolerance for pain, booze, dope and women (but not necessarily in that order, mind you). So this puts me in the position to try and open the windows, except that it's raining outside and we're on the Florida Turnpike, so the Turnpike noise is interfering with Eric Clapton playing on the 8-track. So now I'm under Sensei's skin once again. Carl is sitting in the navigator's seat and is so upset from screaming, he's spitting saliva all over Skeeter who's been driving. Now the death threats have commenced. At this point everyone in the motor home is laughing hysterically at me, except for Carl of course; and I really didn't need this level of ridicule. It wasn't that I was insecure or didn't have confidence in myself, but it really seemed to be agitating Carl.

I thought, screw it—it's time to go to bed. So I headed to the back of the motor home and pulled the bed down on top of the kitchen table so I could climb into it. I couldn't have been in the bunk a whopping fifteen minutes when I decided to roll over, which caused the whole thing to collapse and fall on top of the card players beneath me. I promptly catapulted out of the bunk and hit the floor with a thud, my eyes fixated on the front of the motor home.

Carl instantly whipped his head around to the left to see what happened. I could see the veins in his forehead ready to pop. You would've though someone hit the button to his ejector seat. He came scrambling towards the rear of the motor home, thank God the fellas got to him before he got to me. He was swearing like a sailor in an empty whorehouse on a three-day leave. Despite the fact that they were all laughing hysterically, they managed to calm Carl down.

He ordered me into the bunk above the cab. Great, now I'm directly above him and the driver. Well, I made it thirty minutes this time until I went to roll over just as we hit a small bump in the road and, you guessed it, the bunk buckled and I came toppling out again. Now, both our main bunks have collapsed and are tilted on a 45-degree angle towards the center of the motor home, both rendered absolutely useless. Carl ordered Skeeter to pull over immediately. He then climbed over Skeeter, out the driver's door, and ran around the motor home and tried to enter through the coach door, which, thank God, was locked.

While Carl pounded on the door screaming for someone to unlock it, I used that moment to scurry underneath the wrecked bedding and enter the cab to sit in the passenger's seat. By the time someone unlocked the door and let Carl in, he was pretty worn out from running around the outside of the motor home, beating on the door and screaming. Now he didn't have any energy to climb underneath the bunk and enter the cab so he could get his hands around my neck.

This gave me a little reprieve, but he did order me to stay up there and told me not to touch anything. Now Art switched out with Skeeter and jumped in the driver's seat. I always got along with Arty and he had a great sense of humor, so I knew this was gonna be fun. Now we're rolling down the Turnpike at 70 mph. My one and only job is to take care of the music, so I gotta keep an eye on the radio and the 8-track. Arty insists everything is going to be all right. He laughingly reassured me and tried to relieve my anxiety. Art had known Carl for years, and had witnessed many of these tempered tirades before. After a half hour or so, I am beginning to feel relaxed; I decide to change the music… *Big mistake!*

I reach over and grab Eric Clapton's 8-track to pull it out of the stereo. By the time I get it over to my side of the cabin, I realize the tape's gotten hung up in the player and it's become unwound. It looks like a big ball of spaghetti in the front seat of the cab and I realize I've succeeded in ruining Sensei's favorite tape: 461 Ocean Boulevard by Eric

Clapton. *Can you say Willie and the Hand Jive?* Carl instantly wants to know what happened. Thinking quickly, Art switches the stereo to FM. Arty, never one to miss a beat, hollers back, "It's time to switch the music up!"

Arty and I are now staring at each other with purple faces, holding our breath, trying to keep from laughing. Meanwhile, we've crossed the Georgia state line, and nothing too eventful has transpired. Except, of course, for the reefer-cocktail-poker party going on in the back of the motor home.

At this point, Art has become a little weary; he's been driving for the past few hours. So we decide to switch places. Art's about six feet tall, two hundred and thirty pounds, and built like a refrigerator; hardly a size medium. Nonetheless, we decide we can execute this switch without pulling over. To be honest, Art was extremely limber for his size. More than once I witnessed Art on the verge of a fight and, without flinching, elevate his leg and crack a guy in the side of the head with a round kick, knocking him out cold. Oh, I should mention these adversaries were six feet and taller.

I remember one particular Karate tournament in Coco Beach, Florida where Art was called to the center of the ring. He bowed to his opponent and got into his fighting stance. I'm sure his challenger sized him up as a sweeper/puncher, meaning he was capable of kicking your feet out from under you and punching you on the way down--not a well-rounded martial artist. That was his opponent's first mistake. Although Art had legs the size of tree trunks and was more than capable of kicking your feet out from under you, Arty liked to dance with the best of them. Now a leg sweep and a punch is a great technique, especially in a street fight if you're standing on concrete or asphalt. If you kick somebody's feet out from under them, then you really have to throw a punch to seal the deal.

Once Art and his opponent bowed in, the Kung Fu Killer started moving around Art with his dance of death. Here's where Arty executed extreme patience and impeccable timing. Finally the Kung Fu Killer made his first move; he tried a slide up round kick. Art stepped back and blocked it. As soon as the kick made contact with Art's blocking hand, Art did a spinning back kick catching the guy square in the head, knocking him out cold. While the judges rushed to the center of the ring to Killer's aid, Art turned nonchalantly towards me and shrugged. I remember it was if I drifted off into the Burt Reynolds film,

119

"The Longest Yard." I could almost hear over the loud speaker, *I think he broke his fucking neck!*"

But this was no joke; this kid wasn't moving. Hell, he was barely breathing. So they brought in a stretcher and put him in an ambulance. Now all the black belt judges are in the center of the ring trying to decide Art's fate. Normally, if you punched or kicked someone in the head that hard, you'd automatically be disqualified. But after the big pow-wow, the center referee decided that Art was moving back defensively when he threw the kick, and that Killer had run into it face first. The decision? It was Killer's fault, so Art got a bye.

For those of you that don't know, Karate tournaments are run on a round robin basis. So long as you're winning, you keep progressing, but once you lose, you're out. At the commencement of the second round, Art, Skeeter, David, and myself have all progressed. Art fought first. He went to the center of the ring, bowed to his opponent and then to the black belts, and got into a fighting stance. Now I'm not sure if Art's round-two opponent had been in deep meditation or if he had previously taken an inopportune bathroom break, but when the center judge dropped his hand to start the match, Victim #2 lunged forward with a slide up round kick. Arty stepped back and blocked it. There's a saying, if you find something that works stick with it. Now they're fanning the mediator with a gym towel--he's out cold--while they bring the stretcher back in. Now Art is two for two, but he's disqualified. God, I loved Art.

But back to the motor home. It took us two lanes of traffic, and thank God everybody in the back was drinking or they would've needed seasick pills, but we managed to do the driver switch off without pulling over. Now it's close to 2 in the morning. We're on some Georgia highway back roads, approaching a flashing red light with a stop sign, when the motor home starts rocking back and forth like we're a ship at sea trying to forge through a heavy swell. Something is definitely wrong. So I put the motor home in reverse and back off the side of the road. Everyone piles out of the motor home in anticipation; we had a flat tire. You gotta remember, we were just barely approaching the mid seventies--there was no such thing as a cell phone. We looked around, but we couldn't see a call box. Hell, we didn't see anything—it was pitch black.

Carl assessed our situation immediately and then proceeded to chase me around the motor home. Death threat number two. Going into the third lap I had worn Carl down, so now we could deal with the situation. This was no laughing matter. We were stranded in the middle of nowhere. We needed to think straight, assess our options and come up with a clear plan of action. So we lit up a joint and started passing around cold beers.

Within the hour, David had climbed under the motor home and found a spare tire bolted to the undercarriage. That was the good news. The bad news? None of us could figure out how to operate the jack so we could get the right rear of the vehicle up off the ground. All of a sudden, a dot of light appeared in the dark abyss, approaching swiftly. This was one of those incidents that, as a young man, you dismiss as a coincidence, but as you get older you realize how truly blessed and lucky you are.

The car approached us with its blinking red light. The right turn signal went on, and the car pulled up behind our Winnebago. David and Art moved quickly and stealthily into the motor home to hide any contraband we had lying around while Carl began a dialogue with our new guests: two Georgia State police officers.

These two officers were more than intrigued by the bunch of us. They had obviously heard of Karate before, and seen it in the movies, but they had never met anybody who actually *knew* Karate; and here was a whole motor home full of martial artists, not to mention our chase van. One of Georgia's finest politely offered to go back to his squad car so he could radio a tow truck to come to our aid. In his absence, while talking with his partner, we made reference to all the bullet holes in the highway signs. He chuckled and informed us that out here in the sticks, due to boredom, people would take shots at the highway signs when they drive by, or anything else on the side of the road. He commented we were lucky we didn't all pile in the van and leave the motor home behind; the locals would have turned it into Swiss cheese.

At this point, his partner rejoined us and we had gained their full confidence. Someone made a remark about how lucky we were that no one had driven by and taken a shot at us. Both officers laughed and told us that no one comes out this far without a gun. That's when Carl, feeling pretty confident, informed the cops that he never went anywhere without his gun. That's when an act that I had never heard of before, nor since, took place. The next thing we know, we have a handful of pistols, a rifle, and a shotgun displayed on the hood of the police car.

121

We were exchanging stories with the officers when we decided, "What the hell, there's nobody out here, so target practice it is!"

We were having a ball. Now most people would find this a little alarming, and in this day and age I'd have to agree with them, but back in the mid-seventies on a lonely stretch of Georgia highway, I managed to meet two of the coolest cops that ever walked the face of the earth.

At this point I want to take a minute and remind everybody how quickly life can change. Being the whipping boy of this trip, well, that didn't change... But to roll down the highway with enough smoke in our motor home to take out Cheech and Chong, enough booze flowing to flood the Mississippi, and the illicit poker game going on in the back, then being stuck in the middle of nowhere on a Georgia highway with a flat, only to be rescued by two Georgia police officers who'd entertain us with a firearms display until a the tow truck comes to our aid—now *that's* living.

When the tow truck arrived, they jacked up the back of the motor home and switched out the bad wheel. They suggested that because it was a tandem wheel vehicle (which means two tires deep on each side in the rear), if we were unfortunate enough to experience another flat, we should remove the busted back tire and continue on.

Carl tipped the tow truck driver graciously, then glared at me and said the only thing that was going flat from here on out would be the top of my head from him beating it like a drum. That got a huge laugh. When we turned toward the police officers with a heartfelt goodbye, they wished us the best of luck, and in return we extended an invitation that if they were ever in South Florida to look us up at the Dojo. And with that, we were on our way. The rest of the drive to St. Louis was pretty uneventful, we actually arrived at a decent hour (about 9:00 p.m.), which gave us a good night's sleep before the tournament commenced the next day.

The next morning we piled in the motor home and went to breakfast. As usual, we arrived at the arena where the tournament was being held fashionably late. Thank God tournaments of that size never start on time. Checking out the arena floor, it was like a who's who of Karate. Names like Bill Wallace, Howard Jackson, Jeff Smith, Cecil Peoples, Michael Warren, Everett Eddy... But by far the biggest name in the house was retired Heavyweight Champion, Joe Lewis. Lewis, fresh out of retirement after a hiatus of what was roughly a year, had evidently become restless and bored and now he was back. I had read many

122

magazine articles about the great Joe Lewis, so I was curious to see him fight. Prior to his retirement he had dominated the Karate world. I'm sure Lewis' name being advertised as a competitor brought in a lot of spectators, as well as participants.

Lewis, by invitation, was seeded, as well as some of the other Karate elite in that tournament, which gave them all a huge advantage. It meant that they wouldn't have to compete in the preliminary rounds; they'd only have to fight in the finals. It's always been customary for seeded black belts to act as chief referees during a tournament's competition, which is only fair. Traditionally, black belts are the last to participate in the tournament, so this arrangement lets all the students and spectators watch them compete. Why would you have your average black belt judge a full day of Karate activities and then step in the ring with someone who's been seeded, who's fresh, and a top-rated fighter?

Lewis, however, had come to a different conclusion. He had decided he'd rather fight his way to the finals than spend the day on the arena floor judging Karate underlings. Who can say if he thought it was beneath him to be a judge, or if he just wanted to kick some ass? Ether way, it had to have been an ego-based decision. It was a thrill for me, however, as I got to witness the mighty Joe Lewis fight. In the Karate world, he was a legend of epic proportions.

Yet I was somewhat disappointed. He cut through the competition like a hot knife through butter. Most of his opponents were scared stiff—petrified—so he had his way with them, which aggravated the hell out of me. Sure I wanted to see Lewis pound somebody, but I mostly wanted to analyze his signature moves. One opponent stepped to the center ring and just bowed out, without a kick or a punch having been thrown. And like my mother always said, the big dog might get the meal, but you should always get a bite.

That night at the finals we saw some great action. The grand finale was the heavyweight bouts. Facing off were Everett "Monster Man" Eddy at 6'4" and 240 lbs versus Joe Lewis, 6'2" and 225 lbs. Eddy had all but dominated the heavyweight division for sometime. The short story: Eddy won the match, but had it been a street fight, there was no doubt in my mind; Joe Lewis would've won.

At one point, Lewis had grabbed Eddy by the lapel of his *gi* and head butted and then kneed him across the ring. It was head butt, knee, head butt, knee, head butt, knee from one side of the ring across

123

to the other. It sounded as if a stampede of cattle had entered the arena. Why none of the officials had called a point for a head butt or a knee was beyond me.

After the tournament, Carl had some great news. He had gone to dinner with Lewis during the break between the semi finals and the finals of that evening. Sensei had struck a deal for Lewis to come to West Palm Beach and give the Dojo a training seminar.

Our Karate school, meaning the Dojo, had a pretty eventful day. Even with only eight of us representing our school, we managed to bring home five trophies. I personally was able to salvage second place in spite of the fact that I was disqualified for kicking the first place winner in the head.

Right now, we were flying high. We were jacked up, cranked up and could hardly shut up. We were more than proud of ourselves. To think that one tiny Karate school from the South of Florida with just a few competitors could inflict such damage on a national tournament. We felt it was pretty impressive. Sure, the state of Florida as well as Georgia knew who the Dojo fighters were, but aside from Herbie Thompson down in Miami, we pretty much dominated the Southeastern tournament circuit.

But to be fair, some great Karate people came out of the state of Florida. Don "The Dragon" Wilson out of Coco Beach, Florida went on to become the Light Heavyweight Kickboxing Champion and later move out to Hollywood, California and enjoy a successful film career. Harold Roth grew up in Miami, and later migrated to Los Angeles adopting the name of Harold Diamond and went on to win a Muay Thai kickboxing title as well as do film work. Harold had a black belt in his Miami studio by the name of Tony Palmore who won a heavyweight kickboxing title. Ted Pryor of South Florida won a world kickboxing championship. And the most tenacious of them all, a fellow black belt from the Dojo and close friend of mine Steve Shepherd, won a handful of World Championship Kickboxing titles in four or five different weight divisions.

But you had to tip your hat to Herby Thompson and the ghetto fighters. Although I'm unaware of any of their students winning a world title, he had taken a bunch of underprivileged kids off the street and, through the discipline of karate, taught them honor and respect and whipped them into lean, mean fighting machines. Herbie was a man's man. If he shook your hand, it was his bond. And, like the Dojo, he taught his students how to defend themselves in a bad situation. It wasn't about winning tournaments; it was scientific street fighting. Winning Karate tournaments was a by-product.

Next thing you know, we were on the road headed back to Florida basking in all our glory, but not without a couple of pit stops. One of the things you can't help but notice when you drive through the South is that there are no shortages of firework vendors. These make-shift trailers selling fireworks seem to spring up on the roadside like wildflowers.

So *here I am* with my kamikaze cohorts buying fireworks for what would turn out to be pending chaos. Now with hundreds of dollars of pyrotechnics packed in our chariots of fire, we hit the road. But before we had stopped at one of these ammunitions depots to stock up for some *battle royale* yet to come, we noticed a highway sign advertising Ruby Falls: The World's Only Underground Waterfall. This, we had to check out. After all, seeing is believing. We pulled into the parking lot of the Ruby Falls information building. We checked in and we were given a guide, a kid aged between 18 and 20, who took us to an elevator shaft that dropped us roughly one mile underground.

The elevator hit bottom and the doors opened. *Voila!* We stepped out in what could only be described as a claustrophobic and asthmatic's nightmare. We were standing in one of many narrow cave-like corridors, with stalagmites and stalactites as far as you could see. Experiencing a damp and cool humidity that I imagine only the center of the earth could produce, now it was time to introduce our juvenile guide to the delinquency of the Dojo explorer club.

As if it wasn't already creepy enough being almost a mile underground, while traveling through a maze of caves searching for a waterfall we didn't believe existed, someone lit up a joint. Our young guide beamed with joy. He was looking for the opportunity to suggest he light one of his own. This young kid had no idea what he had just unleashed, nor what he was in for. He spent the rest of our tour time trying to wrangle us in. The minute we killed the roach, we splintered off in our own directions down the caverns and corridors.

David and I, after confronting a few dead ends, decided to go up. We ascended more than 25-to-35 feet into the cavern. While we were up there, we took great joy in watching our guide run up and down the stone corridors trying to figure out what we were up to. After twenty minutes of climbing around through the top of the cavern, we heard

125

Carl's voice summon us through the echo of the cave.

It was time for the unruly renegades to reunite and make a run for Ruby Falls. Our guide led us through a path of stone corridors and pleaded with us—no, he begged us—to stay with him throughout the remainder of our tour. This poor kid thought he was on the verge of being fired for our decision to scatter like locusts in a windstorm; but little did he know, the best of us was yet to come!

The corridor that we had been traveling through suddenly opened up into a huge cavern. And sure enough, about 20 to 30 feet above our heads, out of a sheer stone wall about 8 to 10 feet wide, shot a cascade of water with all the pressure of a fire hose.

We quickly walked over to the stone well that the water had beaten into the cave floor. It was somewhat of a drop to the top of the water inside the well. We were marveling at what we were seeing, as well as inquiring as to where the water was going. As the questions progressed, I heard the western equivalent of *"Bansai!"--"GERONIMO!"* Whose turn had it been to keep their eye on Art?

We wheeled around just in time to see Art, all 230 lbs of him buck-naked and tucked in a ball, hurl himself from the edge of the well. I can guarantee this was more than the tourists had paid to witness this historic landmark.

Well, now we had a problem. We had to figure a way to fish Arty out of the well, and we were eighty-sixed; they'd punched our ticket and kicked us out of Ruby Falls.

We exited the parking lot and watched Ruby Falls get smaller in the rearview mirror. Okay, actually we were looking out the back window of the motor home as we exited the lot, but we were laughing and waving. And we never did hear that cozy refrain, "Y'all come back now, you hear?"

Soon it was time to gas up, and I mean that more ways than one. One thing you can love—or hate—about the South is they're not afraid to mix gasoline with alcohol. Now it's time to relax. We had plenty of dope to smoke, alcohol to consume, and a long drive ahead of us.

Remember, we had stopped by the ammo depot and bought enough explosives to blow up Fort Knox, and you know what they say about idle hands. That led to me being completely ostracized from the motor home. Don't ask me how this happened, but a firecracker had been lit inside the motor home and had blown up, and I took the brunt of the blame. Carl ordered the motor home to pull over on the side of the

126

road and I was ejected.

So *here I am*, standing on the side of a southern freeway as the motor home pulls away and leaves me behind. Thank God for the chase van, and Tommy Fafarco for driving; he pulled over and picked me up. The passengers in my newfound chariot actually welcomed me, so off we went, rolling down the freeway at 70 miles per hour, chasing the motor home. And all of the sudden, out of the side window of the motor home we saw a hand sticking out with something in it.

Everyone in the van squinted to work out what it was, and then it became abundantly clear: it was a Roman Candle and they were in firing mode. Red, yellow and blue fireballs were heading straight for us. *Bullseye!* They hit us dead on. Now we had smoke darts smeared all over our windshield. This constituted an act of war. We rapidly rummaged through our bag of fireworks to see what kind of arsenal we could amass. The very first thing I got my paws on that I thought could be effective was a batch of Roman Candles, but we needed to get within striking range. Driving at 70 mph, with them in front of us, we needed to get closer. Tommy punched the accelerator and said he would try to get alongside them.

"Wait!" I said, "Flash your lights like something is wrong, and we'll try to get them to slow down." They fell for it. We approached the motor home from the outside lane of the freeway. As it slowed, the windows slid open on the driver's side of our van. The plan was for us to move alongside of the motor home. And then, when Tommy yelled out, "Something is wrong with the van!" that would be our cue to light up the Roman candles and commence firing at will. The plan worked! Sort of…

You know when you hang out with somebody for a while and you get comfortable, and then you get relaxed, and then you're taking them for granted and you've forgotten who you're dealing with? Yeah, me too.

Just as we got alongside of the motor home, I could see Carl, Art and Skeeter's faces with a look of concern. Right when Tommy opened his mouth to utter something was wrong with the van, they, being the true warriors they were, decided to finish us off. It was 'take no prisoners and deliver no mercy.' Just as we lit our Roman candles, they unloaded on us with a barrage of Roman candles, bottle rockets and firecrackers. Simultaneously, we fired back with flashes of light, streaks of color and explosions in the air. Had you witnessed this, you would've thought you were looking through the jail cell window with Francis Scott when he wrote those immortal words so many years ago, "Oh, say can you see!"

Tommy instantly realized that they had more firepower, but concluded we had more speed. So he punched it. As we pulled away, all I could see was elated faces. Everyone in the motor home had rushed to the front of it to look out the panoramic windshield. They had won that battle, but the war wasn't over yet. Our van could do close to a hundred. That battleship, or 'May Tag' they called a motor home, would get squirrelly if it went over seventy. We had the advantage of speed, so now we were launching things back at them, which they were driving into. So now they had to come up with something that had enough firepower to overtake us.

Cruising at eighty, we were now winning the second battle. We were laughing our asses off, and actually getting kind of cocky. I mean, what could they do? Suddenly I wished I hadn't said that. I was now laughing so hard I was all but crying. I mean, I almost peed myself. In the middle of all of this, I heard someone say, "What the hell is that?!" I turned just in time to see Arty hanging out the passenger's side window of the motor home firing something at us.

I couldn't make out what it was, but it was the circumference of a Florida orange and about a foot and a half long. This thing had its own launch pad for Christ's sake. It rocketed by so fast, I thought it was Chuck Yeager doing a flyby chasing the sound barrier. It swooped by us at warp speed and thank God it didn't hit us or the coroner would be telling you this story.

The projectile traveled about 60 yards in front of us, skipped off the pavement twice, before making a left arching turn and shot across the grass meridian, which was 60 to 70 yards wide. This scared the bejeezus out of everyone in the van. We watched in awe as this thing flew by us and launched into oncoming traffic on the opposite side of the freeway. For a second it looked as though it was going to T-bone a car, but praise Allah, it just missed it and passed behind it, skipping off into the woods.

As this happened, there was that uncomfortable moment, you know, that heartbeat of stunned silence. We couldn't believe what we had just witnessed. And then, *relief*. We looked at each other and cracked up laughing. Later, I would tell this story and find it hard to believe I was caught up in this delirious frenzy.

Anyway, back to the ongoing battle. That act called for some re-taliation of major escalation. We rummaged through every box and bag of fireworks we had until we came up with a suitable answer to their insult. *Bingo*. We found a missile with its own launch stick. You know, the kind you stab into the ground, light, and then run like hell? This thing was 12 to 14 inches long and just smaller in diameter than a coffee table coaster. Problem was, how to launch this thing from a moving van? You couldn't just hold it in your hand; we needed some-thing we could stick it into. We scoured the van and we couldn't come up with anything, and then we realized we were drinking from it: a 32oz Coke bottle. *Perfect!* We passed the bottle around and drank until it was empty, then we inserted the launch stick down the center of the bottle. The problem was, it was almost two feet long. Then we had a brainstorm; you know the type you get when your adrenaline is going through the roof? We cut off one third of the launch stick and re-in-serted it back in the bottle.

But now we need someone to hold the bottle. Don't ask me why because I can't come up with a clear and definitive answer, but my in-stincts were saying it wasn't going to be me. I believe David turned out to be our guinea pig.

Children, here's another lesson for you: ATF, alcohol, tobacco (and I don't mean cigarettes), and fireworks are not a good mix. We finally got the missile in the bottle and positioned it next to the window. Next came the call, "Anybody got a Bic lighter?" We got this thing lit and David hung out the window and took aim. It took off with such a blast that it almost burned his hand off. David dropped the Coke bottle as soon as the sparks hit his hand, but his aim wasn't true. In hindsight, it was a blessing from Buddha. The missile swept off and hit the motor home on the passenger's side rearview mirror. It sheered off that mir-ror like a samurai sword going through a watermelon. The damage the missile inflicted on the motor home must've incited a moment of clar-ity to those traveling in it. All the sudden, they flashed their lights and put their right turn signal on so they could pull over to the side of the freeway. But we were dealing with our own collateral damage; David had what I was sure was a second-degree burn on his hand.

So *here I stand* on a bayou beltway with a bunch of babbling buf-foons bouncing over each other with joy. People passing by in each direction must've thought that they were witnessing the incarnation of the gay parade. We were laughing and holding on to each other,

129

jumping up and down and hugging one another, until some of us fell onto the hillside the freeway was cut into and the rest of us dog piled each other.

I never quite figured out why we were so elated. Could it have been because we had just coined a new American sport: road rage? Or were we so joyous that in spite of our casualties and collateral damage, no one was killed? Before the thrill was gone, so were our clothes. Four or five of us had stripped down buck naked and streaked up the side of the freeway embankment. (Streaking has just become all the rage.) For Christ's sake… What do you have to do to draw a little attention to yourself? The rest of the journey back to Florida, by these standards, was pretty uneventful. Oh sure, we pulled into a small town or two to gas up, and as we left we'd a light a firecracker and toss it out the window to get a reaction, but over all, we were pretty worn out.

Our exploits ran the gamut from country boy law enforcement target practice, to the Ruby Falls Cannonball, to the Florida boys' version of "Road Warrior," to the nude mountain steeplechase. And let us not forget the purpose of this whole crusade: we were the champions, *and we had the trophies to prove it!* Now back at West Palm Beach, we had to face the reality of our juvenile behavior. The motor home and the van had to go back to the rental place. One guess as to who drew the short straw: the kid with the big, Polish grin.

So *here I am* standing in front of the RV rental office with the owner, who's gone ballistic. And who could blame him? The RV, as well as the van, both look like they've been entered in Death Race 2000 and tied—for last place. There's an old saying: don't make an angry man angrier. You should have seen this man's face when I told him I was instructed to get Carl's deposit money back. I would swear I began to see the blood vessels in this man's eyes pop. At this point, he was so irate that I could barely understand what he was saying. But he was emphatic about not returning any deposit money, and was ranting something about suing. I did my best to try and calm him down, and then asked if I could use the phone to call Carl.

Now explaining the bad news to Carl, I'm trying to defuse the situation and keep everybody civil. But this guy was more than irate. It was like he found out his lemonade snow cone had actually been pissed on. Then he made a big mistake. Carl overheard him say something about kicking someone's ass. Carl slammed the phone down, hanging up on me. What could I do? I turned and looked at the gentleman and informed him, "He'll be right down."

I decided to go outside and wait for Carl. I didn't want to be a witness to this. I mean, I felt bad, but I knew it wasn't going to go this guy's way. Carl was there in a few moments, and boy did he know intimidation––he never even bothered taking his Karate uniform off. There he was in all his illustrious glory, still wearing his black belt with his rising sun headband on. He wanted to know where this guy was. Carl marched into the RV rental office like a proud male peacock in the midst of mating season. It took all of about twelve minutes before Carl exited the rental office with a stack of cash. He got a 100% refund of his deposit and informed the gentlemen there would be no such thing as a lawsuit or he would suffer the consequences.

Later that evening at the Dojo, after classes were over, a few of us gathered in Carl's office to relive the week's events as well as Carl's methods for getting his money back, which busted everybody up.

The following week was fairly mellow, but the one after that stirred a lot of energy. Joe Lewis, the Heavyweight Champion of the World, was coming to the Dojo to give one of his world-class seminars on fighting techniques. Lewis would arrive on Friday and the seminar would take place the following Saturday. Mark and Carl brought him to the Dojo to show him around before they took him out Friday night to show him the town. The good Lord had never blessed a man so much at 6'2" and 225 lbs. There was more fat on the back of his hands than there was on his whole body. He was a rippling rock of muscle and looked like Captain America. I swear they must've taken a mold of his body to stamp our G.I. Joe dolls. With the exception of Paul Newman, no man had ever walked the face of this earth more handsome. With sandy-colored hair and blue eyes, he was confident to the point of arrogance. I was looking forward to learning a lot from this guy.

The problem was, he discovered my girlfriend Ronda, who was a beautiful little Polynesian pineapple—athletic as well as exotic. She had a butt that would make a sister jealous. And we were always on the go with boating, riding horses, water skiing, scuba diving and, of course, she took Karate at the Dojo.

Ronda and I had just gone through a breakup right before I took off for the Top Ten nationals in St. Louis. She could be a little jealous, she didn't like it when I did things without her, and she didn't appreciate me hanging out with my Karate cohorts either. And who could blame her? We did get into a lot of mischief. It wasn't the mischief that bothered her so much; it was all the women around us. (I did mention we were treated like rock stars.) With Bruce Lee's image still prominent on the silver screen, being a martial artist opened doors to the unimaginable (and gave us *all* the keys to the women's locker rooms).

Ronda one-upped me. She accepted a date from Joe Lewis, the Heavyweight Champion of the World. *How do you measure up to that?* And Mark and Carl, my instructors? Well, they just sold me down the river and I understood. Being a black belt back in the day actually meant something––it was an exclusive club that I didn't belong to yet. Nowadays, it would seem black belts are a dime dozen; but back in 1974, you really had to earn it.

Of course I wasn't invited along on their big night on the town, but I *did* hear about the drinking, the joking, and the laughter. And no one mentioned what *they* ordered for dinner, but I ate... crow. Lewis conducted a seminar the next day, and I picked up a few things. But what helped me, as well as hurt me, was that Lewis took a liking to my Karate instructors. So he hung out for the next week and partied with them, but he trained every day. And guess who else trained every day? Yours truly. So I studied his every move. So every night when he was out with my ex-girlfriend, instead of dwelling on it, I was at the Dojo mimicking his every move.

Overall, I felt blessed. For the first time I got to witness a World Champion train and hone his skills, and witness the dedication and discipline it would take to be the best in the world. He was the missing key to the lock on a door I needed to open to further my career. And in many ways, my life was never the same again.

I became more obsessed. I practiced relentlessly. I started running three to four miles a day on the beach in the heavy sand. I would do 500 kicks a day, six days a week with five pound ankle weights on my legs, I'd practice endless punch-kick combinations, and then go to the heavy bag for four or five rounds. Then it was speed drills, and skipping rope for five or six 3-minute rounds. Then I'd do 500 sit ups and leg lifts and stretch for an hour. Throw in sparring a few days a week, and lifting weights four days a week, and that was my routine.

Well, Lewis came and went, and when he left, he took Paul Anselmo, one of our lightweight black belt instructors, with him. Paul was a great athlete and Mark and Carl had taken a liking to him. They recruited him from Master John A. Pochivas' school down in Miami to come up and teach at the Dojo. He had been a gymnast through high
132

school and college and then discovered Karate. Mark and Carl were looking to expand the Dojo from Clematis Street in West Palm Beach with a move north to a second studio in Riviera Beach. Paul was a great martial artist, as well as a good kickboxer. He was bright, clever and witty--a great addition to the black belt panel at the Dojo.

Paul had been with our Karate school for roughly two years before Lewis came to town to give his seminar. Lewis offered Paul a unique opportunity to go on the road with the World Champion for the purpose of helping out with his Karate demonstrations as well as seminars. I don't think Mark and Carl were happy with Paul's decision to sign on with Lewis, but Lewis had made him an offer he couldn't refuse. Whenever a World Champion extends an invitation to travel the world as his wingman, you take the next bus out of town. We wouldn't see Paul again for over a year, but when he got back, he had acquired some of Lewis' arrogance and cockiness.

Paul had also forgotten where he came from; we were a school of warriors. While he was away, Steve Shepherd had gotten his black belt, as well as Rufus Burns (and I was getting close). We had no problem bringing him back down to Earth. The truth was, Paul was a great guy; we loved him as well as respected him. After my days at the Dojo, I lost track of Paul, something you should never do with your friends. I often thought what I wouldn't give to see him once again.

Years later, when I moved to Los Angeles, I became friends with a man named Jimmy George. Jimmy was a good friend of George Benson, as well as his producer; they had released a handful of gold records together. One evening while passing through Coldwater Canyon on our way to Sunset to go out clubbing in Hollywood, Jimmy asked me if I knew Joe Lewis. I laughed and explained my whole experience with the mighty Joe Lewis. When I mentioned Paul's name, Jimmy's face lit up; sure he knew Paul! Then he asked how long it had been since I'd spoken with him.

As you can imagine, I was pretty excited. I mean, what were the odds that we could reconnect? I told Jimmy I hadn't spoken to Paul for over a decade, and then he looked at me with a somber face and gave me the news. Paul had come in contact with the dreaded disease, AIDS, and was gone. I couldn't believe it.

A few years later, in 1997, when I was inducted into the Martial Arts Hall of Fame, both of my instructors were present. When I questioned Mark and Carl about Paul's passing, they confirmed it. I remember I

133

felt just as blown away as the first time I had heard it. What a horrible fate for a talented and great man. Then Mark mentioned that in the end he had gone to live with Renee, his ex wife, so she could look out for him and she said he never once whined or cried. He was a man right to the end. So God bless you, Renee, wherever you are. And Paul, I know I loved ya.

Chapter Thirteen
The Getaway

So *here I am*, driving my car through my mobile home park and it's 1975, on another Easter weekend. I'm on my way to Curtis' place on Good Friday when I pull over, run through the backyards and pull the old "throw the party clothes out the window" trick. Then I get back in the car and pull into his driveway. Curtis exits his home with his *gi* on and his workout bag in hand. We head down to the Dojo and work out. Afterward, it's on to Sensei Herman's house where Curtis cleans up and we're out on the town (early as usual).

Little did I know, we were taking the first step on what would be yet another epic adventure. By ten o'clock that night we had partied at every honky tonk in town and gotten thrown out of half of them. But no problem, Danny Lanes was throwing an Easter party up at the fish house. We got to Acme Fish Co. and the parking lot was full as usual. Curtis, Mark and I made our way up the wrought iron stairs on the side of the building, then I proceeded to pound on the three inch-thick door. The peephole door opened as always, and there it was: that blue, one-eyed, skeptical stare that could only belong to Danny Lanes.

The door flew open, and there was Danny with a cocktail in his hand. He slapped me on the side of my head so hard that my ears began to ring. Then he lectured me, "I dare you to bring Mark and Curtis to a party this late!" That cracked everybody up, and made Danny and I laugh as well. I had never been the first one up the stairs, and what had possessed me this night, I don't have a clue; but I never did it again.

Once inside, the party was raging. There were twenty-five to thirty people, all of our friends and then some. And as usual, it was '3 D':

dames, drugs, and Dopes. Amyl Nitrate had just hit the party scene. They were small ampoules carried by paramedics and used to wake people up from, you know, *serious car crashes!* Snap one of those vials open under the nose of a fully coherent human being, and it was enough to give you the heebie jeebies. Your adrenaline, as well as your beta-endorphins, would shoot through the roof. They called them "poppers," and they were added to the list of the usual party favors. There was cocaine, poppers, hallucinogenics, uppers and downers, and enough booze to flood Lake Okeechobee.

There were more than a few fresh-faced young women present, meaning they were rookies at Lanes' Fish House. So we had to break them in to Danny's party palace. To break them in, a couple of us took turns on the fishnet hammock to lure them in.

Of course, the alpha-female in the group would be the last one in the hammock––she would be the one we tortured the most. We spun this poor girl until she lost her cookies. She threw up all over herself, and when they stopped and finally let her out, everyone was laughing. She was totally humiliated, but it was nothing a little medication and booze couldn't heal.

Next up was the main event: the Mark and Danny knife throwing competition. Anyone who went to the Dojo, who was on the inside circle of this, let's call it "unique" friendship, and who was fortunate or ill-willed and/or ill-advised enough to go to Lanes' Fish House, practiced throwing knives. But you just couldn't beat Danny. He could throw with either hand with precise accuracy. But as you might imagine, we martial artists pride ourselves on hand-eye coordination. So we would try to give him a run for his money. Besides, we had just introduced *shurikens*—razor-sharp Japanese throwing stars—to the competition, so we had all been practicing with this martial arts weapon. Hands down, Danny was the best, and Mark would only stand against the door for Danny. *Imagine that!* But none of the rookies at Lanes' Fish House knew that…

We would convince these unsuspecting girls, the first timers at the fish house, that they had to stand against Danny's bedroom door and let us throw sharp objects at them as a rite of passage. I couldn't begin to contemplate the depth of the scars we left in some of these young women's minds. Deep enough to paddle a canoe through, no doubt… We would do a windup and let it veer off path and stick in the bar, or in a warm up throw, let it get away from us and stick it in the wall behind us. Once we convinced them to stand in front of Danny's bedroom door, they would pose there with their eyes closed and their knees knocking. Then we would make them shriek once our weapon of choice had made contact with something. And of course, everyone would crack up laughing.

But that night I bailed on this bona fide bonzo high wire act at around dawn. I needed a few hours sleep so I could work out. Besides, this circus wasn't leaving town anytime soon. The next day, I was waiting at the Dojo when Carl showed up at the designated time to open on Saturdays: 12:00 noon. Carl looked as if he has just left the party at Lanes' Fish House. By 1:00 p.m., Carl was gone. I think I was giving him a headache from punching and kicking the heavy bag, so he left me in charge of Dojo North, which was okay with me as there were no classes scheduled for Saturdays. I enjoyed an open workout from 12:00 noon until 5:00 p.m., *perfect*. By the time I was done training, I simply locked up and went home. Now my battery was charged for Saturday night. It really wasn't an inconvenience, but of course it wouldn't matter if it was.

I remember when we built Dojo North in Riviera Beach. Back at the Clematis Street Dojo, Carl would announce every night after advanced class that he would supply the pizza and beer for anyone who was willing to come up to the new school and do some construction work. And the whole advanced class would show up and do about thirty minutes worth of work. Then, by that time, the beer, the pizza, the pot and the babes would show up, and it would turn into a three-hour party while yours truly did all the work. I framed all the walls for the locker room, I hung the sheet rock on those walls, I jackhammered the floor up for the shower drains and the toilets, and I did some minor plumbing as well as installing the toilets. Hell, I did it all, with a little bit of help.

Because a large percentage of the advanced class worked in the construction trade, most of the materials used to build Dojo North were donated. There was always a surplus of materials lying around construction sites. If you were building a 30-unit apartment building, you can bet there were 32-to-34 kitchen sinks ordered. Or bathroom sinks, or toilets—whatever you might need. It was easy to end up with a new sink in your kitchen, a toilet in your bathroom, a new tile walkway to your front door, or build a new room addition to your home. Okay, it was stealing, but everyone was doing it, so it seemed to be one of the perks of the job.

At that time, I was hanging drywall at Century Village, an old Jewish retirement community. There must've been ten thousand units to build out there. The subcontractor I worked for actually gave me 200 sheets of drywall that had gotten soaked in a rainstorm. Someone had forgotten to throw visqueen over it to keep it dry—you know, the heavy-duty plastic sheeting they use to cover things at construction sites. I was told it had become damp, but I knew if you let it dry out in the sun it could still be used. Perfect for the Dojo. Trouble was, it had been lying flat on the ground, and had soaked up the water like a sponge. It wasn't damp; it was soggy. It was absolutely useless, but we didn't know that yet.

Carl had rented a 20-foot truck with a hydraulic tailgate on it and had given David and me the keys. We pulled up to the gate at Century Village and the guard just waved us through. Security must've recognized me as being part of the construction crew. David and I stood in front of our designated stack of dry wall trying to figure out how we were going to get it in the back of the truck when it kept breaking apart in our hands. Frustrated and pissed off, I spun around and started cussing when I noticed a brand new stack of dry wall being unloaded from a truck with a forklift. We simply waited for those guys to leave.

As soon as they had gone, we backed up our truck to that stack of new drywall and loaded our allotment of 200 sheets. We rolled down the back door to the truck, locked up the hydraulic tailgate and then we headed for Century Village's back security gate. When we got there, there were two squad cars waiting to arrest us. Someone had witnessed us taking the drywall and decided to call in a theft in progress. This presented us with a dilemma, but thinking quickly I decided to play through.

I told them I had been given the drywall by a subcontractor named Joe; a friend and my current boss. Joe *had* given me the wet sheet rock, and I was betting they wouldn't go on the construction site to investigate which stack I had taken. Now they had Joe on the phone, and thank God he only lived five minutes away so he showed up right away. After a few moments of conversation, we got the green light. Unbelievable as it may seem, as I glanced in the rearview mirror I saw Joe, the security guard, and the police wave us goodbye. Just as I had figured, no one ever left the security gate to investigate. *I love it when a plan comes together.*

Back at the Dojo, I had to back this monstrous truck down a narrow alley and into a parking bay. I misjudged the space and backed the truck right into the wall belonging to the bakery next door. At first, I thought no big deal, I just chipped some cinder block. But when I got out to take a look, I realized the truck's steel hydraulic tailgate had sliced the electrical conduit pipe belonging to the bakery in half. I honestly didn't know how bad the damage was, but I sure found out. Now the bakery had no electricity, which meant no freezers. *Can you say yeast rising?*

The responsible thing to do was to go to the front of the building where there was a number posted in case of an emergency so we could call the baker and let him know that we inadvertently had cut off his electricity. He needed to get an electrician down there right away to avoid a catastrophe. This, however, never entered our minds. We were borderline hoodlums. We quickly unloaded the drywall, at Dojo North, packed up, and hightailed it out of there. I guarantee you, this went against every principle my grandparents had taught my brother Frank and me. Pop had been dead for a few years, so all their standards, principles, virtues, and morals had faded somewhat. What was ringing loudest in my ears was what I had heard from people my whole life. I was stupid, no good, dumb, and I would never amount to anything. Maybe they were right. It might be easier to find refuge in all that they think and say!

The next morning, when the baker showed up at 5:00 a.m., you can't imagine what he found. Carl did his usual morning errands and showed up at the Karate school at noon. The baker was waiting, along with the cops. In Carl's defense, he actually knew nothing about it. (I hadn't bothered to bring it to his attention.) So now Carl and the baker are arguing round and round until the baker insists the police officer arrest Carl. *For what?* They had nothing to charge him with. Everyone walked around to the back of the building to investigate. As soon as Carl laid eyes on the sheared conduit, he knew exactly what happened. Well, all's well that ends well. Ah, not really... The baker stopped sending fresh baked cookies over to us, but we thought that was a small price to pay. If the baker had his way, he would've cut our heads off for cutting off his electricity. He'd have us executed by guillotine.

Well, like the country song says, everything's better when the sun goes down. Curtis called me at sunset, asking me to pick him up from Sensei Herman's house. Evidently he'd blacked out on Mark's couch, and spent the night. When he woke up, Sensei was gone, but had left him a note. Curtis wasn't used to these vampire hours. He was a family man and a construction worker. He was used to getting up at the crack of dawn. But he needed to clean up first, so I told him I'd pick him up within the hour. I arrived at Sensei's house just in time to rendezvous with David Bunning and Skeeter, Mark's younger brother. Curtis answered the door with a towel still wrapped around him. So we entered the house, went straight to the refrigerator, cracked open some beers, and waited for him to get dressed. We left the house, piled into Curtis' car and headed to Palm Beach to some nightclub that Mark said he'd meet us at. Entering the club was no problem. Hell, it was never a problem. But it was only 8:00 p.m. When we saw Mark, it was obvious he hadn't slept. He was still flying from the night before. Worse yet, he hadn't eaten in ten hours. Mark was an amazing human being. People were drawn to his charismatic personality. He had incredible athletic talent, and a bizarrely high tolerance for drugs and alcohol. To say he had a high threshold for pain was an understatement. Then there was his astonishing endurance for partying. Once he put his foot in it, it was through the floor. To this day, thirty years later, I have never met anyone that could hold a candle to him.

But this place was a bore. No one was out yet. So we decided to go get Mark something to eat. We all piled in to Mark's brand new Cadillac El Dorado, which was black on black on black with gangster whitewall tires. With black paint, black leather interior, and black landau roof—the only thing white on it were the sides of the tires. *What a ride!* Then another one of those thunderstorm ideas hit us. Why not go to Fort Lauderdale to party? The night was young, we had a full tank of gas, and by the time we got there the clubs would be a blast.

But first off, we had to grab something for Sensei to eat. We stopped at the 7-Eleven and Mark settled for one of those nasty, shrink-wrapped sub sandwiches at the bottom of the glass refrigerator case. You know, the ones you find below the cartons of milk, bottles of fruit juice, and cans of coke? But it was his stomach and he was happy. We loaded back into the Pimp Mobile, and headed down Okeechobee Boulevard, west to I-95 so we can get to Fort Lauderdale for the evening's festivities. Things seemed to be going well as we approached Tamron Avenue, and then they took a downward spiral. We got lit up by the police for speeding.

This was going to create a huge problem. Curtis was driving, and had left his wallet in his car back at the bar in Palm Beach. The officer approached the car and asked to see Curtis' license and registration. Mark, on the other side of the car eating his hoagie, fumbled through the glove box and found his registration. Curtis handed it out the window to the officer and told him he couldn't find his wallet. The officer told Curt to wait there while he ran the registration. This is where things began to escalate. With the windows darkly tinted, Curtis put the driver side window up and climbed over Mark's lap. Mark slid into the driver's seat and we all waited.

The officer approached the driver's side of the car again and tapped on the window. When Mark put the window down, one look at the police officer's face told me that this ploy wasn't going to work. First words out of the officer's mouth were: "Where's the driver?" Sensei did his best to convince the cop that he was driving all along, but the cop wasn't buying it. He wanted everyone out of the car, and now. We all exited the car and things began to get ugly. An argument ensued between Curtis, the cop, and Mark. Then the cop really got aggravated. He insisted on knowing who was driving the car. No one could ever accuse any of us of not recognizing an opportune moment. That's when Skeeter stepped up and said he was driving. Then I said, no, I was driving. David insisted he was driving, and then it went back to Curtis. Then Mark confessed he was driving all along, and Curtis had nothing to do with driving. That's when the cop stepped across the proverbial line drawn in the sand.

He grabbed Mark by the sleeve and jerked on him, and said something to the effect of, "Look here jackass." That's when Mark stumbled forward in protest. To this day, I truly don't know if it was an accident or a well-conceived plan, but Mark's sandwich ended up open-faced and smeared all over the cop's uniform. We're talking mustard, mayonnaise, tomatoes, and that nasty ass cheese that you can only find on a submarine at your local 7-Eleven store. At first glance, you would have thought that someone threw a bucket of ice water over this police officer. But then he went ballistic. He drew his gun and called for backup. Within a minute and thirty seconds, there were six patrol cars blocking the intersection. But no one was moving too hastily; they all knew who Mark was. At first, they simply demanded that Mark get in the police car. But he wasn't complying. In his mind, he had done nothing wrong. At this point two more squad cars pull into the intersection at Tamron Ave and Okeechobee Blvd with their lights flashing. Now there are a total of nine police cars. Traffic was jammed. No one could move north, east, south, or west. And with all the flashing lights, you would have thought the carnival had just arrived in town. As it turned out, the commanding officer on the scene had known Mark for a few years. He all but pleaded with him to get in the police car, but Mark refused. There was nothing else they could do, so a handful of officers charged Mark. And we stepped forward only to have shotguns pulled on us and told to get up against the wall of the old baseball stadium on the northeast corner of that intersection. We were held up against the brick wall belonging to the stadium.

While four cops held shotguns on us, the remaining officers tried to get Mark in the car, but he was as quick as a mongoose. He knew all those Aikido moves. Every time they got him in a hold, he just broke out of it. They finally corralled him to the back door of the squad car. It looked like they were wrestling with a spider monkey. He had one foot on the rear tire of the police car, and one on the armrest of the back door that was open. With both his hands on the frame of the roof pushing back, the cops couldn't get him in the car. So they took their nightsticks and started beating him in the back of the legs, on the hamstrings and the back of his knees trying to get his legs to buckle. At the same time they were hitting him on top of his forearms trying to get his elbows to give way. When that didn't work, an African American police officer ran around to the passenger side of the car and entered through the back door grabbing Mark by the hair from inside the car, pulling his head down where another officer took a can of mace and sprayed him point blank in the face. That pretty much did it. The black officer pulled Mark into the back seat of the squad car by the hair. When the cop backed out of the car, slammed the door, and turned around, Skeeter was there. And that's when Mark's younger brother said something that was uncharacteristic of him. He blurted out "You fucking nigger!" and that sealed Skeeter's fate. The black police officer pulled out his nightstick and began beating him.

We flinched as if to come off the wall. But the cops with the shotgun swore that if we didn't freeze, they'd blow us in half. And like Confucius says, "A wise man knows his limitations." So now Skeeter's hogtied, and he's in the back of a police car. They cart Mark and Skeeter off to West Palm Beach City Jail, and we're left standing in the middle of the intersection. In the aftermath a police officer that knew Mark approached us. He explained the procedures to us, saying that Skeeter more than likely would be cut loose if he hadn't caused any more prob-

142

lems, but Mark would be in custody for the rest of the night.

So *here I am* at the West Palm Beach City Jail, with my fellow '*kara-tekas*,' waiting for Skeeter to be processed and let out. Just as we were promised, Mark was in for the rest of the evening. By now it was 11:00 p.m. and, despite all the festivities, it was just too early for us to call it a night. So we took a vote. Would Sensei want us to stick around until the next day and his release? Or do we take his car and follow through with our original plan and go to Fort Lauderdale to party? It was a four to zero, one-sided, landslide result. *Fort Lauderdale, here we come.*

Hitting the club scene in Fort Lauderdale was a blast because back then, in the state of Florida, the bars didn't shut down until 4:00 a.m., which gave us time to hit two or three night spots and get our groove on. With the lights going up in the last club we were in, and the door-man ushering us toward the front door, reality didn't strike us until we were in the parking lot. It was now after 4:00 a.m., and we had little more than an hour to get back to the West Palm Beach City Jail and pick up Mark for his release time at 6:00 a.m. None of us wanted to think about Sensei getting released and sitting on the jailhouse steps pondering what it was like to go to Fort Lauderdale and party in his brand new Cadillac without him. By the time we made our little liquor run detour and got to I-95—hell, there was no way we were driving all the way to West Palm Beach without some beers—there was only twenty minutes left for us to get to the jailhouse in West Palm Beach and pick up Mark. Or quite possibly risk our worst freaking nightmare: not being there on time to pick up Sensei. I think the unspoken plan in all of our minds was to go to Fort Lauderdale and have a great time and be back before Mark's release and everything would be fine. He wouldn't know the difference. By the time we got there, it was ten after six and he wasn't on the courthouse steps. We went inside to talk to the desk sergeant who laughingly informed us that they released Mark more than twenty minutes ago. Uh oh. With all of our cars parked in front of Sensei's house, not one of us would escape facing the music. The only discussion in the car was how severe the punishment might be. The only upside to facing our own execution was that Edwards Funeral Home sat on the corner of 58th Street and US-1, roughly thirty yards from Mark's front door. We could be embalmed before rigor mortis set in. Driving north on US-1 we made a right hand turn on 58th Street and crept the thirty yards to Mark's driveway.

What we witnessed as we coasted into Mark's driveway was some-

143

thing quite possibly only seen by the four of us in the history of the world. There was Mark, sitting in the front yard in a lounge chair, beat up, bruised, and battered. His right eye was blackened and the skin was burned off the left side of his face where they had sprayed him with mace. He was laughing with a drink in one hand and a .22 pistol in the other, shooting the fruit from his trees. Stunned and relieved at the same time, the four of us looked at each other and cracked up laughing. *This guy never quits!*

Mark greeted us with drinks. I knew a big part of our joy was a sigh of relief. Mark's first question was, "How'd the party in Fort Lauderdale go?" We told him we'd had a blast, but now we were more worried about him. None of us realized how bad his beating had been. The back of his legs and hamstrings were black and blue as well as his forearms, and his knuckles were bleeding from being beaten with nightsticks. Plus he had a black eye and, as I said, raw skin on the left side of his face. But he was willing to laugh the whole thing off. The cop who knew Mark promised to make sure he went straight home, and gave him a ride home. As soon as the police left, Mark put on a tank top and some shorts. He stepped outside in his front yard so he could watch the sun rise. Sitting in his lounge chair and looking out through the limbs of his orange tree, he realized there were far too many squirrels chowing on his oranges. So he went in the house, grabbed his .22 pistol, came back out, sat down, and started shooting at the squirrels. When the squirrels ran off in fear of the noise, he had nothing else to shoot at, so he decided to pick his fruit with a pistol.

By the time we had downed our first drink in the front yard, we had talked Mark into putting his gun up. We had seen enough of the police to last us at least… a week. At this time, his neighbors were coming out of their homes to pick up their Sunday papers off their lawns. Here I'd like to bring to everyone's attention that Mark's neighbors were pretty used to his bizarre behavior. Oh sure, when he first moved into the neighborhood there were some concern, but because none of his juvenile antics were ever directed towards them, they learned to live with it. As Mark got us our second drink, one of his neighbors picked up his paper and waved at us, and wished us happy Easter. *Easter?!* For Christ's sake, it was Easter weekend and we had forgotten all about it. This one little salutation put Curtis in hyper drive. You'd've thought someone just dropped him overboard into the Arctic Ocean. It was Easter Sunday, a family day, and he had to get home to his wife Lou and their son Chris. Poor Curt. He was torn between two worlds. He was a young man in his mid twenties who loved to go out and cut up with his friends. But he was also a family man with a wife and a young son and a responsibility that he took seriously. Now we had to figure out how to get him back in his house and back into Lou's good graces.

After the five of us brainstormed for at least twenty minutes, Mark decided that it was best if we all went over and then he talked to her. Great idea. I mean really, which one of us was going to piss on that thought? And with that, we all grabbed a fresh beer, piled into Curtis' car, and headed off to his house. Not one of us considered how we were gonna get back, though. So *here I am* in a mid seventies Chevy Malibu, with four other adult males—Curt, Mark, Dave, Skeeter and me—packed in like sardines and headed for Curtis' house. But the Looney Tunes wasn't over yet. Heading north on US-1, we were in the right lane approaching the Port of Palm Beach to the east. In the left lane, also heading north on US-1, was a semi truck that we were rapidly gaining on. All of a sudden, Curtis pulls a .380 from underneath the seat and decides to unload the clip into the box trailer that the semi's pulling. He stabs the throttle and we accelerate fifteen to twenty feet past the big rig. Curtis switched over into the semi truck's lane and then tried to make the left hand turning lane at the intersection of Old Port Road, and US-1, in Riviera Beach. But he couldn't quite scrub off enough speed. As we tried to make our left hand turn, we clipped the rear quarter panel of a oncoming car, spinning it out of control and bringing us to an abrupt stop in the middle of the intersection. The car we hit did two complete revolutions before coming to a halt in the southbound lane, facing north. I could see the shock and bewilderment on the faces of the folks in the other car. Thank goodness no one was hurt. Or at least they weren't bleeding. But I'm sure they felt as if God decided to play a game of tops and spun their car around. One minute they're heading south on US-1, the next they're spinning in circles, and now they're looking in the direction they just came from. We'd cut in front of that semi truck so fast and then tried to make that left hand turn. I'm sure they never saw what hit them and none of us were interested in sticking around until they figured it out. Curtis got his car started in a heartbeat and we took off. We headed west on Old Port Rd and took our first right, which was Avenue E. Heading north and hauling ass, we had two problems; it was a 30mph zone *and* the Riviera Beach Police station sat on Avenue E. We passed the headquarters of our tax-consuming constables just as a Riviera Beach cop was exiting the parking lot in time to see us fly by in our prelude to the Cannonball Run. Sirens blasting, blue lights flashing; he was on us like white on rice. We didn't even make Blue Heron Boulevard, which was a little more than a quarter of a mile from the police station. As the police officer approached the car, Mark had decided that he would straighten the whole thing out—something which we all tried desperately to talk him out of doing.

I can't speak for everyone, but I already had visions of jail cell bars and clanging metal ringing in my head. The first thing out of the cop's mouth as he approached Curtis' driver side window was, "Where's the fire?" Then he referred to Curtis as "Captain." You know, as in "Get your license and registration there, Captain, and come on back to my police cruiser."

By the time Curtis had gone over to the squad car, Mark insisted on getting out so he could straighten this whole thing out. You couldn't talk him out of it, nor could you hold him back. The next thing you know, Mark falls out of the passenger side window of the car with a thud. He was a little more than drunk, barely coherent, and—let's face it—he hadn't slept in three days. This little acrobatic maneuver got the cop's immediate attention. Now let's pause here for a moment of clarity. Sensei would not have been your first choice of mediators between you and the law concerning any infraction you might have committed. Hell, at this point, he wouldn't have made the top 10,000 list. Just when this constable looked a little constipated — oh, I mean irritated—Mark said something that seemed to take all the tension out of the air. He told the cop to call Boone Darden. Boone Darden? The chief of police of Riviera Beach? Huh, I didn't know he knew the chief. And then, by the grace of angels, the officer got a call over his radio; hit and run at the Port of Palm Beach and US-1. He jumped in his car immediately, and told us to slow the hell down.

He peeled off in the opposite direction, towards the Port of Palm Beach and the accident that we had caused. Once the dust cleared, we stood standing on the side of the road stunned. But we still had to face Curtis' wife Lou. We scampered back to the car and skedaddled. We all agreed that our best choice of action was to get as far away from that accident as possible.

So *here I am*, sitting in Curtis' driveway packed in this tuna can better known as a Chevy Malibu. This is not something that I was looking

146

forward to, nor did I even want to do it. Lou was warm, friendly, and welcoming. Despite our childhood antics and our juvenile behavior, she was always gracious and welcomed us in. That's not to say that Curtis didn't get an earful after we left. But I was never there when she let those foul words fly. The Dojo, however, lived by the code of the musketeers: One for all, all for one. So *here we go* marching up the front steps to the porch of Curtis' mobile home. I think I felt worse than the rest of the guys and so be it. 75% of the time it was me who gave Curtis a ride, only to bring him back high with some big story of jive. When Lou opened the front door the mobile home, I could see in her eyes that she was madder than a hornet. But she smiled and graciously invited us in. Unbelievably, after a few moments, Mark actually had her laughing, telling her stories that the rest of us would embellish intermittently. Sensei was quite the charmer, and so it wasn't long before Lou was offering us beer and chips. Of course we accepted, which gave Curtis time to take a cold shower and get his act together so he could follow through on a whole day's worth of Easter activities that he had planned for his family. Our timing was just like a Swiss watch; when he stepped in the living room all dressed for his Easter outing, we were fading out the front door. With hugs and kisses to Lou, and pats on the head for Chris, his young son, we were all but done. Now we were presented with a problem we hadn't addressed earlier. *How the hell were we going to get back to Mark's house?* There was no way Lou was going to let Curt out of her sight again, but like the old saying goes, shit rolls downhill. David and I got stuck with car juggling duties.

Chapter Fourteen
Two Marks and The Real Thing

Not long after this wild and woolly weekend it became a tale of two Marks. Mark Turner was due to be released from the Palm Beach County Stockade, which meant we had to throw him a welcome home party. Mark Herman, on the other hand, had been sentenced for a misdemeanor crime and he was due to start serving his time. Can you guess where? The West Palm Beach County Stockade! It was almost like a revolving door. Sensei Mark Herman had entered the stockade just before Mark Turner had exited it. Their sentences overlapped by about ten days, which meant they got to see each other. Sensei Mark Herman had been accused by the West Palm Beach Police Department for allegedly being involved in half the criminal activity in Palm Beach County. I had witnessed his love for guns, had ingested more than my share of illegal drugs with him, and even received what would turn out to be stolen goods from him. But that didn't make him a bad guy. Besides, who can keep track of these petty details?

The advanced Karate class, although broken hearted that our beloved Sensei was going into lockup, nonetheless had prepared for Mark Turner's release with an all-nighter. But there was one problem. No one had taken into consideration that Turner had been locked up for close to a year without a drink. We laid in wait, in the dark, at his girlfriend Cathy's apartment. When they opened the door and the lights went on, it was, *"Surprise!"*

One thing I can say about being incarcerated, you can forget how many friends you have on the outside. We could have hit Mark with a mothball and bowled him over. He was in total shock—something he

148

got over fairly quickly with a little help from us pouring his favorite brew down his gullet. I think it was around Cerveza número cinco when he started loosing all his faculties, so we just put him to bed and partied for him. In retrospect, I'm sure we screwed the pooch. I mean, the guy had been locked up for a long stretch. He probably wanted nothing more than to spend a nice long weekend in bed with his girlfriend without the hangover. Oops. I'd like to apologize here, and I hope I speak for all my fellow *karatekas* as well as our friends. Sorry, Mark. But who's got time to cry over spilled beer? This derailed freight train from Hell is moving forward at a breakneck pace.

The next adventure on our hit list was how to smuggle contraband in to Sensei while he was locked up. We had three of what we thought were very good reasons to make this daring assault on the Palm Beach County Stockade. One, we didn't want Sensei to go stir crazy because we got lazy. Two, there's nothing wrong with making a dime while you're doing your time. And Three, no one else would dare *think* of this shit let alone pull it. We held a summit meeting. Following a long conversation where we refined and detailed a plan, we arrived at one. Well, not exactly a plan—more of a discovery. Halfway through one of our alcohol-polluted, reefer-fogged evenings, we realized we had the secret weapon: my best friend, Mark Turner. Who knew the lay of the land better than Turner? Hell, he had been locked up at the Stockade twice, the last time for close to a year. Now we had to get to work.

You know the old saying about the best-laid plans? Well I do, and I believe it. I spent my whole life being told I was stupid in reference to me being Polish. As a youngster I fought the stereotype, but as I got older, I learned to flow with it. While everyone's trying to outsmart the other guy, I'm trying to out-dumb him. Turner and I came up with a brilliant, yet simplistic plan and waited until the night of the lowest moon to set it in motion. In preparation, we had removed the interior dome light from my car. We drove out towards the Stockade and entered from behind along a dirt road, approaching stealthily with our headlights off. We could see the sparkling lights from the detention center 150 yards to our right. We coasted to a stop so not to hit the brake lights. Mark got out of the car, climbed through a hole in the barbed wire fence and then disappeared into the dark abyss.

For the thrill, I wanted to accompany Mark, but he insisted I remain in the car and my common sense told me to sit this one out. One person expertly sneaking around a prison yard was far less unlikely to be seen than two. So *here I am* alone on a dirt road outside of a minimum-security prison in the middle of a dark night so that my best friend can break into the prison, creep through the exercise yard, and hide a couple of dime bags of pot in a designated spot for my Karate instructor. Of course, this is more excitement than most people could stand. But we all had to take our hats off to Turner. No one could ever accuse him of not having a set of 'big ones.' It was right about this time that the colors in our world started to fade just a bit.

Two new faces were introduced to our merry band of misfits. Stanley G, and a guy by the name of Tommy C. Tommy I didn't much care for, but Stanley G, aka Stan, was a stand up guy. Stan and Sensei Carl had become roommates and I had quickly grown to like him. Stan was a bookie by trade, and he was fond of the white powder which made him more than popular with Sensei's Carl and Mark, a lot of ladies, and a few of us. Here's a quick story about Stan. I was out one evening at a nightclub when Stan approached me. He had a lady on each arm. He pulled me aside and asked if I had any money on me, as he was broke. I told him I had a hundred bucks in my pocket. He relieved me of it and said he'd pay me back later. The next day when I saw Carl, I mentioned that I'd seen Stan at a nightclub the night before and he had hit me up for a hundred dollars. Carl's response, "You didn't give him any money, did ya?" Baffled, I replied, "Of course! It was Stan," and Carl began laughing. I didn't get the joke. He told me that Stan never paid anybody back. Now I'm broke as well as broken hearted. But that weekend, I ran into Stan again at a different nightclub.

Stan was sitting at a table in a booth, with ladies on each side of him, laughing like a hyena when he spots me and says "Hey kid, come over here." What did I have to lose? It was a table full of ladies and Stan was always good fun. When I approached he said, "Come over here and sit next to me." He handed me a hundred bucks under the table and whispered in my ear, "Thanks, kid. Tonight's on me." I didn't say a word, but I was tickled to death. I couldn't believe it. *Stan paid me back!* After a drink or two Carl showed up with some people, then it was off to the races. Another night in the fast lane. That following Monday when I showed up to class, I stepped in Carl's office and shut the door. I told him what had taken place and that Stan had paid me back. His bottom jaw bounced off the top of his feet. Stan had never paid anyone back, but he paid me and I loved the guy. As far as I was concerned, Stanley G was a stand-up guy.

At this point, most of the black belts and instructors around the state of Florida were bugging Carl. When was he going to test me for black belt? A lot of them frequently made sly remarks to me when I entered a tournament as a brown belt. "Hey Podgurski, have you retired as a brown belt?" I'd just shrug and smile, and then beat up their students. So *here I am* in Coco Beach waiting to enter yet another auditorium to sign up for a Karate tournament, when Carl calls me and my friend Alonso Hall over to the rear of his car. Alonso, whose nickname is Slick, looks at me and I shrug. We both approach Carl and he opens the trunk of his car and pulls out two black belts. He takes the black belts and hands one to each of us then informs us if we don't do well that day, he's going to take them back. Not a traditional black belt test, but certainly no odder than the rest of my life. And a lot less bizarre than the night I tested for brown belt…

A year or so earlier, we were out partying one night, and I had been bugging Carl for almost three months to let me test for brown belt. He was convinced I was lacking the one skill to make brown belt; honing my *katas*. *Katas* are preconceived moves—choreographed series of movements—set in a pattern with variations of blocks, strikes, punches and kicks, which are designated at a certain place and time in the *kata*. The routine is much like a fighter shadow boxing and going through all of his moves, except that each one of these dances of death have their own name, and they progressively get harder as you go up in belt rank. On this particular night, I had been pestering Carl while we were driving. Just as we pulled up to a red light, he said, "Fine!" He had heard enough. He told me to get out of the car and go to the center of the intersection, and if I could perform my *katas* to his satisfaction, he would pass me to brown belt.

I didn't hesitate for a second. I jumped out of the car, walked to the middle of the intersection, and stood directly beneath the stoplight. Car headlights at the intersection going north, east, south, and west were on me. I bowed to my Sensei and the car he was driving and then performed all my designated *katas*. The intersection was at a standstill. Sure there were a few honks of the horn, but then everyone became curious as to what I was doing. When I was finished, I came to attention, once again bowed to my instructor and to the car he was driving. I ran back to get back into Sensei's vehicle and the intersection erupted with horn applause. When I got in the car, everyone in it was howling. Tears were running down the front of Carl's face he was laughing so hard.

Carl punched the throttle on the car and he almost wrecked it, but he told me congratulations. He had just promoted me to brown belt.

Like I said, that was a year or so earlier. So when Slick and I entered that auditorium with our newly bestowed black belts in our hands, there was one thing on our minds, and one thing only; win. And win we did. We fought like demons that day. There was no way we were giving back those black belts. It was our heyday. And like I mentioned before, Karate tournaments are a round robin affair. You're paired up by luck of the draw. So long as you keep winning, you move forward. One loss and you're out. So we were having a ball. I would win my match in the heavyweight division, and then wander over to the lightweight division to see how Alonso was doing. And then when I bowed in to fight my next match, Slick would be on the sideline cheering me on. We both took first place in our weight divisions. Oh no, there wasn't a snowball's chance in Hell, we were giving those black belts back.

Not long after this tournament, Sensei Mark was let out of the Stockade, and of course we threw him a party. Everyone had a great time, but Sensei was one step ahead of the rest of us. When no one was looking, he bailed out of the party. He had decided to take care of nature. Some things were a little more important then the three B's—meaning, booze, bongs, and your buddies. But none of us could have predicted what was going to happen next, although maybe we should have. Things settled down after Mark's party, but then abruptly Curt moved in with Mark Herman. I was never clear as to what exactly had taken place, and why Curtis had left home and moved in with Mark. I suspect that Lou had grown tired of Curtis' juvenile friends and his delinquent behavior.

It was right about this time that I was first approached about beating someone up for money. I was standing outside of a nightclub in Palm Beach when Paul Anselmo approached me. He confessed he needed a favor. His good friend's sister was married to a jerk off and needed to be slapped down for beating her up. Automatically I agreed to do it out of loyalty, but then he said he would pay me. Paul handed me some money, a couple hundred bucks, and then pointed out a guy leaving the club as he got in his car to drive off. I believe things can happen in this life for a reason. Had Paul approached me earlier and pointed this guy out, I probably would have followed him into the men's room and banged him up. But as it was, the guy was driving off, so I laughed and said, "There goes your guy." Paul's response was, "He'll be here tomorrow night."

That gave me more than twenty hours to analyze what was being asked of me, and why I was being paid. The very next evening, I went out, but this was weighing heavily on my mind. Since the clubs didn't close until 4:00 a.m., at around midnight I headed for Palm Beach to see if I could find Paul. I stepped into the nightclub and *bingo* there was Skeeter. My first question, where are the guys? He pointed to a booth that held most of our affiliates: Danny Lanes, Mark Herman, Stanley G., Carl Stone, Steve Masciello, Steve Shepherd, and most importantly, Paul.

I headed over there. I couldn't help but notice as I passed through the dance floor that David Bunning and Mark Turner were dancing and having a great time. As I approached the booth, I saw a couple of faces I didn't know including one that looked familiar. It was the guy I was supposed to beat up. This puzzled me for a moment, but that thought was interrupted with a big jubilant 'Hello! What's happening?' from the guys. They ordered me a drink and wanted to know where the hell I had been all night. After about an hour, I told Paul I needed to speak to him so we stepped outside. I told him I wasn't interested in the job. I tried to give him the $200 back but he laughed. He said, "Keep the money." It had already been taken care of. *Can you say dumbfounded?* It took me about a New York minute to figure out that this is how you get on the strong-arm payroll and take your first step in organized crime as an enforcer.

When you owe a debt for illegal activities to the underworld for gambling, loan sharking, or drugs, there are no lawyers. There will be no courts. You owe the money, period. Which means if you don't pay your debt on time, you will get a visit. And the amount could be your own personal Armageddon. Meaning, the amount of money you owe and the amount of time you're late in paying it could depict the difference between that nagging little squirrel monkey on your back that won't go away, or that 800 fucking pound gorilla coming through your front door. But this is how they recruit you and get you on the payroll. They tell you a story about a guy that bats his wife around or beats on his kids or has abused their sister, or steals from his mother to support a drug habit. Believe it or not, they appeal to your moral conviction. At this point, you're half-cocked, ready to beat the guy's ass on principle. And the icing on the cake is that they're going to throw you a few hundred buck so what do you have to lose? But then you have to ask yourself, "Where does it stop?" Everything in life tends to escalate. Sure, bitch slapping the right guy around and busting his lip is something you might feel good about. Knocking out a tooth or breaking the jaw of some deadbeat, you won't lose any sleep over that. Pretty soon you're breaking someone's leg or neck, and then you're killing people just to try to keep up the lifestyle you've created. You also tend to spend money fast because it comes fast. You're like a hamster on a treadmill. The next thing you know, you're standing over a dead body thinking, "Fuck him, he deserved it."

It becomes all about rationalizing your moral character and, more importantly, your greed. You blame it on the victim. You're pissed off because if this fucker didn't deserve it, you wouldn't be standing here in front of a corpse. Even though I was just entering my twenties, my subliminal binoculars could see the end of this road clearly. *No thank you!* I wanted nothing to do with it. Like I said, I didn't take Karate to hurt people, I took it to defend myself. But that didn't stop them from trying and pestering me. On more than one occasion, Stan would see me and call, "Hey kid, come here. You need some pocket money to walk around with?" In the back of your mind you're thinking, *who the hell doesn't need money?* "What do you mean, Stan?" And he would go into, "I got this guy, he's this, he's that." And he would make up a moral conviction story. You know, to ease your conscience. So your conclusion is, "Hell, this guy needs a good ass whoopin.'" Now you've got one foot on the yellow brick road to a nightmarish existence because you've chosen to punch holes in your soul.

Stan would come to me about every six to eight weeks with the same old proposition. "Hey kid, do you need some money?" I'd just tell him, "Hey Stan, I don't do that. That's not why I took Karate." Then he would reach around to the back of my neck, give it a squeeze and tell me I was a good kid. He'd say I needed to get away from these bums, that I didn't need to hang around with these guys, that I could have a good life...

At this time, my good friend and Karate brother Leon Nubin had joined the paratroopers. Thankfully, he had missed out on all this stuff, because the world around me as I knew it was ready to spiral right out of control. I had tried the real thing four or five times in my life by this point, and although I used a straw, there was nothing thirst quenching about it. Oh sure, I had consumed other kinds of illegal drugs, but cocaine was a little rich for my blood, unless it was free. Not willing

154

to look a gift horse in the mouth, one long weekend that started on a Thursday evening after we shut the Karate school down ended for me on a Sunday morning as a lesson in excess.

Now you have to keep in mind, the only street drugs that were known at the time to be addictive were heroin and opium, neither of which came close to me. Besides, I had a steadfast rule about getting high. If I had to use my body as a pincushion, it wasn't worth the ride. But cocaine, that wasn't an addictive drug—or so we thought. That Thursday evening, we shut the Karate school down at 9:00 p.m. We got cleaned up, and then went out on the town. We started at Big Daddy's and we must've hit half the nightspots in town, picking up different women along the way. By 4:00 a.m., we decided to head back to Stan and Carl's place with groupies in tow. Stan had some coke, and a lot of it. And boy, did we have a good time. We partied 'till the sun came up, and then the realization hit. It was Friday and we had to go to work. Well, some of us... The responsible people, if you could call them that, took one last blast of white powder to try to get them going so they could head off to work. The rest of us? Stan and Carl lived in a beautiful apartment complex for singles, which also had a beautiful community pool. So *here I am* at 8:00 a.m., poolside barbecuing and feeling a little discombobulated. We were having a blast. People were going to work and we were jumping in and out of the pool, goofing around in our swimsuits.

At any given time, one of us would fade away with a different woman to take the short walk over to Carl and Stan's. We'd do a bump (which is a hit of cocaine) and then have our way with her. By midday, all of the people that worked in the evenings who lived at the complex were out by the pool. That would be your bartenders and waitresses and employees of nightclubs, restaurants and hotels. Of course, we got any of the good-looking women involved in our hysteria. Each one of us at any given time would cut one that we found attractive out of the herd and take the short walk to Stan and Carl's apartment. Once inside, you would've thought it was Christmas in Alaska there was so much snow. Of course it only took one or two trips back to the apartment before it was bare-assed on the proverbial bearskin rug.

This behavior continued until about 2:00 p.m. when Carl started bugging me about going to the Karate school and opening it. Sure the Karate school was supposed to be open at three, but why me? So *here I am* at 4:00 p.m. at Dojo North in Riviera Beach right between 23rd

155

and 24th Streets. And who was at the original Dojo on Clematis Street? I didn't have a clue. If I could have anticipated what was going to take place over the next few days, I would have taken full advantage of my little pit stop at Dojo North and gotten some rest. At 6:00 p.m., I closed the Karate school. I rushed home, got something to eat, cleaned up, got some fresh clothes and went straight back to Stan's. I was afraid I was missing something. By the time I arrived at Carl and Stan's the party had moved inside, and it was still snowing in South Florida. I mean, *a blizzard*.

A whole new tide of women were there, smelling and looking good; these ladies came dressed to impress. After a half hour or so, I realized some of these ladies already had their own plans for the evening. They had stopped by to get a jump on their weekend. For the most, we were the hosts and they weren't going anywhere. They had Karate jocks, free flowing booze, and an avalanche that would bury a ski resort in Colorado. At 8:00 pm one of the luscious lovelies mentioned that she was hungry, so we packed up this bunch of bug-eyed beauties and did a caravan to a popular restaurant called The Abbey Road, which just happened to have the best Alaskan king crab legs in town. When we stepped into the bar area of the restaurant, it all but came to a stand still. We were loud, obnoxious, and having more fun than humans are supposed to have. But the *maître d'* overlooked our grand boisterous entrance when he realized we knew the bartender as well as most of the staff.

The first thing Carl did was order our whole party a round of drinks. The second thing that Stan did was hand the bartender a small vial of coke. Now we could do no wrong. The whole allure of doing coke in the 70s was that it was a socially elite drug. It was rumored that the big rock gods of the time—Eric Clapton, Rod Stewart, Elton John, Jimmy Page, David Bowie, Robert Plant, not to forget Mick Jagger, and Keith Richards—were all said to have indulged in many a fun-filled weekend, as well as weekdays. After we'd had all of the seafood we could ingest, it was getting close to midnight, and time for some serious club hopping.

We managed to squeeze in three or four nightspots, each club more fun than the previous. Every doorman in town welcomed us with open arms. It's an interesting study on human nature when you get a sincere respect out of fear. And of course the icing on the cake was in Stan's generous handshake. Name me a guy that doesn't like a man who can beat his ass, but rewards him for not having to do so. Now, close to 4:00 a.m. and, armed with a few new and fresh faces, we caravan back to Stan and Carl's. One realization I had a long time ago: when you're having a great time and a lot of fun, it's infectious. But what we were doing was downright addictive. Once back at the pad, a light snow turned into a blizzard. Then a few of us wandered out by the pool. Who cared if it was 4:30 a.m.? Well it didn't take me long. With the heat of all that dancing, the warm humid air, and the cocaine pumping through my veins, I did what any shy, introverted southern boy would do; I got naked and hit the pool. Something else I picked up early on—it's a lot easier to get a girl's clothes off if you don't have any on yourself. Well, don't blame me if a good idea catches on. Now everyone who is outside with me on the pool deck is skinny-dipping. But were starting to make so much noise, people were waking up. As drunk as I was, I knew if the cops showed up, this was a bust bigger than any of us could talk our way out of. Besides, I wasn't going to bum my buzz with badges and bars. I got everybody out of the pool, we grabbed up our clothes, and all ran back across the lawn to Stan and Carl's place. We entered the apartment through the patio sliding glass doors, laughing like a bunch of high school kids who just blew up the urinals with a cherry bomb. At first, the six of us got a look of shock from those who'd opted to stay in and play in the snow. Then everybody fell out of our chairs laughing. By 9:00 a.m. we were back out at the pool barbecuing. Oh sure, a few faded out and went home. *Pansies!* And more than a few had passed out back at Stan and Carl's apartment. *Wimps!* But for most of us it was *'Man the torpedoes, full speed ahead!'* Our feet were through the floorboards, the throttle wide open and our rev meters were pegged.

So *here I am* at day two of the "three B's:" Booze, Broads, and Boinking with a little nose candy thrown in to help me keep my energy as well as 'bobo' up. At this point I'm sure it's hard for civilized people to understand how you can stay up for days partying non-stop. But for anyone who attended a cocktail party back in the seventies, who stayed up all night snorting coke, busily solving the world's problems only to wake up and not remember the solutions, you know exactly how it's done. Without a doubt we were extremists. We pushed the envelope. Hell, we knew how to blow right through the envelope. But what you have to keep in mind: cocaine use starts off as a very social activity. We all crave the company of other people so we can engage in these philosophical conversations. Then we could go to bed after an all-nighter

157

with warm, self-assured thoughts. The downside was waking up the next morning and only remembering parts of the conversations. And it's always the same; you can never remember the parts with the damn solutions.

But now, it's late Saturday afternoon and the girl I'm with actually lives in the same complex as Stan and Carl. This young lady, who will remain nameless, has called some girlfriends and invited them over. Now, this beautiful young woman has a thing for me and we had been intimate more than a few times. But when her girlfriends showed up, her instincts immediately picked up on an instant physical attraction I had for one of her friends. As luck would have it, as I said, this beautiful young woman lived in the same apartment complex as Carl and Stan. As fate would have it, she had a date that evening with a young man. She reluctantly left the party and came back within an hour dressed to kill. I was already on a roll when she pulled me outside and asked me to reassure her that I wouldn't put my hands on her friend. *Oh, how great!* She's going out on a date and I'm at a party and supposed to act sedate. I told her I couldn't be that fake. She left the party boohooing and I went back to it boogalooing.

Once back inside the party, I had a plan. I isolated this fair young female in Stan and Carl's kitchen and began necking on her. You know, making out. For Christ's sake, for everybody born after 1980, I was macking on her. Once she began moaning, I began groaning in her ear what I wanted to do with her. At first I was outrageous and playful, but she was adventuresome and gainful. Next stop: Carl's bedroom.

Once in Carl's room, I locked the door. Then I swept her off her feet by picking her up and tossing her into the bed. I entertained her with a striptease and this had her laughing so hard that tears were streaming down her face. At this point in my life, I had developed my own seduction technique. Combining the macho masculinity of a Charles Bronson or a Clint Eastwood with the childhood antics and playfulness of the Three Stooges, this turned out to be a lethal combination that worked well on the ladies. *Oh, and did I mention I have dimples?*

By this point I had convinced her to participate in something that would be entertaining to all that witnessed it. I headed off to the refrigerator, but I had to make two or three passes down the hall to grab everything I needed from the kitchen. At one point Carl noticed me and wanted to know what I was up to. So *here I am*, standing in Sensei's hall, all but naked, clutching bowls of fruits, berries, nuts, bananas,

158

and whipped cream. I assured him I'd have his answer in a moment.

After about fifteen minutes, I stepped into the living room and requested that everyone follow me to the bedroom door. At the door I paused briefly and announced to my critics what they were about to witness was truly art and a glimpse of the inner workings of my mind. Without any further ado, I swung the door wide open and introduced to Palm Beach County the very first human banana split.

There was an eruption of laughter and hysteria so loud I'm sure the neighbors thought the Cape was launching another Apollo mission. I had strategically placed fruits, nuts, and berries on whipped cream and bananas to conceal the areas that this beautiful young woman on this particular night would only want me to explore. And with that, I took two giant leaps, jumped up in the air, came down in the middle of the bed on top of her spraying our viewers with ambrosia; the dessert of gods. Knowing when to take a cue, our audience backed out of the room and shut the door leaving us to our ado.

By eleven o'clock I was done with dessert and ready for the main course. Besides, I could hear everyone scurrying around in the living room. It was time to go out. So, I jumped in the shower and cleaned up. When I hit the living room, everyone was amazed. They thought I was down and out. Who cares that I started on Thursday? Who was keeping count of how many girls I'd been with? I was a test tube of testosterone. Like most 19 year olds, I was a walking hard on. It was Saturday night and I was off my stool bouncing around, waiting for the bell to start the next round. When the bell tolled, I kissed my delicious little delight goodnight, and headed out with my Cool Casanovas looking for the big "Three C's:" Clubs, Cocktails, and, ah, Cohorts. Once on the town we did our usual club cruising, bar brawling, lady loving. By 4:00 a.m. we had dragged a whole new group of victims back to Carl and Stan's.

By dawn, those who hadn't blacked out simply crapped out and drove home. At 8:30 a.m. there were just the five of us sitting around the coffee table with drinks. Stan was shaving slivers of coke off a rock the size of a racquetball for us to snort. The coffee table was made from a spool for telephone cables which had been cut in half and polyure-thaned. Those who weren't sitting on the couch like myself were lounging in beanbag chairs. By 8:45 a.m., lines of coke had been chopped up and were being passed around on a mirror for us to snort. When it got around to me I tried to decline. I'd realized that from my top lip

159

to my forehead and from cheek to cheek, the whole front of my face was completely numb. If felt as though my mug had been shot full of eucalyptus. With no sensation at all in the front of my face and my friends badgering me, I engaged yet one more time in euthanasia of the cranium.

One thing I can speak to very clearly—people who are ingesting drugs do not want people around them that are not. By 9:00 a.m. we had another round of drinks and here comes the coke tray. I'm sitting back in my beanbag chair tapping on the front of my numb skull. In retrospect, I'm sure my subliminal mind was tapping out an S.O.S. By this time the coke tray had been passed around yet again and had reached me, but I declined and that's when everyone decided to badger Jeff's behind. You know, my ass. But the more pressure they applied, the more determined I was to deny. After about fifteen minutes of being hassled, I did a few things that were virtually impossible.

Number one (and you have to understand the power structure in the martial arts world is very much like the military): I was a Captain going against his Senseis. I was being insubordinate to not one, but *two* four-star Generals. Number two: I was turning down a very expensive and socially elite drug. And three: at the fifteen-minute mark of me being ridiculed, I went absolutely berserk. I jumped up and flipped over the telephone cable 'coffee table' which had all the coke laid out on it. *Hundreds* of dollars of cocaine disappeared into the shag carpet. The reaction to my aggravation was not what you'd expect. Suddenly there was an explosion of laughter that could have woken the dead. Carl fell back on the couch kicking his feet in the air like a gleeful three-year-old throwing a temper tantrum; laughing so hard I thought the veins in his neck were going to pop. Stan was guffawing to the point that his face turned beet red and he began coughing. Sensei Mark had just taken a drink of his Bacardi and Coke which caused him to loose it and blow the whole beverage out through his nostrils. Everybody was howling, which just pissed me off even more.

I began screaming, "We've been partying for three days straight. We've snorted over a pound of coke. We've drunk every bar and nightclub in town dry. We've drained every liquor store in the city. We've had half the women in Palm Beach County. For Christ's sake, *how much more is there to do?!*"

By this point I had gathered up all my stuff and stormed out the door. By the time I got to my car, I was so pissed off I was yelling at myself. I got the car started and headed for my mobile home. I was so aggravated I was beating the steering wheel and dash with my fist, then I glanced at the rearview mirror. Once I looked into my own eyes, it was like a balloon having the air slowly let out of it. I could see death. I swore right then and there, staring at myself in the mirror, I would never do cocaine again. I was madder than a hornet. I gritted my teeth and made that promise to myself: *never again.* Then I lectured myself all the way back to my mobile home. I could sense something very evil about this drug. I mean, when your closest friends are on it and they don't want you to stop using it, if that's not a red flag then I don't know what is. So that was the beginning and the end. One binge weekend and my dope-snorting career was done.

Chapter Fifteen
Ex-wives, Executions and My Buddies

A few weeks passed after that weekend of drug-filled debauchery. One Monday I arrived early at the Dojo so I could work out before I had to teach class, only to find Carl in his office staring into the air. I greeted him with, "What's happenin'?" As if snapping out of a trance, he looked up at me, asked me to shut the office door, and take a seat. Then he proceeded to explain what had taken place earlier that morning.

At 11:00 a.m., there had been a knock on the front door of his apartment. When he answered the door there were two Italian guys, the size of refrigerators, standing on his porch wanting to know where Stanley G was. Then they proceeded to tell Carl they knew who *he* was but they didn't have a problem with him. They needed to speak with Stan. Now, as Carl related the story, I could sense what was unfolding, but being a naïve kid, I just had to ask what it all meant. Carl, having grown up in Chicago, knew exactly what was going on. The fellas in New York had sent the refrigerators down to give Stan a little message. Then Carl leveled with me and told me what he thought the message might be. Stan's affiliates in New York were in the house of gaming. He wasn't supposed to step into the neighborhoods of drug lords.

It was right about this time that Mark Herman sold his house in West Palm Beach and he and Curtis Lucas moved west out of town near Lake Worth Road. Even though my good buddy, Curt, was now close to twenty miles away, I was happy. To me, that house on Fifty-Eighth Street and West Palm was cursed. On the moderately inconvenient side, Mark had been busted there a few times so I knew the police were watching it. On the extreme, Carl had taken a .32 slug in the chest courtesy of his ex-wife.

Just a few short years earlier, both Mark and Carl had tried to reconcile with their ex-wives. They had taken their lovely ladies out on a double date for a celebration, which quickly turned into annihilation. Carl and his lovely ex got into an argument at dinner, which ended that party. Then on the ride home, I guess things escalated. By the time they got to Mark's, Carl had jumped out of the car and kicked the fenders in. Then with a proverbial Karate chop, he'd sheered off the right side rear view mirror. Then he ran around to the opposite side of the car and punched right through the side window, all the time screaming, "Get the fuck out of the car!"

What he hadn't noticed was that Mark's wife had grabbed his keys and had run the few short steps across the lawn and gone into the house. In the meantime, Sensei Mark was left outside trying to calm Carl down. What happened next could be a chapter in the Lorena Bobbitt domestic violence handbook.

Now, I have to confess; I wasn't there. But I'll tell it to you as it was told me by those who were. Carl raced to the door and began pounding on it, screaming something to the affect of, "Open the fuckin' door. If you don't open the fuckin' door I'll kick the motherfucker in!" With Carl violently pounding and kicking the door, and a little more of his barbarian sweet-talk, someone unlocked the door. Fortunately for Carl's wife, Mark's wife knew where all his guns were hidden. Unfortunately for Carl, when he came through the front door, his wife was standing there with a .32-caliber pistol and let him have it. The bullet struck him on the lower, inside left pectoral muscle, which stood him straight up and then sat him straight down. What happened next was a scene straight out of the Keystone Cops.

Carl's wife runs straight out of the house with Mark's wife cheering her on. Mark is screaming at his wife to call the cops and/or an ambulance. Carl is yelling at Mark to help him into the bathroom because he has to take a shit. Mark won't help him because he heard or read somewhere that if you've been shot and you take a shit you'll die. Carl's now pleading with Mark to get him into the bathroom. Mark won't hear of it. Carl's now screaming he's afraid he's going to shit all over himself once he's in the ambulance. Mark's now yelling at Carl to focus on his *chi* and go into a Zen-like state and fight his natural instinct to relieve himself.

163

While all this is going on, Mark has decided to play Dr. Kildare and has taken his index finger and stuck it in the hole the bullet had made in Carl's chest. By the time the ambulance had gotten there, Mark and Carl were playing slappy hand and arguing as to whose finger was going to plug the hole in Carl's chest. Carl was convinced he could take care of his own hole (no pun intended) so Mark would be free to escort him into the bathroom where he could relieve himself.

Okay, for all of you Einsteins that have kept up, let's take a moment here for the rocket scientists to catch up. Whenever you've experienced a life-threatening trauma or injury and you've just eaten, you're more than likely going to have the urge to relieve yourself. You know the saying, I've had the crap scared out of me. Even a mental midget realizes when you die your brain shuts down and with that you lose all control of your bodily functions. So, this is not a pleasant thought and it's certainly not how we want to be remembered, but for most of us when we pass on we'll make our last deposit on this earth… If you get my drift.

Well, Sensei Mark, in all his infinite wisdom, had gotten a little confused. And how that happened I can only speculate. But for those who partied in the seventies, you might remember that thick white pill the size of a bottle cap called Aurora 714, better known as a Quaalude. You do a handful of those (because God knows one horse tranquilizer will never do) and a few cocktails, and you'd be a little discombobulated too. Sensei had gotten the whole thing backwards. Mark was convinced that if you had been shot and you relieved yourself, you would die. But in actuality it's the other way around; when you die—not to coin a phrase here—you 'crap out.'

Only God himself could have known what the police report would have looked like after the cops got done interviewing the Mark and Carl show. It was probably something on parallel with yet another scatter-brained, tongue-tied manifesto; Ted Kaczynski. You remember him—The Unabomber.

And pardon my pause here for a moment. But as a man who's been involved in the fighting arts for close to forty years, who has achieved a handful of black belts, and been inducted into the Martial Arts Hall of Fame, I would just like to say: had you just eaten and then been shot by your future ex-wife in the chest with a .38, even if you were the Dalai Lama himself you wouldn't have enough *chi*, Zen, or focus to keep from shitting yourself. Okay, it was a .32, but it was still enough to turn you blue. All right, enough said. Let's get back to Stan's story.

There were just a few short months between my first and only co-caine binge weekend and the Miami Beach Golden Gloves Boxing Tournament. Stanley G, being from New York, liked to watch boxing. He loved fighters. A handful of people, including myself, had been invited to go to Miami to view the tournament at the Miami Beach Convention Center.

By this time, Ronda and I had moved in together and we had acquired a boat, so all of our Sundays were reserved for water skiing. Plus, it was my one and only day away from the Dojo and all its inhabitants. I can't honestly tell you how many or who went down to watch that boxing tournament, but even if I knew I'm not sure that I would tell you. But one thing is absolute; after a few boxing matches had taken place, someone approached Stan about going outside for a little pow-wow. Stan never came back. When the tournament was over and they cleared the convention center, they found Stanley G in the parking lot with eight bullet holes in his head and chest.

When I bounced into the Karate school on Monday I got slammed by this news. There was Carl sitting at his desk in his office, staring at the wall. When he looked at me I saw his eyes were red. I asked him what was wrong and he told me what had taken place over the weekend and that Stan was gone. It felt as though someone had punched me in the kidney and knocked all the breath out of me. I fell back in the chair. I couldn't believe it. Stanley G was dead? *They shot him?*

After a few moments, I was enraged. I wanted to know who did this and why. I wanted revenge. And that's when Carl calmly looked up and gave me my first lesson in Mob Etiquette 101. Carl quietly brought me back to those two Italian refrigerators who'd showed up on his front doorstep looking for Stanley G. Stan was getting dirty in someone else's yard. He was from a gambling family, and I don't mean your Uncle Bill and Aunt Gladys. He was playing around with dope. He didn't heed the warning, so he paid with the supreme sacrifice; his life.

As I said, Stanley G was from New York City. He was a tough little street-fighting Jew who, if you played it straight with him, played it straight with you. Although more than three decades that have passed by, I still miss and think of Stan.

Just about the time we were all shaking off Stan's murder, Mark Herman had been indicted yet again, this time for murder; the murder of Richard Kreusler, a prominent Palm Beach resident. Mr. Kreusler had been seeking a political office—I believe he wanted to be the mayor of

Palm Beach. One night, after getting home from a political fundraiser or dinner party, the front doorbell rang. As he approached the front door to answer it, they blasted through it more than once with a shotgun, leaving Mr. Kreusler dead in his own foyer. By now the Deputy D.A. had had his fill of Sensei Mark. He was convinced Mark Herman was Public Enemy Number One in Palm Beach County, so the murder rap got hung on Sensei Mark.

Now you have to bear with me here. This whiz kid of a D.A. had hauled Mark into court more than a dozen times on different charges but could never seal the deal. Mark always seemed to out-maneuver him. You can't imagine how frustrating that must have been to spend the first part of your young adult life in law school only to be out-witted by a street punk.

Before coming back to Florida in the early seventies, Sensei Mark had spent some time in an Arizona prison. Mark had been convicted and sentenced for God knows what. Being very street-wise and bright, Mark went straight to the law section of the prison library and started cracking open the books. He penned a couple of dozen letters before an Arizona Supreme Court Justice accepted one. Mark had found a loophole in the case and the judge agreed with him. So now he was out of his cage. Who says a jailbird can't fly? Mark, like the phoenix, rose from the ashes and was wise enough to leave the state of Arizona and head back to the place of his birth; Florida, land of the flamingo.

But on this rap, he was in for the fight of his life. Florida was a death penalty state and things were really getting weird. As if this wasn't enough to worry about, we had reporters hounding us down at the Karate school trying to get a scoop. Mark had made bail and now everybody was watching every move he made, meaning the cops, the reporters, and us.

My personal assessment of this whole fiasco was that the cops were tired of chasing Mark around. The Deputy D.A. was humiliated and fed up by being outwitted by him. This was a good way to get him off the streets. First of all, the cops didn't have a clue—not one shred of evidence—as to who did pull the trigger and assassinated Mr. Kreusler. But the local police could get rid of this thorn in their side by the name of Mark Herman. The Deputy D.A. could avenge his humiliation over the years by convicting Mark of a murder he hadn't committed. Gold stars all around. But, like I said, that's just my thoughts and assessment.

Mark was convicted in 1978 for that murder and sentenced to prison for 26 years. Close to half a decade later Geraldo Rivera, while working for 20/20, won an Emmy for his investigative reporting on "A Killer in Camelot: the Richard Kreusler—Mark Herman Story." Still, despite these efforts from the outside, Sensei Mark Herman would spend close to twenty years in prison before his case landed on the desk of Governor Childs of the great state of Florida. After reviewing Mark's case, Governor Childs decided that the state of Florida could not uphold this conviction, and therefore granted Mark amnesty.

Mark Herman's case would be unprecedented in other ways as well. His trial would be the first in the United States to permit television cameras from opening statement to sentencing. In the end, more than his life was ruined. His second wife, Debbie, died of lupus before he was released from prison, and the son they had together was a young man approaching twenty before he saw his father beyond a jail cell.

But while Sensei Mark was on trial for murder, as bad as we felt for him, we all had our own problems. A once successful Karate empire, which boasted over six hundred active students and two studios, was now crumbling. The financial stress of mounting a defense for Mark's trial, plus all the negative publicity, had had a dramatic affect. From our viewpoint it was like watching the Titanic sink. And just when you think it can't get any worse, stop thinking because it can.

I can't honestly remember if it was a Saturday or a Sunday but I do know it was the weekend. The phone rang. Curtis was *dead!* I dropped the phone in shock. My close friend—my running buddy, the guy that made me laugh harder than anyone I ever knew, the pit-bull in a bar-room brawl that would never leave you behind—was gone.

I rushed straight down to the Karate school. When I stepped inside, there were a handful of people standing in the middle of the Dojo. The only two faces I could see were David Bunning and Carl Stone. David and I were Curtis' two closest friends, but because of his marriage and his young son, we lived slightly different lifestyles, which would leave David and me to our own delinquency and juvenile behavior and running together, more often than not like Butch Cassidy and the Sundance Kid.

Carl and David immediately pulled me into the Dojo office and shut the door so they could explain to me what had happened. It turns out the new house that Mark had bought out west of town off of Lake Worth Road was no luckier than his place on 58th Street in West Palm Beach. Curtis had turned south off Lake Worth Road onto the access

167

road to Mark's new neighborhood. A couple of hundred yards further along there was a barrier where you had to take a right hand turn; a 90-degree angle. A few hundred feet further than that, on the left, was Mark's new house. Curtis never made that 90-degree turn. He slammed through the barrier, roughly traveling ten yards through the sugar sand, and had flipped his car upside-down into the canal that lay beyond. The police said there was no sign of a struggle. Curtis never tried to exit the vehicle. He catapulted into the canal upside-down, was knocked out cold and drowned. The only comforting fact that I have is my friend never knew the sheer panic of drowning. He just didn't know what hit him.

I had no official responsibility in Curtis' funeral, thank God. Curtis had family in Palm Beach County and the Hawaiians are a very noble and stoic people. They take care of their own. So, all that week I showed up at the Karate school with my game face on and taught class. Every conscious moment I kept convincing myself I was going to be okay. I kept trying to picture my friend in a casket. I kept picturing Curtis dead. I was going to be okay.

The day of his wake came. Ronda and I pulled up in front of the funeral parlor and it seemed like everyone we knew were there. I think at most funerals, there's happiness as well as sadness. There's the joy of seeing people you might have lost touch with who you're glad to see are okay, but all the while you're hating the fact that it took the death of a loved one to bring you back together. I stood outside the funeral parlor greeting friends and Curtis' family, reminiscing over stories about Curtis and his antics. I deliberately waited until the last minute to step inside the funeral home and when I did, it felt as if half the blood drained out of my body. I remember I got a little dizzy, so I held my ground in the back of the funeral parlor. After about fifteen minutes, I seemed to have caught my balance and my breath and I felt as though I was ready to view Curtis in his casket, so Ronda and I headed towards him.

With every step I felt the blood leaving my feet, my legs. My knees began to buckle, my chest was heaving. And then there he was. I really thought I had prepared myself. I had envisioned Curtis in every state of death I could think of. When I looked into his casket, I all but blacked out. Ronda was standing in front of me. I had my hands on her shoulders to steady myself. My knees buckled and all my weight came crashing down on this five foot two, hundred and ten pound girl. Her

168

only response: "God!" And she shrugged me off as quickly as I fell on her. Thank God Tommy Fafarco and David Bunning were standing there as they saved me from hitting the ground. They caught me and all but carried me back out to the front of the funeral parlor.

So *here I am*, an absolute basket case, standing on the front steps of the funeral home, shaking so badly that I couldn't even drive. Tommy and David had to go get my car and Ronda had to drive me home. I couldn't bear to go back in. In fairness, Ronda and Curtis never quite cared for each other. They constantly got into little verbal sparring matches. He thought she was a controlling bitch and I'm sure she felt that he was a crude redneck. But either way, it doesn't matter now.

The next day was Curtis' burial. The whole advanced class chipped in and we bought a bronze plaque engraved with our school insignia, which is mounted on his headstone. That was the first and last time I was ever at Curtis' gravesite. It's far too painful. To this day when I think of Curt Lucas I either laugh hysterically or I want to cry. At a mere 27 years of age, Curt had way too much potential to have been taken away from us so soon. It's funny, but years later I heard something that struck a nerve. Dan Aykroyd spoke about his good friend, John Belushi, who Curtis resembled quite a bit, saying, "John was a bad boy, but a good man." He could have been speaking of my friend, Curt.

By this time, though, we had all but shut down the original Dojo in West Palm Beach, and with Mark's huge legal problems and the bad publicity Karate had been receiving from the local press, Sensei Carl was struggling to hang onto Dojo North in Riviera Beach. Carl was forced to take on some investors, the first of whom was George Mc-Clease, a fellow that Curtis introduced to the Dojo in 1973. Later on he became my dearest friend; my partner in a Karate school and my cornerman in life. George came to Carl's rescue by financing a few thousand dollars' worth of Karate equipment and supplies. It doesn't take a Donald Trump to figure out that if you're going to sign up new Karate students, you'd better have Karate uniforms to sell them along with mouthpieces and jockstraps with cups, also foam rubber gloves and boots—called safety chops and safety kicks—that we wore when we sparred to keep from killing each other.

George's arrangement with Carl went something like this: George would have the only key to the locker where the new equipment was stored. The display case in our showroom would have a variety of

169

equipment to display. When someone new signed up for lessons, they would get the equipment in the display case. George would come in a bit early before his class and check the display case. If it needed restocking, George would take care of it. At the end of the evening as we were locking up, George would check the display case yet one more time. What poor George couldn't have anticipated was Carl's love for grandeur.

This arrangement between Carl and George lasted for quite a few weeks. But then a big Karate tournament, the U.S. Grand Nationals, was due to be held in Miami Beach. The entire Karate world in South Florida, if not the state, was aware of Mark and Carl's troubles. Carl, a little desperate and understandably so, was signing up new students who could barely afford the lessons let alone the uniform, the *gi*. At the time I was a little young and naïve (okay, ignorant) to heed the warning. But I can testify now, years later, that your pride will get you in trouble.

Carl was determined to put on his game face and make a big impression in the Karate world. So what did he do? He came up with a plan to make a grand entrance at the U.S. Grand Nationals. He had every student who was planning on participating in the tournament meet bright and early at Dojo North on Saturday morning where he promptly took a pair of bolt cutters and cut the locks off the lockers that held George's investment. And in case you can't see where this is going, look to the right and get out of the passing lane because *here comes a semi!* Every participant got a brand new *gi* compliments of Sensei Stone, financed one hundred percent by the George McClease Foundation for Wayward Karatekas.

Carl was hell-bent on walking into that tournament and creating a lasting impression that nothing was wrong. The Dojo was living on borrowed time and Carl refused to see it. He was living like it was 1973 and Bruce Lee was still dominating every movie theater screen in the country. But boy, it wasn't. It was 1976 and whenever someone in Palm Beach County heard the word "karate," or worse yet "the Dojo," they thought "criminals."

By this time the press was butchering Mark. Every arrest that he'd ever had was being splashed across the media. It would seem as though newscasters opened their broadcast every other night with the oft-repeated line, "Dojo owner, Mark Herman, suspected of *this*, arrested for *that*, and indicted for *whatever*..." Looking back at it now, I can understand how the press was intrigued. The martial arts world, to westerners, has always had an air of mystery about it. But I can tell you this: human beings are inexplicable mysteries. Like when a car on a jack stand collapses pinning a child underneath it, only to have the mother run out of the house in a state of panic and lift the car off of her child. Or when someone is struck by lightning only to come out of their coma and have gained a deeper intellect than they had before the storm. Or explain this: a child afflicted with autism sits down behind a piano for the very first time and plays Mozart or Beethoven better than the masters had written it. Having said that, I can assure you of this: in the martial arts world people cannot pass through walls, levitate, nor do they possess 'death touches.' It's quite frankly some Asian mystique.

Now that George has been burned, he and Carl are no longer speaking to each other. Let's take a look at a few other gentlemen who are no longer communicating with Carl, although for totally different reasons. Let's take Gary Sproul, who grew up in Jupiter, Florida and was the son of a wealthy family. By middle-class standards, Gary was considered a rich kid. I was told his father was in the gas and oil business. Gary was a gifted high school athlete and later became a nationally rated East Coast surfer. Gary was introduced to the Dojo in 1973 and trained alongside George McClease in their beginner white belt class. It was obvious from the beginning that Gary came from money, so he and Carl got along great.

Fast-forward a few prosperous years and a few dozen problems, and now Carl's offering Gary shares of the Karate school. Gary doesn't bite at the bait—he swallows it hook line and sinker but now his ego's the size of a beached whale. Oh sure, he was fine with me because I could have spanked him like a red-headed stepchild. And he left the bulk of the advanced class alone because most of them had been there years before him. But to all the under belts, he had assumed a position of dictator. He would pass through the Dojo with the swagger of a black belt martial artist and the air of a sensei, of which he was neither. He hadn't earned or achieved the rank of black belt, nor had he earned the respect or honor it takes to be a sensei.

I sensed things were going into a downward spiral one evening when I stepped into the Dojo to find a whole class of students, including Gary, down on their knees while he was instructing them on the correct way to fold their *gis*. For Christ's sake, for a moment I thought I was standing at a military memorial ceremony with Gary teaching the

171

cadets the proper way to fold the flag for our great nation. The problem with this was that he was full of shit. He was making this crap up as he went along. And besides inventing etiquette rules of the ancient Asian arts, he had a habit of showing up high on Quaaludes to help teach class and take beginners through their warm-up exercises. The problem: he would take beginners through his dictator death march. By this point there was no mystery why everyone appreciated me when I stepped on the mat to teach Karate. I was the only one making any sense.

But the proverbial straw that broke the camel's back was one Saturday when a handful of us went up to Cocoa Beach to participate in a Karate tournament. I was the only black belt representing the Dojo. At 8:30 a.m., prior to the tournament, Gary pulled into the parking lot of the facility where the tournament was being held and pulled up along side of us. He promptly got out and stepped back to the rear of the car where he opened the trunk and pulled out a brand new black belt, still stiff with starch, and wrapped it around his waist. At first I congratulated him. I thought Senseis Mark and Carl had had a private black belt ceremony that I hadn't been invited to attend. After talking with Gary, I came to find out that the night before the tournament Gary had decided he wanted to compete as a black belt so he promoted himself. This was more than unprecedented; it was downright unheard of. If you went back a thousand years to the very monk who originated this Asian art form of fighting, the smart money is you couldn't find one student who'd had the audacity to promote himself a black belt.

Gary actually did well in the tournament. He took third place. But the next day when Sensei Stone found out that Gary had showed up at the tournament wearing a black belt and had promoted himself, he went ballistic and into orbit. Carl chased Gary right out of the Karate studio and up US 1 screaming obscenities and vulgarities that ended with, "You're kicked out of the Dojo!" A mental midget could have predicted Carl's reaction but I'm sure Gary didn't realize the repercussion of his actions. Now that Gary was kicked out of the studio, I would bet that in Carl's mind that took him off the hook from ever paying Gary back.

And then there's Steve Shepherd. Shep, as he was affectionately known, was preparing to test for green belt—which was halfway to black belt—when I entered the studio and began my training. Steve had never bought into the mystical intrigue of the martial arts world.

He was there for one reason and one reason only; he wanted to learn how to fight so he could kick everyone's ass. And who could blame him? I mean, that's why I was learning karate, although, I was hoping I wouldn't have to kick anybody's ass. But knowing how Shep thought, he wasn't bowing to black belts; they were bowing to *him*.

After Steve Shepherd was promoted to black belt, Mark and Carl were looking to move south into Lake Worth, which is where Shepherd had grown up and basically knew everyone in town. So a Dojo South in Lake Worth, with Shepherd at the helm, made perfect sense. The plan was to find a suitable space of 1500 to 2000 square feet. Carl would have to gut the place, build an office, add men's and women's locker rooms, mat the floors, stick the mirrors on the wall, hang some heavy bags, and then turn the whole thing over to Steve. But Shep had other plans. He was pretty shrewd. He saw no reason to give Mark and Carl money that he was generating.

Shep had acquired quite a reputation at Lake Worth Beach as a surfer who loved to scrap. There was a whole army of young beachcombers from Lake Worth that followed Steve into the Karate school for training. He called then friends but in reality, they were more like groupies. Every small town in America has someone; that ever-popular guy who's so cool that everyone wants to be his friend or the guy who can kick everybody's ass so everyone wants to be his pal. In the small town of Lake Worth, Florida, Steve Shepherd was that guy. Shep could wear both shoes. And who could blame them? Shep could look at your arch nemesis and tell them to lay off and the next day they'd be trying to be your best friend. And if he didn't like the guy, he'd beat the hell out of him on principle.

Anyway, when Mark and Carl finally agreed upon the spot they want to call Dojo South, Shep went around Carl and talked to the owner of the building and worked out a deal for himself. Once the place was up and running, Shep dropped a dime that dropped the bomb. He called Carl and informed him the place would no longer be called the Dojo but rather Steve Shepherd's Karate and Kickboxing Academy. As you might imagine, Carl went into orbit. Before the end of the Dojo era, which lasted roughly seven years, Carl had been in orbit so many times, he could have given the people at NASA some lessons. But then who could blame the guy? Nothing he seemed to do worked out.

But Carl wasn't taking this lightly. This was rank insubordination. Although they'd never signed a contract nor made a handshake deal,

Carl felt as if Shepherd was ripping him off. So Sensei persisted in informing Shep, over the phone, every which way he could have his ass kicked. Shep actually had his hand over the mouthpiece of the phone, chuckling. Shep gained great satisfaction when he got a rise out of people, especially when he knew there was nothing they could do. Once the smoke cleared from Carl's ears, Shep asked him if he was through. Then Shep politely gave Carl the address to the new Steve Shepherd Karate and Kickboxing Academy... You know, just so Carl wouldn't get lost.

And now fast-forward to the present and we're in the middle of a shit storm. The original Dojo in West Palm Beach has been shut down. And with the lease coming up on Dojo North in Riviera Beach, Carl decides to shut the doors and move south down US 1 about a half a mile and open up on the opposite side of the street. About the time all this had taken place, I had finally put together enough money to have my teeth extracted. You know, the broken ones I had obtained on the future site of the happiest place on Earth: Orlando, Florida. You remember that clan of people that resembled the cast of "Deliverance" and would feel right at home in the front row of the Country Bear Jamboree?

So *here I am* playing instructor for my classes (which are three to four sessions per night, five nights a week) with between twelve to fifteen students per class, and I have no teeth. Once Dojo North had relocated, the end was near. I don't think it lasted a year. I was the last of Carl's entourage to leave. I was the last remaining member of the original Clematis Street Dojo. But your loyalty will wither when you can't feed yourself. I hadn't been paid on a regular basis for some time, so I had to go back to hanging drywall to make a living. But now I had to drive all the way to Lake Worth, to Steve Shepherd's place, so I could train. Shep, always one to look out for himself, was great and surprisingly generous. He welcomed me with open arms and never asked me for a dime.

By this time, Shep was not only competing in kickboxing events, but also promoting them. Shep had met a local businessman, an entrepreneur named Don Haynes, with whom he formed a partnership and a company to promote kickboxing events. Among other things Don owned a local Nissan car dealership in West Palm Beach. Don was great; a straightforward, self-promoting businessman with high energy and a terrific sense of humor. Don was a Southerner all the way,

174

an Alabama man, and to this day the best storyteller I ever met.

By this time, my good friend George McClease had been stopping by my house every other day to talk to me about opening a Karate school. It took George a couple of weeks to wear me down. I was pretty burnt out by all that had happened. I just wanted to get back to focusing on myself and sharpening my own skills. Thank God for George's persistence because after a while it started to sound like a pretty good idea. At this point I already had a handful of kickboxing matches under my belt and I was undefeated. I was on my way to becoming one of the best black belts in the nation. *Why not open my own school?*

Besides, I had to do *something*. I was coming to the end of my tolerance with Ronda. At this point we had been living together for a little over a year. I had boxed myself in by selling my car. I had a handful of bench warrants out for my arrest for various traffic violations, and I still didn't have a driver's license.

My previous car was a '66 Mustang that I had bought from a friend of mine at the Dojo, Chuck Walken. The car had some minor front-end damage due to an accident he'd been involved in, but otherwise it ran fine. The problem was that it looked like a hot rod. One Friday evening, I was on my way home after hanging drywall all day. I had drywall dust caked all over me and my hair was pulled back in a pony-tail. Suddenly I got lit up by the F.H.P. (Florida Highway Patrol). Did I happen to mention I was doing absolutely nothing? I had just seen him on the corner of Okeechobee Road and Military Trail, sitting in a gas station. I was facing east in the left-hand turning lane on Okeechobee Road ready to make my turn and proceed north on Military Trail. The F.H.P. officer was sitting opposite of me at the gas station on the southeastern corner. When I got the green arrow, I eased my clutch out so I could make the turn and head north on Military Trail. I glanced at my rear-view mirror just to double check. I could almost see him salivating; a hippy in a hot rod. I barely made a hundred yards. I was watching him in my rear-view mirror when I saw him exit the gas station in a quarter slide sideways and, with the flip of a switch, my weekend plans had been canceled. With Christmas lights flashing, I slowed down to pull over. I had about a nickel's worth of pot on me, enough for a couple of joints, which was in a plastic bag. I fumbled with the pot, trying to tuck in underneath the custom shag carpet that Chuck had so patiently and creatively cut out for the floor of the Mustang. When I finally pulled over, I shut the car off and immediately looked

175

in the driver's side door mirror and watched the patrolman take what seemed to be ten minutes to get out of his car.

When he finally cleared his vehicle, he stood up straight and adjusted his cowboy hat. He then sauntered up to the driver's side door of my car and, in the process, eclipsed the Sun. Anybody from Texas, or anyone who's ever drove through the great state of Texas and has been pulled over by one of their troopers, can envision the massive man standing outside my car window. This Florida Highway patrolman towered at over six feet and well over 200 pounds. With me still sitting in my car, I found myself in a vicarious position that no man wants to get caught in: staring at another man's crotch. At this point Officer Bunyan put his forearm on the roof of my car and leaned down into my window, which totally obscured the view out my driver's side door. And the very first question he asks me (or should I say tells me?) could have been the dialog from a Burt Reynolds' movie.

"You like to spin them tires, don't you boy?" Me, full of shock and awe because the whole world to my left had disappeared, foolishly stuttered, repeating his question.

"I like to spin my tires." That's when the pace quickened just a bit. In a heartbeat, it seemed as though he'd ripped the door off of my car and grabbed me by the handle (my ponytail) and jerked me out of the car and to my feet. And that's when I heard those immortal words that must be chiseled in stone in every Police Academy in the South: "Shut the Hell up, boy. I'm asking the questions here, not you."

And next came the question that has always presented a problem for me. He asked for my license, which of course I've never bothered to get. So naturally, I told him I left my wallet at home. He asked me where I lived. When I told him, he just smiled and said, "No problem. I'll follow you there."

For all you 70s country western fans out there, you'll get this. I started stuttering like Mel Tillis. At my first sign of weakness, he grabbed me by the shoulder and spun me around so fast I thought the world was spinning off its axis and giving me vertigo. The next thing I know I'm handcuffed. This trooper had gone into hyper-drive. Now he's not waiting on my answers, he's telling me I don't have a driver's license and I'm under arrest, which means I'm a criminal. Which means he can search my car.

So *here I am,* standing on the side of Military Trail, handcuffed and under arrest, watching Officer Paul Bunyan rummage through my car. I'm sweating profusely like a Klansman at a Black Panther Rally, knowing that any minute now he's going to flip up the shag carpet on the driver's side of the car and find that nickel bag of pot, which I'm sure in his mind will give him the right to publicly execute me, a commie pinko fag, right there on the side of the road. But my angels were watching out for me (well, sort of). He never found that baggie of pot but I did get to go to jail for the whole weekend. Oh, I got my one phone call, which went to Ronda. But she didn't have the cash to bail me out and they had confiscated all my money, along with everything else I had (except, of course, the pot), when they took Public Enemy Number One of the DMV (me) into their custody.

When I got out on Monday, it didn't take a whole lot of talking from Ronda to convince me to sell that Mustang because we had a car that was always referred to as 'our car.' (Except, of course, when I wanted to use it. Then it was *her* car.) That one weekend in jail told me everything I needed to know about being incarcerated: it's not for me.

Chapter Sixteen
New Friends, Missed Friends and The Crown

Just about the time George and I started to do all the legwork to prepare for opening up our own Karate studio, I started to develop two new friendships. One was Larry Thomas, who was United States Senator Jerry Thomas' oldest son. The other new friend was Skip Walls, who would later turn out to be one of the greatest friends a man could ever have.

I met Larry through Ronda's best friend Kim Regulman. Kimmy had been dating Larry since high school, and in one meeting you could see why. Like a shorter version of Tom Selleck, with a mustache and dimples and lots of wavy hair, women found him irresistible. He had a devilish sense of humor and enough personality and charm to fill a room. Oh, and I did mention, he was a Senator's son? Larry was a blast and borderline fearless. Ronda and I, more Sundays than not, would find ourselves in our boat cruising the Intracoastal from Riviera Beach to North Palm, where we would beach the boat on Kim's parent's property, roughly a couple of acres right on the Intracoastal Waterway. Kimmy's horse had free rein of the whole property and they lived in a beautiful custom-built, hand-cut log cabin that Bob Regulman, Kim's dad, had built with his own hands. Every third or fourth time we went to pick up Kimmy, there would be Larry standing on their beach with a grin so big it was blinding. Larry loved the water; hell, we all did! We were Floridians! If it floated, and you could fish off of it, water ski behind it, scuba dive off of it or sail it, Larry could master it. We spent many a Sunday, on the Intracoastal, ripping up the water all the way from Palm Beach Gardens to Jupiter Island. Larry had tons of charisma; people were drawn to him. When you were in his presence you felt that there's something special was going to happen. And eight times out of ten, it would. Larry had such life and spark in his eyes, not that you ever saw them because he always wore mirrored sunglasses; but his spirit radiated the enthusiasm of a five-year-old at a Fourth of July fireworks show.

One Sunday afternoon, Ronda and I were cruising the Intracoastal up by Jupiter Inlet when we witnessed Larry and Kimmy struggling with a catamaran. Larry had turned the Hobie Cat around in the middle of the Jupiter Inlet. He was trying to sail south back to North Palm Beach and Kim's house, but the tides were changing. It was going into low tide, and the current was too strong. It was pulling him and Kim out through the Jupiter Inlet and into the ocean. There just wasn't enough breeze to tack that Hobie Cat back to Kim's place. So we tossed them a rope and pulled them over to the shore. Just north of the Jupiter Inlet and on the west side of the Intracoastal Waterway was a handful of tall pine trees. Someone, no one can recall who, had taken a 30-foot rope, about the thickness of a man's wrist, and tied it to a branch on one of those trees. On any given Sunday you can find one or a whole flotilla of boats tied off to each other at that rope swing. It seemed as though you could spend days at that swing. You could drop from twenty feet of air into the beautiful turquoise blue water that was a consistent 78 degrees year 'round, and for Christ's sake without a mask you could see twenty feet in front of you underwater. Best of all, it was the people. You always knew at least two other boat owners and it didn't matter anyway. We all tied off to each other and everybody drank out of everybody's beer cooler, everyone ate out of everyone's picnic basket, and anybody who had a radio we would set their stereos on the same rock station and let it blast.

It was one of those Sundays when we pulled up to the swing with Larry and Kim in tow. We tied off the bow of the boat then Larry and I dove into the water and swam over to shore. We scaled up the rocks and roots to the trees and got in line for that rope swing. That's when Larry first mentioned his big going-away party. After a few hours, when completely exhausted, we decided we better tow Larry and Kim back to her place before the sun went down.

When we finally got back to Kimmy's place it was well past twilight, and we found her mom and dad sitting in lounge chairs on their beach with a fire going. We anchored the stern then we tied our bow off to their tree, moved the Hobie Cat up on shore past the high tide mark and then, of course, we joined Kim's mom and dad for cocktails. Kim's dad, Bob Regulman, was a great guy, and a fascinating man to talk to. He was a big game hunter as well as a master carpenter, hence the log cabin he had built with his hands for them to live in. Every year Bob, along with Jeff Sullivan's dad and a few other guys, would go to Alaska to hunt. Once you got him wound up he loved to hear a good story as well as tell one. He was like a wide-eyed enthusiastic kid. After a couple of cocktails, a few stories, and more than a successful day, I promised Larry I would show up for his party, and then Ronda and I headed home. How do you cap a perfect, fun-filled Florida day? You cruise the Intracoastal Waterway heading home at idling speed on a perfectly moonlit night.

A couple of weeks had gone by, and *here I am*, standing at the Juno Beach Club in Juno Florida. The Juno Club sat right on the beach sand of the Atlantic Ocean with access courtesy of Alternate A1A. And like any tropical beach, with every breaking wave you could feel the mist of sea spray embrace your body. Larry was leaving town, and he was leaving in a big way. Everybody at the party had a blast, although I didn't know too many people there. That was mainly because most of Larry's friends were from Juno and Jupiter—what a West Palm Beacher considered the wealthy north end—and I was definitely from West Palm Beach (more blue collar). But I had fun anyway. Ronda had run into some friends that she had graduated high school with and that was fun to watch. Later, during the party, I asked Larry where he was headed. He said Alaska. *Alaska?* To a southern Florida boy that sounded like another planet. Larry assured me there was a lot of money to be made working on the Alaskan Pipeline. And for a sideline, he was going to pan for gold. The party ended with hugs and "best of lucks" and Ronda and I headed for home.

On Sunday, as usual, Ronda and I prepared the boat. We dropped it in the water, and then cruised north along the Intracoastal, straight to Kim's house. When we had reached the Regulman's there was Kimmy, standing at the water's edge wearing that big warm beautiful smile, as bright as a lighthouse beacon, and a two-piece bikini, with her water skis and ski vest in tow, ready to cut up some water. We idled up, Kim hopped in, and we headed north. We took turns in a three-person rotation, water skiing all the way to Jupiter Island. It was such a beautiful day. When we got to Jupiter Inlet, we looked out into the ocean and it was laying flat. So we decided to try out the inlet and take the ocean south to Palm Beach. We weren't more than half way to the Palm Beach inlet, somewhere around Lost Tree Village or Air Force Beach—better known to all you Yankees that have migrated to my tropical paradise hometown in the last twenty years as MacArthur Beach—when we decided to shut the boat down and just drift. We popped the ice cooler open and raided it for sandwiches and beer. Floating aimlessly in the Bermuda Triangle, we started laughing about the grand party Larry threw himself. That's when I posed the question to Kim about how long Larry had been planning to go to Alaska. She chuckled and looked at me with a big grin, and replied that the first time she heard anything of it was the day we were all at the rope swing. I couldn't believe my ears, "Did I hear you right? You mean the day I found out about it was the moment you found out?"

She just laughed and shrugged her shoulders and said, "Yeah, that's Larry." I have to admit, it dawned on me then that Kim was very mature for a girl who was just going into her twenties. If it ever bothered her, she never showed it. Looking back, I never witnessed Kimmy being unhappy. She was always smiling with a positive disposition.

Now with Larry on hiatus, George and I got down to the business of finding a location for our new Karate school. It had to have been in the stars that Larry had left town at that moment. We had just started developing our friendship; we really only knew each other from our girlfriends and the boating world. And as I've said before, I'm no criminal, but I am juvenile and Larry had the makeup for the pair of us to get into a whole lot of trouble. As it would turn out, this wouldn't be the last time Larry and I saw each other, but right now, George and I buckled down and we found a place in North Palm Beach; an upscale, middle class area with plenty of commercial buildings. At the time, Ronda worked for a realtor. Jim, her boss, and I had become friends. Real estate sales were slow and he was looking to downsize his office space. He had about 3,000 square feet in a two-story building and he wanted to sublease 1,500 of it, on the second level, to George and I. *Perfect!* The building had its own parking lot and every business in it shut down at 5pm, and our classes wouldn't start until 6. Well, almost perfect, until we went to the township of North Palm Beach for licensing and permits. It didn't seem quite as cut and dry as we'd thought.

181

They had George and me attend three or four town council meetings; they were fighting us all the way on this. Finally the clown in charge looked right at us and said, "Okay, what are you really going to do up there? Punch boards in half and kick holes in the wall?" Man, the ignorance of some people. I started to lose my temper when my friend George put his hand on my shoulder to interrupt the conversation I was having with this ignorant idiot, so he could enlighten this gentleman that we would simply be teaching the art of self-defense to women and children. They denied us anyway.

So George and I left the meeting rejected and looking back on it now I guess you really couldn't blame them. Although it was unwarranted, all the bad publicity my Sensei at the Dojo had gotten, it was pretty obvious why the town council didn't want a Karate school in their city. But George, never one to be outsmarted, said, "Screw them! We're going to open up anyway! Because after all, what they don't know won't hurt them." Jim had rented us the second floor space because his office, as well as the rest of the professional building, shut down at 5; right about the time we'd be coming alive. So we figured the city of North Palm Beach could keep all their jive. Besides, take a guess what time bureaucrats in this fair city say, "Bye bye."

By the time I'd severed my relationship with Sensei Carl Stone, I had given up all illicit drugs. Pot smoking, however, was the last to go. My common sense nagged me, how could I compete at the top of my level while clouding my lungs? So one night I did the old mirror trick. After closing down one evening, I stood within a foot of the panel mirrors at our Karate school and stared myself down. I looked myself dead in the eye and swore I would never smoke grass again. Not that I have anything against pot smokers; hell, I would rather people smoke grass than drink. I've witnessed the poison of alcoholism first hand and the havoc it can wreak. People who smoke pot do not become aggressive behind the wheel of an automobile and cause drunk driving accidents. They don't rob liquor stores, and they don't beat their wives. Booze, on the other hand, can give you liquid courage mixed with alcohol aggression. After a few months on the straight and narrow, my relationships with some people had changed. Oh sure, I still had all the old friends; I just didn't hang out with them much anymore. They were constantly trying to get me to party. "Aw, come on! Take a couple of hits—it's just one night. I've got extra Quaaludes—it's just one night." The problem is, that one night is a long succession of consecutive nights. Get it?

My argument to my friends was, "What in the word 'quit' means 'continue'?" And I hate to admit it, but Ronda had me on somewhat of a short leash. She knew my friends from the Dojo. Hell, she knew a lot of them before I did. I'm sure she felt that my partying behavior with my friends was a threat to our relationship. These were the heydays of sex, drugs, and rock and roll, and I was more than happy to indulge. Ronda never really hammered (criticized) any of my friends; she just didn't like me around them. So I would find myself more and more in the company of her friends, who were a lot of fun and liked to party but it just wasn't their every waking moment's agenda. Besides, you could hardly blame her for wanting me around people who were in steady relationships that were solid.

At this time, every weekend was booked with water sports and boating. There was scuba diving, water skiing, and tubing. Tubing was a blast. We'd go out to the local truck stop near 45th Street and military trail and buy an inner tube from a semi truck tire. Then we would blow it up, take it out in the boat, toss it in the water, let a ski rope out for 20 to 25 feet and tie it off. Then we'd play "rock, paper, scissors" to see who would be the first victim. With someone on the tube and the boat floored, going close to 70 miles per hour, the game was to see how long you could hold on. What was really fun was putting one of the girls on the tube; none of them weighed much more than a hundred pounds. At close to full throttle in a wide part of the Intracoastal we would bang a U-turn, which would take the girls and the tube two to three feet off of the water and slingshot them past the bow of the boat. With them clinging on to this rubber projectile with all their might, rapidly approaching three digit speed, it was anyone's guess what was going to happen next. They were screaming like hyenas. Ronda and Kim caught on pretty quick. It got to the point where neither one of them would get on the inner tube without the other one being with them. That way, they had just enough weight to keep the tube down on the water. That kind of ruined our fun. But when we felt like things were getting kind of stale, we'd run out one of the inlets and out into the ocean where we could chase down cruise ships and yachts. The cruise ships could leave as much as a six-foot swell behind them and some of the yachts would leave close to four foot. *Perfect!* We'd run up behind some of the bigger yachts at full speed, position ourselves about twenty feet off their stern, and then we'd turn out, which would catapult us five to six feet up in the air, and easily launch us twenty yards out. If we were lucky enough

183

to spot a cruise ship I'd get giddy, because I'd apply similar techniques for lunar launch time. But despite all this weekend fun in the sun, I'd still like to go out to a nightclub occasionally, which is where I met Skip Walls.

We had been introduced to each other by mutual friends, and although I can't speak for him, the second I shook his hand, I knew this guy. Even though we grew up in totally different economic backgrounds, we shared some parallel experiences. While Skip did grow up with his real father, he moved around somewhat: Parallel number one. Parallel number two: Skip's father, as well as his mother, both suffered from alcoholism. Plus, when Skip's father was drunk, he wreaked havoc on Skip, his brother Richard and his mother Kathleen, so we had violence in the home in common as well; that's parallel number three. *We just hit the trifecta.* But all of this didn't come to my attention until some years later. Still, meeting Skip was almost like that experience of *déjà vu*. You know, that first time experience that you could swear you've had before, or that feeling when you're introduced to someone for the first time but you could swear you've known them your whole life. Then you brush it off that you must have met in a former life. Well, as inexplicable as it was, I had that moment when I met Skip. It would take a few months of us bumping into each other, however, before we actually struck up a friendship.

I was pretty busy trying to help George build and run our Karate school. After hanging drywall all day, I'd get home to Ronda only to hear her protest every move I made and fight me every step of the way. At first she thought the new school was a great idea, and was enthusiastically behind it. But after a few short weeks, she realized she wasn't going to have any day-to-day involvement or control of any kind, and that it would pose a threat to our relationship, which had been deteriorating for some time. What she didn't know was I was already done. And how do you explain it? As much as I loved her, I wasn't in love with her any longer.

When we first started dating, her little demands were kind of cute and sassy. Then, as our relationship went on, it turned into domineering and brassy. And here, at the end of a couple of years, it just turned ugly. But I loved her, and I wish her well to this day, because after all, her instincts were right. She was constantly trying to get me away from the Dojo and all its hijinks. And though it's been years since I've seen some of my good friends, and the fellows I used to train with at the

184

Dojo, we all share the same bond, although you had to have been there to see it, to experience it, to share it, to understand it. To this day I have to say, I still love my Dojo brothers. But let's face it, we weren't serving—nor were we a credit to—our community.

It was around this period that my good friend Leon Nubin came home on leave from the Paratroopers unit. He had brought a beautiful young woman home with him so he could introduce her to me. He was looking forward to introducing me, his best friend, to his future bride. What *did* happen kills me to this day... When Leon showed up to our house, unannounced, Ronda and I were in the midst of a fight. The atmosphere wasn't simply gale force; it was a class 5 hurricane. So, when I heard a knock at the door, I jerked it open like I was trying to pull it off its hinges. Low and behold, there was Leon's smiling face. Leon's unexpected appearance had the equivalent effect of dousing me with a bucket of ice water. I quickly regained my composure. Shutting the door behind me, I stepped out on the front porch to talk with my old friend. Leon, as happy as I had ever seen him, told me he had brought the girl he was planning to marry home so she could meet his family and friends. I hesitated for a moment, and then apologetically explained what was taking place inside the house. It was a horrible predicament to be caught in, not being able to invite my friend and his future wife into my home. This is a moment that I would regret for the rest of my life. Leon was such a great guy. Being the beautiful human being that he was, he simply invited me out to the curb to meet his fiancée who was sitting in his car.

So *here I am*, standing in front of my house underneath a streetlight. I'm meeting this beautiful young woman who has consented to become my best friend's wife, and I'm unable to have the decency of inviting her in to my home so I could get to know her.

This embarrassing episode would come to haunt me for over thirty years. Something that Leon and I could not have possibly predicted; *this would be the last time I would ever see him again.*

It wasn't long after this incident that Ronda and I broke up, and I moved out. Things were moving pretty fast. The Dojo was shutting down, and there was no longer an address for it. That, plus me changing my residency, meant that Leon and I lost touch. If we were ever afforded the opportunity for do-overs in this life, Leon wouldn't just make the top ten; he would make the top two. As in, second only to me telling my grandfather how much he meant to me before he died.

The last place I knew that Leon was stationed was Fort Bragg. I tried writing him once but the letter came back. I still have a couple of letters Leon had written me from when he was completing basic training out in Fort Hood, Texas. I can only pray that my friend's service in the military was good and that he's had a great life.

Chapter Seventeen

Not long after splitting up with Ronda, George McClease and I had gained some momentum with our new Karate studio. By this time, it seemed as though we had every redneck in the north end of Palm Beach County taking Karate classes with us—and I use that term "redneck" lovingly. These guys loved to hunt and fish, work hard, and play harder. We had the Penders, the Sullivans, and the Edwards boys. Ray Edwards, who was one of George's friends, had brought in his two younger brothers, who were around my age, as well as his sons to learn Karate from us. Ricky and Randy, the two younger of the Edwards brothers, were already veterans of 'Bar Wars.' There was the time they paid a visit to Crown Liquor, which was a local hang out with a package liquor store attached to it. Evidently a close friend of theirs—I believe it was Roker, a fellow they had gone to high school with—had gotten into a little scuffle, which then escalated into a beating from the doormen. Now you have to understand, all these boys had a very definitive view as to what was fair and what was not. Now if Roker had gotten his ass handed to him by one guy—and one guy only—no one would have batted an eye. They would have taken him out drinking the following weekend and teased him about it. But that's not quite what happened. If you go out to nightclubs, or drinking establishments, on a regular basis, you should already know this; and if you're a young man planning to pursue this type of entertainment, then listen up. The security staff at any nightclub, pool hall, or drinking venue is exactly like a pack of wolves. You can be assured that if there is a problem, they will all get involved. Plus, there are two types of door guys. There's the guy who wants to pick up a little extra money on the weekends and hopes that everybody has a good time. And then there's the other type—the majority—the guy with a chip on his shoulder and something to prove. He now has a built-in gang, so you don't want to give him a reason to take out his frustrations on you. And of course, the one thing they have in common is chicks. If you're attractive in any way—say the ladies like your looks, or you make the ladies laugh, or you're a good dancer, or you're a sharp dresser, or you have deep pockets—you're making waves in their chick pool. You have a target on your back. Now I don't know exactly what took place the night the wolves fed on Roker, but what I do know is this; there was more than one canine in that dog fight. And if I've got this right, they got more than the attention and the ears to stand up on Ricky and Randy Edward, Jeff Sullivan, and Buddy Huey. In their minds, in the world of our western heroes, John Wayne and Clint Eastwood, and the code of the Magnificent Seven, this was deemed as unfair and called for retaliation.

As luck would have it, I had a friend that worked as a doorman at Crown Liquor right at the time Roker got jumped. My friend was a fellow student at the Dojo by the name of Jay Collins. Now, Jay was no small man. At six foot four and 235 pounds, he had left the state of Florida as an All-American to attend UCLA with a full-ride football scholarship. Jay had once told me he chose UCLA so he could pursue a degree in psychology. But by the time Jay had gotten to Los Angeles, people were already experimenting with a hallucinogenic drug called LSD. And this is where the old saying, 'Don't bite off more than you can chew,' comes in. Jay had mentioned to me that he had decided to do a paper on the psychological and social impact of this new drug. At some point during his research on LSD, Jay decided he needed to experience the drug first hand. This contributed to his downward spiral. A couple of years later, Jay came back to West Palm Beach weighing a little more than a hundred pounds and, by his own admission, somewhat fried. Jay explained to me that LSD had opened up doors in his mind to rooms he didn't know existed. The problem was it became a big maze; he kept trying to unlock the next door to another room. Bottom line—some doors need to remain locked.

But back to the night of retaliation. The boys had pulled into the parking lot of Crown Liquor, parked their pickup truck, and gone inside. At best, it was Pearl Harbor. They didn't go in to have a drink; they went in to bust some heads. And from all accounts it was a humdinger. Jay had been backed into a small hallway that led from the bar into the packing store. Within such close quarters, Jay was doing everything he could to keep the punch-happy rednecks off him when he got pushed backwards through the door and into the liquor store. Evidently his brain wasn't as fried as he thought. Just like in the George Thorogood song, he saw a few good friends. He grabbed the necks of the Walker brothers—Johnny Walker Red and Johnny Walker Black—and started heaving them. Then he saw an ol' pal, Jim Beam, and threw him into the mix. And then, for a somewhat subtle diversion, he tossed in a little Canadian Mist. By the time he got to the back of the store with Jack

Daniels and threw 'Old lucky No. 7' down the track it turned out to be just that. The fight was over and the cops were on the way, although by now Jay had destroyed one third of the liquor store. Crown Liquor on US-1 and Riviera Beach would never be the same. Jay had no idea who the rednecks were he had been serving booze to, but two things he felt pretty sure of: one, he had an excuse for a long stay in the hospital, and two, I would be likely to know who those rednecks were. I did, and so did my partner George.

In fact, George had grown up around all of their older brothers; he was the squirt that got to tag along. A few short years later, *they* were the squirts hanging around George. So I called him up to smooth the whole thing out. George, more as a favor to me than our friend Jay, had a pow-wow with the Edwards brothers, Jeff Sullivan, and Buddy Huey. With a great respect for George's fairness and sensibility, a truce was worked out. The funny thing about it, the night Roker got jumped at the Crown Liquor I don't believe Jay was even there. He had the night off. Two days after this incident, Jay shows up at the Karate school as nervous as a Florida cockroach when you switch on the lights. He wanted to know how things were going and I saw my chance to have a little fun. I said if I were him, not only would I quit working at the bar, I'd move out of the county. Jay's eyes got as big as softballs. He started running off at the mouth so fast it would have taken a speed freak to decipher his chatter. I managed to catch something to the effect of, "Podgurski, you know these rednecks, can't you talk some sense into them?" That's when I started laughing, and he assured me there was nothing to be laughing about. He opened the door to his VW Bug and pulled out a pistol from underneath the front seat. Jay had decided he wasn't going down without a fight, which got me laughing even harder. When I stopped laughing I told him to put the gun away, he wasn't going to need to be packing heat. The whole affair had been taken care of. As he tucked the revolver back underneath the front seat he informed me I must have had something evil happen to me to have developed such a wicked sense of humor. We both laughed at that but I told him he should plan on quitting the Crown anyway. Then I shared my experience at the Crown Liquor a year or so earlier.

One night I was out with the usual suspects: David Bunning, Art, his buddy Aaron, plus another friend of theirs, and yes—we were drinking. Aaron had been taking Karate at the Dojo for about a year. I believe he was a pool contractor by trade. He had the first van conversion I'd ever seen. This van was beautiful, in a trailer park kind of way. It had a plush 'leather' (Naugahyde) sofa that ran from behind the driver's seat all the way down the driver's side of the van and wrapped around in front of the rear doors, plus thick shag carpet and drink holders for your cocktails. That luxury van had one of the best sounds systems of the day, fully equipped with multiple speakers, an 8-track quadraphonic tape deck and an AM/FM radio with equalizer and power boosters. Throw in a couple of captain's chairs to navigate this battleship, a multicolored metallic paint job with custom rims and tires—the only thing missing was a mirrored disco ball.

The night in question David and I went out to meet Art, Aaron, and their friend for drinks at the Bacchus House, a nightclub in an open air bazaar shopping plaza across from the Port of Palm Beach. This was back during the time Carl was trying to recuperate from what could have been a permanent sedative administered by his future-ex wife, compliments of a .32 slug in the chest. So I was driving Carl's van, which in turn was the Dojo's van: a mid 60s Econoline Ford van with windows that wrapped all the way around it and a two-inch wide orange stripe right beneath those wraparound windows. With two huge orange and black Dojo insignias modeled after our school patch painted on the two front doors, it had all the subtlety of a garishly colored Versace shirt. If you didn't pick this up on your radar you must be reading by Braille.

After David and I hooked up with Arty and the fellows for a few drinks at Bacchus House, somehow—and it's still a mystery to me—we all ended up at the Crown Liquor drinking with the bouncers from Bacchus House. We blew through the door and went straight up to the bar. After entering this fine drinking establishment, if you chose to drink at the bar you had to take a couple of steps up because there was a rise there. The bar was along the left side of the room, which followed the wall all the way down to the end of the pub then made a 90-degree turn which protruded out into the room creating an "L" from which you could drink from either side of. Now you had two bar tops where customers could face each other and the bartender could serve either side from going down the middle. On the main floor there was an assortment of tables and chairs as well as two pool tables. When we barreled into the place, had we made a right, we would have been facing the infamous corridor where Jay Collins, in the not-too-distant future, would later get backed up into and dragged into the liquor store and

190

try to hone some of his 'bar-tending' skills. If you stepped toward that infamous corridor and took a hard left, you would have a clear path between the railing on the rise to your left and the pool tables on your right all the way to the rear of the club. Take another hard left at the "L" leg of the bar and to your right were the restrooms. If you continued past the restrooms on your right and the backside of the bar on your left, you would eventually come to an emergency exit that only opens from the inside. Step through that door and you find yourself locked out behind the shopping plaza.

Okay, the stage is set. We had just settled into our barstools and ordered our first round of drinks when we noticed down at the "L" leg of the bar there was a little celebration going on. None of us paid a whole lot of attention to it because we were on our own roll. At least that's how it seemed until Aaron leaped off his barstool like somebody lit a match under his ass. All of a sudden there was some serious profanity being thrown back and forth across the bar between Aaron and the biggest guy in the group celebrating at the "L" leg of the bar who, I realized after a moment or two, was wearing a tuxedo. And after another moment or two I realized the woman standing next to him was in a gown. Then I realized that this guy was celebrating his wedding vows at the Crown Liquor. Even with me being Polish it only took a millisecond, like a flash of lightning, to realize this matrimony was doomed. And then I heard those four infamous words that no man can ignore, words I had heard many times before: *I'll kick your ass.*

Aaron spun around and was off like a speeding locomotive towards the front door. Problem was, given no warning, no one cleared a track for him. He bounced off a table, stumbled over some chairs, tripped going down the rise and fell to his knees, bounced up, took a hard left between the rise and the pool tables and tangled with more than a few pool cues. More than winded and almost completely out of gas, he took a hard left at the "L" leg of the bar and fell flat on his face. With his last burst of adrenaline, he jumped up and waded into the middle of the wedding party. While all this is going on, the whole place was frozen in time. It was as quiet as a funeral except, of course, for Aaron stumbling over things.

At this point our crew, Arty and the fellows, including the bouncers of Bacchus House, decide that Aaron might need a little backup. They rushed over to the railing on the rise and climbed over to the main floor where the pool tables were. David and I stood up from our barstools and looked at each other completely slack-jawed. We must have looked like a couple of flycatchers. After staring at each other for a moment with our mouths gaping wide open, I could see it in David's eyes; *it's on.*

We snapped our attention back to the "L" leg of the bar and the celebration party, which was quickly deteriorating into annihilation, just in time to see Aaron fly into the big guy head first, chest leveled, only to be swallowed up. Then Arty got into the mix with reinforcements right behind. David and I shot another glance at each other then we climbed up on the bar. With a leap of faith, David launched first. But at only 140 pounds, David wasn't heavy enough to penetrate the crowd. He landed on top of them and they passed him hand over hand like a conveyor belt right out the exit door.

Just as my feet left the bar for what is commonly known as a *"Geronimo,"* I witnessed some guy in the celebration group grab Art by the bottom of his shirt and pull it up over his head. If I close my eyes and think about it to this day I can still hear Art's robust laughter as he blindly got pushed through the men's bathroom door with his shirt pulled up over his head.

So *here I am*, shoved into this tight ball of human spaghetti. This was nothing like the Karate you've ever seen in the movies. All I could do was throw elbows and knees and an occasional punch. Now we've fought our way to the emergency back door exit where we encounter a doorman who, amazingly enough, separates us from the wedding celebration and pushes them out the back door. After a brisk and lively debate with the doorman it suddenly hits me; David's locked out and in the back parking lot all alone. I yell to the guys, "David's out there!" We turn to bolt towards the front door. That's when Art emerged from the men's room still laughing with his shirt pulled up over his head, asking for some help. I blew right past Art and hollered for someone to give him a hand. I made a beeline for the front door. By the time I made it to the parking lot, Arty was right behind me.

When our feet hit the asphalt we turned right and sprinted down the front of the building. At the end of the plaza we took a hard right and headed towards the back parking lot. By the time we cleared the rear of the building the cops were already there. Arty and I never even slowed down. We simply made an arching left turn and headed back towards the front of the building. Once we cleared the front parking lot we were pretty winded and there was nothing but parking lot and cars; nowhere to hide. Then I remembered I had Carl's van.

We ran straight to Carl's vehicle and jumped inside, along with all his personal belongings which means a lot of laundry. So Art and I climbed into the back of Carl's van and pulled all his dirty linens and clothing over the top of us and lay quietly and listened. The police pulled into the front parking lot and came straight over to the van. You could just imagine what was going through their minds. 'Gee, I wonder why this van is here? Dojo North is right there in Riviera Beach on US 1 less than a mile away.' Thank God somehow we had the presence of mind to lock the doors once we got inside. With the cops outside banging on the windows, neither Art nor I flinched. They were yelling at us to unlock the door but neither one of us budged. Then we heard David knock on the door and tell us to come on out, but we weren't buying it. After a few moments, we heard David and the rest of our wedding crashing party tell the cops that if we were in the van, we would have come out by now so we must have sprinted for home.

Then we heard the voice of one of Riviera Beach's finest tell our wedding crashers, with no uncertain terms, that if we were ever caught fighting in the Crown Liquor again we were going straight to jail. We heard the police cruisers leave the parking lot. We laid still for a moment or two longer until the fellows started beating on the doors again, informing us the cops were gone. We slowly peeked out from underneath Carl's laundry, and low and behold yet one more narrow escape.

So *here I am*, standing in the middle of the Crown Liquor parking lot after another barroom brawl along with my unscathed Karate cohorts. Well, we knew that Crown Liquor wasn't going to let us back in to drink so we pondered what to do. As we stood in the parking lot weighing all of our options, we all turned at the same time and looked across US 1, and with all the subtlety of a pie in the face it dawned on us: there's the Schooner Lounge.

Perfect! We didn't even have to get in our cars. All we had to do was dodge the traffic as we crossed the Highway. We entered the Schooner Lounge with all the energy of a toddler on Ritalin. We had a war story. And you know that old saying, 'Great minds think alike'? Well so do dopes, because here comes the wedding group. When we turned and saw the wedding party we had just been in a fight with come through the door, everybody on both sides cracked up laughing. Since no one had gotten hurt seriously (oh, Aaron had a black eye), no one could carry a grudge. The whole thing was just too funny. So we drank the rest of the evening away as part of the wedding celebration.

This story had my friend Jay crying. He was laughing so hard tears were rolling off his face. These stories were typical at Palm Beach County in the 70s especially if you hung out at the Dojo. This stuff would happen almost weekly but neither Jay nor I in our wildest dreams could have predicted what was about to happen to us in the very near future.

Chapter Eighteen
Smugglers, Mafia 'Capos' and Triumph

The drug trade was beginning to cook in South Florida. Anyone with a 20-foot boat or bigger could make it over to the Bahamas and a lot of guys started coming back to Florida with a very profitable stash of marijuana. Mostly it started off innocently enough. They'd head out to the islands for a weekend of scuba diving and fishing and on the way back pick up a little marijuana for their own personal use. Then the light bulb went on. Why not bring back enough to set off their personal expenses? Once again, it's not a slippery slope—it's a free fall. Why not bring back a whole lot and make it a profitable adventure? Then they figured out a pound is a pound, so why not make the best of your round? Trip, that is.

So now they've shifted gears from the sweet weed to the cocaine candy. And why not? Smuggling is smuggling. Cocaine, when packaged, is more condensed and much easier to get rid of if the authorities are pursuing you. With a much higher profit margin, it didn't take a business degree from M.I.T. to figure out that bales of marijuana are big and bulky and kilos of coke, like bricks, are small and compact, hence that the same amount of weight in coke in your boat brought back ten times the profit. And believe me, the big three Latin American countries, Columbia, Peru, and Bolivia, were watching. It took the criminals all of a heartbeat to figure out that the Bahamas was a great port for distribution of their product to the country with the most disposable income; the good old U.S.A. And for all you people that haven't been to a third world country I can tell you this: the honey handshake works. And I'm not saying that all the officials, including the police, in the Bahamas are corrupt. But it would seem as though the more money you hand out, honey, the more they tend to see things your way. Anyone who's traveled in third world countries, including the islands in the Caribbean and most of Latin America, will tell you it's not in your best interest to take guns into those nations.

By 1978, with my martial arts skills honed to the sharpness of a Samurai sword, I was being recruited almost weekly to go on some of these smuggling endeavors. If it wasn't someone trying to get me into their boat, they were trying to get me to collect the bad debt on their dope. But my instincts kept me clear of most of this rhetoric. My grandfather taught my brother and I never to rat out anyone, especially your friends. And for all I might have gained from a criminal career—and trust me there were a lot of guys who hit the jackpot—I knew I couldn't do the time if I got caught doing the crime. Your freedom in America, second only to your health, is the most valuable asset in the world.

Don't they say a good man knows his limitations? My Achilles heel: there was no way my ass was going to be locked up for 20 years over a drug conviction. I would sing and hit octaves that a canary couldn't reach. If I may quote the great fictional crime fighter Dirty Harry, a good man always knows his limitations and when it comes to jail, mine's about a weekend long. It's a fine line to walk, but I've always prided myself on being one of the world's biggest juvenile delinquents, as you may have guessed by my antics. But when it comes down to being an actual criminal, I'm out. Believe it or not, I would occasionally hear disgruntled whispers of criticism, but no one dared confront me face to face.

Take this story my friend, Jorge, had told me. Now Jorge had extensive involvement in this kind of illicit activity. Some dealer who owed Jorge money tried to negotiate with him. The dealer happened to have a bad debt owed to him for the exact same amount of money he owed Jorge. The dealer tried to trade the debt off, even-steven, but Jorge declined. He didn't care who owed the dealer money; all he knew was that the dealer owed *him*. No dice. Jorge had won this round, but then the dealer threw my name into the mix. The dealer then suggested to Jorge that he have his good friend Podgurski collect the debt. Jorge immediately informed the dealer that his friendship with me was none of his concern and that I didn't do such things. And then this clown

196

tried to play the macho card and suggested that if I was afraid, maybe they'd have to get somebody else to collect the debt. Jorge, enraged, came down on this guy like a ton of bricks. He told this joker that I had nothing to do with the business, so I had nothing to profit. And if he insisted on questioning my manhood, Jorge went on, then all he had to do was not cough up the money by the end of the day and Jorge would be happy to pass along these insults and point me in his direction. By the time the sun had set in the west, Jorge had his sack of money. I didn't find out about this incident until much later. One evening, over drinks, Jorge explained the whole thing to me and then apologized for using me as leverage. I told him "anytime" and laughed it off.

Our friend Jay, on the other hand, wasn't quite as lucky... Jay wasn't a bad guy; he just made some bad choices. He was no different than a lot of guys in this country who have a lot of potential and start off on the right foot but somehow end up on the wrong path. Good old Jay was actually a decent guy—maybe a little gullible—but he had a tremendous sense of humor and would do anything for his friends. *Therein lies the key.* You have to be able to determine who your real friends are.

I had left Palm Beach County, Florida to move to Las Vegas, Nevada in 1979 and hadn't seen Jay in over a year. Before that, Jay had switched over from the Dojo when it went under to come and train at the Karate school George and I started; Southern Pro Karate and Kickboxing. Jay trained with us a few months but then he disappeared. I had heard through the grapevine that he was making money collecting bad drug debts, but by the time I left town for Vegas, like I said, I hadn't seen Jay in quite a while. On some of my vacation trips home, and through phone conversations with good friends, I heard that Jay had got in pretty deep. I was told he'd been riding shotgun, doing security for a smuggling operation. Then there was the story about Jay, and one of the yahoos he was running with, shaking down a Bahamian citizen who they suspected was trying to rip them off in a dope deal. After a few days of stalled negotiations—on his home turf in the Bahamas—they determined it was time to sweat this guy out. They came up with the brilliant solution of tying a rope on the man and dragging him down the beach behind a rental jeep. When that didn't work, they moved the operation to the Bahamian cobblestone streets, which caused two very detrimental repercussions. One: they almost killed the poor bastard, and two: whenever you mess with a native of an island community, you can guarantee that somewhere on that island he has a relative in high places. Sure enough, as Jay's luck would have it, this poor bastard's cousin was the head of the Port Authority.

The minute they unchained this poor soul from the back of the jeep, it was abundantly clear that they had screwed up; he apparently looked like a piece of tenderized meat. They needed to get off the island *and quick.* They'd barely got their boat untied and were headed for open water when the Bahamians were on to them. The chase was on and believe it or not they ducked their pursuers. Well, sort of...

The Bahamas are a string of islands, most of them small, and the Bahamian tourist industry only promotes the larger ones. Jay and his cohort ducked into the bay of one of the tiny outer islands that all smugglers were familiar with, ditched their boat, covering it with palm fronds and vegetation, then holed up and laid low. But now they were stuck there. About a week went by before the story reached some of my friends in Palm Beach County. A friend of mine named Avon, who had ancestral roots in the Bahamas, realized how grave the situation was, so he decided to take action and head over there to retrieve these two dopes. Believe it or not, after some quiet searching of the known smuggler's coves, Avon managed to find our two mental midgets in their self-imposed exile. They were approaching close to two weeks stuck on this tiny island out in the Bahamas. Avon said when he found them they were as nervous as a couple of Chihuahuas at a Mexican barbecue.

But Avon couldn't persuade Jay to get into the boat. Jay was convinced the Bahamians were watching them and that as soon as they hit open waters, the gunboats would blow them out of it. Avon finally got Jay to climb in the boat and was talking some sense into him when he realized it was going to be a long ride home. That's when a better plan flashed through his brain. Avon put a worried look on his face and gazed past Jay's shoulder, exclaiming, "Oh my God!" When Jay turned to look, Avon clocked him and knocked him cold as a cadaver. He told me this story almost two decades later and was forever convinced that it was the only way to get Jay and this yahoo out of Bahamian waters and back to the relative safety of South Florida.

Fortunately, from what I understand, that was the end of Jay's smuggling days. You couldn't put a gun to his head to make him return to those islands. Unfortunately, he discovered that collecting the money on bad drug debts on the mainland of Florida was almost as profitable.

198

Well, that along with ripping off the competitors of whomever he was working for...

Jay went out one night for a rip off, or to collect on some deal; it would be anyone's guess as to which one was the case. It was alleged that he set out that night with Gary Sproul as his wheelman. Yes, that Gary Sproul; the same guy Carl Stone kicked out of the Dojo for promoting himself to black belt. Rumor had it that they found their mark's house and cased it out for an hour or so until someone came home. When the presumed inhabitants got out of their car in the driveway and went up the walkway to their house, Jay grabbed a gun from underneath the seat, jumped out of the passenger's side of the car, and raced up the walkway after them. Now, with everyone entering the house and totally oblivious to Jay's pursuit, just as the front door started to close, Jay came busting through it. Now in the foyer, Jay confronted a handful of people. The group consisted of a couple of women, who I believe were in their mid to upper thirties who happened to be mothers, a man of similar age, who was the husband of one of the women standing there, as well as the father of at least one of the grade school children who were also there with them. And yes, there were other children present who happened to live in the home. Only a handful of people can testify to the nightmare that was about to take place but from what I can gather it went something like this: Jay was waving the hand cannon he was carrying, screaming at the man in the foyer, "I want the dope or the money motherfucker!" At that instant, sensing something was wrong, the family's Great Dane entered the picture and attacked. When the family pet latched onto Jay, he didn't hesitate in shooting the dog dead.

The actual homeowner, who was somewhere in another part of the house, heard a shot ring out, so he immediately ran to his rifle rack and grabbed a weapon. He sped to the foyer. Jay saw him brandishing a gun and shot him dead in an instant. Can you imagine watching someone you love get killed right in front of you? This traumatic horror is beyond what anyone should ever have to witness, let alone grade school-aged kids from both families, plus the wife and close friends.

Jay now exits the house, runs for his car and high-tails it out of there. The police arrive at a scene right out of a Sam Peckinpah movie, only it's real. The first move the police make is to notify all the local hospitals to be on the lookout for a man with a severe dog bite.

So what's the first thing Jay does? I mean, after getting rid of his wheelman, whoever that was. Oh, and you can bet that dumb bastard never imagined that when he woke up that morning he would be involved in a murder. Jay, minus his chauffeur, heads straight over to the Palm Beach Gardens Hospital. *Busted.*

This is a horrific story, but it gets worse. The real tragedy is this: our two rectum hole retards were in the right neighborhood, but they picked the wrong house. Their mark? The guy they were after? Well, he lived two doors down.

Now I haven't been an advocate of the death penalty since I was in my late twenties, but if Jay had been sentenced to death, I wouldn't have shed a tear for him. But I sure woulda cried for his family. And if I could say this: The Jay Collins I knew in his mid-twenties was not the Jay that shot and killed that man.

People tend to be a product of their environment, and therefore influenced by their surroundings. There's an old saying that a wise man can learn from his mistakes, but a genius can learn from the mistakes of others. Jay wasn't paying attention to the environment he stepped into. It's one thing to dabble in a little extra-curricular entertainment, but it's a whole other story to advance to the level of major profit. You've now entered a shark frenzy zone. I can tell you from my own experience: karma is a strange animal, but it can be tamed by putting out a positive glow, therein you will live a positive life. That's not to say you won't hit a pothole or two in life, but those sinkholes? You'll see them coming. The misuse of recreational drugs, and that includes alcohol, can drop a cloak over your inner light, which means you're navigating in the dark.

Jay ended up spending over a decade in prison; I haven't seen or talked to him in over two. I heard his mother passed away and had left him and his sister a substantial inheritance. When Jay was finally released from prison, unfortunately he picked up right where he had left off. I couldn't testify to this, but I was informed that Jay had gotten into a shootout with the cops, and you wouldn't have to be *summa cum laude* to guess who won that battle. And although I do not follow a religion, I do believe in God, and I would find myself praying for all those people Jay had hurt, including himself. And if nothing else, I hope the Lord took Jay into his kingdom and healed his torment.

Ten years after Jay's passing, I was staying at the home of my good friend, Alex Diaz. Alex told me that the last time he had seen Gary Sproul was roughly a year earlier. He'd spotted Gary walking westbound on the side of Okeechobee Boulevard pushing a shopping cart with an old automobile transmission in it, talking to himself. Yes, the world can work in very mysterious ways.

Chapter Nineteen

Years before all that had taken place, Skip Walls and I had sealed our friendship. Not only was he tall and good looking, but also he was as smart as any Harvard graduate whiz kid. And for the first time in my young adult life, I had a running partner who was confident enough, not to try and compete with me over women.

I remember one of the first times Skip and I were out together when we encountered some ladies. One of them had caught his eye, but she had expressed an interest in me, so he stepped back and built me up. I picked up on that right away, and made a mental note, because that's the way I had always behaved, but I'd never had a friend extend this grace to me. I was more than anxious to return the favor to him, too, because Skip and I recognized something very early on: Men Don't Get To Choose. Every guy has got that boneheaded friend whereupon spotting a group of attractive ladies, this bonehead screams out that delusional battle cry, *"She's mine!"*

Whether she is a blonde, a brunette, or the redhead, a Black, a Latin or Asian beauty—or possibly a Scandinavian—it's time to douse the bonehead with a cocktail and bring him back from never-never land. Because the longer he stays in that delusional state, the worse he makes it for all who involved. And the longer you wait to ask for that date, the more insurmountable the odds become, courtesy of a cock-blocking snake.

So boneheads, get a clue—it's always ladies' choice. But now, *here I am* in between Larry Thomas, with his good looks and charisma, and Skip Walls, who's approaching six foot five and is as handsome as he is tall. Between the two of them, I could hardly keep up. The one thing I did have in my favor? I had lived in over half the coastal communities in Palm Beach County and, at one time or another, attended a school in almost every zip code. Add to that the fact that the local paper, the Palm Beach Times had begun reporting on my kickboxing career. So with a little PR behind me, I guess I was holding my own. *Wink wink.*

At this point people who recognized me, or knew me, were happy to see I was doing well. Well, not everybody... There was more than one occasion where some guy would walk in off the street and challenge me in my own Karate studio. I mentioned this to my good friend Steve

Shepherd and he cracked up laughing.

Evidently it had happened just once to Steve as well before he had gotten his message out loud and clear. Whereas I would take a moment to try and explain the ramifications to my soon-to-be floundering foe, Steve saw no sense in prolonging the inevitable. Steve would push his chair back from his office desk, and then proceed to march his victim into the kickboxing arena. Once the gloves were laced up, Steve was more than happy to demonstrate why he was on his way to becoming a world champion. He'd let fly an onslaught of jabs, punches, and kicks, delivered with all the accuracy and skill of a surgeon. More times than not, once the anesthesia wore off (okay, when they woke up), they couldn't remember why they were in a Karate school in the first place, let alone how they ended up in the ring with a future world champion. As for myself? I'd tell these newly Everlast punching bags if they came back after my classes were over, I'd be happy to work out with them. I'd use the term "work out" to try to keep it professional, hoping that after a few hours of deliberation, they would either lose interest or come to the conclusion they might better be suited to another sport to prove their masculinity... Like checkers.

Of course, my hopes were never realized. They'd show up later that evening, flanked by cars full of people, thinking I was going to get slaughtered. What they failed to realize was they were walking into the Lion's Den. And it never ceased to amaze me how many friends they would invite down to witness and cheer on their heroic efforts and, for whatever reason, try to humiliate the local Karate school instructor. And it was always the same; I would step into our office to get my sparring gear, and I would look at my good friend and partner George McClease and ask, "Can't these people read the newspapers?"

George would look at me with a smile from ear to ear. Personally, I think he loved this stuff. But George was rarely, if ever challenged; for some reason, unbeknownst to me, I seemed to have a target on my back. Either way, after I put my gear on, I would step out into the center of our Karate school, which was 1400 square feet—1200 of it was matted training space. Our mat was sand color, so I would advise these future brain scan recipients to wear boxing gloves because we didn't want to get blood all over the mat. Of course they were convinced it was *my* blood that was going to paint the floor. Now, I had three definitive reasons why I talked them into using boxing gloves. One: I didn't wanna kill anybody. Two: I didn't wanna take a chance on hurting my hands, and 3: most of these mental midgets had no idea what it was like to go a three-minute round wearing a sixteen ounce boxing glove. Not that it was gonna last that long...

I beat these guys across every inch of those 1200 square feet, from one end of the Karate school back to the other. Unlike my friend Steve Shepherd, I wanted to punish them. I wanted them to remember exactly where they were and what happened to them. Every time I knocked one down, I would back off, so George could come in and administer a little cold water and fan them with a towel. Once they were on their feet, I would pick up where I left off, with a barrage of punches and kicks. This would last just long enough for me to break a nose, crack a rib, or loosen a few teeth. Boy was the whole audience quiet, their hero's hopes dashed. After witnessing the ugly beat-down of their man, the whole place would empty in silence. They would go out to the parking lot, and get in their cars without uttering a word.

Then there was the time a police officer entered my Karate studio along with one of my students, Joe. This officer had done some boxing in the military as well as in the police academy. Now he was stepping into my Karate school because he wanted to test his skills against me. We agreed upon a night for him to come to my studio after I was done teaching classes so we could spar. And once again it was the same scenario, on that designated evening after classes were over, cars started filling up the parking lot. Johnny Law showed up on time with his brother in tow as his designated cornerman plus a few spectators. We had previously agreed to just go against each other just with our hands, since his expertise was in boxing. By the end of the first round, I had knocked Johnny Law down more than once. I noticed during the second round that Johnny Law's brother was screaming "Foul!" at me for punching him in the back of the head. Which I was. But I spat out my mouthpiece and gleefully said that if he'd quit turning his back on me and trying to run, and turn to face me, that I'd be happy to punch him in the front of his head.

This got a laugh out of some of my students, as well as from some of the spectators, but it must have humiliated the guy. Once he was on his feet, he made one gallant charge towards me. I cracked him with the right hand, and he went down to the mat... And then we all went home.

At this point, in 1977, I needed to take a little sabbatical. Between leaving the Dojo, breaking up with Ronda, hanging drywall all day, opening a Karate studio, training for fights—I was exhausted. That's when Larry Thomas came to the rescue. Yes! Larry was back. Larry had been working for his dad, Senator Jerry Thomas, and studying Karate with me. The Senator had expressed interest in hiring another person to help Larry maintain their Jupiter Island estate, as well as keep up their yacht.

And what an estate it was! Arguably one of the most beautiful waterfront properties in the country with a private dock for his yacht, the Intracoastal Waterway as its front yard, and the Atlantic Ocean rolling all the way to the Bahamas as its back yard—well, the suggestion box is open as to what you might find more beautiful. We often referred to it as "White House South" because of the big white pillars at the front door.

As you approached the Senator's estate along the main road that split Jupiter Island, the only thing you could see from the road was a beautifully manicured hedge that stood about ten to twelve feet high. When you left the main road and turned east to approach the Senator's home, you then had a twelve-foot wall of green on each side to escort you up the driveway to the Senator's estate. The driveway then opened up into a circular courtyard that had a fountain in the middle of it. Looping around the fountain set you right in front of the stoic white pillars flanking the Senator's home. Standing on the entryway steps between the white pillars, looking past the fountain, you couldn't help but notice a beautiful pool and pool deck, with a rock garden plus pool house big enough to live in. Believe me folks; if this ain't heaven, you'd be a fool not to settle for it.

Just beyond the pool deck and the rock garden was that twelve-foot hedge, which separated the estate from the main road. On the other side of that main road that split the island, the property continued another thirty yards through a coconut tree forest to the Intracoastal Waterway, where you would find the Senator's dock and his fifty foot yacht.

Which I'm sure cost a lot, but on any given weekend, more times than not, you could find me Larry and Skip down there with our guests after the nightclubs had closed. It was close to a hundred yards of distance from there to the main house, and with the Atlantic Ocean gently breaking in the background, the privacy of twelve-foot high shrubs, and the three of us loose on a million-dollar boat with the opposite sex—I'll leave it to you to take a guess as to what we were up to.

With the main house set up on a bluff with its rear side exposed to the Atlantic Ocean, it made you wish you had the Senator's luck. Actually, luck had nothing to do with it. Senator Thomas was a former Marine Corps Captain who retired from the armed forces before he entered the world of Politics and became a Florida State Senator. Later he was brought in to President Gerald Ford's Cabinet and became one of his closest confidants.

Senator Thomas knew how to focus and dedicate himself to hard work. I think he sensed some of those traits in me, but he also recognized that I was somewhat of a loose canon. If someone was to ask me to do something, I'd be more than happy to break my back to help them get the job done, but if someone tried to order me to do something, I figured they could do it themselves.

Nevertheless, I think he recognized that I was having somewhat of a positive influence on his son Larry. I had convinced Larry to come down to my Karate school and take some lessons. He actually enjoyed working out, and he was a good athlete, which meant he backed off the throttle on partying during the week.

That's not to say that Skip, Larry, and myself didn't go out on the weekends and have a good time, because we did. The weekend started on Thursday night at the KiKi lounge on Congress Avenue. The KiKi—or as we lovingly referred to it, the Kai Kai—was the great Hawaiian nightclub which had nothing to do with Hawaii. That was our inside joke, but it had two very strong things going for it. One: Wet T-Shirt Night, which we referred to as Wet Titty Night, and two: Live music on the weekends, with a band Palm Beach County seemed to anticipate the most: Truc of America, a southeast touring rock band which put on amazing theatrical performances. And although they only performed cover tunes, more times than not they played them as well, if not better than the original artist.

They were fantastic and not only were they great players, they were highly creative. They were the only nightclub rock band in Palm Beach County that would perform amazing theatrical stage shows along with their music.

So one Thursday night, I'm supposed to meet Skip and Larry at the KiKi Lounge for the wet t-shirt contest, and I'm the first one there. After I say all my "Hello's" to the door guys, I walk up to the bar, and I see Gary Sproul's roommate, an old surfing buddy of his. Gary had been a top-rated east coast surfer before he had taken up Karate. I say
206

"Hello" and start to order a drink when I realize, Gary's roommate is having problems with a guy I recognize. Mark Herman's alleged Mafia buddy, Tommy C.

First of all, for the record, I never cared for this Mafia wannabe. He was rude, obnoxious, and intimidating. He liked to push his weigh around, but of course the only time I saw him was when he was with Sensei Mark, and he could afford to act that way. As I leaned on the bar, I started to get an earful of what Tommy C was trying to lay on this kid. Just as all this was happening, my friend Skip showed up. Rumor had it that Tommy had studied Karate under Sensei Warren Siciliano. Sensei Warren was a man to be respected: he had once been a bodyguard for President John F. Kennedy. So my suspicion was this: Tommy C had gotten himself a dollar fifty's worth of Karate lessons, seen one too many Clint Eastwood movies and now, with Mark Herman in prison, he fancied himself the fastest gun in town. To top all this off, with Mark behind bars, and on account of their close association, Tommy C was trying to adopt Mark's persona and slip into his shoes. He was no Mark Herman. In the midst of terrible Tommy's tantrum, I leaned over and whispered into Sproul's roommate's ear, "You can take him, don't put up with his shit."

This kid was strung as tight as a piano wire; he must have surfed every day. He was all knotted up with muscle, yet not real tall; about five foot nine and only 145 pounds. But I had faith he could handle old terrible Tommy. Feel free to do the math: you've got a kid in his early twenties who works out and surfs daily, and then you've got a Michael Corleone wannabe, the guy of excess who smokes, drinks, and parties too much.

About then, Skip leaned over to me and asked what was going on. I told him to hold on a minute and just listen. I leaned into the kid's ear again and told him to not take this shit. "He's bluffing. He's got nothing to back it up and you can take him," I urged. Right then Terrible Tommy took a sip from his cocktail, set it on the bar and then squared off with the kid. What left Terrible T's mouth next could have been the dialogue out of a bad B movie. He told the kid, and I quote here, "Don't even think about it, I'm too fast for ya. Don't even flinch, none of you stand a chance."

Did I just hear none of us? Or was that the bell for round one? That's when I slid to the left, placing myself between the kid and the bar, pushing the kid aside with my left forearm. Then I placed both of my hands on the bar where Terrible Tommy could clearly see them. Then I posed the question, "What about me? Do you think you're too fast for me?" His response? *Who the hell did I think I was?* I grinned and replied, "I'm the guy that's gonna knock you out."

I'd slapped my hands down on the bar so he could see them. But in the blink of an eye, I threw a left-handed back fist that struck him somewhere around the temple on the left side of his head. When his knees buckled, I threw a right hand and caught him right on the chin. *Boom boom!* Out go the lights. When the bouncers ran in and picked this idiot up off the floor, they looked at me and asked me what had happened. I told the bouncers that this idiot tried to start a fight with my friend, and when I intervened and tried to calm things down, he tried to sucker punch me. Since the bouncers knew me never to be a problem, they picked up Terrible Tommy by the scruff of the neck and the ankles, and took him out the front of the club.

As I turned back towards the bar, Skip put one of his mitts on my shoulder. When I looked at him, he told me he was glad I'd taken care of the situation. With a big grin he added that he was growing weary of Terrible Tommy's hot air and was just about ready to take action himself. Skip only weighed a buck eighty, but he was pushing six foot five, wore a size 48 long jacket, had played High School football, and then later rowed for the University of Central Florida's crew team.

Anyone who's ever put an oar in the water can tell ya: the guys who row crew are in insanely good shape. Although it mighta gotten a little messier if Skip had stepped up, basically I think the outcome woulda been the same. When the kid tried to thank me, the sarcasm of my Scots-Irish blood came out. I lifted my hands and showed him both sides of them, and then stated, "I go nowhere without my surgeon's tools." Everyone got a big laugh out of that. But as the laughter died down, and the front door to the nightclub opened, in spite of the people coming in, you couldn't help but notice there was a commotion outside.

The next time it opened, I saw Terrible Tommy outside the nightclub, arguing with one of the doormen. That did it for me. I made a beeline for the front door, and as I approached it, I heard Terrible Tommy tell the doorman, he was going back inside, because somebody sucker-punched him and now he was gonna kick their ass. Did I just hear the bell for round two? This is when I glared old Tumbleweed Tommy down and told him I was the ass he was lookin' for, so he'd

208

better start kickin'. Then Double T steps back and demands, "Who the hell did I think I was?" I cracked up laughing and asked if he stuttered because that's what he said ten minutes ago when I knocked him out the first time! Before he could think up a rebuttal, I shoved him back and threw a roundkick up by his head. Then I told him if he didn't get the hell out of there and stop bothering people I'd be more than happy to hand him his head on a plate.

That's when his friend, trying to get my attention, grabbed me by the shirtsleeve. I bitch slapped him with the back of my hand on the side of his face. Now he started whining like a little girl trying to tell me who Tumbleweed Tommy is and what a heavy connection he has. This clown was trying to do me a favor! I told this gopher I knew exactly who he was, and with Sensei Mark in jail, I had no fear of retaliation because let's face it, who's gonna retaliate; the two of them? Then this clown tells me that Tumbleweed Tommy's got a pistol in his car. My response? "He's never gonna make his car, and you're gonna give him a ride home."

Next Tumbleweed Tommy pipes up with a question, was I one of Mark's students? I acknowledged Double T's question with a grin. That's when he threatened that Mark was gonna hear about this. "Perfect," I replied. "Tell him the Flying Pollack knocked you out." That was a nickname I got tagged with after the barroom brawl at Big Daddy's. You remember—when I went to Skip's side, kicked one of the doormen, only I over-amped and leapt so high I landed on his head and shoulders and we both went to the ground? The guys at the Dojo had a field day with that. They graffitied my safety kick, which was a foam-rubber boot you wore over your bare feet to protect you and also keep from killing each other when you sparred. Someone, and I never found out who, came up with the idea of taking a red and blue felt pen and drawing a circle with a "FP" on the front of my safety kicks with wings on either side. It looked like a superhero's insignia. "FP" stood for—yep, "Flying Pollack." With Terrible Tumbling Tommy getting in his gopher's car, he yelled out that Mark was gonna hear about this, and it was not the last I'll hear of it. You know what's funny? I never saw nor did I ever hear of Terrible Tommy C again.

But now, back in the nightclub. Skip and I had barely gotten back to the bar when Larry Thomas showed up, and oh what a scene he walked into! Now I had my new best friend on one side (surfer dude), and what turned out to be one of my oldest and dearest friends, Skip

209

Walls, on the other, along with everyone else at that end of the bar, trying to convey to Larry the first round knockout that he just missed. Like I said before, Larry's enthusiasm was that of a ten-year-old child. His eyes got as big as softballs. No way he coulda missed that! But he did. By the time the story telling had dissipated, we were well into the night and having a pretty good time. Then the lights went out, and the cover band Truc of America started playing the song "White Punks on Dope," which is where they went into their theatrical performance of Star Wars.

Through the darkness a spotlight would hit center stage, and there would be Darth Vader brandishing his laser saber with smoke and steam billowing up behind him. All of a sudden, out on the darkened dance floor, another laser saber would appear. At that point, Darth Vader would leap off the stage and engage in a laser swordfight with the lead singer of the band. Of course, we had seen all this before and it was highly entertaining, except for this night. It became *insanely* entertaining. All of a sudden there was a third laser saber in the fight. After more than a few minutes of hilarious chaos, the doormen ran in and grabbed the third laser saber, and dragged our swashbuckling anti-hero out the front door. Then the stage lights came up, and the band kicked into "Just What I Needed" by The Cars, and everybody went right back to dancing and having a good time.

But who in the hell was wielding the third laser saber? I was about to find out. Midway through "Just What I Needed," one of the doormen came into the club and grabbed me. My presence was requested. I was taken to the front door of the nightclub. There, in all his glory beneath the neon lights, was Larry Thomas with his laser saber, demonstrating how one might go about killing Darth Vader. Larry had witnessed this stage show more than once and had decided to go out and buy his own laser saber. And now, after more than a few cocktails and God knows what else, Larry had decided to inadvertently integrate himself into the show. You know, just to joke the band, and snap them out of what he felt was their predictable, repetitive routine. The issue was, he had never cleared it with the band. And for anyone who knows performers, a problem starts when you begin to upstage them.

So *here I am*, standing underneath the neon lights outside the front entrance of the KiKi Lounge with my good friend Skip, and we're holding each other up; we're laughing so hard we're about to black out. Larry's popularity was at a high point in Palm Beach County, so a signifi-
210

cant amount of spectators who had witnessed his improvised behavior are now outside the nightclub giving him 'high fives.' Oh this is just what the doctor ordered, and a doorman's nightmare: encouragement and moral support for juvenile behavior. Now the burden is placed squarely on my shoulders to talk the doorman into letting Larry go back into the club.

After a few minutes of friendly, jovial conversation with the doorman, I had convinced him to let Larry back into the club, but they confiscated his laser saber and checked it at the front door. Larry agreed to submit to that, but he assured the doorman he'd be taking it with him when he left.

Chapter Twenty

It was during this time frame that my good friend Steve Shepherd had come across some amateur boxing matches being held in Northern Miami. Steve had found a boxing trainer by the name of Johnny O'Brien, a former contender in the lighter weight divisions when he fought back in the fifties. Poor Johnny! He had taken on the daunting task of coaching Steve Shepherd. Under normal circumstances you'd refer to Johnny as your trainer, but Steve was no normal circumstance. Steve had his own mindset; he couldn't be trained. But coaching? He'd take suggestions.

Steve began traveling south about once a month to Northern Miami so he could compete in these amateur boxing contests. By the second time he had gone to Miami and came back, raving about what a great time he had (you always have a good time when you win) I couldn't resist going down and giving it a shot myself.

So *here I am*, packed in a car with Steve Shepherd and Johnny O'Brien, headed south to Northern Miami, to climb in the ring with God knows who, armed with absolutely zero boxing skills. *Oh, what the hell?* I was in great shape and I'd been trained to fight. Sure, the demographics were off slightly... In Karate and kickboxing we fight from longer range, meaning there's more distance between you and your opponent because of the kicking element. But my basic thinking was that this factor could work for me, not against me. I figured I wouldn't have as far to travel to strike my opponent, and this logic proved to be somewhat correct.

But the interesting thing about amateur boxing is that it somewhat parallels the experience of fighting in Karate tournaments as a white belt: it's a mixed bag of nuts. You could be getting into the ring with a guy who's been training for a year and is somewhat polished, or find yourself up against a guy who's got something to prove to his ex girlfriend and only started boxing yesterday. Sometimes your opponent may have no sense of rules at all. So when the bell rings, sure he's trying to punch you in your head, but he's going about it by beating you in your balls, punching you in your ass, putting knots in the back of your head... He's just throwing punches indiscriminately, hoping a haymaker will find your button, meaning your chin. After a while, you're feeling like a piece of tenderized meat and you're just trying to stay one step ahead of their scattergun approach. So, after winning a couple of fights with no actual boxing skills, Johnny O'Brien talked me into entering the Miami Beach Golden Gloves tournament. Let me tell you something, we're all proud of our Olympic Athletes, but you should also hail our Olympic representatives in boxing.

Fighting in a series of Golden Globe tournaments is a tough way to distinguish yourself from the rest of the crowd. After my first couple of wins, my third opponent was a southpaw, meaning he fought with his right side forward. Again, with no boxing skills, I held my hands low because Karate punches are thrown from your hip, which turns out to be a bad tactic in a boxing ring. I also had a tendency to drift to my left, which gave my left jab a little more extension, and I was a firm believer in Muhammad Ali's philosophy: you can't hurt what you can't hit. And tipping the scales at a whopping 188 pounds, I was a little light. Okay, I was too light for the heavyweight division. After doing the science, in spite of me being Polish, I decided movement was my best defense.

But you have to know the right movement. So *here I am*, an amateur in the ring, basically a Karate champ with an illusion of boxing skills, going up against more seasoned fighters and hoping that the skills I did have might gain me a win. By this stage I'm facing opponents with far more skills than I had. I lean to my left, flip out one of my half-backfist half jabs, and my opponent timed it just perfect. I had retracted my left jab just a little low, and it was hanging just above my ribcage. My opponent stepped forward with his right foot, and let go with his right hook, that hit me right on the button, which, by the way, I was moving into by moving to my left. I would find out later that was a cardinal sin in boxing.

So now, with the door wide open, I was inadvertently being introduced for the very first time to what Muhammad Ali would refer to as "The Room." Upon entering "The Room," funny things begin to happen. First there's an unexpected flash of light, which seems to be from a lightning bolt, and then everything becomes surreal. You're aware of everything that's going on around you, but everything seems to be moving in slow motion, and you can hear none of it. You're coherent enough to realize where you are, and what's at stake, so you summon all your energy to focus on your opponent, but you can't help but be plagued by the daunting strangeness and the haunting weirdness of it all.

Again, I have to say, this being my first time, I never saw the punch coming, but I sure did hear it. It sounded like the faraway whistle of a bomb being dropped in a Second World War movie. And then *shwack!* The whole place went silent.

So *here I am*, in a strange cartoon setting, trying to defend myself. I can see my opponent, clear as day, but it's surreal; we're moving in slow motion. I notice the referee out of the corner of my eye, but I couldn't see beyond the boundaries of the clearly lit ring. I could sense the crowd, although I couldn't hear them. It was as if I was surrounded by a black curtain, enclosing all four sides of the ring.

I was now fighting more from instinct than skill, but I must have done all right. It was the biggest con job of my life, because by the time the bell rang and ended the second round, I had all my faculties restored, in three distinctive waves. The first wave was the shocking sensation of being jolted back to reality. I was suddenly acutely aware I was in some type of arena, auditorium, or convention center. The second wave was the crowd. All of a sudden I had the awareness that there were thousands of people yelling and screaming, although the roar of the crowd was muffled and dragging, like a 45 rpm record being played at 33⅓. Then came the third wave, which I found to be the most peculiar: all of a sudden I heard *chuwack!* and suddenly everything was moving at full speed and at an ear-piercing volume. Then the bell rang to end second round, so I walked back to my corner and sat down. With Johnny O'Brien pouring ice water over my head, he asked me what happened. "What happened? What happened is I took a leisurely fucking stroll down Queer Street and I don't mean the gay part of town!" At this point I'm feeling pretty relaxed, because I'm convinced I've got the secret weapon in my corner. I've got Johnny O'Brien, one time world contender, with possibly as many fights under his belt as he had years on this planet.

So now, when he tells me he's gonna tell me what to do, I sit up and my ears perk up like a bluetick coonhound. This could be one of those defining moments. My mind is racing, my adrenaline has peaked. So what does this Patton of Pugilism tell me? This Buddha of Boxing? This Confucius of Combat? The ten-second buzzer went off, I stood up and turned towards my corner, I looked straight at Johnny, and the advice he then gave me baffles me to this day. He tells me to go out there and punch until I drop.

That's it?! The bell rang and my opponent was all over me like a wet shirt. In the midst of tearing into each other like a pair of rabid dogs, I was thinking, "My fucking instincts coulda told me that!" But when it was all over, and the smoke had cleared, I had to stand and watch them raise the hand of another man in victory. And me? I got to make that lonely one-hour drive home in silence and defeat. Defeat, to me, felt like disgrace.

No, I never acquired a taste for it. It was like anchovies on a pizza: hard for me to swallow. I had always prided myself on doing more, on training harder than the other guy, but I was forgetting the fact that I had never trained as a boxer, nor had I developed any boxing skills. In my mind, I should have won that fight. All the criticism that had ever been directed towards me, starting way back when I had entered the first grade, no one, and I mean no one, was harder on Jeff, than I was.

A few days had gone by, and I was shaking off the loss. I had gone back to my first loves, teaching Karate and training as a kickboxer. Boxing had been a little sideline, somewhat of a parallel entertainment. I was through with it. *Little did I know.*

One weekend Skip Walls had talked Larry Thomas and me into driving to Orlando, up near central Florida, where he had attended college. The biggest night in Orlando to party happened to be on a Sunday Night. And the biggest place to party? Rosie O'Grady's. Neither Larry nor I had ever been to Rosie O'Grady's, but we had heard a lot of great things about it. And the icing on the cake? Back when Skip had attended college in central Florida, he had been a doorman at the place. *Can you say carte blanche?*

The joint was a riot. It had four or five nightclubs under one roof. Whatever your musical taste, you were in the right place. They had a New Orleans ragtime jazz bar, a country and western saloon, a riotous rock and roll nightclub and, if you liked to dance, hang on to your pants because they had a discotheque too. We had a ball, because we hit them all, but our favorite by far was the New Orleans style jazz bar. This was the first place I was ever able to climb up on a table, or get on the bar and dance, without having my reality jarred and promptly being escorted out to my car. At Rosie's they actually instigated this type of behavior, so we didn't hesitate. We had a blast!

There was a horn player, blowing his heart out, who stepped down off the stage and started a conga line, which we stepped into. After a lap around the room, he jumped up on a chair, and then proceeded to dance a lap across the tops of people's tables, with the whole conga

215

line in pursuit. Next thing I realized, our fearless horn player had used a bar stool to step up onto the bar and—you guessed it—we weren't far behind. Now there are more than twenty people dancing on the bar. With the bar now far too crowded with dancers, our serenading saxophone player stepped down off of it, and went right out the front door, and into an adjoining nightclub. And of course we were having far too much fun to let our magical musician get away, so we joined him. It took all of one lap around that nightclub before the conga line grew longer. When we got back, the Jazz bar was packed, and of course the band hadn't missed a beat, which left me pondering, how did they do that?

The next thing I know it's 5:00 a.m., and Rosie's had closed at four, but I'm standing in yet another line to go into another nightclub. It was a bottle club, a private club, that just happened to be a gay club, but it was the only place in town still jumping. Now we were surrounded by college coeds, and most of these were girls that Skip had gone to school with. One of them just happened to be a member of the club. She wasn't gay; she just liked to party with them. For her, it was a safe bet. She could party and dance the night away with no fear that someone would try to pull off her drawers or take advantage of her.

Now I can't speak for Skip or Larry, but this would be my virgin voyage. This was the first time I'd ever gone into a gay nightclub to sit down and have a drink, and I have to say, what an experience. The rule was, if you were straight you had to walk in with a chick. Okay, it wasn't a rule... I guess it was more our paranoia than anything, but there was no way that one of the three of us were gonna walk into this dump without holding the hand of a lady. At this point, there were seven or eight of us walking into this gay night club, and we were treated warmly. That was mainly due to the fact that we were there with a member: Skip's lady friend.

Now bottle clubs do not sell liquor. You have to bring your own bottle, hence the name. But they do sell you the mixers, at the full 1977-78 nightclub prices. So you might pay two dollars for a coke or a glass of orange juice to mix with your rum or your vodka.

About halfway through your first drink, when the hair starts to go down on your neck, you start to have a pretty good time. At least I did. Oh sure, out on the dance floor you'd see a little male grab-ass, and deep in the shadowy part you'd almost make out a couple of guys making out, and you know, speaking as a straight male I really don't care

216

to see two men trying to molest each other. Then again, I'm not big on public displays of affection anyways. I don't even like seeing a straight couple maul and grope each other.

I just focused on the party at our table and we all had a great time. But now it's 6am. We've got a two-hour drive back to West Palm Beach, and Skip's supposed to be on a construction site at 8am, while Larry and I are supposed to be working on his dad's yacht. Larry and I had it easy: we'd climb up on the boat and piddle around, and as soon as his dad left we'd slather ourselves in suntan oil, find a cot, and take a nap. *Can you say as bronzed as a beer bottle?*

Sometimes the perks are worth more than the salary. All that week I hadn't heard a word from Skip. He had signed up at Southern Pro Karate and Kickboxing to take lessons but he hadn't shown up for class. That weekend, I decided to call him to see what was up. I had to talk him into meeting me that Saturday afternoon for a drink over at a place called the Crazy Horse Saloon, off Northlake Boulevard and US1. Over our first drink I found out that he had spent the whole week trying to find a new job. He'd lost his construction job mainly due to our Orlando - O'Grady overstay. So, after consuming a few beers, we had discussed his options, which weren't many. I told him to cheer up, promising something would happen. And it did.

His mom, Kathleen, worked at the Tequesta Country Club in Jupiter, which was full of high-end clients. One of the members mentioned to Kathleen, Skip's mom, that he was looking for a young, executive trainee, someone who was bright, energetic, and creative.

Talk about hitting the trifecta; he was describing Skip Walls and he didn't even know it! Next time I talked to Skip, he was on his way to a meeting with this older gentleman at his home on Jupiter Island. And oh, what a meeting it turned out to be. This old gentleman was pretty sharp; he hired Skip on the spot. Next stop: New York City.

And *here I am*, seeing my friend off to the Big Apple where he gained training and became a Junior Executive in a business that later became very lucrative for him: the department store fixture business. Skip went on to design and construct the interiors to department stores.

In the meantime, one morning I was abruptly woken up after I had spent the night at the Senator's home. The bedroom door flew open and in came Larry, buzzing like a swarm of hornets. He had grabbed a handful of things that belonged to him, and although I was discombobulated because I had been woken up from a dead sleep, I think I heard him mutter something to the effect of, "I don't have to put up with this shit any longer." Then he rushed out of the room as fast as he had entered it, taking a few of his belongings with him. Senator Thomas tried to intercept him in the hallway, but Larry wasn't having any of it. Then I heard the front door slam. I got dressed and tried to slip out of the mansion unnoticed. You have no idea how uncomfortable it was trying to sneak out of that house… I had been spending four nights a week at the mansion by this time. Just as I crept to the front door, Senator Thomas called out. I turned around and he was right behind me. He had a peculiar yet pleasant smile on his face. Then he asked me what my schedule was for that day. I had to have had an expression of shock when I replied, "My schedule?!" I had assumed that with Larry out the door, I'd get out too before it hit me in the ass. The Senator reassured me that he wanted me to stick with the program, and go on with the work scheduled for that day. Then he asked if I minded stopping by his office at the end of the day so he could speak with me.

After the Senator retired from his seat in the Senate, he had become the President of a chain of banks, First Marine Bank, which I got a charge out of because he had been a Captain in the Marine Corps. I headed over to the bank for our afternoon meeting. *Here I am*, being escorted into Senator Thomas' office, witnessing more grandeur than I had ever seen. And you can believe me when I say this, when you're a former United States Marine Corps Captain—retired—and a former United States Senator—retired—and finally a sitting Bank President, you get some nice perks.

I remember sitting down and thinking, *"How in the hell did I get here?"* A kid that grew up with eight people in a two-bedroom house, a sand lot in the front yard with no grass, a kid with no formal education… A kid that was picked on, spat on, and told he was stupid simply because of his ethnic background. But now the real bomb was about to be dropped. Senator Thomas wanted to know if I would stick around and handle security around his home, as well as doing my daily labor. He was concerned that all of the kids were now out of the house. Well, all except Cindy, Larry's younger sister, but she had a boyfriend so she wasn't around much. Now that Larry had taken off, the Senator didn't like the thought of Mrs. Thomas being alone at the Mansion.

Jupiter Island was a very beautiful and very exclusive enclave, but it was also highly isolated. With the ten-foot wall of shrubs blocking the view from the road, and the long winding driveway leading up

218

to the front of the house, plus beach access at the rear of the house, bad things could easily happen. It could be hours before anyone knew something had gone wrong. There were no words to describe how flattered I felt that Senator Thomas was placing Mrs. Thomas' well-being in my hands. He couldn't have picked a more loyal person, either. The trust and sense of pride that I felt would have driven me to protect Mrs. Thomas to my death. Then he requested that we keep this arrangement between ourselves, as men. We shook on it. I left his office a foot taller and walking on air. The dignity I felt was indescribable.

A few years later, when the hit TV show "Magnum, P.I." came out, it instantly became my favorite show. I responded to the whole idea of running around in shorts, a tank top and Hawaiian shirts. Okay, so I didn't drive a Ferrari, and I didn't live in a guest house, but I did spend nights on the yacht, and I did have an island compound right on the ocean. And I pretty much had free rein of the property. I was beginning to wonder how much better life could get. Working for the Senator by day, teaching and training in Karate during the evening, I was living in a place most people would consider a tropical paradise. But like the saying goes, all good things must come to an end, and my dream life suddenly came to an end one Friday afternoon. Senator Thomas called me up to his house. He explained that he and Mrs. Thomas were going away on vacation and he wouldn't need my services any longer, at least for a while. I thanked him and he returned the gesture, we shook hands and I said goodbye.

I didn't know it then, but it would be the last time I would ever see the Senator. A couple of days earlier I'd noticed that their mailbox wasn't quite up to par. Like the house, the mailbox was white, but its paint was flaking off. Unlike the house, it wasn't trimmed in black. Before I left, I scraped off all the old paint from the mailbox, repainted it sparkling white, and then trimmed it in black. There were numerals above the mailbox in single digits, so I painted them black as well so they would stand out. That was my parting 'thank you' gesture to the great Senator.

As life would have it, it would be just a few short years later that the Senator would be diagnosed with terminal cancer. Knowing he was taken by cancer kills me to this day. Senator Thomas was the first man of great esteem who actually gave me respect. And I will say this to all that didn't know him: we lost a fair, decent, and honest man. He was a straight shooter. When Jerry Thomas stepped down from the Senate, they say the state of Florida—as well as our great nation—lost a great leader. I would go so far as to say that when Senator Thomas passed away, mankind lost a true champion.

In the meantime, even though I now needed a job to supplement my basic income, the fact that Senator Thomas let me go kind of played in my favor. It was 1978. I had committed myself to fighting Dave Rupert in a kickboxing match. Rupert was six foot seven, two hundred and twenty five pounds. He was rated number three in the world as a heavyweight by the only governing body at the time: the PKA, Professional Karate Association. Steve Shepherd and Don Haynes were promoting kickboxing events at the West Palm Beach Auditorium, and I'd signed up to be the semi-main event on the next card.

As for the main event? Steve Shepherd, of course! But with Rupert rated number three in the world, and me at number twelve, beating him would break me into the top ten ranking, something that had to be done if I wanted a chance to compete for the heavyweight title of the world.

I'd witnessed Dave Rupert in action in Atlanta. I had participated in the Battle of Atlanta Karate Tournament during the day and then attended the kickboxing event that evening. Rupert was on that card. Watching him in the ring, I knew I possessed the skills to beat him. I was roughly six foot three and weighed 193. And although Shepherd and I argued over the purse (my fee), I ended up taking the fight just to catapult myself onto the world platform.

But in the meantime I needed a day job, so I went to work with my old compadre, George McClease. In addition to being my partner at our Karate school, George had started a small air conditioning company. He had bid on and won the contract to outfit a town home community called Live Oaks, right on the Intracoastal Waterway and the PGA Boulevard. *Here I am* in 90 degree weather, shirtless in 100% humidity, cutting fiberglass board which gets turned into an air duct system, which I will haul up into the one place that was hotter than where I was just standing—the attic—and mount them to trusses before the whole mess is hidden with drywall. It was my second favorite thing to do… My first? Pretty much anything else.

Although I was hot and sweaty (and you're pretty much always hot and sweaty when you do construction work in Florida) and those fiberglass threads would stick to me and make me itch like a bitch, it still was a lot lighter work than drywall, and that was important. As unpleasant as the work was, it left me with some energy to train for my up and coming kickboxing event. Not only that, but George would let me off by four o'clock, which meant by four thirty I was rinsing off the itchy sweaty mess, and by five I was entering my zone. *God bless George McClease!* I would leave George's duplex and run the distance of roughly four miles over to our Karate school, Southern Pro Karate and Kickboxing, where I would go in my office, wipe down, put on my *gi*, and step out on the mat and teach three one-hour classes.

At nine p.m., when classes were over, I would step back into the office, put on my workout gear, and start my training for my up and coming fight with Dave Rupert. Friday afternoons, Saturdays, and Sundays were my fight days. You would find me at Steve Shepherd's Karate Academy sparring with none other than a future world champion, Steve Shepherd. For roughly my entire kickboxing career, and a large majority of his, Steve and I were each other's main sparring partners. Oh sure, we used other sparring partners, but Steve was the only person who could match my tenacity, and quite possibly surpass it. Although only a middleweight, he was six feet tall with blazing hand speed, and he could hurt you with either hand. Remember, being roughly six-foot-three, I weighed in at 193 pounds.

This all played to my advantage. Being lean for a heavyweight only made me faster, and speed was the key to my game. On those weekends I'd travel south to Lake Worth and down to Steve's Karate studio. Once inside, I would do my warm-up, do a few rounds of shadow boxing, spar for six rounds, do a kicking routine of no fewer than 300 kicks and finally stretch for an hour. Then it was back up to George's house in Lake Park, where I'd pick up George's Doberman Pinscher named Bronco, and then Bronco and I would run the three miles to Singer Island Beach. We would run a further three miles along the beach sand, and then it was time to cruise the beach. If you're like me and you like meeting new people, especially the ladies, then gentlemen, this is my humble advice: Take a dog to the beach.

But now it's fight night. The West Palm Beach auditorium holds close to 5,000 people, and tonight it's packed. This, in itself, was mind numbing. This was the biggest venue in Palm Beach County at the time, and *here I am* one of the headliners. As a kid, I had attended professional wrestling matches at the West Palm Beach auditorium. I'd experienced my first live concert, Steve Miller, at the West Palm Beach auditorium. Later, I would work security for rock promoters who would hire the Dojo members to assist with crowd control for major rock acts at the West Palm Beach auditorium. Did I ever dream I'd be the attraction? *Here I am*, a kid who found himself pointed in this direction, though never having had it suggested or even being directly encouraged to study the martial arts. The sandlot, blue-collar kid with the funny last name; the kid with no education and no direction. He now finds himself as one of the headliners on the marquee on the West Palm Beach auditorium.

Knowing now what I, of course, didn't know then was that it's the little triumphs in life you should try to savor. Right at this minute, I'm the third fight up, so I'm sitting quietly in the locker room when the door opens and my cornerman in life steps through it: George Mc-Clease. And the first thing out of his mouth? "I just saw Rupert, and he's not so big."

I just grinned and nodded, but in my mind I was thinking: he's the height of your average home's doorframe, and his shoulders were almost as wide. Do me a favor, when you're done reading this page, go look at your front door and investigate the size of the frame. If that's not big, then I've taken one too many cold showers, and I've been following Alice and that rabbit around some Scandinavian wonderland, where the average height is just under seven feet tall.

The second fight had just ended when I finished up my warm-up exercises and shadowboxing. Then they called us out. Eager to get this over with, I was the first one through the door and into the ring. Since this was my hometown, there was plenty of applause and raucous cheering when I entered the ring. I circled the ring twice and then headed to my corner, with my back to my opponent's corner. Then all of a sudden 5,000 people erupted into a chaotic roar. I started to turn to glance over my shoulder to see what the commotion was about. Then it dawned on me; I had seen this act before. After clearing the steps, Rupert made a grand entrance paired with intimidation by simply stepping over the top rope, where it barely caressed his crotch, and casually entering the ring. (He's not that big, George—*not much!*) I remember how that stunt affected me; it felt like the ultimate put down. It dawned on me that I wasn't big enough to be taking him on, and that possibility brought on a swell of emotion and aggression that I immediately had to channel. What rushed through my mind was the memory of every person who had ever tried to hurt me, hate me, or humiliate me. And with the crowd's eruption of adulation for my opponent,

222

it was like throwing kerosene on a fire. *My own hometown wasn't giving me a snowball's chance in hell of beating this guy!* Then the referee called us to the center of the ring for our last minute instructions. Rupert met me in the middle of the ring, glaring at me with his nostrils flaring. He was looking down his nose at me, adopting the scornful intimidation tactics a father would use on a school-aged child.

Gazing back at him, in my eyes lay the still calm before the rage of a tropical storm. I couldn't tell you one word that the referee had uttered. In my mind, I was going to make him pay for stepping over the top rope and grandstanding, for all that posturing before the fight had even started.

The bell rang for round one. As we closed in on each other I hesitated just for a moment to size him up. Rupert threw a left jab and a right cross, and the right hand caught me underneath my left eye. It burned as my head snapped back. I immediately danced out of harm's way and I remember clearly thinking, that will be the last solid punch you land on me. Blessed with great timing, and being more of a defensive fighter, with clean counter striking, I went back to that old Muhammad Ali adage: you can't hurt what you can't hit.

So I got on my bicycle. I used every inch of that 22 square foot ring. All that sparring with Steve Shepherd—who had the blistering speed of a middleweight—almost made this guy seem slow. The burn I had suffered almost daily from running miles along beach sand had put my legs in great shape, and I was gonna need 'em.

After this fight, someone had given George a snapshot of me making contact with Rupert's body with my lead left leg round kick, and him leaning over and hitting me square in the head with his left jab. For Christ's sake—his arms were almost as long as my legs!

By the end of the first round, I had settled into a strategy of making him miss and pay. As soon as he'd miss, I'd make him pay with a two to three punch combination and then dance back to the outside. Rupert was strong, powerful, and a good athlete, and I knew he would wear me out if I stayed on the inside and wrestled around with him.

By the second round, I had loosened up, and now I had some feints working. I would throw a right shoulder fake, and then skip into him with a left front kick, which was off of my lead leg. This approach was really punishing his body, and it quickly started wearing him down. When the bell rang to end the second round, I headed back to my corner. Before I sat down I looked at George and asked him, "How big does Dave look now?" George did a little double take and grinned. Then he got back to the business at hand; administrating aid to me as my cornerman.

As the fight progressed, Dave got more desperate. His combinations had slowed. He was now throwing fewer shots, but the punches he did throw were much harder. By now my right shoulder fake had him reacting. When I threw the fake he would drop his guard to protect his body, and then I would unleash a kick that I'd learned from Jeff Smith the hard way.

I remember taking a little trip up to Washington DC with Ronda, to train at Jhoon Rhee Institute of Karate. I was hoping to get a little one-on-one with the light heavyweight kickboxing champion of the world Jeff Smith, which by chance I did. During our sparring session, the light heavyweight champ threw a right shoulder fake, which I went for, and then he stepped into me with a lead left leg round kick which caught me square on the side of the head and spun me around in a circle which had me staggering towards the front door, more than a little discombobulated.

I never forgot that lesson. I might not be a quick study, but I sure recognize what works. But now the final bell rings, and George bursts through the ropes and hits me like a linebacker. He throws his arms around me and lifts me in victory. The thunder from that auditorium must have shaken the angels in heaven. As it turns out, I won the fight by a unanimous decision. My greatest victory, achieved here at the West Palm Beach auditorium, but it would be somewhat short lived. Just a few short years later, though, the West Palm Beach auditorium would hand me my greatest defeat…

But right now, I'm the winner, and people are climbing over top of each other trying to get into my locker room. George, as well as security, pushes everyone out of the locker room door, and finally my dressing room has been cleared. I now have a moment of serenity. George turns and looks at me and asks if everything is all right. In my mind I was reliving everything it took to arrive at this moment of pure victory. I looked up at George and said, "Can you believe this?" Forever the optimist George replied, "Yeah, I can believe it. You've worked hard, you deserve it." But what was about to take place in the next few minutes, neither George nor I could have anticipated.

Chapter Twenty-one
The Signing

In the middle of a congratulatory hug from George, Steve Shepherd stepped into my locker room accompanied by two middle aged Italian gentlemen who had asked to meet me. One gentleman, who was doing most of the talking, introduced himself as Carl Duva. It had turned out that Carl and his brother Lou—who would later handle Evander Holyfield, Boxing's Heavyweight Champion of the world—trained professional fighters. Professional, as in *professional boxing*. Carl asked if I had ever considered entering that arena. I chuckled and said 'No.' He then handed me his card and asked me to call him. He wanted to set up a luncheon on Sunday, at his town home overlooking the Intracoastal Waterway, so we could explore the possibility. I looked up at George and that's when he stepped in. He thanked Mr. Duva, took his card and assured him we would call either way.

Well, we had a hell of a party that Friday night. Then George and I mulled the idea around all day Saturday. And our conclusion? As George pointed out, we had nothing to lose. What the hell? Let's go to lunch and see what the man has to say.

So *here I am*, sitting in Carl Duva's town home, staring out at the sparkling Atlantic Ocean, listening to him give me a sales pitch on why I should become a professional boxer. George and I left that luncheon with the understanding that we would call Mr. Duva in a few days and give him an answer. Carl assured us he would be in town for at least another week; he was vacationing with his wife and friends. After a few days of deliberation with George, we made the call.

We told Mr. Duva we were interested in his proposition, but we weren't willing to make a commitment until we had further investigated his proposal. He seemed to be more than pleased. He wanted everyone to be happy with the arrangement, if one eventuated. The plan was to fly me into New York and head over to Patterson, New Jersey. That was where the gym they wanted me to train at was located, as well as the neighborhood I'd be living in.

This is where my guardian angel and my cornerman in life, George McClease, went into overdrive. He called his old high-school friend Keith Pender, who was a buddy of mine as well. Keith had friends in the New York Tristate area. Pretty soon my friends were circling their wagons around me.

Keith had attended the fight when I beat Dave Rupert the week before, and he was excited to hear that someone like Carl Duva, who had a lot of clout in the arena of professional boxing, was interested in me. So here was the deal: Mr. Duva was gonna fly me to New York and back, picking up all my expenses, so I could get the lay of the land. Carl's plan was to pick me up in person when I arrived at the airport, and then take me out to Patterson New Jersey. I was to spend a week getting acquainted with the neighborhood they wanted me to live in, as well as getting to know my way around the gym they wanted me to train at.

Carl was also looking forward to introducing me to a lot of people. His brother Lou Duva, who I had met briefly after the fight, as well as some boxers, and the President of Madison Square Garden. Both George and Keith were determined I wouldn't go to New York without an outside contact number.

When I first stepped off the plane, I was met by Carl and his daughter, a young lady who was roughly a few years younger than myself. After our greetings, my contact rolled up on me. This was a gentleman of heavy influence that I had never met before, and who shall remain nameless. Mr. Duva couldn't hide the look of astonishment on his face; I don't think he believed that a Florida boy had tentacles that reached that far north. After a few introductions, everyone seemed to relax.

Following a discussion of our agenda for the week, my northeast connection inquired where I would be staying. This guy was way ahead of the game. He knew every location that Mr. Duva had mentioned, so he insisted that I ride with him. And *here I am*, with my newfound northeastern connection, following Mr. Carl Duva and his daughter to Patterson, New Jersey and heading to what could be my new career.

The whole way to the motel in Patterson, the place I would be calling home for the next week, my new best friend of the northeast was giving me the pep talk, or should I say the 'deterrent' talk. He kept describing the ugly side of boxing, and insistently asking me if I really wanted to do this. He was hell-bent on pointing out all the degenerates and lowlifes I'd be exposed to, that I'd be stepping into the ring with child molesters and murderers. To these men, fighting itself wasn't an option; it was more of an absolute. When we finally pulled into the motel, I thanked him for his positive support and cheerful encouragement, saying it was time for me to take off the rose colored glasses. I declared I needed to take this shit seriously and focus. We both cracked up laughing. As I was getting out of his car, he gave me all his contact numbers, and asked me to call him in the morning.

I watched him drive off, and as I turned and walked towards the motel I remember thinking: for Christ's sake, we're fighting with boxing gloves, not dueling pistols, and I seem to remember there is a referee... We're in a ring, and there are rules! Then I wondered—*could they really sneak a horseshoe into a boxing glove?!*

The very next morning, Carl Duva picked me up bright and early, at 7 am. We went to eat breakfast and get to know each other, and then he proceeded to drive me around the Patterson Area, introducing me to the environment in which he expected me to live and train in. Well I can tell you this: New Jersey is a beautiful place, with some wonderful people, but Patterson is not the Garden of Eden of the Garden State.

Over the next few days, I was introduced to a variety of people, most of them Italian. Carl even introduced me to his wife again, like I was joining the family. I was introduced to a multitude of boxers, as well as union officials. Carl pulled out all the stops, even arranging an introductory lunch with the President of Madison Square Garden. As the week unfolded, I had been wined and dined, I seemed to have met all of the right political connections, plus I struck up a friendship with Carl's sweet daughter. And oh yeah, I trained. Let me tell you without any hesitation, straight out of a Florida boy's mouth: getting up at 5:00 a.m. and running through the snow and jumping over rocks in the Patterson park is not my idea of a fun-filled winter vacation.

By week's end, I sat down for dinner with my New York connection, and that's when he made me an offer I couldn't refuse. He suggested I take a ride with him. He told me he had made the decision to take a trip to South Florida in his brand new BMW, and he offered me the shotgun seat. It was the lure of a road trip, coupled with the bonus of saving Mr. Duva my return-trip fare. *Did someone say "road trip?"* To me, this is the equivalent of asking a five-year-old if they want an ice cream. I was in. I said my "Goodbye's" to the Duvas and thanked him for the week. Now *here I am*, on my way to South Florida, in a new BMW 6-series (with a giant Schnauzer in the back), with my new northeast connection behind the wheel, gunning it up to 95mph, getting on I-95.

What I came to realize en route was that my newly acquired chaperone was a drug mule. For those of you who might not know, drug mules are the transporters of contraband from point A to point B. They are the shipping agents of drug smugglers. And the giant Schnauzer in the back was, in fact, *not* my chauffeur's; he was a hostage, to be held till my chaperone-slash-chauffeur retrieved the money he was owed for his last delivery. By the time I had gotten back to West Palm Beach, I wasn't the least bit amused. At this point I had gotten an earful, and had heard just enough horseshit to be able to connect the dots. While I was appreciative for all their help, I was a little agitated with my friend Keith for his responsibility regarding the transportation arrangements to get me back from New York. I had called and cleared the ride with him before I had accepted the offer, but he hadn't given me the whole picture. But I never said anything to him about it, because my chaperone was also affiliated with another friend of mine: Jorge.

Now Jorge was a great guy, and everyone who knew him spoke very highly of him. But Jorge was in the drug business as well, so I kept somewhat of a buffer between the two of us. I never got involved in that business, and Jorge respected me for that. Whenever we bumped into each other socially, the subject never came up and we had a great time. He was always interested in our Karate school (Jorge had studied a little Karate himself), and he would inquire how my training was going and who was on the agenda to fight next. Oh, and we couldn't avoid the topic of women, and of living in paradise as well.

Right before I left New York, Mr. Duva presented me with a contract, which I declined to sign. I reminded him of our original agreement, which had been for me to come up in good faith and take a look around. But I told him I'd be more than happy to take the contract back to Florida and give it serious consideration.

Keith mentioned that he had once dated an attorney named Patty Ryan and that her father, Frank Ryan, had been involved with some prominent sports figures, negotiating their contracts. I believe this was a gesture of goodwill on Keith's part, trying to ease what little tension there was between us. If I remember correctly, Frank Ryan had acted as legal representative and brokered deals for Hall of Famers such as Ted Williams for Sears, and for Baltimore Orioles pitcher Jim Palmer. And oh yeah, he had negotiated the sale of a basketball team from Minnesota to Los Angeles that you may have heard of; the World Champion Los Angeles Lakers. Not to mention he owned a stable full of record-holding race horses.

So my friend Keith makes yet another phone call on my behalf, this time to Mr. Frank Ryan's office. Now by the age of twenty-two, I had pretty much lived the whole length of Palm Beach County, from as far south as Boynton Beach, and as far north as Jupiter, and I had pretty much attended schools in every town in between. I'm talking about Boynton Beach, Lantana, Lake Worth, West Palm Beach, and Riviera Beach. 'Ryan' was a prominent name in Palm Beach County. If you hadn't gone to school with one of the kids—and I believe there were ten—then chances were you knew someone who did. It would seem as though one out of twenty people in Palm Beach County knew who the Ryans were. To me this was the 'Big Leagues.' These people lived in a big beautiful house on Singer Island, right on the Intracoastal Water-way. As luck would have it, they lived right down the street from my ex-girlfriend Ronda. She had grown up with them, having attended school with some of the younger Ryan siblings.

So *here I am*, sitting in the North Palm Beach Penthouse Law Office of Mr. Frank Ryan, with my old friend George McClease and our bud-dy Keith Pender. It was a brief but cordial meeting, which took about a half hour, where I explained my situation and the offer that had been made to me. Mr. Ryan politely took the contract, and advised me not to speak to anyone until he had had time to look over the contract and get back to me. A few days later I received a phone call from Keith down at the Karate school. He explained to me that after examining the contract, Mr. Ryan had found it almost laughable. Mr. Ryan dis-covered that the contract stipulated that I would be bound to the Du-vas *eternally*; that if Mr. Duva died, his wife would retain me, and that if Mrs. Duva died, his daughter would retain me. And God forbid their daughter should die because then I'd go straight to their dog. I could theoretically find myself managed and trained by the family mutt! So that was that. I dismissed the whole delusional affair from my mind, but I cherished the adventure.

I went right back to teaching Karate classes and training myself, supplementing my income with construction work, in the hope that one day our Karate school would gain enough momentum to financially support me. But fate wasn't done with us yet. About a week later Mr. Ryan's office called; they wanted to schedule an appointment with George and me. This puzzled the hell out of both of us; *who the hell were we?* We showed up on time, in our 'Sunday best' sports coats, trying our hardest to look professional. So *here I am* once again, with my good friend George, sitting in the North Palm Beach Penthouse Law Office of Mr. Frank Ryan, with both of us a little bewildered as we stared across the desk at Mr. Ryan.

What was about to come out of his mouth caught us both by surprise. It was no Pearl Harbor, but it was more than enough to blow us right out of our seats. Through careful explanation, Mr. Ryan laid out the formula for a limited partnership in which he would raise a few hundred thousand dollars to sponsor me in my efforts to win the Heavyweight Boxing Championship of the World.

I snapped my attention to George so fast I think I got whiplash. Though I can't speak for him, I did see the blood drain from his face. I swallowed so hard I thought I'd sucked my brain through my windpipe. While we sat there in shock, Mr. Ryan went on to explain that he had contacted his friend Mr. Rosenblum in Los Angeles, who just happened to own a football team called the Los Angeles Rams. Mr. Ryan had asked Mr. Rosenblum if he could contact his friend Howard, to enquire as to who might be the best boxing trainer for a young, up-and-coming heavyweight fighter. You know, as in *Howard*, the greatest fucking sports commentator on the fucking planet, *Cosell?* While I was hubada hubada hubading, George stayed cool. He asked Mr. Ryan to give us a few days to think about the proposal. We needed time to try to digest it all.

We stood up, shook Mr. Ryan's hand in good faith, and walked to the elevators in silence. Once inside the elevator, I started to speak, and George put one finger up to his mouth for silence. Once outside the building, we shuffled towards George's truck with the quickened pace that only the threat of a proctology exam would bring. For those of you who have been goosed, you'll know exactly what I mean.

Not until we were safely inside the truck, with the windows up, did we dare to erupt. We exploded with a jubilant flurry, laughing and

230

roughing each other up. What a sight it must have been for anyone passing through that parking lot. Here were a couple of crackpots, shut inside George's truck with the windows wound up, laughing and cavorting as if we'd just won a Las Vegas Jackpot. Oh, did I mention it was a typical August day in Florida, meaning 90 degrees with 100% humidity? *Crazy!*

In a few short weeks I was back in the Penthouse Law Office signing contracts. Mr. Ryan and his son Michael had rounded up a few investors for the limited partnership. Some high-powered businessmen. One of the Executive Board Members, if I remember correctly, was the grandson of the founder of Coca-Cola. Another heavy hitter was the President of the Oldsmobile division of General Motors. Plus one of my favorite members of the limited partnership, who had the greatest name in spite of the fact that he knew nothing about boxing, was Charlie Knuckles, who actually trained and managed racehorses.

Now only the rich can involve themselves in this type of frivolous endeavor. Just for fun, Mr. Ryan owned a stable of racehorses; a couple of which I was told were track record-holders. If this contract and opportunity was not mind-blowing enough, there was a clause attached, much like a ballplayer's signing bonus, that stated that if I did not succeed in boxing, I would receive a substantial about of money to get me started in a new direction in life.

As soon as all the 'T's were crossed and the 'I's were dotted, the signing was over, and we jubilantly shook hands all 'round. George and I went back to his place. I had decided to stage a party true to our Dojo tradition: George and I made phone calls to everyone involved to join us for a grand celebration. Dinner on me at Yesterday's, down in Fort Lauderdale right on the Intracoastal Waterway.

Now it's Saturday night, and we're pulling up in front of the restaurant Yesterday's. None of us are feeling any pain; we'd been drinking since we left West Palm Beach. We are being escorted to our table, but the party has already started. So *here I am*, sitting on the edge of the picturesque Intracoastal Waterway, on a moonlit evening, enjoying dinner and drinks with a disco pumping away on the second floor above us. Keith had invited my New York connection-slash-chauffeur as well as his drug connection Jorge and their dates. What could I say? We were having such a great day, and they were somewhat instrumental, so *what the hey?*

By eleven o'clock we were clearing the check, and we were ready to head upstairs and do some dancing. Throughout the evening, various people at our table would get up to go powder their noses, if you get my drift. Then—and this would be the first and only time Jorge had ever done this—all of a sudden, Keith, my New York connection, and Jorge cornered me, each with a Cheshire Cat grin. They produced a vial of cocaine they promised would choke a goat, claiming it was the purest snow you could find in the Northern Hemisphere. I declined, telling them "Not here," so they suggested we go to the men's room. I glanced over and caught George's eye. Now, I had no intention of snorting coke, but I was buzzed and it was a celebration. But by catching George's eye, I was reminded of the day I looked inside and made a conscious decision that alcoholism—which ruined my family—and substance abuse—which proved to be of no use to friends and family throughout my life—was in no way shape or form going to be part of my professional athletic life.

To keep the party going, I looked over at George and gave him a shy wink. I entered the restroom with them all, took the vial of coke and went into a stall. I made a snorting sound and dumped some of the coke into the toilet. I came out coughing, and tossed the vial to Keith. I went straight over to the sink and ran some warm water on my hands, pretending to snort a little to rinse my nostrils out, which is a common thing to do when coke is too strong and it burns your sinuses.

Later, in the disco, George asked me what had taken place up in the men's room. When I told him, we both started laughing so hard we started to cry! Later, when the second round came at me, I had an excuse. I told him it was way too strong and since everyone knew I hadn't snorted coke in years, I convinced them it would be wasted on me and went back to my beer.

It turned out to take a few weeks before they finally got me on payroll, and that was a long month and a half. But *here I am*, at the tail end of morning rush hour traffic driving to Miami Beach every day to spend four hours training at the Fifth Street gym. Then, after becoming completely exhausted, I'd get in my car and hit what would be the beginning of rush hour traffic for everyone trying to get home.

I determined very quickly that my '67 Mustang, although in mint condition, wasn't going to be able to keep up with this pace. After the first few weeks had passed, I called and scheduled an appointment with Mr. Ryan and his son Michael; Mr. Ryan's oldest son, an attorney at the law firm, and one of my limited partners. They listened to my grievance, and a few short weeks later, I had a brand new Oldsmobile Omega automatic. Of course, I'd requested something a little more sporty; the Oldsmobile Cutlass. But the Ryans felt that the Omega, which was on line with the Chevy Nova, was a little more economy minded, and therefore a better choice, and who the hell was I to complain? In the world I came from, there was no obtaining a brand new car unless, of course, it was by gunpoint. But the best part about this whole arrangement? I mean besides receiving a brand new car, it was F-R-E-E. *Bingo!* It didn't cost me a dime.

Chapter Twenty-two
Viva Las Vegas

For my professional debut, I was scheduled to fight at the Miami Beach Convention Center, on the undercard of the Canadian Middle-weight Champion against Sugar Ray Leonard as the main event. Yes, the same Miami Beach Convention Center where I'd suffered my only boxing loss, and yes, the same Miami Beach Convention Center where I lost my good friend Stanley G, courtesy of eight bullets to the head and chest. All those haunting memories could wreak havoc on your mind and spirit... *ya think?* On the way down to Miami, I had a three-step thought process going 'round and 'round in my head. Number one: did I train properly and hard enough? Am I in good enough shape to step into this arena? Number two: this is where I suffered my only loss in the first encounter I had with the boxing world, and number three: Stanley G.

When we got to Miami, it was a media circus. This was a big deal in the world of boxing. This would be Ray Leonard's first big step on the march to winning the world's Welterweight Championship. Once I was inside the arena, I needed to clear my head, I needed to get focused. I headed for the locker room to escape the insanity.

It was a huge sports media event. I remember one of the big three networks was there covering the event. I believe it was NBC, and I believe they had sent Dick Eckinburg to do the announcing. The door to my locker room opened, and Mr. Eckinburg quickly stepped in to check his suit, makeup, and hair in the mirror before he stepped out to go on the air. I remember seeing Kenny Norton, the heavyweight boxer and former World Boxing Council Heavyweight Champion, who looked as big as a house and was in his prime and thinking, *I wonder if I'll see him a little later down the line?*

Well, Ray Leonard and I both had a great afternoon. I won my fight by a decision, and he won his by a knockout. But throughout the journey back to Palm Beach County, although jubilant, something was needling me in the back of my mind. Although it was no fault of Ray Leonard's, in preparation for my first professional bout I had twice been derailed from my workout. In the weeks leading up to the event, after Ray Leonard had gotten into town, on two occasions trainers had come over and removed me from the equipment. Once was when I was in the middle of working the heavy bag, and then the second day was when I was using the speed bag. The trainers had asked me to step aside so they could get publicity shots of Ray Leonard using that apparatus.

Ego is a huge part of professional sport. You have to have one or you wouldn't be a competitor. Besides, my common sense was offended as well. At the ripe old age of 23, I was almost too ancient to be starting a career as a professional fighter. My instincts were telling me I needed some attention, and not to take a walk until the cameras stopped flashing. But I really didn't have a choice.

My second fight took place about six weeks later, at the Sunrise Musical Theatre in Fort Lauderdale. This time I knocked Greg Henderson out in the fourth round. But it would be my third profession fight, which was also held at the Sunrise Musical Theatre, that would drive a wedge between me and my trainer and promoter, Chris Dundee.

Ten days prior to this bout, I had come down with the flu, so I had not made the drive to Miami to train. A few days before my bout, I had gone out and run five miles, trying to clear my lungs. Then I went to my Karate school and shadow boxed a few rounds, hit the heavy bag and skipped some rope, trying to compensate for the week of training I had missed in Miami.

But now it's fight night, and I pull into the Sunrise Musical Theatre parking lot and look up on the marquee, and there's my name listed as the 'Ten Round Main Event.' I was more than shocked; I was livid. Not only had I been sick the week before—and Dundee knew it—but after only two professional fights, I was already being moved up to the main event? Which is ten rounds or more? I was pissed.

You need to understand the world of professional fighting. You

235

wanna move up to the main event gingerly, not only because of the conditioning that's involved, but because of the caliber of opponent you'll be fighting.

Just as I suspected, when I finally tracked Chris down inside the Arena, he informed me that I'd be fighting the Caribbean Champion. *Are you kidding me?* Only two professional fights and I'm already being matched up with the Caribbean Champ? An argument did ensue. In fact, our discussion started out on a level that a marriage counselor would not only have suggested—but would have *insisted* on—a divorce.

Then Chris persisted by pouring gasoline on the fire, threatening to go over my head to the Ryans and telling them I wasn't cooperating. This is where a strange and eerie calm came over me, as if an angel had placed their hand on my shoulder. Having gained some maturity in life, I can look back at every bleak moment I've ever experienced, whether it be physical, emotional, or financial, and each time a strange eerie calm of clarity came over me that I can only attribute to a higher power. My angels.

And *here I am* in that moment, at this time. This is where I inform Chris Dundee of the benefits of a Limited Partnership 101. Most fighters that find themselves in this position have a sponsor and a trainer who will pull their proverbial strings and keep them dancing to their tune. In my particular situation, I had showed up in Miami with my own backing. Our limited partnership stipulated I was an equal partner, therefore I had no boss, and no one was pulling my strings. Delivering this conveyance had the equivalent effect of throwing iced water on a dog in heat. The look on Chris Dundee's face said it all.

He chilled out. But I was looking Chris dead in the eye and I could see his brain trying to calculate his next move. He immediately tried to negotiate with me, "Okay, eight rounds," but he still didn't get it. Not only had he pissed me off, he had proven he couldn't be trusted. It was obvious he didn't have my best interests in mind; only his, as a boxing promoter. He then tried to negotiate six rounds, but I wasn't going for it, so we eventually settled on four. I was scheduled to be the fourth fight up, so by the time I went to my locker room, I thought I had calmed down.

But now, *here I am* inside the ring. The bell rang for round one to begin and I was all over my opponent like a cheap suit. Somewhere, halfway through the first round, I had knocked my opponent's mouth-

236

piece out. So now I pressured my opponent into the ropes, until a hard right hand blow hit him square in the philtrum. The philtrum is that vertical groove underneath your nose that goes down to your top lip. My right hand slams into the lower half of his mouth. His head snaps back, when it bobbles forward, he's spitting blood and looks like a jack-o'-lantern. I had sheared his two front teeth off at the gum line.

I had him ready to go, all but down and out, when the bell rang to end round one. Round two would not be as fortunate for me, and I knew it. When I got back to my corner I was wheezing. The flu had sapped me of all my endurance. When the bell rang for round two, his experience started to show. I didn't possess the strength, energy or speed to keep up with my opponent. When the bell rang to end round two, I walked back to my corner seeing white spots. Not so much from the punches he had bounced off my melon, but from the oxygen depletion in my brain. I now had the deep burn with every inhale, that felt as if an acetylene torch was being held against the bottom of my lungs. If round two looked like a losing battle, round three looked like the ending of a war. I'm sure his cornermen were preparing the peace documents for me to sign. What they couldn't have known was that my corner was telling me something I didn't wanna hear, nor would I accept. As usual, everyone underestimated my Polish-German-Scotch-Irish-Jewish blood. My corner had flat out told me I had lost the fight, so when the bell rang to start the last round, I stood up and turned around and declared, *"No I didn't!"*

I stepped to the center of the ring with the same intensity I'd had in round one. It was cheap suit time and I was the tailor. I draped this guy with a barrage of punches that had him stuttering at the end of the last round. When the bell rang to end round four we went back to our corners. Then they called us to the center of the ring for the decision. They raised both our hands, a draw. I had won the first round, he easily took two and three, and I'd overwhelmed him in the fourth. I salvaged the fight, which is amazing when you look back at my lack of experience. Besides, he's the guy that lost his teeth in the boxing ring.

Despite the fact that technically I didn't lose, in my mind, I had a blemish on my record. I was pissed off, and I could see which way the tide was going. I never talked to Chris Dundee again, although I would see his brother Angelo many times. In fact, it was Angelo who had been recommended to me by Howard Cosell and who was supposed to be my trainer—not Chris!

When I signed up for this deluded boxing endeavor, I was under the impression that Angelo Dundee would be working with me. I only got to train with him one glorious day. Years later I would learn that Chris Dundee had come down with cancer, so when I saw his brother Angelo, I asked how he was doing and sent my best wishes.

One thing that connects us all is that we have these little struggles and sometimes major battles in our life. The one thing we have in common; we're all just trying to survive.

Later that week, following the fight, I had an appointment with Mr. Ryan and his son Michael to discuss what options we might have for someone new to train me. They were going to put their feelers out in New York, Philadelphia, and Chicago. In the meantime, that weekend there would be a heavyweight title fight between Ken Norton and Larry Holmes which would decide who would be the WBC Heavyweight Champion of the World. Leon Spinks had vacated the title by giving Muhammad Ali a rematch, instead of fighting the WBC number one contender Ken Norton. The number two contender; Larry Holmes.

Leon Spinks had won the WBA as well as the WBC title, but by giving Muhammad Ali a rematch—and losing—he basically handed Kenny Norton the WBC belt. He was bound by WBC rules to fight the number one contender. But instead, he opted to give Muhammad Ali a rematch (which Ali went on to win). So now the stage was set for the match between Ken Norton and Larry Holmes.

As I was watching this battle of Titans take place in Las Vegas something dawned on me. My friend Danny Tischler had once told me that his uncle and father trained fighters in Las Vegas. It seemed like a interesting prospect to pursue.

Meanwhile, my good friend Skip had come home for the weekend for a visit. I remember how surprised and how stunned he was at all that had taken place with me since he'd been gone. Skip had always thought that I was lucky. At this point we were young men, and we hadn't shared all of our backgrounds with each other yet. We both had personalities that tended to look forward at the possibilities, and not backwards or dwelling on the detriments. I don't think he'd have felt it was lucky to have grown up with a stepfather who was a hick idiot, without a lot of confidence that you were gonna eat half the time, where you were sent to multiple grade schools and junior highs where you were constantly ridiculed and picked on, mainly because of your last name which sticks out like a sore thumb. Or having grown up fighting to protect yourself and your brother if not weekly, then daily. So ready or not, you leave home at the ripe old age of fifteen because you can't stand the drunken ridicule of a hillbilly any longer. Where you find yourself regaining consciousness, aged seventeen, in the midst of a nightmare of 'no good deed goes unpunished,' finding yourself sprawled across the hood of your car with half your teeth bashed out, where you're told later it was courtesy of the Ku Klux Klan. And while the severe beating is happening, you're totally convinced they're trying to dismember you. But somewhere in your frontal lobe, you hear that distinctive cry, "You must survive." So you walk into a Karate school in good faith to learn self-defense so you can prevent such things from happening to you again, only to end up as the Dojo punching bag for the next two years courtesy of the advanced class.

Being called 'lucky' didn't even come close… As the years ticked off, I came to realize that luck had nothing to do with it. I was blessed. And like any good poker player will tell you, it's not the cards you're dealt, it's the way you play your hand.

But right now, my friend Skip Walls was home for a visit, so we were celebrating. He had come home simply because his company was transferring him from New York to Burbank, California, and so he wanted to make one last run through South Florida before he headed out to the West Coast. Not being sure if or when he might make it back, we spent his last day in town on Juno Beach, just south of Jupiter. Together we ran a breezy five miles along the beach. The last thing Skip said to me before he took off was that when he got to Burbank he would call and leave me his phone number so that we could stay in touch, or in case I ever made it to the West Coast.

Neither one of us could have predicted how long or short that would be. Some weeks later, a decision had to be made. I was either going to Philadelphia or Las Vegas, and in my mind, Vegas was the Mecca of boxing. Why? Gambling, that's why!

So the decision was made: Viva Las Vegas! So *here I am*, all alone, with everything that I own packed into my car, on my way to Nevada to rendezvous with my friend Danny Tischler, and his gorgeous wife Terri, so he can give me an introduction to his uncle Stan and his father.

I left West Palm Beach, Florida on Tuesday morning, to arrive in Las Vegas at 2pm on Friday. And that was after a five-hour visit with my brother Frank, who was living in Houston at the time. And don't even ask me how I did it. I remember snapping awake behind the wheel in West Texas and in parts of New Mexico and not recognizing a thing around me. And with my foot flat on it and traveling seventy-five to eighty miles per hour, thank God that the I-10 is flat and straight in those areas. This was a feat I would repeat some twenty years later, only extending my trip further to Los Angeles, courtesy of Red Bull and Protein bars. P.S… *Not* recommended.

I remember stopping in Boulder, Nevada, a little town that sits above Las Vegas, overlooking Lake Meade. Boulder is the only town where gambling is not permitted in the state of Nevada. It was a town that took shape when they were building the Hoover Dam.

I stopped at a trading post to buy my Grandmother and my mother some Indian jewelry, to commemorate my landing in Nevada. Boulder is a cute, quaint little town that sprung up from a tent city when they were constructing the dam. Evidently, the women and children of that day needed a safe haven from gambling and gunplay. Some place devoid of the debauchery that gambling, drinking, and prostitution would bring. Oh, and did I mention dodging bullets from the occasional gunfight?

I was in the Wild West and couldn't be happier about it. In my mind, I was in an occupation parallel to a hired gun without the pistols. So *here I am*, traveling north on Boulder Highway, which will eventually turn into Sahara Avenue, turning left onto the Las Vegas Strip. And, oh what an eyeful that is.

Practically everything I own is in my car, including a piece of paper with a phone number on it for Stan Tischler, who would eventually become my trainer. Arriving in Vegas was when the reality of it hit me, *how in the hell did this happen?* But before I can answer, here comes the Stardust Hotel, which is where I'm supposed to rendezvous with my friend Danny Tischler and his wife. I make a right into the parking lot, and go straight in to check-in for what will turn out to be a week-long stay at the Stardust Hotel. First thing up: go straight up to my room and dump my stuff so I can hit the buffet. I'm starving and exhausted. Second thing on my agenda: back to my room for a four-hour nap. When I wake up, I call the only number I have for Las Vegas, which is Danny's Uncle Stan. He tells me we're all meeting in the lobby of the Stardust at eight o'clock, so I shower, clean up and head down.

Evening has set in, and the gamblers are out. Passing through a Casino for the first time is like walking through the magical land of Oz.

You can't quite focus with all the lights flashing and people laughing. Bells and whistles are chiming, and slot machines rhyming. Some folks are swearing while others are staring, and some woman is screaming at the top of her lungs. And you pass through all this before you've even reached the front desk.

Then I see Danny and his beautiful wife, Terri. I notice two middle-aged couples accompanying them. Danny embraces me warmly, and then he introduces me to his dad Harvey, and his Uncle Stan, and then to their respective wives. Harvey is warm and friendly and I like him immediately. Stan, on the other hand, is standoffish and stoic, sizing me up and looking me up and down, much like a racehorse trainer would peer at a thoroughbred. After we're all acquainted and somewhat comfortable, the suggestion is made to get something to eat.

The decision was made not to eat at the Stardust, so out to the Strip we go. Much as I'd thought the impressions were over, we stepped out on the Las Vegas Strip at night and *shazam!* My brain was on instant overload.

If you've never been to Vegas, nothing can prepare you for the Strip at night. There were so many bright colors of neon, I wasn't able to focus. I couldn't begin to tell you what was said in the car on the way to dinner. *So this is what it's like to hit the big time.* I felt as if I was sliding down a rainbow in all its kaleidoscope colors with a leprechaun in my lap, so when my feet hit the ground, all I had to do was collect my pot of gold.

The big discussion at dinner was how I got involved in boxing in the first place. After a long explanation, all the wives agreed: I was too good looking to be a fighter, which suited my vanity just fine. But I informed them that as soon as my mug started to pay my bills, I'd retire.

After dinner Stan told me to rest up to get my bearings and recuperate from my drive. He promised he would meet me at the Silver Slipper casino on Monday at noon, where he would be training my future stable mate, Earl Tripp. Stan and I shook hands in good faith, and then he and his lovely wife disappeared into the Vegas night. Danny turned towards me and informed me that he had gotten tickets to a sold out event the following night at the Aladdin Theatre for Performing Arts: Gino Vanelli. Gino had a top ten hit playing on all the FM radio stations, "I Just Wanna Stop," which was a love ballad that holds up well to this day. At the time, I didn't know who he was. I was familiar with the song and dug it, but I thought he was a guy who played keyboard and sang love ballads. Man, was I in for a surprise.

Since I had just gotten into Vegas, and I had stopped drinking and I didn't gamble, I had nothing else going on, so I was happy Danny invited me along. Danny, being the owner of a chain of record stores in Palm Beach County called Sergeant Peppers, had pulled some strings to get these tickets. Dan was pretty excited about this event, but not one of us, including his stunning wife Terri, could have been prepared for this concert.

Lights were out, and when they came on, it was with an explosion of music. There was Gino, front and center, with the spotlight glaring on him. Long brown curly locks down to his shoulders, with a white lace french cut shirt unbuttoned down to his navel, wearing white spandex pants that looked as if they were painted on him. Then he broke out in dance moves that would make any hip-hop artist jealous. He literally jolted Danny, Terri, and myself out of our seats. Ever since my mid teens, when my good friend Chuck Muck had his own band, I was a big music lover. I had attended thirty, maybe forty rock concerts over the previous ten years, but nothing compared to this. Danny and I glanced at each other throughout the concert with our mouths gaping wide open, clearly thinking the same thing, *"Is this for real?"*

After the concert we couldn't stop talking about what we had just experienced. I immediately went out and bought the album "Brother to Brother" which Gino was on tour promoting. And I've spent my money on this album four or five times, buying the audiocassette and going all the way up to buying the CD.

I still think to this day that it's quite possibly the best live performance I've ever witnessed. It's hard for me to believe I only ever knew one song, which was a love ballad. But if you want my opinion, and let's face it your opinion is the only one that matters to you, I feel fortunate that on that one night in Vegas with two friends, I got to experience one of the greatest shows ever performed. *Gino, you were electrifying.*

Sunday came way too soon. I saw my friends Danny and Terri off at McCarran Airport and then mentally tried to prepare myself for Monday and the beginning of my new life. Monday morning came and I had to pinch myself. The reality of living in Las Vegas was now real.

Me, a kid from a mosquito-infested, small, south Florida coastal town, alive and well in Sin City. *Show me the lights!* When you look back, you have to realize that, although always a tropical Paradise, West Palm Beach was not always the tropical hot spot it is today, with its entertainers, sports heroes and CEO's. *Damn Yankees!*

Once I came to my senses, I got down to business, which is why I was here. I started my day the same way it would start for the next few years: roadwork, aka hitting the road. I ran out the front of the Stardust Hotel and turned left, and made what was barely a two-mile loop. Up the Las Vegas Boulevard, left on Sahara, and then down Industrial, which runs behind the Casinos on the Las Vegas strip, then back to the Stardust. I barely ran two miles, but that high and dry desert altitude was something totally new to me. Now when I speak with athletes, or I see them discussing their training programs on TV, and hear of the geographic places they've chosen to train in for their up and coming competitions, I almost chuckle. Listen, if you're an athlete and you can live and train in Vegas or the surrounding mountains, you can compete anywhere.

But now it's high noon, and *here I am*, entering the Silver Slipper Casino, which is owned by the Summa Corporation, and part of the Howard Hughes Empire. I head upstairs to the Burlesque Room, which is where they hold a 'boylesque' show with men in drag. There's a makeshift boxing gym with a ring, dead center of the room in front of the stage. What a paradox.

There's a young black fighter shadowboxing in the ring, about 195 pounds, five foot eleven, maybe six foot, and there's Stan Tischler, my new trainer. Stan waves me over. We shake hands, and Stan introduces me to the young fighter shadowboxing in the ring, who will become my stablemate, my main sparring partner, and my close friend for the next couple of years; Earl Tripp.

I liked Earl right away. He was a tough kid from Rockaway Beach, New York, with a good set of values and an engaging smile that reached from ear to ear. The second thing I noticed about Earl was that he had hands as thick as pork chops. And I would find out soon enough, he could throw those hands.

Then Harvey showed up, Danny's dad. But after some discussion, Stan had decided he wasn't working with anybody until he had a signed contract. I thought, "Fair enough," but I was there to see what he had to offer. I wasn't signing anything without the Ryan's approval. So I benched myself that first day, and sat and watched the whole training session.

When it was over, I got up and shook everyone's hand and told them I would see them tomorrow. The next day I showed up with all my gear. I wrapped my hands and started working on my own. Eventually Stan drifted over and started giving me some pointers.

Just as I suspected, or should I say *hoped?* After that first week, I got on the horn and called the Ryans. I told them, "We have our guy." Stan and Harvey were a couple of Jewish kids from Rockaway, as well. Their father had them boxing professionally around the days of this country's depression, before they were teens. They could have quite possibly forgotten more about boxing than most people will ever know.

Those two would eventually migrate over to the camp of the legendary and possibly the greatest heavyweight champion of all time: Joe Lewis, the "Brown Bomber." Stan fought and successfully competed back during boxing's heyday, with over sixty professional fights and only a handful of losses. This was the guy I needed. Stan was a boxing teacher—not a trainer—and believe me, there is a difference.

Stan's first priority was to sharpen my already-quick left jab. He wasn't happy with it stinging; he wanted it to punish. As every knowledgeable expert in boxing will tell you, the key to a good fighter is a great jab. Why? Because it sets up every other punch and punch combination that follows. After six weeks in front of a mirror, practicing popping my jab as well as blocking one, which is called a parry, Stan finally set me up with my first Las Vegas fight: Cowboy Mike Creel, whom I outfought and stopped within three rounds with a TKO. *Jackpot!*

Now I felt like I had my feet on solid ground. With my first Vegas fight—and win—under my belt, I needed to fly home to tie up a few loose ends. On the flight back, I sorted out and arranged in my mind how I would like to see this next chapter in my life go. During the last few months I'd lived in West Palm Beach, I had rented a house with my old friend Mark Turner. Or should I say, Mark and his older brother leased a house to live in, and when his brother moved out to live with his girlfriend, I took his spot.

Now back on my old stomping grounds, everyone who knew me approached me wide-eyed and wanted to know about my journey. With reality pending, George and I finally sat down and discussed the future of our Karate school, Southern Pro Karate and Kickboxing. George insisted he didn't want to continue without me, so we decided to shut the doors down, which was an incredibly selfless act on his part. George had invested thousands of dollars so we could open our own Dojo, and now he was willing to flush the whole thing down the toilet for the benefit of me.

One good selfless act deserves another. I had made my old friend Mark Turner an offer I was sure he couldn't refuse. I was convinced Mark had gotten a couple of bad breaks in life, and all he needed was the door for opportunity to open. He was working a job going nowhere as a doorman at night, and attending poker games during the day. He was bouncing at a place called Ricky D's, which was formerly the Cock and Bull, a country and western bar where more than a few fist fights had taken place, and occasionally someone was mortally wounded during combat. One time they actually found a guy shot dead, his corpse left underneath a car in the parking lot. And that's not to mention all the stabbings. Oh, the games people play...

So I made Mark an offer to come out to Vegas, and stay with me until he got on his feet. I reasoned, "If you love gambling, then why not get paid for it? Come out to the Silver State, where you can attend gaming school, and then break into one of the casinos as a dealer, where they'll pay you to gamble with their money. Besides, you can make a fortune in tips." It was a lucrative offer.

Still, Mark was a little apprehensive. I was convinced he needed a fresh start, to get away from all the old influences, and have a change of pace in order get excited about life. So *here I am* on a jet airliner headed to Las Vegas with my good friend Mark Turner in the seat next to me, just excited enough to pour back a few cocktails and ponder his possibilities.

By this time, I had already seen my good friend Skip Walls, now living and working in Los Angeles. Entering my second week in Las Vegas, I had to find a place to stay; I obviously couldn't continue living at the Stardust Hotel. As soon as I got anchored, I made that call to Skip. "You'll never guess where I'm at!" He hadn't a clue—we hadn't talked in months—but he took a couple of stabs at it and then finally I told him, "I'm right next door in Las Vegas." He almost leapt through the phone.

The following weekend, Skip was knocking on my door. He had been to Vegas only once before, so we did the low-dollar tour. The next weekend, I drove over to Burbank, and then we went to Mammoth Mountain and skied for two days. On the way back to LA I told him my plan. When I got to the part about Mark, he just looked at me and grinned.

Skip didn't know Mark real well, but I think he sensed this wasn't the best move on my part. But he smiled and he wished me luck, and told me to call him when Turner got into town.

Skip would end up with what I'll call a more Republican attitude: you get your boat up and afloat and sail on your journey. Once you succeed, you hand-pick the chosen friends you want on your vessel for the rest of the voyage. As for me, I always enjoyed sharing my good fortune with my friends. My instincts told me there was no guarantee that any of us would make it until tomorrow, and there's no right or wrong here, it's simply the choice you make.

Chapter Twenty-three
Vegas Victim number Bazillion

It was early in the Summer of 1979 when Mark and I landed in Las Vegas. The weekend was here, so we hit the ground running. First up, I showed him the apartment I'd rented across from University of Las Vegas (UNLV) and the surrounding area. That evening, I gave him the Rat Pack tour of the Las Vegas strip, hitting all of the high-end hotels. The next day we had Sunday brunch at the Sahara Hotel, and don't ask me how this happened, but by one o'clock we found ourselves in the Sahara pool, frolicking with a bunch of topless tourists. *Ain't Vegas great?*

Now it was down to business. Mark entered gaming school to learn how to deal craps. As for me? After my third fight in Nevada, I had stopped three opponents in a row. TKOs. I was well on my way to becoming one of the popular young fighters of Las Vegas. And why not? I was making a lot of people money. All of the high-rollers that sat ringside would make side bets on the fights, and I was a consistent winner.

By my fifth fight in Las Vegas, and my eighth overall, I was already being recognized around town at the grocery stores, the dry cleaners, or the movie theaters. Why? Because there are no professional sports teams in Las Vegas. So if you were a sports fan living in Vegas at that time, you had two choices: Jerry Tarkanian's Running Rebels at UNLV and/or to learn to love the local fighters like me. At this point the future was so bright I needed shades. I had begun dating what would end up being the love of my life, a beautiful bombshell redhead named Dana Cartwright. Although it was a strange meeting (we met in the back parking lot of the Red Rock movie theater after a show) I was instantly attracted to her. Not just because of her looks—like I said, she was a bombshell—but because of her sense of humor. And she had the same engaging laugh as the movie star Dyan Cannon.

Dana had beautiful legs and a flat stomach that I'd later find out came from studying jazz dancing. And oh yeah, she had a pair of headlights that could blind those who could see, if you know what I mean. In my personal opinion, there are two types of redheads: ones that aren't so attractive, and then there are the ones that men want to put their hands on, and Dana was definitely a "hands on woman." Her hair was more beautiful than the movie star Ann Margret, with a Farrah Fawcett feathered haircut, just like in that famous poster where her hair rained down in three shades of silk.

But by far the coolest thing about Dana was her fun-loving, tomboy streak. She loved to ride horses, mountain climb, snow ski, play softball—you name it, she was up for it. She went on to become a 5-0 tennis player at the age of forty. But back in the day, every time I went to pick her up, she would descend the stairs of her parent's townhome, and bring a new meaning to the word 'breathless.' I used to love to watch her stop traffic when we were out on the town. Unlike a lot of men, I'm not jealous. I expect men to look at my lady; I take it as a compliment. If I find her beautiful, why wouldn't they? Whenever we were out dining, if I got up to go to the men's room, when I returned I had to break hearts. There would be a line of men competing for her attention. Dana was always amazed at my patience, even with guys that persisted with questions like, "What's she doin' with you?" That's where I grinned and said I was lucky. When it came to her, I totally wished I had recognized how lucky I was.

Now we're into December of '79, and I had just stopped another opponent with a TKO. Skip and I had planned to take a week off between Christmas and New Years to take a snow skiing trip up at Lake Tahoe. Now, let us take a moment here to connect the dots. Both of us were from south Florida: this was an undertaking neither one of us had much experience at. I did have one surprise for Skip—or should I say a fly in the ointment—because I had invited our old friend Larry Thomas to escort us into this journey of the little known.

The day Larry was scheduled to arrive just happened to be Dixie's birthday, better known as Dana's mom. I had refined that entire day's activities down to the accuracy of a Swiss watch, which was my mistake. I had been away from South Florida for just long enough to forget that Floridian time doesn't run on a parallel universe with the rest of the country. I show up at McCarran Airport and search high and low for Larry, and can't find him. Just around the time I'm about to give up, I hear a young woman shriek: *Bingo!* I turn and stare in the direction of the squeal, and there he is: Larry Thomas in all his glorious behavior, trying to climb over the rental car counter to get to the young lady standing behind it, which is thoroughly entertaining to the two young women assigned to work the Budget rental car booth.

As I approach, Larry turns and spots me. He's got his red, white and blue ski sunglasses on, which are mirrors, and I know what that means. He grabs me with a robust hug as a hello, and then informs me that the two young ladies behind the counter, who are laughing so hard they're due for an unscheduled restroom break, that unbeknownst to them they are leaving with us.

My first question to Larry was, "Did you bother to ask them? Or inform their employer, the Budget rental car company, of their untimely departure?" At this point he's got one of the young women by her wrist. He looks at me and says, "It's cool man, they wanna go with us," and then turns, and politely starts kissing the young lady on the back of her hand, traveling up her arm to her cheek, which is where she lets out another shriek.

Now with half the airport staring at us, and most of them finding it amusing, I felt the timing for an exit was perfect. I pick Larry up by the waist, and start dragging him away from the counter, promising the girls I'd bring him back when he was a little more coherent, though when that might be, God only knows.

Had I known what the next ten or twelve hours were going to bring, I'd have left Larry right there at the airport. Larry insisted on knowing what the hell I was doing. I told him it was my girlfriend's mother's birthday and we had a party to go to. We had to stay on schedule, which suited Larry just fine, since he had begun the party before he even got on the plane. Larry had rolled one of his famous fatties and smoked it before he even got to the West Palm Beach Airport. Then, after boarding the plane, he'd started ordering cocktails, which he proceeded to down over the next four and a half hours till he landed in Vegas. My suspicion of the mirrored sunglasses had been confirmed. *Oh lucky me!*

Once back at my place, I had to try to straighten Larry up, as well as get us both cleaned up, so we could go pick up both Dana and her mom Dixie, so we could escort them to a high-end conservative restaurant called The Library for the birthday celebration.

Larry and I are running a little late by the time we get over to the town home community gates, but it's all right, because Dana and her mom are also running a little behind. By the end of 1979, the Cartwright's were living in an exclusive high-end, two-story town home community.

When the door opened, Dana greeted me with hugs and kisses. As we stepped inside I introduced her to Larry, and then laughter ensued. As I had mentioned earlier, Larry was quite the charmer, and Dana had quite a sense of humor. We hear a voice from the top of the stairwell. As we turn and look, we see Dixie start her descent from the second floor.

Now Dixie was not your average mother. She relished in the fact that most people thought she was Dana's sister, another stone cold babe. Dixie was a slender, blonde-haired, sapphire blue-eyed beauty. Larry leaps up off the couch and about out of his skin and proceeds to lose his mind, running halfway up the staircase to meet Dixie, yelling, "I owe you buddy."

He's on Dixie like white on rice, yelling something about, "How am I ever gonna repay you, man?" and "*Va va va voom,* this is gonna be a great date!" At that point, Dana retreats to the couch adopting a fetal position, laughing so hard that I begin looking around the room for something to use as a bedpan, for fear she's gonna spring a leak!

Dixie was a young and hip mom, with a great figure, who went to the sports club and played racquetball daily. Thank the fitness gods that she was totally flattered by Larry's attention. Dixie was a stone-cold looker, all right. Oh, and did I forget to mention the fact that she has four kids? Nevertheless I had to break the bad news to Larry; she was Hank's date, not his.

When I told Larry that Dixie was Dana's mom, he couldn't believe it, but then neither could anyone else. He thought she was Dana's sister, just like everyone else did. So now he's requested a drink for the road, you know, to help him get over his shock (or disappointment).

Here I am, chauffeuring Hank's wife and daughter around, in his Lincoln Continental, pulling up to The Library with Larry Thomas in the seat next to me. Dana chimes in with, "There's daddy," with Dixie simultaneously harmonizing, "There's Hank," who was standing right in front of the fancy restaurant, The Library. Poor unsuspecting Henry was quietly smoking his pipe. As we proceed to pass Henry, Larry promptly rolls down his window and yells, "Hey Hank!" Henry's first reaction was to look up, smile and say hello, but with Larry hanging out the window with his tongue wagging like a Weimaraner, clutching a cocktail in his hand, you could see the cheerful expression on Hank's face slowly melt to: *Who the hell is that in my car?*

Of course the ladies in the back are finding this hilarious, but I'm only finding it somewhat amusing. After stealing the apple of his eye, and then meeting Hank, I wasn't exactly on chummy grounds with the man. I was still earning his respect. Hank was a straightforward business man and an entrepreneur, and even though he had a great sense of humor, I would come to find out that off the wall, over the top, off the charts, out of control, slapstick Florida boy shenanigans weren't exactly his cup of tea.

How successful was he, you wonder? Well, he was the guy who started Pizza Hut down the franchise road, and then he opened up a chain of taco stands that would eventually be called Taco Bell. In the 90s, for round three, Hank and a man named Eisinger would merge their two video companies together to create a super store you've probably heard of: Blockbuster.

And at the time, I'm sure it was constantly going through Hank's mind, "Just who was the apple of his eye dating, and why?" The term 'Daddy's Little Girl' doesn't even come close. Dana worshipped her dad, and he was her top priority, until I came along. And it's not for me to say, but she was his favorite. They were more than father and daughter; they were great friends. I'm sure it crossed Hank's mind, like any good father, was I dating her to get close to him and the pot of gold? And I'm sure I wasn't helping matters any by being brash and cocky at times. But hell, in my mind I was on my own road to millions; I didn't need his.

As we entered the elegant restaurant, I had the highest hopes that we had hit bottom on Larry's behavior. *Wishful thinking on my part...* With Hank's family and business associates seated at the table, Larry proceeded to plunge me into the bowels of hell. Although Dana's brother Terry got the biggest kick out of Larry laughing his ass off, everyone else was bewildered.

We hadn't even ordered appetizers when I looked at Dana and saw an S.O.S look, one I had never seen on my lovely redhead's face, which screamed: Daddy's getting upset.

But before I could get up and get to Larry, it was already too late. Larry was already at the table with the vice president of Hank's company. Already down on one knee, kissing the hand of none other than the VP's wife, assuring her of her beauty, and whispering loud enough for everyone to hear, how he'd like to make sweet love to her.

Now I'd like to pause here in Larry's defense, because in all honesty she was enjoying the attention. I walk over and grab Larry by the shoulder and give him a nudge. I tell him we have to go, insisting, "Let's get out of here." And may I pause yet again. I have to take the bullet; I should have predicted his response. He glanced at me briefly, and turned his attention back to the VP's wife saying loudly enough for everyone to hear, "Not yet, I'm on the verge of an orgasm."

Game over. That sent fireworks through the room. Larry always had a few things going for him. One was his looks: women found him attractive. Two was his charm: people could find him irresistible. And three, in case you forgot, his father was a United States Senator, representative of the State of Florida.

His inebriation canceled out the first two, his charm and good looks, and as for number three, we were now next to California and the West Coast. No one had ever heard of—nor did they care—who his father was, which definitely canceled out his trump card.

If I may, let me share a lesson I learned long ago: never mistake your environment for the way the world is, because no matter how good it is, someone's got it better, and no matter how bad it gets, someone's got it worse. And Vegas was a world within itself—one Larry would find out soon enough that he wasn't very familiar with.

So *here I am*, on the I-15 headed north towards Utah, with Larry on the verge of blacking out. I had told him we were headed to a nightclub, but in reality we were taking a wild spin through the desert and I was hoping he would pass out. I almost had him when his head bobbed forward for the fourth time and he asked, "Are we almost there yet?" I said yes, and he reached down and pulled something out of his pocket. It was a black pill. This sent a shockwave through me, as if someone had hit my funny bone. I desperately made a grab for it, but Larry popped it in his mouth and started laughing. Even though I'm sure I didn't wanna know, I had to ask, "What was it?"

This made him laugh even harder. It was a 'Black Beauty;' a diet pill that was an upper. Now with Larry amped up and wide awake, I had

252

no choice. I turned the car around and headed back towards my house. Not far from my home was a little Mexican cantina on Paradise Boulevard. Although Larry was not in the mood to eat, I was hungry. Our dinner had been abruptly interrupted. While I sat down to eat, Larry headed to the bar to try to work the crowd. Fifteen minutes later he came storming right back with a woman in tow. Once we were introduced, he said her and her friends were going to a popular nightspot called the Brewery, right on Paradise. Then he wanted to know if we could meet them there. I said yes, but I warned him we couldn't be out all night, because we had to meet Skip at the airport at 7:00 a.m. When we pulled up in front of the Brewery, I warned Larry once again, he had to be at McCarran Airport at seven to meet Skip.

He jumped out and said to give him five minutes. He wanted to run in and collect her, because she said she wanted to leave with us. Big mistake on my part. I wouldn't see Larry again for close to seven hours. After waiting twenty minutes, I decided to park the car and go into the club, looking for Larry.

I wandered through this Las Vegas hotspot aimlessly looking for my friend but to no avail. I talked to every bartender, doorman, and restroom attendant, but no one had seen Prince Charming. Now with the clock approaching 3 am, I threw in the proverbial towel. I went home and set my clock for 5:30 and got in bed. The thought was, if Larry didn't miraculously appear at my front door by 6 o'clock, I was going to go to McCarran Airport, meet my friend Skip, fly to Lake Tahoe, enjoy our skiing trip, and not bother to mention the exploits of Prince Charming to my good buddy until our flight back.

In spite of the fact that I was more than aggravated, knowing Larry as well as I did, I should have expected it. With my alarm clock set, I got a restless night's sleep, hoping miraculously that Larry would remember my phone number, or show up at my front door.

The alarm went off. I hopped in the shower thinking, "If Larry's not available by 6am, I'm going to the airport without him." I had just gotten dressed when the phone rang. Hallelujah! Praise Allah! It's Prince Charming, but I could tell by his voice his state of coherence was somewhere between drunkenness and hangover. Added to that, he was more than pissed off. I tried to follow his conversation, which was scattered and scrambled. I remember thinking in the back of my mind, "How in the hell can you be pissed off, when it's you that's wreaked havoc on our schedule?" and then through all his babbling, he got his message across: he had been robbed. *Welcome to Sin City, naive Prince.*

The good news? (If there can be any good news in this situation…) Larry had tracked down the girl of his dreams, the girl he had been looking for. He ended up at her hotel room, and my guess is that he sealed the deal. But this is where our nightmare begins; she was sharing the room with some friends. When Larry woke up from his drunken stupor, they were all gone, and so was his money. *Wake up, oh sweet Prince!*

This is one of those situations you have to prioritize your actions. First pressing issue, where was Larry located? Since he had never been to Vegas before, it was anyone's guess. I had him describe the surrounding area, and what he was looking at. In less than 30 seconds, *bingo.* I worked out he was less than 100 yards from the Mexican cantina I had dined at, and where he had met his one-time alimony recipient dream girl. Thank God he wasn't that far away.

I lived right across from the University, on Maryland Parkway, a block north of the Tropicana. I took Harmon, which cuts across the UNLV campus to Paradise. When I got to the light at Paradise, I looked to my left and across the street and *shazam!* There was Las Vegas victim number bazillion.

When I got Larry in the car, his shorts were torque! He was more pissed off than a bucking bull at the rodeo finals. He now wanted to search every hotel and motel in the Las Vegas area, which would present a hurdle you couldn't get over if you had 24 hours, and we only had 45 minutes before our rendezvous at the airport with Skip.

We went back to my apartment, and Larry got on the telephone. He was convinced he could track down his Florence Nightingale and her merry band of bandits. I tried explaining to him vastness of overnight lodging in Clark County. I told him we didn't have time to even call every major hotel, let alone motel in Las Vegas. It got to the point where I told him to get in my car, or he could stay here for my Ski Vacation.

We got to McCarran Airport just in time to greet Skip getting off his plane from Burbank. Skip was bowled over that Larry was in Las Vegas, and now the three Florida Amigos were gonna make their mark skiing in Lake Tahoe.

I looked Skip dead in the eye, and said, "If you only knew! You don't have a clue!" and went on to regale him with the previous night's adventures. As we stood in the boarding line to get on the plane, I looked behind Larry to see Mac Davis walk up. You remember Mac Davis, the country western star who had his own television show, as well as a film career that included one of my favorite movies, "North Dallas Forty" with Nick Nolte? Not to mention writing a songbook full of hits, including one of Elvis' biggest, "In the Ghetto." He had a traveling companion with him, a young man about twelve or fourteen years old. We ended up in conversation with them, and Mac turned out to be a pretty decent guy. He invited us to the show he was performing in Lake Tahoe, but we never made it.

Now on the plane, Larry gets up and goes to the restroom. I look at my pal Skip and say, "It's your turn." He looked at me, puzzled. "It's your turn to babysit," I insisted. In all fairness, Larry was a blast to be around, and he was pretty handy if you didn't have to babysit him. Skip was always pretty organized, and I had a structured life, so getting a dose of Larry Thomas after not seeing him for close to a year? It could throw you a little off balance.

We land in Reno. We grab a rental car and, just as the sun starts setting, it starts to snow. So *here we are*, on a dark twisted mountain road with it snowing just shy of a blizzard. We decide to pull over and put on chains, and Larry comes alive. I haven't seen him this excited since, well, since Dixie started coming down the staircase.

Larry's not only got it under control, he's come to our rescue. He leaps out into the snowstorm and puts the chains on the tires, while Skip and I sit in the cozy car with the heater on and let him. Pretty soon he's affixed those chains to all four tires by himself. How can you not love a guy who's got a bizarre sense of humor, and loves a challenge?

All that aside, after everything I'd been put through in the last twelve hours, and not being sure if I'd be welcomed into my girlfriend's home when I got back, I thought it'd only be fitting that I sit in the warm lap of luxury. I deserve this.

Now we've completely blown our ETA, and we're moving at less than half of the posted speed limit, but we found a liquor store, which is essential. We stop and pick up a couple of cases of beer; this could be a long trip. We finally spot our hotel, nestled in between two enormous snowdrifts. We pull into the parking lot and unload our stuff. By the time we had unpacked our things, we made a decision to stay in. It was late and none of the restaurants in town appeared open. By now it was snowing hard.

Besides, we wanted to get up at dawn and get the jump on all the other skiers. Next thing you know, Larry had stuffed his ski parka full

255

of beer bottles and started heading for the door. Skip asked, "Where ya goin'?" His answer? "To find some people and party!"

This was so ridiculous it sounded ludicrous. Skip asked him where he thought he was gonna find some people. Larry declared he was going to go out and stand at the roadside, and wait for some good looking chicks to come by. We found this amusing but tried to talk him out of it. "In the middle of a snowstorm? Like that's gonna happen!" But off Larry went, right out the door!

Skip and I had barely got in our beds and got warmed up, when the door flew open and the snow came flying in with Larry. He made a beeline for the beer cooler and started rifling through it, searching for more beer. When Skip asked what he was doing, he replied that four hot chicks in a customized pickup truck had stopped to pick him up, and now he was going off to party. Then Larry spun around enthusiastically and left the room, slamming the door. Skip and I laid in the dark silence for maybe thirty seconds when Skip exploded out of bed, saying he had to know if it was true.

He went over to the window and pulled the shades back, and almost immediately fell to the floor in what would parallel an epileptic fit. I bolted out of bed to go to his aid, when I got there he kept pointing at the window. He couldn't even catch his breath he was laughing so hard. I opened the blinds just in time to see a customized pickup truck with four ladies in it, and Larry sitting between them, grinning at me through the back window as the truck drove away. And with that, I was struck with epilepsy myself, and joined Skip on the floor for the finale of the floundering fish act.

So much for hitting the sack early… That kept us up for the next few hours, we were laughing so long and hard. When we finally did fall asleep it was only to hear Larry come stumbling in a short time later. Just as Larry settled, the alarm went off, and Skip and I both bounced out of bed. We had taken our showers, and we were getting ready for a fun-filled downhill day. Throughout our preparation, I kept trying to wake Larry and get him on his feet. We were in the car with it started and warmed up when Larry comes stumbling out the door. I guess the thought of us skiing all day without him got the better of him.

We skied all morning and had a blast, if you could call what we were doing skiing. Then we went down to the lodge at 12:30 p.m. for lunch. At 1:30, Skip and I left the lodge to go up to the chairlift, while Larry stayed in the lodge. Although Larry stayed ahead of his hangover that morning by keeping beer stuffed in his ski parka, beer could only prevent the inevitable for so long…

Skip and I had a great day, but now it was 5:30 p.m. and we were back at the lodge, searching for none other than who else: Larry. The last we had seen Larry was at lunchtime. As we'd headed back out to the slopes and looked back, we were just in time to see him nuzzled between two young ladies, raising a toast to us. Now he was nowhere to be seen. We searched the area high and low, including the ski lodge locker rooms. Finally, out of frustration, we rolled outside onto the deck, and there was Larry, "P and P"; passed out on a picnic table.

By day two, Larry's batteries had been recharged, and everything clicked. For the rest of the trip, we all had a great time. We'd ski all day and go to dinner, then find a resort with night skiing. Skip and I were stuck picking up Larry's hotel and ski tab. In the name of fairness, although somewhat lopsided, every time a round of drinks was ordered, Larry would hold out the same twenty-dollar bill, proclaiming it to be his last.

Now this was the end of Christmas of '79, with the new year of '80 upon us. When we got back to Vegas I gave my two friends a hug goodbye, and we discussed when we might get back together again. And here we are at the beginning of 2013, and neither Skip nor I have seen Larry since… Though neither one of us expected to be paid back, it would have been nice. And though I cannot speak for Skip, Larry you were worth the price. To me it was a bargain admission. You couldn't find a more entertaining, nor worthy one-man show than hanging out with Larry.

Mark Herman. Dojo South, 1973.

Carl Stone. Dojo South, 1973.

Mark Herman in action. Dojo South, 1973.

Paul Anselmo, Carl Stone, Mark Herman.

Dojo trophies.

LeeAnne and Ronda.   *Me and Ronda with trophies.*

*Leon Nubin and me
Dojo North.*

*Me with Gary
Sproul Karate
Demonstration.*

*Me with George McLease
Southern Pro Karate and Kickboxing.*

Me and Jay Collins at Dubois Park, Jupiter Beach, FL.

Ronda (dark hair) and sparring partner at Singer Island.

Gram in Boynton Beach, FL.

Dana Cartwright in Las Vegas.

My brother Frank and me.

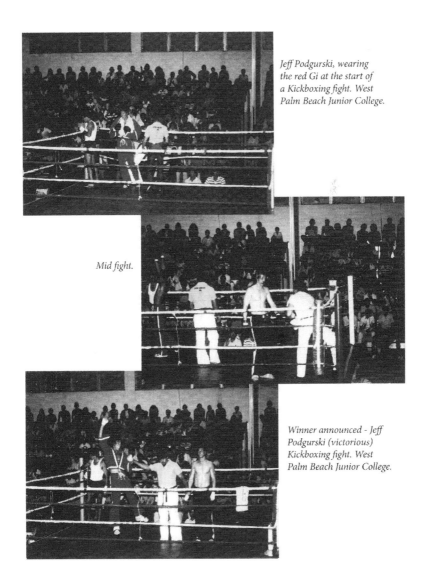

Jeff Podgurski, wearing the red Gi at the start of a Kickboxing fight. West Palm Beach Junior College.

Mid fight.

Winner announced - Jeff Podgurski (victorious) Kickboxing fight. West Palm Beach Junior College.

Me, my niece and Mark
Turner, Florida 1978.

Mark Turner, St Nick and me,
Las Vegas 1979.

George McLease 1977.

Me with The Great Lorenzo (Larry) Thomas, shark fishing. Jupiter Island, FL.

Leon Nubin over the Rio Grande River.

Ronda, at her parent's home, Singer Island, FL.

Mark Turner and me.

265

p. 45 "The Ring" magazine – profile on Jeff Podgurski.

Article about me in "Official Karate" magazine – first page.

Fight program - Leonard vs. Marcotte, with Jeff Podgurski on the bill (lower right).

Fan letter from radio personality Mike Lopez.

PART THREE

Chapter Twenty-four
Substitutes and Nightmares

Eventually I found myself preparing for my biggest boxing opponent. Not by name, but by size; 6'6, 258 lbs. Once we entered the ring, we were introduced by name and our given weight, and the crowd went, "Woooo." I don't think they gave me a snowball's chance in hell of surviving. *Again!*

Here I am, 6 foot 3 and tipping the scale at 195 pounds. My opponent? He's one Big Mac and an order of chili-cheese fries away from 260. The interesting thing about boxing in the heavyweight division is that there is no weight limit. Unlike the other divisions, once you cross that line to heavyweight, there's simply no maximum limit to how big your opponent might be.

When the bell rang, I came out moving to my right. My opponent threw a left jab, which I parried, and then followed it up with a right hand, which hit me squarely in the chest. The classic one-two punch. Except the number two punch, which caught me in my chest, lifted me off my feet and knocked me back a couple.

Again the crowd "Woood," and, just like in the Dave Rupert fight, it flashed through my mind: don't get hit with another solid punch. So I returned the favor, throwing a classic one-two punch myself, except my right hand caught my opponent squarely in the head, which enraged him. That's when he charged me. We ended up in a clinch just off the center of the ring. We wrestled for a moment, and then we both sensed the referee stepping forward. I started to relax my hold on my opponent, which caused him to release me completely.

I instantly jumped back and fired a three-punch combination that hit him right on the button. *Timber!* He started to fall like Washington's cherry tree. I jumped out of the way, and when he collided with the canvas with an almighty crash, the referee and I both bounced up in the air.

My dearest friend, and cornerman in life, George McClease had flown in for the fight. He was sitting ringside, three rows back, with my girlfriend Dana, who had him by the arm in a vice grip that cut the circulation from his hand. While the referee was introducing my opponent and me to the crowd, she had that death grip on his arm. He kept trying to reassure her everything would be all right; he had seen me slay a giant once before. After the fight he jokingly informed me I had saved his arm from certain amputation. He didn't know how much longer he could stand the tourniquet that Dana had put on him.

But back in the ring I was ordered to go to a neutral corner. They started the count, and by the count of six he was back on his feet and bouncing mad. I instinctively knew that he was going to charge me, and charge me he did. When the referee waved for us to continue, I took three steps from the neutral corner, and planted my feet like a matador waiting for the bull. And he didn't disappoint me. He came right for me, raging like a wild buffalo with his nostrils flaring.

Just as he got to me, I deftly hopped to my right and threw a left hook that bounced off his forehead, snapping his head back, which sent him into the ropes chest first. As he bounced off the ropes, he started turning to his left to try and spot me, and he didn't have far to look. I opened up on him with a five-punch combination that sent him home for the night.

The crowd's eruption was deafening, only to be matched by my relief. And then they began chanting my name, which in case you can't guess, will do more than a little for your psyche.

It was a Wednesday night, the Strip's 'Fight of the Week' at the Silver Slipper. My other cornerman in life, Skip Walls, had flown in from L.A., along with my good buddy Mike Brucker to see the fight.

We had met Mike through Dana; he had dated her best friend in high school, Regina Medina. And though they were too young for the relationship to work out, he was now one of Hank's favorite gambling buddies. After the match, we all went out to eat and to celebrate, but it was a short celebration by Vegas standards. We had to get Skip and Mike back to McCarran Airport by midnight for the last Southwestern flight out to Burbank.

Thursday morning came, and since George had never been west of Texas, I decided to take the weekend off. By midday on Friday, we found ourselves on a plane to Los Angeles to hang out with Skip and Mike for the weekend. Three Florida swamp rats and a Bakersfield hick in L.A. A great time.

We did Malibu, Magic Mountain and the late Hollywood nightclub scene. It was a quickie; I had to have George back to Las Vegas and Mc-Carran Airport for a late night Sunday flight back to West Palm Beach.

But no one felt cheated, especially my buddy George. When you hang out with my good pal Skip, you find yourself doing three days' worth of activity in one. In those days, I had more than enough energy to keep up with him. But poor George, by the time he got back to WPB, I'm sure he needed a vacation from his vacation.

And me, I'm back to waking up at 4:00 a.m. to do roadwork. I'm now training for what would turn out to be the most bizarre fight I ever had in the ring. The boxer I was scheduled to fight had to pull out last minute because of an injury. The emergency substitute turned out to be Keith Moore from Long Beach, California.

I was scheduled to be the fourth fight up, but due to the fact that we had to find a last minute substitute, we had to wait for Moore to fly in from Long Beach, which made us the main event. Oh, what an event it mainly became, undoubtedly the biggest spectacle the Silver Slipper had ever seen.

Sometimes fate, and/or nature, is undoubtedly the best barometer for what could have happened. My personal routine was to get to the fight venue a little bit early. No matter how big or small the venue was, I always liked getting there before the crowd so I could climb in the ring and move around, to get the sense of it, to feel if it was a fast or slow ring. A fast ring would be minimal padding, with the canvas stretched tightly across it; my personal favorite. A slow ring would be thicker padding, with the canvas merely draped across it and tied down and, in my opinion, more suitable for professional wrestling.

I'll try and break it down. Picture the difference between running on a racetrack, and running on beach sand. I think now you get my drift. Quietly sitting in my locker room as the second fight begins, the promoter Frank comes in and apologizes; he's not sure that Moore's gonna make it in time. By the end of the fourth fight of the night, Moore is there. How do I know? I can hear him beating up the lockers. I can hear him yelling, "I'm going to kill him."

270

Then Moore proceeded down the hall, mutilating the lockers along the way, screaming, "Where is he? I'm going to kill him!" As he passed by my door he yelled, "You're going to the hospital. I'm going to kill you!" Then he continued to molest the lockers. Stan looks over at me, and I just grin. Lockers don't punch back. In my mind I'm thinking, he's scared. He's trying to psych himself up, as well as psych me out. The average person looks at boxing as a brutal sport, and it is, but as I've said before, it's also a chess game.

Move number one: Moore is trying to get into my head. That just amuses me because obviously I'm already in *his*. Also, what he doesn't know is that I already had the privilege of seeing Mr. Moore fight at another event. I'd witnessed what he was capable of. His opponent then was slightly more than a light heavyweight, at 188 lbs. Moore, however, was tipping the scales at 230 pounds plus.

When they stepped into my locker room with the pre-call to the ring, I stepped out into the hall and walked past his locker room door. As soon as he saw me, he started pushing his cornermen around yelling, "Let me at him!" then he slammed his boxing gloves into the locker room door, and then yelled again, *"I'm going to kill you!"*

I never flinched, nor did I even look his way. While they were announcing us in the ring, Moore was busy punching out the turnbuckles in his corner. Then he turned to stare at me, began to pound his gloves together and, like a broken LP, once again reassured me he was going to kill me. *Yeah, yeah—I heard you the first time.*

Once the referee is through with his final instructions, it's customary for the two fighters to touch gloves. Mr. Moore, however, had decided that shoving me in my chest was more appropriate. Joey Curtis, it turns out, was our referee, and he warned Moore right then and there to knock off the roughhousing. He would find out soon enough that it was falling on deaf ears.

So *here I am*, moments before the bell sounds for round one, and what Mr. Moore is convinced will be my public execution. Facing my corner with my back to the ring, Stan rinses off my mouthpiece and plants it firmly in my mouth. And then in a low baritone whisper he says, "Remember what he did last time he was here."

And *ding!* Round one is on. I take three steps from my corner and firmly plant my feet. And just as I had witnessed in one of his previous fights, here comes Mr. Moore raging like a charging rhino. Luckily, a few months before, I had witnessed Mr. Moore on the winning end of what could possibly have been the quickest knockout in heavy-weight history. When the bell rang for round one, Moore took off in a sprint across the ring, and caught a young up and coming heavyweight named Bowman as he turned around, clocking him with one punch.

And in case you hadn't guessed, my previous experience with charging animals was to step to my right with my right foot, pivot, and immediately throw my left hook. And I'm sure Mr. Moore was thinking; 'When you find something that works, stick with it.' But put yourself in my shoes for a second; you had to have nerves of steel to stand in front of the raging rhino up until the last possible moment.

Just as Moore gets to me, I hop to my right and throw that left hook. Now if I'd just dropped my punch 3-5 inches, I'd have hit him right on the button and we'd have all gone home, because believe it or not, there's no overtime in boxing. But that's not what happened. Once again I threw my punch, and it caught my opponent high on his forehead, snapping his head back, and dazing him—but only for a heartbeat. Now imagine this; I'd pissed him off. I'd not only hit him and hurt him, but I'd made him look like a buffoon. So he charges me with flailing punches that I somehow avoid getting hit with, as he bulls me into the rope.

Now Joey Curtis, the referee, tries to step in and break us up, but Moore is having none of it. He keeps throwing punches at my head as he struggles to grab me by my neck so he can prop my head up. You know, so he can get a clean shot at my melon? The referee finally gets between us and breaks us up, and he warns Moore once again to knock off the roughhousing. The ref walks us to the center of the ring and waves for us to continue. I snap out a couple of jabs, one of which catches him, and incites another charge, back over to the ropes.

This time I don't wait for the ref. I step to my right and spin him off. Then I hit him with a two-punch combination, and then I run him into the ropes, just to prove to him that he can't out-muscle me. Now he's got his right arm around the back of my neck, pulling my head down.

The audience responded favorably with a "Woo" when I hit him with a two-punch combination, but he's shaking his head no, like it didn't hurt him. In my mind I'm biding my time. I'm betting that as soon as the referee breaks this up, the next one's gonna do some damage. The ref breaks us up. I step back a few feet.

As soon as the ref clears, I pump a fake jab at him. He goes for it. Then I throw a three-punch combination—two out of three find their targets. I find him with the left jab, and I crack him with the right hand. I throw the left hook but it misses. He falls back into the ropes and gets away from the punch. I slide forward with another jab to find my target, and he grabs me. Now we're in a clinch for a moment. Then our ref finally intervenes and breaks us up. He walks us to the center of the ring and tells us, that's it, no more roughhousing. But again, that instruction falls on deaf ears. Ref Curtis waves for us to continue...

Moore charges me. I tag him with a left jab on the way in, but now he's got my back pinned against the rope. This is rapidly deteriorating into a street fight. He's got his left hand wrapped around my neck and digging his left thumb into my throat. He's trying to waylay me with rapid punches off his right hand, but I turn my left shoulder into him, and tuck my chin in behind it, so all he succeeds in doing is punching me in the shoulder and the top of my head, which is doing no real damage, but aggravating the hell out of me.

When the ref tries to wiggle between us like a slice of Swiss cheese on a heavyweight sandwich—and by the way our ref is only 5' 9" and tipping the scales between 160 and 170—Moore reverts back to dirty tactics number 101, and proceeds to give me a facial with the laces on his glove. When the ref finally squeezes between us and separates us, he's not mad, he's pissed off, bellowing at us to "Knock off the rough-housing!" but Moore is desperate. I can feel the wind leaving his body. He's in no shape to go any distance.

At this point I'm feeling the relaxation that only the confidence in your skills and your conditioning can give you. My senses are telling me: get him into round three, and he'll fall on his face by himself. I won't even have to throw a punch.

When the ref says continue, Moore charges me like a linebacker, only this time I end up with my back in my own corner. He's trying to get a hold of my throat again with his left hand, so he can hold my head still enough to throw his right. I pop him with an uppercut, and he falls forward with his head resting on my chest.

The referee moves in to break it up, and Moore reverts back to football practice. He's got the rope on either side of me, and now he's ramming his shoulder into my solar plexus and chest repeatedly like a battering ram, trying to knock the wind out of me.

Poor Joey, as he tried to break us up he weaseled in between us, so now Moore is using him as part of his battering ram system. About the second time he rammed the ref into me, I had gotten my right hand free and threw it over the top, which hit Moore in the head. It wasn't a particularly hard punch; it just felt good to strike back. Now Joey's facing Moore. Pushing him back by the chest he tells him to knock it off. I start to move forward out of the corner, that's when Moore throws a right hand over top of the ref and tries to sucker punch me.

I shrug it off my left shoulder, and it glances off the top of my head. He tries to follow up with a left that completely misses me, and then continues on with a right that hits the ref. *That's it!* Joey's had enough: He calls the fight. It's a TKO; I win by disqualification.

Joey somehow wrestled Moore all the way back to his corner, and explained to his cornermen, "That's it. He's disqualified. He's not fighting by the rules." Moore's guys jump up on the ring apron intending to argue. Stan, being the sharp old boy that he is, cuts my gloves off. Now there can be no change to the decision.

The crowd has gone crazy. Moore is pacing back and forth on his side of the ring, livid. I glance across the ring; Moore's eyes meet mine. I shrug, as if to say, "Play by the rules," He starts slamming his gloves together, growling he'll kill me. So I blow him a kiss.

Moore starts towards me, I start dancing around like Muhammad Ali. The ref, Joey Curtis, is still arguing with Moore's cornermen, so he doesn't see this. I wave Moore on. In my mind, the boxing match is over; this is now a street fight. The crowd has gone ballistic, and only a handful of spectators in the arena are aware that I have a second-degree black belt. It's anything goes when the whistle blows. I badly want Moore to charge me one more time, because what he doesn't realize, and most of the crowd couldn't possible know, is that I'm preparing to plant a sidekick square between this idiot's teeth, something he'll never see coming. But his cornermen can tell him all about when he wakes up.

Just as Moore approaches center ring, and as I set up my timing to kick his teeth out, our ref, Joey Curtis, jumps in front of him again, intercepting potential mayhem. As Joey shoves him backwards, he orders Moore's cornermen to take him back to his side of the ring. Joey then turns and jumps in my face, screaming, *"This fight is over!"* Fine with me; I'm the winner. But somebody needs to break the news to the moronic malicious Moore.

At this point the crowd is just shy of chaotic. I'm told to stay put in the ring, as they have to separate our exits. They're taking Moore out first, and what ensues is something you might expect on a WWF

SmackDown event. Moore steps through the ropes, and takes the three steps down. But before his foot can hit the main arena floor, the crowd begins to bombard him with anything they can get their hands on. Now he's taking a soda pop and beer bath with a hot dog mustard relish shower. Then it started raining Raisinets. It got so bad that when the angry crowd started throwing chairs, casino security had to surround Moore just to get him back to his locker room in one piece.

By the time I exited the ring, the crowd's mood had turned from fury to celebratory. Now, thank God, they were cheering me on! When I got to the corridor that lead me to my locker room, there was a flood of security guards. They were blocking Moore's door in the hall that I would be passing through. As I passed by Moore's door, I glanced in. The moronic malicious meathead Moore was still having a meltdown. Even with his cornermen restraining him, he was still screaming he was going to kill me. Yeah yeah, Moore like I said, I heard it all before.

Security personnel had to sneak Moore down to the first floor, by way of the kitchen elevator. This put them out in the kitchen, and gave security a perfect exit out the back of the casino. Which I'm sure, given that crowd, prolonged Mr. Moore's health and welfare.

Now there's no question in my mind you'd have to question the sanity of anyone who got in a street fight with Keith Moore. But given his below-average boxing skills, he relied on a big punch and a Pearl Harbor sneak attack. But you have to have a bigger arsenal than that if you're going to take professional boxing seriously. When I look back, I personally think he threw the fight because he knew the odds were certain he'd lose. But my gut feeling says Keith and his band of buddies had a great laugh over cocktails on his flight back to Long Beach.

What a fiasco! A great night, a fun story. A couple of fights later I find myself facing yet another substitute. *Can you see the pattern here?* I had dinner with Harvey, Danny's dad. Something I frequently did before my fights. Stan had me doing something that was totally against my instincts; he insisted on me eating red meat a couple of hours before each of my fights.

It was between four and five in the afternoon, on the day of the fight, and normally I'd show up at the arena between 6:30 and 7 p.m. Even though I'm scheduled to fight as one of the main events, this time I showed up a little earlier as usual.

I never saw my opponent when he arrived at the venue, but Stan and Harvey had gotten a glimpse of him. They came into my locker room and told me it should be a short night: he was still sporting what was left of a black eye.

The arena was sold out, as usual. Through the locker room walls I could hear the muffled sounds of the preliminary bouts and the cheering crowd. As always, it was customary for Stan and Harvey to bet on preliminary bouts, so Harvey had gone out into the arena to keep an eye on their investment.

Now normally, after I was done warming up, I would go to the men's room to relieve myself before they put the boxing gloves on me, as I can't hold Mr. Happy after I'm gloved-up. But on this night, Harvey comes busting through my locker room doors in a state of hysteria. The fight before mine had ended in two rounds, and I quote Harvey here, "He knocked him dead!"

Forgive me if I'm pointing out the obvious, but this is not the type of excitement you want in a professional athlete's locker room, prior to them going out to compete in their given arena. Nor is it the preferred terminology you want to use in front of your boxer prior to him coming out to fight.

So *here I am*, having my boxing gloves taped onto me before I had the proper time to warm up, and oh yeah, I never got a chance to go shake my snake, if you follow me. Harvey Steichen, my opponent, was somewhat stockier than me, over 200 pounds. My weight? As always 195, although they would inflate it during the announcement to make the contest appear more even.

Steichen stood at around 6'1", so at 6 foot 3, I did have a height advantage and I wished I had used it. Being completely focused on the boxing skills that Stan was trying to teach me, I had neglected two of my greatest assets; my legs. Stan had trained me into a fighter who constantly moved forward and pressured his opponent, something that works much better within the parameters of the smaller weight divisions.

Being on the lighter end of the scale when I entered the heavyweight kickboxing arena, my greatest defensive skill was movement. Again: you can't hurt what you can't hit. And so I brought that instinctive skill to the boxing arena for my first handful of fights. When I chose to fight defensively, and didn't want you to catch me, you'd have a hard time hitting me in my ass.

By the second round I had regretted not making that pit stop in the men's room. My back teeth were floating, and things were not going

276

well. Every muscle in my body was burning, as if depleted of oxygen, and my boxing gloves felt like cinder blocks taped to my hands. Plus, Stan had me so amped up with enthusiastic encouragement, such as— and I quote here—"Knocking this bum out!" I was pushing forward and getting hit with punches that should have never landed. By the last few rounds, I could sense the ringside crowd, which mainly consisted of gamblers, was not being their usual support group. *Ah, how quickly things change when money's involved...*

Harvey Steichen got the favorable decision, and I was more than disgusted by my loss, but I had a more urgent issue pressing me at that moment. I needed to get out of the ring and into the men's room, *fast!* Now here are some words of wisdom for you: when you need to urinate, don't procrastinate for ten rounds while someone beats you in your kidney and bladder. Unless, of course, you enjoy the embarrassment of leaving a liquid trail for people to retrace your steps back to your locker room. Yes, there's nothing quite like the humiliation of losing an athletic competition, unless you top it off by going one step forwards towards degradation by pissing yourself. Which would leave one to ponder... *Why, Polish? Why me?*

Steichen had won fair and square, so God bless him. I had hoped to fight him once again but on that particular night, I learned a lesson. After a few days of analyzing the fight in my head, I got on the telephone with my friend Skip. I was explaining to him the fatigue, how exhausted I felt through the entire fight, and how my muscles were burning, which made absolutely no sense given how hard I had trained for that bout.

In passing conversation with my friend, I had made mention I was thinking of seeing a nutritionist. Skip agreed. After diligently listening, he was convinced I was depleted of something.

A few days later the phone rang. It was Skip. He'd tracked down a nutritionist in Marina Del Rey, a Doctor Rob Krakovitz, who had a string of Olympic medalists under his supervision. And my buddy Skip, being one who always moved forward, had already gone out on a limb and scheduled an appointment for me. I also later met one of Doctor Rob's cohorts, Olympic medalist Russ Hodge. Russ was a track and field competitor who had won the U.S. a bronze medal in the shot put in the 1968 Olympics in Mexico City.

Russ and Doctor Rob were both excited about working with a boxer. All other athletes compete in one of two states: aerobic, or anaerobic conditioning. In the fighting sciences, however, you have to be able to compete in *both* the aerobic and anaerobic states. As a fighter—whether it be boxing, kickboxing, or the ultimate fighting sports that you see today—you must possess the conditioning and the ability to pace yourself like a long-distance runner, then, at any given moment, you might have to explode with a flurry of punches, kicks, and/or throws, which now puts you on an anaerobic level equal with that of a sprinter. Then on top of that, you must develop speed, flexibility, and power in addition to your aerobic and anaerobic conditioning. All this makes the fighting arts the toughest job in sports. These five things are the key to a fine-tuned, perfectly conditioned human being, and/or athlete.

After five days of testing—which included hair, fingernail, urine, and stool sampling, not to mention a barrage of physical stress tests—it turned out the most detrimental hindrance to my quest was dehydration. Sure, I was lacking a few vitamins, but more critically my mineral pool had been depleted, mainly due to my state of dehydration. Additionally, I was overtrained. I was working out way too hard, and not permitting my body enough time to recuperate. And then, twenty years later, I was diagnosed with a blood imbalance.

Doctor Rob's approach was to strip my body of all impurities, and then rebuild me. Following a two week fast, I was to embark on a very strict and structured diet. I was instructed by Doctor Rob not to compete, nor to accept any new fights, for the next few months, until my body had gained the chance to rebuild and acclimate itself to the new dietary programs.

I left Marina Del Rey for Las Vegas ecstatic and enlightened. This all made perfect sense to me. Coming from a martial arts background, I already had awareness of diet and flexibility training. Not to mention a familiarity with weight resistance program, as well. I had lifted weights for years, until Stan had steered me away from them with his old-school thinking: lifting weights would make you musclebound, tight, and slow.

Next, to complement Doctor Rob's dietary regimen, Russ Hodge put me on a weightlifting and flexibility program to develop my quick twitch muscles. I'm talking about your reflex muscles. This new training program mainly consisted of Olympic and powerlifting exercises. When I showed up at the boxing gym on Monday with my newfound knowledge and a one-gallon jug of water laced with chlorophyll, vitamin C, and honey, Stan went ballistic. He exploded with—and I

278

quote—"Where the fuck did you dig these guys up, who the hell are they?" and "I'm your goddamn trainer!"

I tried to calm Stan down by explaining the whole program to him, but he looked at me as though I was speaking Cantonese. He wasn't buying into any of it, especially the weightlifting part. But it made perfect sense to me. The stronger you are in any athletic competition, the better you're going to perform. Especially those sports with brutal contact like boxing!

Nevertheless, I embarked on my fast, and I lost about eighteen pounds of garbage. Then I started the slow rebuilding of my physique to become a more effective athlete. Over the weeks, Stan and I had been arguing quite a bit. Much like Dundee, he was from the old school, where the managers and trainers controlled everything, and the fighter danced at the end of their strings and unquestioningly followed orders.

If you look at all the ethnic backgrounds in boxing you'll find two things in common: one is economics, in that they don't have any. Two is education: they don't have one. But that doesn't make this Pollack stupid. In fact, I was trying to step outside of the box and bring the latest research and science to one of the world's oldest combat sports.

Knowing Stan as I did, he wasn't going to tolerate me being out of the ring for a couple of months. As soon as I was done fasting, Stan had me back in the gym and training. Instead of giving my body the proper time to acclimate, I'm now prematurely back in the gym, and on the road to destruction.

So *here I am*, stepping into the heavyweight arena again, 10 pounds lighter than my original fighting weight and now at a whopping 184. My opponent weighed in at 205. I ended up winning the fight, with just a few abrasions on my face, but none of them came from punches my opponent had thrown at me. In fact, my opponent was black, and had decided to shave his head four days before our fight. Now, with a four-day stubble on his head acting as a scouring pad, every time we got into a clinch, he tried his best to polish my face—with his head! Nevertheless, I won.

Now I had a fresh win under my belt… and a new facial. Stan had been talking with the Ryans, and they had decided it was time to promote a boxing event in West Palm Beach, my hometown. Now all this might look good on paper, but I doubt it. I wasn't 100% fit; I hadn't bounced back yet. I sensed I was on a runaway freight train and I was riding in the caboose. And if you think about it, the conductor doesn't drive the train…

I left a week earlier than everyone else. My stablemate, Earl Tripp, was also fighting on the card. Stan and Earl followed me a week later. I got there early to do some publicity. I also felt it was a good idea to get reacquainted with the Florida humidity. By the time I stepped off the plane in West Palm Beach, I had no idea I'd be stepping into one of the strangest odysseys of my life.

The first sign of turbulence in paradise came when my sponsor-slash-promoter didn't want the expense of renting me a car. When I protested that I had no way to get to the gym, I ended up with Tommy Ryan's vehicle, Michael Ryan's younger brother. When Thomas handed me the keys, he informed me his air conditioning was out, with no apology. He told me that if it was good enough for him to drive around in the sweltering heat and humidity, then it should be good enough for me.

The next expense-cutting trick was they didn't have a place for me to stay. So now I'm expected to burden my mom, who lives way down in Boynton Beach, or mooch off my friends. Which left me wondering, were they this good to their racehorses, which they left back at their air-conditioned stables? It would seem they also expected me to impose on my friend Steve Shepherd and train at his gym, which I did, but I made sure he got paid.

After switching residences every two days for the next ten, it was finally time to weigh in, and I knew it wasn't going to be good. I could see the veins running through my pectoral muscles as well as through my abdominals, and my biceps had shrunk down to the size of my wrist. For Christ's sake, I made Bruce Lee look fat.

I had weighed myself the night before and I was 177 pounds. I showed up the day of the weighing wearing a jogging suit with rolls of quarters in my pockets to edge me up over the 180 mark. I tipped the scales at a whopping 182 (with an extra pocket full of quarters just for the psych!) My opponent weighed 212, and that was just in his skivvies alone.

Now it's fight night. I show up at the arena a little early, as always, so I can get up in the ring and feel it out. Then I go to my locker room, where I plan to sit and quietly wait. A fighter's locker room can take on the air of death row; it's like you're waiting on an execution, and hopefully it's not yours… Professional fighting is unlike any other sport;

there's only one reason for you to be in the ring, and that is for the dismemberment of a fellow human being. This is not about sinking baskets, scoring touchdowns, or hitting home runs. It's about inflicting punishment, and it's a game as strategic as chess. You must be able to endure as much punishment as your opponent may be able to inflict on you, while you masterfully try to cause more damage to him.

Here at the arena, Stan and Harvey Tischler show up with my good friend and stablemate Earl Tripp, as well as Mike Morton and his heavyweight contender, Larry Frazier. Frazier was scheduled to fight in a preliminary match with local Miami boxer Jeff Sims, who had been knocking everyone dead. But then, so had Frazier.

Mike Morton, one of Stan and Harvey's friends, was a successful Portland, Oregon businessman who owned a stable of fighters, two of which were heavyweight contenders; Larry Frazier, and my pal, Willie "The Cannon" Shannon. Mike's nickname in the press was "Motor-mouth Morton." He would finance all his top prospects to come to Vegas and train with Stan. So in a sense, Larry and Willy were my stablemates as well, although Tripp, "The Cannon," and myself had become great buddies.

As a side note, Willy's brother, Henry Lawrence, played football for the World Champion Raiders. Now *that's* an athletic gene pool. But now with all the players here, the stage has been set for what will become a bizarre, barely noticed pugilistic event.

Now it should almost be obvious, and more than important, that a competitor needs to stay loose and relaxed before an event. George and Skip, plus Steve Shepherd and my brother, all stay out of my locker room so I can focus on the task at hand. Once my hands are taped, Stan and Harvey decide to go out into the arena and watch the preliminary bouts, as well as take their Vegas habits with them, which means… Betting… And big.

So *here I am*, in my locker room, staring at Larry Frazier, halfway across the room, laid out on a table half asleep. I lean back in my chair and try to relax, but the locker room door opens, and who steps in? Right out of a B movie nightmare, it's a guy I haven't seen in a decade, and could have done without seeing in a hundred: Jim Ward, my stepfather.

And some things just don't change. He's red-eyed, and stumble-footed drunk. His next move was just as unbelievable as him being there. He grabbed a chair, set it down in front of me, and then proceeded to try to discuss his divorce from my mother. He starts going through every problem they ever had in their relationship, as if on any normal day I would give a shit. I guess this boob forgot that the last time I saw him we were in a fistfight and I had to dive through my bedroom window. And despite any lack of help from him, I had made it this far. Just as my blood pressure was starting to rise, Stan and Harvey came through the door to prepare Larry Frazier for his fight.

So I bit my tongue and tried to relax. About the time Larry was done warming up, Stan and Harvey were stepping out of the locker room. They looked over at me on their way out. I guess they could sense something was wrong, so Stan asked, "Who the hell is this guy?" I told him, "My stepfather, get him the hell out of here." But the "get him the hell out of here" part came just as they were called to the arena. So they shook it off, and they headed towards the ring.

So *here I am* with this shithead formerly known as my stepfather sitting in front of me, red-eyed drunk and whining about his relationship with my mother, on what could be the biggest night of my life. While I listen to this wino whine and wallow in misery, the locker room door flies open. Frazier had knocked Simms out in one round. Well, kinda-sorta… Larry let go with a punch that cracked Simms and knocked him to his knees, which is where Frazier should have stepped back and waited for the ref's count. But in all this excitement, Larry let go with another punch, which put Simms in fairytale land.

The original call is a knockout in the first round. Larry Frazier's your winner, which left Stan and Harvey ringside, collecting all their money. I had now drifted away from Daddy dearest, and begun my warm-ups by shadowboxing. He was still moaning about something, but at this point I wasn't paying a lot of attention. I was trying to get my head back into the task at hand. Stan and Harvey once again enter the locker room, grinning from ear to ear, with a bankroll big enough to plug the hole in the Titanic. Just as my boxing gloves were tied off and taped on, Stan and Harvey were called back out into the arena, where their presence was requested ringside. While Larry Frazier was celebrating his first round knockout, and Stan and Harvey had been counting their money, and I had been putting up with derelict daddy dearest, the ringside officials out in the arena had decided there had been a foul. Frazier had struck Simms when he was down, so now the call was a 'no contest'; a disqualification. Which meant Stan and Harvey were gonna have to give all that money they had just got done counting back to the people they had bet with.

I'd like to stop here, and forgive me if I'm pointing out the obvious, but I had no idea all of this was going on. I'm back in the locker room trying to stay warm and loose, and shake off all the distractions. So *here I am,* with a celebration and champagne corks popping on one side, and a drunken degenerate downer on the other.

But wait! *It gets better!* The party had just gotten started. Right then the locker room doors comes bursting open, with Stan and Harvey running in and eight guys chasing them. Stan and Harvey, a couple of tough little Jewish guys from Rockaway Beach in New York, had evidently refused to give the money back. They felt they were being cheated because they were on Jeff Sims' home turf. They were old school—streetwise—and they weren't gonna be railroaded. All of the sudden, it's like *déjà vu,* as if we're back at Big Daddy's lounge in the mid 70s. I've got eight or twelve guys brawling right in front of me, so what's a fighter to do? Stand by and watch his trainer, who's approaching 60, and his older brother get annihilated?

So with my boxing gloves still on, I get in the brawl and crack a few guys. Thank God Larry Frazier never hit anyone; he had already taken his boxing gloves off. What I didn't realize until we had wrestled the whole thing to a standstill, was that George, Skip and Mike had all witnessed the whole thing ringside.

There's something to be said for street smarts. They instantly realized what was about to take place. As they rushed to my locker room, they picked up security along the way.

Now at this point you might wonder, why would your trainer drag all this chaos into your locker room, and dump it in your lap just moments before you are ready to enter the ring?

I know it flashed through my mind, but I really didn't have time to think about it. But more than likely Stan and Harvey thought the security that was afforded fighters in Las Vegas around their doors to protect them from the public applied here. I'm sure they felt they could exit the arena through the locker room doors, and security would handle matters from there.

You know those days when you ask, what the hell else can happen? And then you realize you shouldn't have asked? Right after everything had calmed down, and moments before we were called to the ring, Stan turned to talk to me, but I couldn't hear a thing he was saying.

I had just gotten a whiff, and my eyes immediately jumped to Skip and Mike. Skip mouthed to me, "Stan's drunk," with Mike nodding in confirmation. And right then we were called to the ring, so we made our entrance into the arena of the West Palm Beach Auditorium.

After being announced, and moments after the bell rang for round one, I found myself stepping back away from my opponent. I had caught him with a punch as he was moving back, and he stumbled and fell into the ring ropes. Now with his ass sitting on the bottom rope, and his arms tied up with the middle one, I had decided to step back, fearing after what had taken place in the Frazier-Simms fight that the crowd might suspect the bouts were fixed.

Rule number one in boxing: when you get a fighter in trouble, you take him out. Let the chips fall where they may. I would come to regret my clemency soon enough. Technically, since his ass never hit the canvas, the referee had him stand up for an eight count. He wiped his gloves off, checked his eyes, and instructed us to continue.

He started to circle the ring for a moment, and all of a sudden I was the most relaxed, peaceful, and calm I had ever been. I wanted to stay like this forever, then all of a sudden I heard it: five... six... seven... *Holy shit!* I'm in a fight, GET UP!

I sprang to my feet somewhere between eight and nine, but the referee was already calling the fight, waving his hands in the air. The fight was over. I grabbed his arms and pulled them down. I argued, "You can't stop this fight, I'm up!" At that point, my opponent was already sitting at his stool, and his cornermen were cutting his gloves off. As I had mentioned before, this was a wise old trick.

By the time I got back to my locker room, it was as chaotic as I left it. George and Skip were more than pissed off, but they wouldn't let it show. Like my brother and other close friends, they were more concerned with my personal wellbeing.

The press was pushing through my locker room door; they wanted an interview and pictures. Stan and Harvey were arguing with boxing officials on whether the fight should have been stopped or not. For the first time in my life, my mother, my grandmother, and my brother attend one of my fights, and I suffer a knockout.

Years earlier, my mother and grandmother were planning to attend my first kickboxing bout down in Miami. And all of a sudden, two weeks before the bout, my brother had a change of heart and decided to marry his girlfriend, who was pregnant with their first and only child, on that very same day. *Can you say upstaged?*

284

But now, like everyone else, they're outside my locker room door trying to squeeze their way in. So I send my pal Skip out with a message to my mother that I'm all right. Luckily an hour later, everything had calmed down, and I'm sitting in the locker room all alone. Now for the first time since my arrival I have peace and quiet! But oh how lonely life can be...

So *here I am*, sitting by myself with a flood of emotions going through my mind, and a stinging and burning sensation in my right shoulder, as if it had been hit with a cattle prod. As I tried to stretch my shoulder out, I couldn't help but think, how could this happen here, of all places?

It was hard enough to swallow that I lost in my hometown, but being knocked out in the first round? It just couldn't happen. But there's no changing history; it took place. And now I have two losses on my record to a couple of fighters that shouldn't have been able to beat me on my worst day.

Of course we had a big celebration planned. I was supposed to win. Mike and Skip had flown in all the way from Los Angeles, what else could I do? I had to suck it up, get cleaned up, and go out on the town.

Every restaurant and nightclub we went in to, it was as if people were staring at me with the thought, "You're a loser." I tried to put on the best smiling mask that I could, but I was in no mood to be out. Besides, my shoulder was really starting to bug me. Somewhere among our group we had scraped up a couple of painkillers, but that just caused me to retreat further into my mind. I went back and analyzed everything from the first day of training, and all that had transpired along the way.

At 5:30 a.m., I found myself alone in a car, on my way to Singer Island, so I could sit on the very beach I had done so many miles of roadwork on as a young man, and contemplate it all as I watched the sun come up.

That next day would turn out to be somewhat hectic. First, my shoulder was swelled up in pain to the point that I started to look like Quasimodo, the hunchback of Notre Dame. Meanwhile I was ducking phone calls from Stan. By the end of that day, I finally took Stan's call. He expressed to me that the Ryans had set up a meeting the next day, and expected all the players to be there. I was livid. I told Stan in no uncertain terms I wouldn't fucking be there; I was injured and in a lot of pain. Sitting with my friend George, we discussed the nightmare that had taken place the night before, which caused us to re-evaluate a sequence of events that had taken place in the last few months.

And with my friend Skip weighing in, it only crystallized a very clear conclusion: Stan wanted complete control. As it was, the limited partnership would send me money at the beginning of every month, and I would pay Stan. From almost the beginning Stan protested this arrangement. He felt it would be better if the Ryans sent the money to him, and then he dispersed my living expenses to me. That way, he could control the fighter by way of economics, by pulling the proverbial purse strings.

It had stuck in his craw that I stepped over him, and gone to a nutritionist and fitness coach. Stan felt threatened. He saw it as losing control of his fighter instead of recognizing the benefits that would be gained. So he started to schedule me for fights way too soon. He anticipated it being in a win-win situation. If I win, it's another "W" in the right column. If I lose, he goes to the Ryans and complains I'm not doing things his way.

So now I'm expected to go to a meeting and sit there in pain for what would turn out to be a separated right shoulder, and participate in a verbal battle as to why things should remain the same. Think about it. Who do you know that would volunteer to sit in physical agony, while being lectured at the same time? Besides, I knew I couldn't be in the same room as Stan at this point.

After hanging up, the very next thing I did was call Dana. I asked her to get my car back from Mark. I had left the keys in his hands, so he had transportation while I was away. Then I explained everything that took place in Florida, and brought her up to speed. I told her I didn't know what was gonna happen next, but the last thing I needed was for Mark to wreck my car. The phone went silent. I called out, "Dana!" And she replied, "I'm still here, baby."

You ever feel like you're in a shit storm, and it's hailing elephant manure? Well that's where I am, standing right in the middle of it. And from the weight of this situation, it feels like the elephants haven't dislodged all their feces yet. *Can you see this coming?* The next words out of Dana's mouth were, "It's too late. Mark has already wrecked your car." Is it me? Or does this shit happen to everybody? Either way, I'm ready to wake up and get past this nightmare.

Okay again, the good news if there is any: It wasn't a bad accident, and no one was hurt, thank God. And the car was still drivable. But what really pissed me off was Mark came up with a scheme for Dana to bite the bullet so she could cover his ass. In Mark's delusional mind, he came to the conclusion that if Dana wrecked my car, I wouldn't be pissed off, and he'd be right.

But Dana pointed out this scheme would never work, because if she truly had wrecked my car, she would have told me, and it would have been fixed and painted by the time I got back, and I never would have known by looking at it. So now I'm on the phone with Mark, and I'm getting a little agitated, because Mark takes a Billy Badass attitude. You know the old adage; the best defense is a strong offense? Well, I wasn't buying that either. I told him he was a real tough guy over the phone. Then it went quiet… Then we had a civilized conversation. I insisted he turn the car keys over to Dana, which made him none too happy. Which left him with three choices: catch a cab, ride the bus, or rely on a friend.

Now it's Sunday. My friend Skip was dating a young lady whose family had a ranch right next to Burt Reynolds' place. And believe it or not, with my arm jacked up and tied to my chest, we went horseback riding. My two friends were determined to keep my mind occupied, although their choice of activities bordered sanity. Really, what harm could it be to take a horse through a relaxing trail ride through the woods with one of your appendages tied to you?

Famous last words… Skip and I had taken to each other like brothers, and when we were younger, like brothers, there was that constant competitiveness. Skip was a gifted athlete and, truth be known, a much better one than I. Having said that, what followed probably doesn't require a lot of imagination. So with a Bakersfield hick and two Florida swamp rats, the pace began to quicken.

With the three of us astride, running full gallop, and the theme to the Magnificent Seven ringing in our ears, Mike's horse pulled a head length in front of me. Now mind you, I was fresh out of the emergency room, and diagnosed with a separated shoulder. My arm was jacked up in a sling and tied to my chest, and I had a healthy amount of pain-killers running through me.

All of a sudden Mike's horse shies—you know, spooks—and makes a ninety-degree right hand turn in front of me. Mike is now airborne, but before I can laugh, my horse rams right into his and hits the brakes. Now I'm flying the United skies along with Mike, before I hit the ground with my feet stretched out in a seated position, and my good hand on top of my head trying to save my cowboy hat. Skip goes by at full gallop, and I can swear he AND his horse were both laughing.

Mike and I both hit the ground, *whaBAM!* Mike rolls to his feet, laughing. At first I was in shock at their lack of concern for their friend, namely me. But what Mike, Skip and his girlfriend found so humorous was me, flying through the air by the seat of my pants with my left hand, my one good hand, on top of my head trying to protect my cowboy hat. But all's well that ends well. None of us got hurt and we had a great laugh (though we did decide it was time to put the horses up).

Now it's Monday morning, and Mike and Skip have to catch a plane back to the West Coast so they can get back to work. I put my friends on a plane headed back to California. This had been a Labor Day weekend I'm sure none of us will ever forget.

The next day was a pressing day. I had to see an orthopedic surgeon, get X-rays and MRI's. The results? Just as the emergency room technicians had guessed, a separated right shoulder. Doctor Ford, the orthopedic surgeon I was sent to, said I had one of two options. The first one was surgery, which he pushed for. That meant he needed to open me up, and then go in and tighten up the tendons and ligaments in my right shoulder, a process that would take me five to six months to heal.

The second one? Put a new sling on me, jack my arm up and tie it tight to my chest so I could only wiggle my wrist, and then wait to see if it heals, in six-to-eight weeks, with no guarantees. I told him I'd think about it.

So with Stan safely back in Vegas, my next pressing issue was to call Mr. Ryan's office and schedule an appointment. I booked it for the following evening, and just like the first time I was in Mr. Ryan's office, my good friend George McClease was sitting right next to me.

The first thing on Mr. Ryan's punch list was to review the fight that had just taken place. At the end of the fight review, I had my first question, and unfortunately the answer was a bomb. I enquired, who was the referee, and what were his qualifications? Mr. Ryan's answer; Captain Jack Smith. I almost went down for the count again. CAPTAIN JACK SMITH? You mean the local fishing reporter who did the fishing report, right after the sports report on local news, back when I lived with my grandparents during the 60s? My next question was, *what in the hell was he doing in there?*

Evidently, Captain Jack used to box back when he was in the service. Meaning, during the war. As in, the SECOND WORLD WAR! Some-

288

how, Captain Jack heard that there was going to be a boxing promotion held at the West Palm Beach Auditorium, so he promptly called the Ryans and insisted that they use his expertise at their venue.

So let me get this straight. My match is being refereed by a former G.I. who used to box in what the military called "smokers;" a three-round event back during the Second World War? You mean to tell me that you got a guy to referee my fight from back when the United States of America DECLARED WAR ON THE NAZIS?! You know, Adolf fucking Hitler? *Hey—wasn't anybody available from the Spanish-American War?!* This would be where my good buddy Francis Frank Ryan goes on to explain that our partnership wasn't working. Earlier in my career when I came down with the flu, and I fought to a draw, I apologized to Mr. Ryan, and I quote his reply here, "We are not fair-weather friends."

As I listen intently, while he tells us he doesn't think the fight game is for me, I couldn't help but think, it's a shame no one told that to me, when I was training myself and fought my way to the top of the world as a professional kick boxer. And as I might have mentioned before, you do not get to apply your achievements from another form of fighting when you enter the arena of boxing.

I had to start all the way from the bottom. So gee, I wonder what the people over at Sports Illustrated could have possibly been thinking when they gave me the number 10 ranking? But every time I made a motion to interrupt with a counterpoint, my buddy George would just give me the signal to sit and listen. By the end of the meeting, Ryan had pulled the carpet out from under me, and it became abundantly clear, I was the one doing the high wire act, without a safety net beneath me.

I guess they thought obtaining boxing's most coveted prize, the Heavyweight Championship OF THE WORLD, was going to be easy. Using me as a tax write-off, what did they have to be paranoid about? The Ryans and their multi-million dollar friends were putting up a little money, I was the one putting up the blood, sweat and tears, as well as my physical wellbeing.

So *here I am* again, in the elevator of Frank Ryan's law building, with my good friend George, this time headed for the bottom floor. I was injured, I had no source of income, and very little money in the bank. And oh yeah, they had no insurance on me. Again my mind drifted to the racehorses back in their air-conditioned stables. I wonder if they had insurance. If so, they totally had better attorneys than I did.

That whole week felt like a descent into hell. I had to take what little money I had and fly out to Las Vegas. Mark hadn't paid the rent. When I arrived in Vegas, Dana picked me up. After a quick stop at my place, I asked her to take me to the casino where Mark was working. As soon as she parked, I went straight inside and right to the craps tables and there he was. I think I blew him right out of his socks. I was probably the last person he expected to see. I had just spoken to him on the phone from Florida less than twelve hours previously. I had told him I needed his keys to the apartment to get in, that I had left my keys back in Florida, which was a total lie. But I couldn't afford to float any more weight. My ship was sinking.

As soon as I got back to the apartment I had to shift into hyperdrive. I had to drag all of his personal belongings from his bedroom with one arm, out onto the sidewalk between the pool and the apartment. And it was apparent to me I couldn't drag all his stuff out to the pool deck and fight with him at the same time with only one useable arm.

Actually, moving his stuff out went pretty swift. All he owned were some clothes. Everything else in the apartment was mine. So then I sat patiently and waited for him to come home. When he finally came up the sidewalk, and saw all of his stuff sitting on it, his first reaction was, "What the fuck?" By the time he got, "What the hell is going on?" out, I had met him at the door.

I told him he was going to have to find another place to live, that I couldn't afford him any more. He tried to argue with me, but I interrupted. I told him I had brought him to Las Vegas and had supported him for close to a year. As a friend, I felt that I had done everything I could do to help him get a new foothold on life. This would have been the third time this year he would have had to pay rent. I'd gotten him into gaming school, and had been happy to get him auditions on craps tables at different casinos. As well as given him his black and whites, meaning black pants and white shirt, better known as a uniform when he did land a job. Not to mention furnishing our apartment with brand new decor for him to adore. When he first landed, if I ate steak, he ate steak. If I had lobster, he had lobster. And when I went off to go skiing, horseback riding, or mountain climbing, he was welcome to come along. Broke or not, he was my friend.

But now that the world had taken a meat cleaver to me, he'd wrecked my car and expected my girlfriend to take the hit. I told him I was done arguing, and shut the door in his face. His first move? He went and complained to the apartment manager. Now there's a knock on the door. When I answer it, it's M and M: Mark and the Manager. When I had left, he had told the apartment manager that I didn't leave my half of the rent, which was technically true. But since he owes me money, he was supposed to take care of my half of the rent that month.

He really didn't have an argument. He didn't have a leg to stand on. The apartment was in my name, and the brand new furniture had been ordered and delivered right before, and just after, he had gotten to Las Vegas. The short story, we had befriended our neighbors, a couple of UNLV baseball players. Mark moved in with them until he could get on his feet. For Christ's sake, how long does it take for a grown man to stand up?

So I end up paying the rent out of my pocket, but now I've gotta get back to Florida to see my orthopedic surgeon. You know the old saying, when you look back you have 20/20 vision? Well, it's true.

At the time, I was reacting under heavy stress, and we all know what that can do to logical thinking. I was a man in the middle of the ocean in the middle of the night, coming up for the third time. So in Mark's defense, he really wasn't a bad guy. I loved him then as I love him now. I really hope good things have happened for him. But back in the day, he just didn't read life well, nor did he know how to counterpunch it. When there were things he shoulda stayed away from, he just couldn't help himself. He just couldn't do it, and it would turn around a bite him. And when good things fell upon him, instead of working hard and taking advantage of it, he'd put his feet up and cruise. So when things didn't go his way, it seemed to be everyone's fault but his. But of course these are my personal views, and my thought is that we all sometimes fall prey to bad habits.

Back in Florida, I opted not to have surgery. My instincts were telling me my body was healthy and strong, and I could heal on my own. Of course, Dr. Ford tried to talk me out of it. With my arm strapped to me in a sling, if it didn't heal in a couple of months I'd have to have the surgery anyway, which would just set me back that much further. But I stuck to my guns, and I can say my instincts were right.

Chapter Twenty-five
Mini Me and Big Jerry

I wasn't in Florida long, and now that I knew the program, it just took time. I needed to get back to Vegas, and in doing so I found out that Dana was an angel sent from heaven. Not only did she help me with mundane things like bathing and getting dressed, she would frequently have me over to her parent's house for dinner, and when I didn't eat at her folk's house, she insisted on bringing me dinner. Even though I could drive, she was determined to take as much stress out of my life as possible by offering to chauffeur me around.

And all of a sudden my birthday was upon us. It was November 5th, and I'd had my arm tied to me since Labor Day Weekend. Dana had made us dinner reservations at the Bacchanal Room at Caesars Palace. I had decided there was no way I was going out on my birthday with this sling on. I wanted to look presentable by wearing a sport coat, so I took the sling off myself.

To tell the truth, I wasn't that good of company. Despite all the preparations Dana had made to make my day special, I couldn't get my brain to switch tracks. I kept mulling around what had taken place in the past couple of months. I couldn't help but feel the isolation of a castaway that had been discarded in the middle of nowhere. And then, at dinner, she presented me with I think the most amazing gift I've ever received: She had gone to a friend who was a jeweler, taking a publicity shot of me from Ring magazine, and had him make a miniature gold sculpture silhouette of me, which would hang from a gold chain around my neck.

My mind was so preoccupied that at first I didn't realize what I was looking at. So I don't think she got quite the reaction she expected. But then the realization of what I was looking at pierced my thick head and I was stunned. A lot of professional athletes will choose to wear a necklace that promotes their chosen athletic career. I had seen chains dangling from the necks of a variety of athletes, with charms from their adopted professions. Such as baseball gloves, tennis rackets, scuba tanks, downhill skis, and racing's checkered flag. But Dana, never being the one unable to read my personality, not only hit the target, she hit the bullseye. While every other boxer I had ever met, including Sugar Ray Leonard, had a simple gold chain with gold boxing gloves hanging from it, I was the only one with enough confidence (okay, so I had an ego, but it was never out of check and I never treated people as if they were less than me) who would, and I did, wear myself around my own neck.

Mini-me was beautifully sculpted, I must say, from my pageboy haircut to the muscular definition in my legs from years of Karate and kickboxing. We went back to my apartment and I'm sure you can guess the rest. But in the middle of the night, I got up and went into the bathroom and shut the door looking down into my hand at Mini-me. Realizing the thoughtfulness it took to create this beautiful gift, I began to break down. It was the most heartfelt gesture I had ever experienced. I spent the entire next day with my arm free of the sling and it felt pretty good.

So that was it. Goodbye Mr. Sling and hello rehab, which I would embark upon myself. Ever since the Ryans had pulled the carpet out from under me, I didn't possess the money to go back to Florida to see Dr. Ford, nor did I have the insurance to seek out another doctor's help. Dana, being a long time student of jazz dancing, was recruited by the Sporting House to teach aerobics. It was the most hip fitness center in all of Las Vegas, with more than twenty racquetball courts, a full gym weightlifting facility, an indoor basketball court, with a full size Olympic pool, and an outdoor jogging path which circumvented the perimeter of the property, with fitness stations scattered throughout. Not to mention a sports clothing boutique and health food restaurant. Their gym at the time had a full array of state of the art, Nautilus equipment and enough free weights to make Governor Arnold Schwarzenegger drool.

Between attending two or three of Dana's aerobic fitness classes a week, swimming in their pool, and using their state of the art Nautilus

293

fitness equipment, this was rehab heaven. Now approaching the end of November, I was broke. With no source of income and my bank account about to run dry, this would be the first time my friend Skip would throw me a rope.

Skip's company was sending him to Corpus Christi, Texas, where a rebuilding effort was taking place after a hurricane had struck the Texas Panhandle and had all but wiped out South Padre Island. Skip was in the position to get me, as well as an old high school buddy of his, Ken Shot, construction jobs rebuilding a department store. Skip had the gift of being an incredible salesman; he could sell refrigerators to Eskimos. He had Ken and I both believing we were going to be foremen on a construction site that he was the supervisor on. Once we arrived, however, it took Ken and me all but a heartbeat to realize we were his main labor fools.

But before all that, Ken had to make it to Vegas. He was going to drive across country from West Palm Beach to Sin City. We had discussed him residing here for a year or two as an adventure. Since I now had a spare bedroom where Mark had stayed, I told him he was welcome. I could use help paying the rent.

So *here I am* sitting on pins and needles, anxiously waiting for Ken's arrival. Ken shows up right before Thanksgiving weekend and I feel as if the Cavalry has arrived. But to my surprise, it would turn out to be more like F Troop. Ken had been living off of granola bars and peanuts and had to dig underneath and between the seats for change to use for gas money since he had left New Mexico. This was a real dilemma. With Ken in a state of panic tearing up the carpet in his car and digging between his seats scrounging for change to make it to Las Vegas, my spirit sank faster than a lead zeppelin. Rent was due in about five days and obviously Ken wasn't going to be any help. Now I'm really scrambling. Oh no, not to pay rent but to find enough money to feed Ken and me and have enough left over to put gas in the car so we can meet Skip in L.A.

That night, as I laid down to go to sleep, I couldn't help but think, "What type of mental midget takes a journey from South Florida to Las Vegas without calculating how much money he's going to need to gas his car, let alone feed himself, and you might consider having a little money for lodging when you get there." Oh sure, I had an apartment for him to land in, but it wasn't free. And he was considering living here for the next year.

294

And then it struck me. I laughed so hard I began crying. It's Florida-itus. Natural Floridians have enough optimism to save the world and when I lived in Florida I was guilty of it too. On more than one occasion I took off on a journey I was ill-prepared for, yet here I am. So I have to believe in Hank Williams Junior's jive: a country boy will survive.

I woke up the next morning with a new outlook. I had to get back to my roots. If Ken can make it 3,000 miles on spare change and granola bars, I could certainly make it to Los Angeles. Now Ken and I are collecting up all of my spare change and thank God there was a lot of it. Back when I was making money I never spent my change. I kept storing it in glass jars. Dana would laugh at me until one day she showed up with a five-gallon glass pig. She told me I needed a bank to deposit my spare money in; a piggy bank. Over time I had neglected to keep count of how much money I had deposited into the bank. Now, counting it out with Ken, I had close to 500 dollars. *Thank God for the Pig!*

Ken and I cruised easily into Los Angeles and the very next morning, the three of us piled into Skip's Audi and headed off to Texas. With the three of us Texas-bound listening to the radio, we heard the shot that no one in the world could believe. John Lennon had been killed; shot dead in front of his Dakota apartment building in New York City. In my short life we had now lost four great men to assassinations: one of our greatest presidents, his beloved younger brother, a revered reverend, and a popular poet; all who dared believe in the same thing for this world: love and peace.

By the time we got to Corpus Christi, Skip had calculated how many hours we were going to work that first week and then fronted Ken and I our first week's salaries. The whole experience was bearable but barely. Oh sure, it wasn't all bad. At the end of each workweek we went up to San Antonio to unwind. Why? Because most of Corpus Christi had been destroyed during the hurricane.

But neither of them was aware that during the week I wasn't sleeping. I would wait for my friends to fall asleep and then I would get up and pace the floors all night. Sometimes I'd get so worked up I'd be afraid I was going to wake the guys up, so I'd go out the door and walk until the sun came up. It was hard for me to get past how hard I had worked only to suffer what I would call a mutiny and have someone else wreck my ship onto the rocks. And of course, during the day I was barely functional, walking around in a fog. This caused more than a problem for my perfectionist friend Skip, who had no idea I was operating on zero sleep. He just came down on me harder.

By the Christmas of '80, Ken and I were both back in Las Vegas. John Lennon had just been shot, we still had hostages in Iran, and I was still tormented in dealing with my own crisis. After the New Year, Stan approached me. I was still on contract with him and he wanted to know if I was healthy enough to box. While I was away healing and trying to make a living, Stan had found some investors who he felt were interested in sponsoring a slightly damaged young heavyweight. So *here I am* shaking hands with Jerry G., "Big Jerry" as he was known (which is not his real name because he's an alleged mafia boss). Apparently Jerry was the criminal underworld's Number One man; the kingpin of a major metropolitan East-Coast city. Jerry turned out to be, in my opinion, a great guy and so was his son Jan, which is not his real name for obvious reasons.

Standing tall at NBA height and tipping the scales at NFL weight, Jerry was an imposing man, and a jolly one as well, thank God. I never witnessed the man in a bad mood, and he was very respectful of everyone. But then, everyone was respectful of Big Jerry. Stepping in to Caesars Palace with Big Jerry, or any other major casino on the Las Vegas strip, was like witnessing the parting of the Red Sea. The moment he was spotted by a pit boss or concierge, the word would travel throughout the casino with the buzz of a telegraph wire. It was always the same: men with immense power within the casino industry would rush over to his side to shake his hand. And this courtesy would continue with pit bosses, hotel managers, concierges, *maître d's*, right up to the biggest man in the house, the casino manager. They all wanted to know what they could get Big Jerry. And with a big smile, his response was fairly consistent, "Nothin'. I came to play with the dice," or "I came to play some cards."

Big Jerry didn't drink, at least not in public (which I thought was pretty smart if you're an underworld boss). Then, referring to me, he'd ask them if they had met "The Kid." And if they hadn't met me yet, he'd introduce me to them and then announce I was a fighter. Not *his* fighter but a fighter. These guys didn't get to where they were by not being able to connect the dots, because after that grand introduction, they couldn't do enough for me.

At this point I was also hiring myself out as a sparring partner. I got picked up by Larry Holmes' camp, the Heavyweight Champ of the World, for a week. I was at Caesars Palace one day watching the champ train for an up and coming fight. When he was through, I got in the ring and moved around with one of his sparring partners, Jody Ballard. I must have impressed Jody because from what I understand, he mentioned to the champ that I might be good to use. What Jody didn't know, and no one ringside suspected, was that I had a jammed capsule in my right hand, which is the fluid sac in your knuckle that lubricates the joint (can you say OUCH?! It's extremely painful when you punch), and I couldn't use it.

So *here I am* with my good buddy, Earl Tripp, and we both landed jobs in the champ's camp. It was customary for Larry Holmes, the heavyweight champ, to carry a couple of sparring partners with him. Jody Ballard and Marvin Swinton were his mainstays, both of them tremendous fighters in their own right. But then the champ would want the best to keep his skills honed and sharp. It's always been customary for the heavyweight champ to carry two or three sparring partners with him, often hiring a couple of local fighters to work with, as well, from whatever venue the fight was being held at.

That whole week I showed up to Caesars Palace training room early. Over the first few days, I had warmed up, shadow boxed, and was ready to get in the ring with the champ but they never called my name. By day four, they had called out the usual suspects and also my friend Earl Tripp, so I began to run my mouth. By day five, they booted me out of camp. To tell the truth, Larry Holmes would have punched me drunk, but it would have been a great honor and a great test because I would have been in his ass. Sometimes you just have to find out what you're made of. Speaking as a man, we're in constant search for the answers to these questions. And stepping in the ring with possibly the greatest heavyweight champion of all time might give you a clue…

Under Big Jerry's sponsorship I'd had a couple of wins, actually stopping one guy, so the shoulder didn't seem to be an issue. After this knockout, Stan approached me and he was more than excited. He said we were going to fight Billy Baxter's kid next, Anthony Davis. I knew Anthony from the gym, Johnny Taco's, and we got along fine. I actually liked him. He was a tough Oklahoma kid who had gotten in some trouble when he was younger but had come out the other end with his head screwed on straight and had taken up professional boxing. Now, with both of us on the rise, whoever won this fight would more than likely get a shot at Carlos "Sugar" de León's cruiserweight title, and I had to admit in the back of my mind I was thinking, with all the prospective fighters out there you could match me up with, why match me with someone from my own gym? But the truth is, in the world of professional fighting, if I may paraphrase a line from "The Godfather:" It's business. It's not personal.

The fireworks between Stan and I had calmed down but there were still sparks. So *here I am,* training at Johnny Taco's Ringside Gym at Main and Charleston, sparring with Joe Bugner. Joe resided in London, England. He was a former top-ten contender back in the 70s, one of Muhammad Ali's sparring partners, and then later down the line one of Ali's opponents. At 6 foot 3, Joe had a fluid but lightning quick left jab, which I'm sure he learned from Ali. With his smooth body movement and a razor sharp left jab, if you were going to classify Joe as a fighter he was a boxer not a puncher.

Anthony Davis, on the other hand, was quite the opposite. Just approaching 5'11" and a little over 200 pounds, Anthony was a little more gritty and liked to mix it up. My good friend and stable mate Earl Tripp was out of town; he had gone home to visit with his family. Earl was 5'11" and 198 pounds and would have been perfect for me to work out with. Do you see where I'm going here? In the world of professional fighting, styles can make or break a fight. Here's an example: George Foreman bounced Joe Frazier around the ring like he was a big kid playing with a teddy bear. And Joe Frazier gave Muhammad Ali all the Hell there was on this Earth. But then Ali knocked George Foreman out as cold as a block of ice, something he could never accomplish in three fights with "Smokin' Joe" Frazier.

So *here I am* sparring and training with Joe Bugner, who I've struck up a friendship with, as well as with his trainer, Chuck Bodak, who's got a great demeanor. At this point, Stan and I are barely getting along as usual. Suddenly, just two days before my fight with Anthony, Stan has a mild heart attack, which throws everything into a power struggle. Johnny Taco insists on working my corner but Stan won't hear of it. Stan and Johnny had a love-hate relationship. They fought like cats and dogs, but when the fireworks and smoke all cleared, Chuck Bodak had assumed the corneman position with Johnny as my cut man.

The fight was being held at the Sands Hotel and Casino. After the weigh-in that morning I went over to Stan's to see how he was feeling. He was laying low and on medication but he assured me he'd be at the fight. I told Stan to relax and not to worry about it but he made his intentions very clear.

The day before, my good friend George McClease had flown in to see the fight with another buddy, Larry Fagero, better known as "Hot Curl." Larry was charged with his nickname in Palm Beach County for his surfing ability.

The night of the fight, after all the well-wishers had cleared my locker room, I began to warm up. As I started to shadowbox, Chuck Bodak called me over and then started to apply something to my face. When I questioned him he told me it was cocoa butter. What happened to the Vaseline? As it turns out, Chuck never used Vaseline. He liked to use cocoa butter on all his fighters. We should have stuck to Vaseline…

After the bell ended round one, I came back to my corner with a cut underneath my left eye that would eventually take twenty-two stitches to close. This, my friends, should have been an omen. In round three, I had my mouthpiece knocked out of my mouth, not from a hard punch but from being lazy and not biting down on it. The referee kicked it towards my corner and the fight continued. When the bell rang to end that round, I went back to my corner only to be greeted by a full-on shoving match between Stan Tischler, Johnny Taco, and Chuck Bodak. Stan, who had been sitting ringside, all of a sudden decided he didn't like the way the corner was being run so he jumped up in it. Now you have three veteran cornermen fighting for the top dog position.

Meanwhile, while all the pushing, shouting, and shoving is going on, I'm waiting patiently for someone to pretend they're a cornerman. I need some water administered, my cut attended to, and my mouthpiece rinsed off before it's put back in my mouth, which basically didn't happen. You only get one short minute between rounds and they had used up 47 seconds of it staging their own fight. Now there's a pounding on the ring apron, which is the 10-second warning, which seemed to snap everybody to attention. I get sprayed in the face with water, my mug wiped off, and my mouthpiece shoved back in my mouth without it being rinsed.

Now for all of you who have never attended a live boxing event, there is a shallow box, one and a half foot square and four inches deep, that sits in the neutral corner. Prior to the first bell, each fighter is to go over and step in that box and grind their feet down into a grainy powder that resembles rock salt but is rosin; it's used to keep the slick leather sole of your shoe from slipping as you move around the ring. With my corner preoccupied with their own skirmish, no one seemed to remember the purpose of a cornerman, which is to assist the fighter. In his haste, someone had shoved my mouthpiece back in my mouth without rinsing it off first. I turned to face my opponent with what I'll describe as the foul and pungent taste of ammonia pudding. *Can you say choked up?* But through my gagging and gasping I had a more prevalent issue to deal with, like the world contender coming straight at me trying to use my head as a piñata.

We went straight into the ropes in front of Big Jerry, who was sitting ringside. I grabbed Anthony in a clinch and spit my mouthpiece trying to catch my breath. All of a sudden Big Jerry stands up and starts taunting Billy Baxter from across the ring. In doing so my spirit's dropped. The way he was conducting himself seemed to indicate to me that he didn't think we could win the fight.

It was a long and brutal battle; a great fight for fans to watch. A couple of times I had backed Anthony into the ropes and we were trading punches back and forth as the crowd went crazy. And in spite of the severe cut I'd acquired during the first round, I battled on and won a few rounds. But then Anthony's corner, run by veteran fight trainer Jesse Burnett, sensed the urgency and got Anthony to pick up his pace and by doing so, he captured a few rounds of his own.

Then, with ten seconds left to go in the 9th round, the referee stepped in to break us from a clinch, scrutinized my eye and stopped the fight. The baffling thing to me was the ref's call. He ruled that my ribs were broken, and although my body was sore from Anthony pounding away at it, my ribs were not broken. Now I'm baffled. I battled into the 9th round with a gash underneath my left eye only to have the fight called due to broken ribs. But that's it. That's the ruling. So I'm heading for the showers.

So *here I am* sitting in the locker room, pissed off and confused when Anthony Davis sticks his head in to see how I'm doing. We spoke for a moment and I thank him for stopping by. Anthony and I had been friends before our fight and now we can be friends again. He told me he wanted to quit a couple of times but his trainer, Jesse Burnett, and his manager, Billy Baxter, wouldn't let him. I don't know if he was telling me the truth or he just didn't want me to feel bad, but either way I told him I wanted a quiet word with those two and we both laughed.

Anthony went on to fight Carlos de León for the cruiserweight title and he recruited me to help him get ready for it. But right now, with ice on my face, I'm on my way to my general practitioner's office before my eye swells up so badly they cannot administer the twenty-two stitches it will require to close the gash beneath my eye. Once I was back in my apartment, I laid in my room in the darkness with an ice-pack on my face. I hear my front door open and a moment later I hear a voice from Heaven enter my room and then the touch of a red-haired angel as Dana softly caressed my arm and shoulder and gently whispered, "What can I do?" I told her I would be okay, and that she should go out with her friends, and that there was nothing she could do. Then I reached over and kissed the palm on her hand and said I would call the following day.

The next day I got out of bed, or should I say crawled? I felt as if I'd been hit by a Mack truck. I was pissed off. Whenever they stop a fight, it goes down on your record as a knockout and then they suspend your license for 60 to 90 days, which means you can't fight. When I got to the bathroom I gazed in the mirror. It looked as if someone had embedded a black and blue softball into my eye socket. But I was still pissed. I jumped in the shower and cleaned up and, with my eye swollen shut, I put on a pair of shades and went straight to the boxing commissioner's office. My protest fell on deaf ears. Even with me beating myself in the torso with my own fist to prove that my ribs weren't broken, they thought it was a just call. Now I have loss number three on my record.

When I get back to my apartment, my phone rings. It's George. He wants to know if I'll go out with him and Larry that evening to see Redd Foxx. As you might imagine, I didn't feel much like going out but George and Larry had flown all the way in from South Florida in anticipation of a celebration. So what was I to do? Give them a declaration of depression? Well, I thought, better shut up, get up, clean up, and suck it up. We went to see Redd Foxx.

George and Larry had a room at the Sands Hotel and Casino on the eighth floor. Coming down in the hotel elevator, we stopped around the fifth floor to pick up a passenger; a beautiful young woman in a sleek evening gown. I had tinted glasses on but she had noticed my eye by doing a double take. She reached up to touch my face and asked me what happened. When I told her I was a professional fighter she asked me why I would pick up such a profession? Not being the best of moods, I snapped back with: It beats yours. She then quietly pulled her hand away from my face and stepped back. When the doors opened to the elevator, we all stepped out into the casino. I had been in Las

Vegas long enough to recognize a call girl; not a hooker but a high-end professional. Of course, I never saw that young woman again but if she reads this book I'd like to sincerely apologize. It's not for any of us to judge. Somehow and in some way we all prostitute ourselves. Is being paid to go out on the town with a stranger and have a good time, ending the evening with sex any less moral than two men climbing into a ring and trying to beat each other into submission? What about the crowd who paid to witness and cheer the destruction of one or the other? Or could it be the cat who spent way too many hours at work chasing the materialism of the American dream while their child sits alone at the ballpark or a ballet recital with no one to cheer them on? These are the questions America needs to answer.

But *here I am* again: injured and with way too much time on my hands. All I could do was sit around and think how a once promising career could get so far off track. I just kept mulling over all that had transpired in the last year. What was it that had tripped me up? One name kept rising to the top: Stan Tischler. A week or so later, I showed up at the gym where Stan was working with my friend Earl Tripp plus a new fighter. Boy, did we have a blow out. My argument: how did a young promising prospect for the heavyweight division show up in Las Vegas, bringing his own sponsorship, and deposit himself in his lap only to have him screw it up? Stan's argument? Well, he really didn't have one. I didn't smoke, drink or do drugs. I had witnessed what that lifestyle could do to you and I had put it behind me. I didn't gamble, stay up late at night, or hang out at whorehouses. I had known fighters—even some Stan had worked with—who constantly had to be taken to doctors to receive shots to ward off venereal diseases. I was always at the gym on time. He never had to search for me in bars or casinos, nor did he have to show up at my house first thing in the morning and kick me out of bed so I would go do my roadwork. Quite the contrary, I was the athlete that would show up at other fighters' homes before dawn so I could wake them and we could all run together. His big counter argument was that I went around him to find other trainers. I was dumbfounded; I couldn't believe my ears. You mean Dr. Rob Krakovitz, my nutrition coach, who's got a trunk full of Olympic medal winning athletes? Or Russ Hodge, my strength coach, who just happened to be one of those medal-winning Olympians? Even though he had never met one of these men, Stan viewed them as a major threat to him. Through Stan's eyes, my collaboration with them meant he was losing control.

As the argument escalated I felt the anger and testosterone in my 20-some year old body rage to the point where I was seriously considering crushing his head like a fucking grape. Thank God some people stepped between us. As I turned to leave I told him I was going to speak with Big Jerry. That's when Stan made a statement that I didn't catch at the time but later, after some thought, realized it could work in my favor. His retort: He didn't give a shit who I talked with and Big Jerry could be taken care of, too. Now I don't know exactly what Stan meant by that comment, but I know how I presented it to Big Jerry.

But before I could come to my senses, *here I am*, ten days later, sitting in my car a block and a half away from Stan's house with a .32 caliber pistol in my lap. My intentions were to wait patiently for Stan to pull up in his driveway and then casually walk up to him and put a cap in his cranium. There's an old saying, idle hands are the devil's workshop, and it's true. With my boxing license pulled, being injured and unable to train with nothing else to do, I found every conscious thought was dwelling on the negative. Add to that the fact that I was still not sleeping at night, I was prey to every chaotic thought that blew through my mind.

With my brain simmering in this poisonous stew, I found myself teetering here on the edge of murder and mayhem. And then it hit me, something my good friend George had said to me during a previous trip to Las Vegas to watch me fight—a fight I had won by a unanimous decision. Now normally after one of my fights, we'd all have a little get-together, kind of a celebration. But on that occasion I told all my friends, as well as Dana, that I just wanted to have a quite dinner with my buddy George. After being seated at a booth at the MGM Grand on the Las Vegas strip, George looked across the table and sensed something wasn't right. "'Gurski, what's going on with you?" He always dropped the "Pod" when he was speaking frankly with me. I told him I wasn't happy. I didn't like the boxing business, nor the people in it that had surrounded me. I told him I thought I was dealing with snakes and that no one was looking out for my best interest. I felt as though I was floundering and surrounded by sharks. George fell backwards in the booth and began to chuckle. I asked him what was so funny. That's when he told me that if someone took a survey of all the people back home in South Florida who knew me, I would be voted the happiest guy they'd ever met. This left me speechless. Not because I couldn't think of anything to say, I was choked up to the point I just couldn't get anything out. So I sat quietly and listened. Then he pulled the word out of the air I never would have thought of: *Quit.* He reminded me I was a martial artist and that I never set out to be a boxer and no one would hold it against me if I stopped.

Then the conversation reverted back to how all of this started, which brought me to a discussion I'd had with our mutual friend Jorge on the phone. After my loss in Palm Beach County where I separated my shoulder, Jorge had called George and requested my phone number. He simply wanted to see how I was healing. Then he asked how everything else was going. I chuckled and told him of a conversation I had with Tommy Ryan. With no insurance, no source of income, my arm tied to my chest to heal, and what I felt was the limited partnership pulling the carpet out from under me, they were now requesting the car back that they had acquired for my use. When I pointed these issues out to Tommy, his response was one only a kid of privilege could respond with, and I quote here; "Can't you get a job?" I snapped to look at the phone. I couldn't tell if this guy was numb or he just didn't hear what I just got done explaining. But either way, in my mind, I'm convinced I've found the missing link! Upon hearing this, Jorge goes off like a Chinese New Year's fireworks display. His mind is working so fast his mouth can't keep up with him. He keeps criss-crossing the language barrier between Spanish and English. And I don't know Spanish, but I know this: he was willing to kill Tommy Ryan. After I had calmed him down, he assured me that all I needed to do was give him the word.

The Latin community, in general, is passionate about their fighters, and Jorge was no exception. If I had simply said, "You do what you feel you need to," there's no doubt in my mind, Tommy Ryan would be dead. Besides, a little thing like that might come back to haunt you. One day Jorge might request something from me I wouldn't be willing to do. Then there were the legal issues of the cops showing up at your door, and then the biggest issue of them all, the moral issue of you taking something that's not yours, like a life. And with all this echoing in my mind I looked down at the gun in my lap and thought, "What the hell are you doing?" Was I willing to climb into a sewer and swim with these rat fuckers so I can kill this cockroach but ultimately ruin my life? The answer to that was 'no.' So I started my car, drove out of Stan's neighborhood, and went home.

304

The next morning I called Big Jerry and scheduled a meeting with him for the following day. When I got to Big Jerry's, we sat down and I explained my situation with Stan. And then I dropped the bomb. I was fed up. I knew I couldn't work with Stan any longer and I needed to get my contract back from him, and there was only one way I could think of doing it. I relayed the statement that Stan had made regarding Big Jerry, only I might have phrased it a little differently… So I relayed Stan's retort about Big Jerry in this way, "I don't give a shit who you talk to. And if Big Jerry gets in the way, he can be taken care of, too." That's when his eyebrows rose and his eyes widened. And then he inquired, "What did he mean by that?" Jerry was no fool; he could see my potential. Plus, he liked me. I made sense to him. As it turned out, Big Jerry was not a big fan of Stan, but he didn't know that until he got involved with the guy. But getting back to Big Jerry's question, I just shrugged and said I didn't know, but I sure knew what it sounded like. Big Jerry concurred with a nod and a big smile. Then he asked if I could come back tomorrow and that he'd have his wife contact me with a time. He told me he had to fly back east to take care of some business but that he'd be happy to call all parties involved and put us on speakerphone.

Now let me share something with you, and no disrespect intended, but Big Jerry could pick 'em. His wife was attractive with street smarts hidden by elegance, and ferociously loyal. She had his back, 110 percent—something every man dreams of having. The next morning when I woke up, I felt the beginnings of a migraine headache, something I've been plagued with my whole life. Nonetheless, I showed up at Big Jerry's at the designated time, feeling borderline nauseous. Big Jerry's wife greeted me at the front door and invited me in. She shot me a second look and asked me if I was all right. I told her I had a migraine coming on. She offered me a seat, and got me something cold to drink. And as punctual as a Swiss watch, the phone rang.

Big Jerry was not one to pussyfoot around. He told me he had come up with a plan; he was going to straighten this mess out. He informed me he was going to call Stan and inquire exactly what he meant by that statement he'd made. Jerry wanted me to listen in on the speakerphone and not to interrupt, no matter what. Now Stan's on the phone, and Big Jerry point blank asks him what he meant by that statement. Stan replied it was taken out of context, which started Jerry on that robust laugh of his. Then the big man told Stan, "Yeah, let's not get stupid, you don't want to start this kind of war." You know that old saying; I shot myself in the foot? Well, this was where Stan blew off both of his feet. Stan continued by telling Big Jerry nothing good about me, and then he made the statement of statements. He blurted out: "You have to listen to me here, all fighters are whores." It took everything I had to keep from going through the phone lines after Stan's throat. Thank God Big Jerry's wife was by my side. Her presence had a calming affect on me, reminding me I had promised Big Jerry I wouldn't say a word no matter what happened. After Stan hung up, we continued our conversation. Big Jerry got it. He knew I was a clean living kid, and if I was so bad, why did Stan convince Big Jerry to buy into my contract in the first place? At the end of our conversation I apologized to Big Jerry, but I told him straight up; if I had to continue fighting under Stan, I would stop fighting. Big Jerry's response: "Kid, you do what's best for you." There was no way I could express how much I appreciated that.

This whole scenario played out better than I hoped. Stan called me a day later, and told me he was going to release me from my contract. His heart was bothering him, and he didn't think I was worth the aggravation. *Bingo!* We had dissolved our contract, and I was now a free agent. It felt as if a building had been lifted off of me.

Chapter Twenty-six
Karma with Goliath

While I was benched, my eye had healed but I was still on suspension from the TKO. First things first, I had to feed myself and pay the rent. The company Skip worked for had won a contract to build a Bloomingdales in Dallas, Texas. Oh sure he could use some help, but to me, this would be the second time my friend would throw me a rope. So I packed up some personal things and I was off to Dallas, for what would turn out to be a year's hiatus of spinning my wheels. I made good money but I was burning through it. I had kept my place in Las Vegas but my living expenses were in Dallas. I can't really say Dallas was a mistake because we only know the path we take. But I did come away with an absolute, it was abundantly clear; I absolutely did not want to make a living in the construction trade. This was not a new revelation; after all I did hang dry wall for years. But after such a steep fall from grace, I needed to look around to reassess my place.

Skip was one of the best friends a man could ever have, but we were so close we were like brothers, and that can make it tough for one to take direction from the other. Looking back on it now with 20/20 vision, I can clearly see he was learning the ropes and putting the building blocks together that he would later use to build his empire. But for me, my Dallas experience was more stalemate and heartbreak than it was checkmate. Finally, after paying double rent for ten months, I dumped my place in Vegas. Skip bought his first home in Dallas. Now he owned a house with no furniture. I, on the other hand, had a house full of furniture with no home. So, on a three-day weekend, and I believe it was Labor Day, I flew to Las Vegas by myself, rented a truck, moved out all my furniture, and drove back to Dallas alone.

Towards the end of my Dallas hiatus, we had built a Bloomingdales and five Mervyn's stores; all which had their grand opening on the same night. So now, we're in a dilemma. Which grand opening do we attend? *Not!* We put on our best tuxedos, which we rented, and went straight to the grand opening of the Bloomingdales store. And what a night that was. They had invited the great Broadway stage entertainer, Peter Allen, to perform for all of Bloomingdales' guests. But before all that, they had five of the top fashion designers of the day, each one arriving in his very own jet black, jet ranger helicopter, which landed single file on the roof of the Bloomingdales parking structure. *Can you say grand entrance?* Then the mega rich were allowed to browse the virgin store as they were served food and cocktails. Oh and did I forget to mention, for one night only, it was fifty percent off anything in the store? Is it just me, or has anyone else noticed that the more you seem to have, the more you seem to get?

After the grand opening, Skip informed me that we'd be doing a Sakowitz store next, in Tulsa, Oklahoma. And I informed him it would be the last store I'd build. We were finished with the Sakowitz store in Tulsa right at Christmas break. After we packed up to go back to Dallas, I made the decision to sell everything I owned.

So *here I am* back in Dallas, in more than a heated discussion with my friend Skip, who doesn't understand anything I'm about to do. I sell the classic mid-seventies Dallas Delta '88 Oldsmobile convertible, which was chocolate brown with camel colored interior, to our pal Larry Edery for a few hundred dollars. Not to mention selling all of my furniture to Skip, including a sofa I had custom ordered—all for dimes on the dollar. Poor Skip. He was a young man of high intelligence and immense logic; none of this made any sense to him. But I never based my worth on my monetary gains, nor anyone else's.

My brother and I both have my granddad's old school thinking burned into our mind. The four most important things every man should carry with him through this life: morals, virtues, standards, and honesty. Dropping the bar on any one of these starts chipping away at your self-respect. I knew I wasn't happy going in the direction I was headed, and there was no amount of money or material possessions that could change that. So once again I flew out to Vegas to pick up the Oldsmobile that the limited partnership had acquired for me, having just dropped a new motor in the vehicle so I knew it was road worthy. You can make it from Las Vegas to Dallas Texas in 24 hours—if you don't sleep. After arriving in Dallas, I spent one full day in the city that hosts 'America's Team.' I had packed up the car with all my personal belongings and at the dawn of the next morning I started my solo race, heading west, back to Las Vegas.

For the first time in a long time I felt as free as the prairie eagle. I could head off in any direction; north, east, south or west. I didn't have a tie to anything and that's when it hit me, I had let all the material things I had acquired through my years of boxing hold me back. I was scrambling to hold on to possessions that really meant nothing if I wasn't happy. So I did what always worked for me before, my standard check. I looked myself dead in the eye through the rear view mirror and I swore that I would never get attached to material possessions like that again. My new resolution was if I acquired something I liked, and had to give it up, I'd just work a little harder and obtain it again.

My stay in Vegas was a short couple of months, and once again, my red-haired angel came to my aid. Dana opened herself, as well as her apartment to me; which looking back on it now, was pretty remarkable. Somehow, we'd maintained our relationship mostly by phone. Being gone most of the year, I had only gone back to Vegas a couple of times. Knowing now, what I didn't know then, it's more than doubtful I will ever find another woman who loved me as much as Dana Cartwright did. But at this point I had to hit the ground running. My wallet was thin and I needed to get some revenue. So I went straight to Main & Charleston Johnny Taco's gym and hired myself out as a sparring partner.

While I was away, I'd worked diligently to try to keep my conditioning up, so it didn't take me very long to get back into fighting shape. But now I was running into another obstacle; none of the promoters wanted to talk to me. They insisted I have a manager or trainer who they could negotiate with. And in case you can't guess, I was more than apprehensive about signing with anyone. Then I remembered a phone call, much earlier when I was still living in Dallas, from my buddy Gary Kastello. Gary was a friend of mine in Las Vegas who was involved with his brothers-in-law, Len and Marty, in a tool rental company off of Boulder Highway. And in case you haven't noticed, this is how crazy my life can be. Gary knew a fight promoter in Los Angeles by the name of Dan Goossen who shared the same hair stylist in Las

Vegas. In conversation during one of his haircuts, Gary happened to mention that he and I were friends. So the next time his stylist was cutting Dan Goossen's hair she asked Dan if he had ever heard of me. Dan expressed a little interest by calling Gary. This prospect seemed to have some potential.

So, after training in Vegas for a couple of months, *here I am* on the road again, driving through the smoldering heat of the desert headed for Los Angeles with a phone number in my hand. The first stop was Newhall, better known today as Valencia. I had called my friend Mike Brucker, and he, in turn, invited me to stay at his place until I had time to investigate the possibilities. I drove into Newhall and pulled into Mike's driveway at roughly one o'clock in the afternoon. Mike's then girlfriend greeted me at the front door in her bathing suit. This would not be the first time I was at Mike's home. I'd actually been there a few times. It was a beautiful customized tract home on a corner lot. There was a smoke-glass mirrored wall, which stretched the length of the living room, which was beautifully decorated with custom furniture. It was a three-bedroom two and a half-bath home with sliding glass doors that opened up to a back patio and pool deck with a Jacuzzi that sat six comfortably. His place was a mess, though, and I would soon find out why. His then girlfriend had three things she liked to do: she would lie in bed all morning, lounge at the pool all afternoon, and then snort cocaine all night. But at this point none of this is my concern. I had business to take care of and I wanted to wrap it up within a week.

Within the week I had found the Ten Goose Boxing Gym in Van Nuys, California, I had discussed the possibilities with Dan Goossen of him managing my career, and found the time to work out at the gym for a couple of days just to see how it felt. Things looked promising.

So *here I am* on the road back to Las Vegas, to pick up what few belongings I own. A few years earlier, I had introduced Skip and Mike to each other, they had become friends and roommates. Now I was discussing the possibility of renting the room that Skip had vacated since he had bought a house in Dallas Texas. This seemed like a perfect fit. Mike needed a roommate to offset his expenses, and since I didn't know anyone else in Los Angeles, I now had a safe place to land. Once I was back in Vegas, I could tell, this did not sit well with Dana. And who could blame her? I was gone almost a year and continued our relationship primarily by phone and now after only two months in Las Vegas I was already packing up to move to Los Angeles. But amazingly enough, she understood. How, I don't know. And if the Pope ever looked at me to nominate someone for sainthood, I know one red-haired angel that would get in on the first tally of the votes.

So *here I am* going south on the I-15 headed into Los Angeles, when I decide to do another self-check. I looked myself dead in the eye, in the rear view mirror, and swear that if this doesn't work out I'm through with boxing and going back to the martial arts world, which was always my real love. As I cross the state line, I have no idea what's waiting in front of me. But what I do know is I can see Primm, Nevada in the rear view mirror behind me, and the Doobie Brothers are cranked up with "It Keeps You Running," and I'm in a great mood.

I headed into Baker, a small town on the way to Los Angeles from Las Vegas that was no more than a gas stop. It lays claim to the world's tallest thermometer, and by God they need it. With summer temperatures hovering around 122 consistently, the other detrimental thing about Baker is the sandstorms. Living in Las Vegas I'd heard of them and I had been through Baker a dozen times but never experienced one. But on this particular trip I charged head-on, straight into one. I'm no expert on weather phenomenon but back home when the thunderstorms hit and the rain was coming down so hard you couldn't see past your hood, it dawned on me that there's not a whole lot of difference between a thunderstorm and a sandstorm. When you can't see past your hood, you can't see. Except for one small detail. In Florida, when it was raining heavily and you're traveling at speed, and then you slam on your brakes you tend to hydroplane, and then spin out. In a sandstorm, you have quite a bit more traction. Back home in Florida, during a thunderstorm people would pull over to the side of the road until the storm passed by and I couldn't help but notice people were doing the same thing in the sandstorm. This brought me to a conclusion only my heritage would deem logical. With everyone heading south on the I-15 to Los Angeles pulled over, that meant the road was wide open; I could gas it.

So *here I am* on the southbound I-15 heading into Los Angeles at close to 70 miles an hour driving blind with the Doobie Brothers cranked high and, I might add, appropriately singing "What a Fool Believes." By the time I got to Victorville to take my right hand turn to hit the 138, better known as the Pear Blossom Expressway, the sandstorm had subsided. Once I got to Newhall, off the 114, I went straight to Mike's house and pulled into his driveway. Mike answered his door and greeted me warmly. Then he insisted on helping me unload my car. I spun around and we headed down the walkway leading to his front door. When I stepped out to his driveway, I saw for the first time the repercussions of driving through a sandstorm at warp speed. Mike asked me what the hell happened and I was stunned. I was missing the paint job on the whole front end of my car. *Holy Earl Scheib! Can you say 200 miles of sandblasting?* Because that's exactly what it took to blast the paint off the front of my car. There were even little patches of chrome worn off the front bumper. Mike was laughing so hard he had to use me as a crutch; I was stunned. My mind was still racing, trying to connect all the sand granules. And then, after we were done unloading the car, Mike was polite enough to point out that my windshield had been pitted as well. Later that evening at dinner, Mike asked me why I didn't pull over and stop like everyone else. I told him, hell, I couldn't see the front of the car, you know (to assess the damage). And with all that sand blowing around I hadn't even noticed the windshield becoming pitted. So my personal advice to all you desert cruisers, if a sandstorm starts, and you're not in need of a new paint job, drive gingerly.

My first month in the Valencia/Newhall area was somewhat productive. Los Angeles is a massive place, so just figuring out the lay of the land is somewhat of an accomplishment. I now knew the most direct route to Ten Goose Boxing Gym, located in Van Nuys, as well as figured out all the main streets and roads in the Newhall area. I also joined Mike's weight lifting gym: Valencia Health Club. And oh yeah! It took me all of two weeks to figure out the pattern that Mike's girlfriend had established. While she whined, bitched, and moaned Monday through Thursday, convincing Mike he was inadequate at providing her a lifestyle she was sure she deserved, she managed to get taken out to dinner nightly, and preferably out to Beverly Hills, which was a 20-mile journey in one direction. She would start her day at noon, quietly lounging in his pool all afternoon, waiting for him to get home so she could inflict her demands on this oil-filled workingman.

She'd wait patiently for Thursday afternoon when Mike got home, so she could start a knockdown, drag out fight and then demand to be taken to her mother's house out in Thousand Oaks, easily a forty mile trip in one direction, where she'd spend Thursday, Friday, and Saturday. *Can you say party weekend with my friends?* Then on Sunday, after brunch, the phone would ring. She'd want Mike to come out to Thousand Oaks to pick her up. All had been forgiven, she needed a place to chill out, and she wasn't gonna hang out with her mom.

After Mike had chased his tail for well over a year, he finally had someone to bounce the logic off. He scratched his head and asked me if I thought it was him. And I asked him, "Have you noticed a pattern?" Mike paid attention, but it took him a couple of more weeks before the lights went on. Eventually he could clearly see what was more than obvious to me, so he did come to his senses and let her go. And I think a lot of us are guilty of this same crime: holding on to someone we love even though the relationship is toxic. But in the meantime, after grocery shopping one afternoon, Mike suggested we stop by some guy's house because he owed him money.

So *here I am*, at the front door of some deadbeat's house with Mike knocking. When the door opens, Mike barges in so I instinctively follow. And what do we see when we step inside? A handful of guys who snap to attention, with one of them snorting cocaine off the living room coffee table.

Let's just freeze here for a moment. I don't know about you, but to me this is so *déjà vu*. The hairs on my neck are standing erect. This is where Mike begins questioning the kid sitting on the couch snorting the dope, when he might be able to pay back the money that's owed him.

It's been over a decade since I got my teeth extracted and rearranged, and I find myself standing in the middle of another bad-debt drug deal. Only this time, I'm more street-wise. So why not nip it in the bud? A strong offense is the best defense.

Here is where the kid gets belligerent, and jumps up in Mike's face. Forgive me if I seem a little edgy, but this has way too many traces of familiarity about it. My knee-jerk reaction is, let's get the party started! I batter Sparky with the back of my hand, who then rolls over the coffee table and falls into the couch. This gets everybody's attention. Sparky bounces back up like he just sat on a tack. And that's when all his friends grab him, and Mike puts his arm in front of me.

It turns out, Sparky here had been over at Mike's house, partying with Mike's girlfriend, snorting cocaine. Mike had put the money up for the coke with the understanding that Sparky was going to pay him back.

The way Mike entered the house told me something was up. And once I stepped in and saw the dope on the table it was too late to back up. So in for a penny, in for a pound, but you can imagine the conversation I had with Mike in the car on the way back to his house.

You wish your friends would clue you into these things before they got you involved, but then you might not get involved... But no harm no foul. A few days later Sparky, showed up with the money he owed Mike and that was the last either one of us saw of him.

On the positive side of that first month, I landed a job. I took a position as a doorman at a rock club called Stage West. My thinking was, if I worked in the evenings, it would leave my days free for training. But here's where I find out, you can never be too careful when you answer a newspaper add for a job.

What I couldn't have known was, this rock club had been a biker bar for over two decades, and a pain in the LAPD's ass, but all that was about to become abundantly clear.

When I applied for the job, I met a man by the name of Sam Skinnard who was the manager of the club. I quickly found out I wouldn't be taking orders from him; rather I'd answer to George, the club's owner. Sam had a no-nonsense air about him. He didn't suffer fools easily. He was a stand up guy, and expected you to be the same.

Sam had played a rookie year of baseball with the Dodgers, and they compared him to the great Willie Stargell. This guy could hit a baseball. But he was a victim of his times. The Dodgers management came down and told him to shave his sideburns and his mustache, which he had grown into a long, Fu Manchu-style. He simply refused, so they suspended him.

With a back as wide as a billboard, he was such a great hitter he was sure they would call... They never did. Deep down, I think Sam was a little resentful, but he never showed it. He was a man; he sucked it up and never complained. He made his choices, and if I hadn't dug it out of him, I wouldn't be able to tell you this story.

The first night I was called to duty at the rock club, they held a wet t-shirt contest. It was the three B's plus one: Bikers, boobs, and booze. *Can you say bedlam?* The club's owner George was from Hungary and, in broken English, he would officiate the pageant. He also entered one of his waitresses into the competition, and she had, well... a Nice Rack. The winner would be decided by audience participation. The bimbo, I mean broad, I mean Barbie, who got the most applause would win the competition. *Can you see where this is headed?*

Now if it had been left up to me, Monica, George's employee, would have won the competition hands down. She had what can only be described as a perfect pair of melons, though my personal taste runs toward a full, perky breast over girth any day. The princess who actually won the competition by audience applause, was some biker's old lady. But unfortunately for me, George deemed her the runner up and instead anointed his girl Monica as the winner. And since the grand prize was more than a few hundred dollars, the biker was slightly more than outraged. *The fix was in!*

So *here I am* between George, the club owner, and this 240-pound, bad breath, foul-mouthed, tattooed up bearded biker who's on the verge of a catastrophic eruption! Did I mention his breath stinks? But believe it or not, I manage to calm the guy down. Just as I got this guy to relax and back off, George sticks his head over my shoulder and screams with his thick accent, "Get out of my club, you dog-faced American!"

Did I mention George is from Hungary? I couldn't believe what I'd just heard! I just stopped this biker from chewing George's face off with his jagged rotted teeth, and this honky couldn't leave well enough alone. But since I'm the buffer between them, he feels it's okay to throw gasoline on an already raging fire.

So now I'm the pinball, getting bounced around between these two Buddha bellies, trying to keep one from getting to the other. Well, actually it was the biker who was trying to get to George, but George was determined to keep me between them. Somehow, and believe me it's a bigger mystery to me, I talked the guy down. I got him to go back to his table and I bought him a round of drinks. I went straight to page one in the self-defense handbook. One of the things you learn in the martial arts world is how to redirect energy.

So with Biker Billy Badbreath focused on his free round of drinks, amply-endowed Monica can dance off the stage with her first place dollars.

Then Billy bad-breath Badass wanted to know when I wasn't working… That was a puzzling question. When I told Billy Badass I only work Friday, Saturday, and Sunday, he informed me he's coming back to burn the place down on Monday. And of course I humble myself and I say, "Excuse me Bill—I mean Mr. Ass—if you do that then I won't have a job."

And so goes night number one. Night number two? Well, the pace quickened. When I first started working nightclubs, my MO was to lay low. I like to watch the crowd and see who knows who, and I prefer to stay under the radar. Normally it doesn't take long to figure out who the potential troublemakers might be, and who might be backing them up.

So it's Saturday night, my second night of employment at Stage West. I'm standing on the dance floor talking to Bo the DJ, who's up in the DJ booth, which happened to be two-thirds of the way into the club. A few guys go by me briskly, passing the band that is on stage and turning left down the hallway behind the stage, where the liquor supply room and the restrooms are located. My subconscious immediately picked up on this, but I really didn't focus on it until a couple more guys went running by me.

That's when I thought, "That was strange." I turned around just in time to see them hit the brakes and take a hard left down the hallway, towards the restrooms. I followed them down the hallway just in time to see five guys trying to break the men's room door down. I shot straight down the hallway yelling, "Knock it off! Knock it off!" And just as I got to the men's room door, they busted it in. Just like a vacuum, it sucked the five of them and me in with it.

There was a full-on brawl in progress. Somehow I got shoved from my right, and my back got pressed up against the wall. Now backed up against the wall, I had nine guys throwing punches at each other right in front of me. We were all packed so tight in that tiny room that I couldn't pick my arms up to do anything.

With my back slammed against the wall, and my arms pinned to my sides, all I could do was yell, "Knock it off!" Somewhere around my third "knock it off," I shouted, "That's it! We're calling the cops!" One of these bathroom brawling buffoons had his right forearm pressed up against the side of my neck so hard that now my head was pinned to the wall.

In between throwing rapid-fire punches with his left hand at various people, he looked up at me for a moment and muttered, "You're not calling anybody." That caused me to bust up laughing because he was right. I wasn't in a position to call anyone and I knew it. With the bathroom filled to capacity with grown men throwing punches, and the bathroom door ripped almost off its hinges, the whole riot spilled out into the hallway. Now with my arms free I could set forth with trying to do my job. But how does one man stop or try to break up a fight this size when everyone else's intent is to continue?

316

It seemed like every time I tried to pull a guy off someone, another guy would jump on. You have to remember your job description, as a doorman, is not to beat people up but rather restrain them if need be and keep them from hurting each other. Suddenly someone bounced a punch off the back of my head. That was it. I'm not being paid enough money to let people take punches at me. I turn around and crack the first guy I see, and all of a sudden he's out of the fight. Now that my first punch had been thrown, I feel liberated to continue. Out of the corner of my eye I see two doormen running down the hall towards me. *Thank God, the cavalry has arrived!*

One of the other doormen, who was over six foot, wore a size sixty sports coat and weighed well over 200 pounds, grabbed a guy by the scruff of his neck and the seat of his pants, and used the guy as a battering ram to open up the cigarette machine. *Game over!*

It turns out there were nine full-grown men throwing punches inside that men's room. And I felt like a spectator in the bleachers! All I could do was watch from the cheap seats. But once it spilled out into the hallway, and with a little help from the cavalry, we cleaned it up pretty quick.

My backup at the club (but only for the first couple of weekends) was a great guy. Like I said, he was a little over six feet and closer to three hundred pounds than two. I'll never forget him grabbing that kid by the scruff of his neck and the seat of his pants and lifting him up about waist height and then using the kid's head as a battering ram to open up the cigarette machine and then dropping the kid to the floor like a used toy.

At the end of the evening we all had a great laugh, but I wasn't sure if the staff that worked there was laughing with me or at me. I had worn a cowboy style shirt to work that evening with, snap pearl buttons. At the end of the night the only thing left of that shirt was the collar, the button line down the front, and one cuff. The rest of the shirt was missing.

I told the manager, Sam Skinner, as he cashed me out that evening that if I had to wear my own wardrobe to work, I couldn't afford to keep the job. Sam tucked his chin down and chuckled as he counted up the money he owed me for that evening's work. Then he promised to supply me with Stage West rock club t-shirts to work in. That was my first weekend working at Stage West, which should have been an omen for what was to come.

In the meantime, by day I was training at Ten Goose Boxing, trying to sharpen my skills so I could get back in the ring. After about two weeks of working out, Dan Goossen approached me one day as I was hitting the heavy bag, and asked if he could speak with me a moment.

We stepped outside, and that's where Dan proceeded to be one of the most direct and upfront people I had ever met in the boxing world. He went on to explain that he'd talked to some fight promoters who knew me and said they liked me. Dan, being a good manager, was trying to get his fighters in to the boxing capital of the world, Vegas, and I was trying to get out. So both parties could see we had a conflict of interest.

I thanked him for his honesty and shook his hand, and went straight back inside to pack my bags. I didn't even finish my workout. I headed north on the 170 to catch the 5 into Newhall. And I didn't have one mixed emotion. I knew I was through. I would later come to realize, boxing had simply provided me with a vehicle with which to arrive at the West Coast. I had already made up my mind to go back to my first love, Karate.

Since I had a weightlifting membership at a gym, Valencia Health Club, that had an aerobics room with four mirrored walls that no one used during the day, this would provide me with a place to go through my moves until I could find a Karate school that was suitable.

Every day after working at the gym, I would stop at a different Karate school to see if I could start training at their studio, but I kept getting stonewalled. At this point I had been away from the martial arts world for quite a few years, and evidently it had changed quite a bit.

Back in the 70s, if you were driving across country and your car broke down and you had no money, all you needed to do was find a dojo. Walk in and introduce yourself, and as soon as you proved you knew what you were talking about, more than likely they would welcome you with open arms. It was a true brotherhood. If they hadn't invited you to their home, and in most cases they would, at the very least, they made sure you had a place to sleep at their dojo.

At first I didn't understand their attitude. I had brought all the press I had received throughout the years to prove my worthiness. I had been featured in articles from major publications, such as Ring magazine, Sports Illustrated, and Official Karate, not to mention the slew of newspaper articles I had received from Miami all the way to Las Vegas. I was under the impression that this would surely speak volumes for

318

my credibility. But then reality slowly crept in: this was hurting me more than it was helping me. Now how can I put this politely? Most black belts have a healthy ego, and few would welcome someone into their Karate studio who knew more about the fighting arts than they do.

So *here I am* knocking, but I can't get in. Despite my proven background, no one was eager to introduce me to their Karate studio. So I switched to Plan B. I acquired a heavy bag, and hung it off the overhang of Mike's pool deck. With Mike at work during the day, I'd slide open the double glass doors to his pool deck, crank the stereo, and rock the house.

This arrangement worked pretty well for quite a while. With Mike leaving for work at about 5:00 a.m., and not getting home until 2 or 3 in the afternoon, we only crossed each other's paths for a couple of hours before I headed off to work at night. And boy, did I need to stay sharp.

For the next two weeks I watched to see who were bar room buddies, and which ones could be potential problems. As I mentioned before, I stayed underneath the radar. No one had a clue what my background had been, and my senses were telling me this would serve me well. Instead of running my mouth like a big shot, and telling everyone I had been a professional fighter, and to what extent, I just kept my mouth shut, and observed. That is, until one Saturday night when I had to clear everybody out of the bar before two am, closing time. I would come to find out that L.A. County has stringent liquor laws. If someone were caught at 2:01 a.m. in a nightclub with a drinking glass in their hand, the nightclub could not only be fined, the nightclub could lose its liquor license.

The week before, I'd had the same problem with this guy. He had dragged his feet at the end of the night, until he stepped out right at 2:00 a.m. Now it wasn't unusual for people to move towards the front door in a slow fashion. These folks had been drinking and partying all night, and they didn't want it to end. But this one guy was that belligerent drunk that everyone recognizes. The rules weren't for him. He wasn't going to leave until he was ready. It was pretty standard for me to have to walk through the club three or four times announcing that we were closing and that everyone needed to move towards the front door.

On this evening there were thirty to forty people gathered around the front entrance of the club, trying to make their way out the front door, when this Numbnuts decides to stop at the front bar and suck on his ice cubes. As I had mentioned before, Numbnuts here had agitated me the week before, but I have always prided myself on having extreme patience with people. So I politely ask him to move towards the front door again. His response? He'll move when he's ready. This arrogance made the hair follicles on my body stand at attention.

Once again I politely request that he put his drinking glass on the bar, and move towards the front door. His second response was more arrogant than his first! This time he tells me he'll leave when he's ready, he's not through with his drink. This is where I politely point out he has no drink left, that it's only ice. This is where he smirks and tells me to fuck off. Then he raised the glass up towards his mouth as if he was going to take a drink. I grabbed the glass with my left hand and pulled on it. He pulled back. Now at this point in the story I can't argue as to what happened. But I'm going to tell you my side of the story and I'm stickin' to it.

I jerked the glass out of his hand, and when I did, he came with it. I took that as an attack, so I threw a right hand, cracked him on the chin, and dropped him like the sack of shit he was. His buddy who was nearby stared at him on the floor for a couple of moments, and then looked up and started screaming, "Sucker punch!"

I demanded that everyone leave the bar, and with a shock of the reality they had just witnessed, there was a stampede to get out the front door. I grabbed Numbnuts by his belt buckle and hair and carried him like a piece of luggage to the front door. As I passed his buddy, I told him to stay right there, and I'd be right back to show him a sucker who was going to get punched.

I opened the front door using Numbnuts' head and dropped him out on the sidewalk. When I did, Numbnuts' friend ran right by me. So much for loyalty… I slammed the door and locked it from the inside. Moving like a man with intent as I passed the front bar, I looked over at Sam and told him I was sick of taking this crap from these assholes.

Sam began to laugh, and then he applauded. I found out that no doorman had lasted more than a few weeks at this establishment. For the next four or five months, I'd find myself in at least one fight a week and, back when I first started, sometimes three in one night. I would come to find out there was an overabundance of arrogance and stupidity in the San Fernando Valley.

Take the belligerent drunk one of the barmaids refused to serve one night. Behind our bar, like in a lot of taverns, was a liquor shelf. And the wall behind that shelf was mirrored. This belligerent clown, after being refused service, grabbed someone else's beer bottle off the bar, and threw it at our barmaid. Thank God it missed her. But it didn't miss the liquor shelf and mirror. Now part of my job description was to restock the beer coolers when they got low. I had just locked up the liquor stockroom, and was headed up to the front of the nightclub with two cases of beer in my hands when I heard an earsplitting crash. I dumped the two cases of beer on a table and immediately ran for the front bar. When I arrived, the mirror behind the bar was shattered, as well as liquor bottles on the shelf. The barmaid pointed at a man who was steps away from exiting the building, and then she told me he'd thrown a beer bottle at her for refusing to serve him.

I took off like a shot. Just as he was about to step outside, I shouted, "Hey!" and then he made a big mistake. He spun around and threw a right-handed punch at me. I threw a left-handed knife-hand block, which pounded him on the shoulder and stopped his punch dead in its tracks. I slid my left hand up behind his neck and grabbed him, then threw a right uppercut that buckled his knees. But I wasn't done with him yet. Now I had him by the front of his shirt shaking him and lecturing him at the same time. Every time he became coherent enough to try and fight back, I popped him with another uppercut and lectured and shook him some more.

After a few more shakes, a couple of uppercuts, and a lot of lecturing, I pushed him out the front door. Now you would think that by then this belligerent fuck would have come to the conclusion of "Hey, maybe I'm in over my head. Maybe this guy knows something." But nooooo, not Mr. Belligerent.

I pushed him out the front door backwards. He staggered back a couple of paces, and took one quick step forwards and tried to kick me in my onions. Now here's one part of the male anatomy you will guard at any cost. You take a hard enough hit in the family jewels and you could be shooting blanks. So you instinctively move a little faster when someone targets that area. Ah, to know Karate. I step back on my right foot and throw a left-handed low block and hook his legs.

Now with his legs trapped, and his foot about shoulder height, judging by the size of his eyes as wide as softballs, it's now perfectly clear to him that he's in trouble. Just as I glide in for the kill, I hear Mr.

Belligerent whine, "I'm fucked up!" like, at this moment, this excuse is some sort of an apology. Just before my right palm connects with his chin, and my right leg kicks his supporting leg out from under him, I tell him, "You are now."

Let me pause here for a moment for a brief description. Anyone who's ever been to the tropics and tried to break a coconut open by smashing it on a curb or a rock, knows exactly what a human skull sounds like when it bounces off concrete. And for all those who haven't been to the tropics, it's not a comforting sound. It's almost always one big hard thud, with two follow up bouncing thuds. It's a little disturbing, and enough to make you feel nauseous.

But believe it or not, it wasn't always this chaotic. A lot of nights were pretty mellow and a lot of fun. You just needed to have your senses turned on at all times, because at any minute, anything could happen. By far Monday nights were my favorite. It was Jam Night, and Tim Bogert, former bass player for Vanilla Fudge, would come in with his band, which included one of the lead guitar players from Three Dog Night, and one of the best drummers in rock, Chet McCracken, who played with the Doobie Brothers.

At any given Monday evening, you could stop in and possibly hear some of the greatest players in rock. It never ceased to amaze me how many great rock musicians would stop into the little dive bar just to jam. It wasn't unusual to see band members from groups like Foreigner, Journey, REO, and Rush; all of them playing for free just to have fun. There were so many I couldn't keep track of them all. But one thing I did know, I was privileged to witness such a show, week after week.

After working at this fine establishment for close to half a year, things did seem to settle down, but then a new problem presented itself: the old 'fastest gun in the west' syndrome. Now all of a sudden I had guys coming in just to challenge me. I never had any problems with the Hell's Angels, but I did with some of their prospects, as well as some of the guys that like to hang out with them.

Prospects are, well, just like it sounds: prospective members. They had to prove their worth as probationary members and jump through designated hoops before they could join the group. One night, I had just stepped in through the front door when the bartender called out for me. I walked up to the bar, and there was a guy sitting to my right, who reached up and shoved my right shoulder. I looked at him and smiled; I thought it might be someone I knew. Believe it or not, the first words out of his mouth were, "I bet you think you can knock me out."

I glanced down the bar quickly, to see if there was anyone I knew. I thought someone might be playing a joke on me. Then my smile quickly turned to a grin, and I turned to the man and said, "C'mon man, drink your drink and have a good time." When I turned back towards the bartender, he shoved me again. Now I turned to face him, and he repeated himself. "I bet you think you could knock me out." I just smile, and tell him not to put his hands on me. I can already see where this is going. Keeping my eye on him, I turn back to the bartender when he puts his hand up to shove me again. So I turn to square off with him, and once more he says, "I bet you think you could knock me out."

I just smiled and replied, "Yes, I can," only the "can" part hit his ears just as I punched him on the chin. He must have thought a lightning bolt struck him. He fell forward and I grabbed him by the collar and jerked him back. Across the aisle from the bar was a poolroom, which was enclosed by a four-foot high wall, separating it from the rest of the club. That wall had a two-by-ten cap on it, which acted as a counter for you to set your drink on while you shot pool.

The entrance to the poolroom was directly behind me, so when I jerked the guy backwards, instead of going through that opening, he bounced off of that chest-high counter, and right into my front kick, which caught him square in the forehead, and snapped his head back with the violence of a rear end collision.

He was out cold, face first on the carpet. I grabbed him by the back of his collar and the belt of his pants and once again I feel like a luggage handler down at LAX, opening the front door with his head and tossing him out on the sidewalk. As I turned to go back into the nightclub, I noticed a couple of people outside smoking a cigarette and talking.

After a few moments, a young woman burst through the door and asked me to call an ambulance. I said, "For what?" She said the guy I had just brought out of the club was making weird noises and she thought he might be dying. I started to chuckle and replied, "He's not dying" and she said something that chilled me right to my bones: "How do you know? Are you a doctor?"

I jumped on the phone and called an ambulance. The local hospital was less than a quarter of a mile away, thank God. An ambulance arrived in moments and they took the guy away. Fortunately for me he turned out to be all right.

But now *here I am*, standing in front of Stage West, being grilled by the LAPD and they're more than happy to inform me of all the charges that can be brought against me. My response? "For what?" They went into the legal ramifications of me punching out a customer. Just because I'd been hired by the nightclub to do security, it gave me no more legal right than the next guy to strike someone. These were all things I was acutely aware of already.

This is where I interrupted. I politely explained to the police officers that if I was supposed to wait until someone struck me before I took action, no one was paying me nearly enough money to afford that privilege. Besides, like I said, the guy had put his hands on me three separate times. One officer looked at the other and shrugged. Common sense wins out again.

Then there was the night of a biblical tale; David versus Goliath, with me starring in the role as David. By this time I had thinned out most of the riff raff that had been coming since before I started working there.

At this time, Stage West was as popular as it would ever be. Weekdays, the rock club would get filled to its maximum capacity of 215 people. On weekends we were pushing well over the limit, with as many as 250 to 260 partygoers on a Friday or Saturday night. The fire marshal was now on us like a dog in heat. I now had to keep a click counter at the front door at all times, just to keep track of all the patrons.

One weekend night, as I was standing at the front door, a massive man walked up. I think he was the biggest guy I had ever seen; over seven feet tall, and over 400 pounds. We were packed, so I had to deny him entry, which didn't seem to bother him too much. He turned around and began to mingle with the crowd that had begun to gather out front. By this point we had hired a few other doormen. Glen Wagner and Lou Vachon were my two favorites. Leaving Glen at the front door, I stepped inside for about fifteen minutes to make one of my rounds. When I got back, it was just in time to see a pretty young blonde girl lead Goliath in by the hand.

I had to stop them, but she pleaded with me to let him use the pay phone. I was told his car had broken down, and he needed to call someone to come and pick him up. I thought, fair enough. With the pay phone just inside the front door, I thought, "What harm could it do?" *Little did I know...*

He had to duck down just to get through the front door. A few moments later I happened to glance to my right just in time to see him hang up the phone, do an about face spin, and head directly into the nightclub. I rushed in to cut him off, but by the time I got to him, he'd already passed the poolroom and was approaching the far end of the front bar. I jumped in front of him. I tried to explain, firstly there were way too many people inside the club, and secondly, he needed to pay the weekend cover charge if he wanted to gain entry. Judging by the look on old Goliath's face, "No" was not part of the verbiage in his language.

He proceeded to walk over me, and so I reached up and put my hand on his chest. Out of the corner of my eye, I could see Sam Skinner wiping off his hands with a bar towel, instinctively picking up that he was going to have to back me up. Right then Goliath grunted, and tried to wrap his arms around me. I stepped back and tried to leg sweep him. But with my adrenaline pumping so hard it was drowning the hair follicles in my scalp—I missed the sweep.

Still grunting and in pursuit, Goliath again tried to wrap his arms around me. I jump back and plant my feet, only this time I fire a right cross that hits him square in the cheek which drops him straight to his knees. You know when you pop a guy with your best shot and all he does is fall down on his knees, and now is staring you straight in your eyes? Yeah, I didn't think so...

But this is where I find myself. Sam, being accustomed to me hitting someone and knocking them out cold, had already turned around and headed back behind the bar, which has presented me with a problem. Even though I dropped Paul Bunyan here like one of his trees, all I did was bring him down to my size. Quite honestly, now he was able to look me square in my face.

Thank God for Louis. He happened to be in the club on his night off, shooting pool, when he looked up and witnessed what was taking place. He walked out of the poolroom, and pushed Goliath from behind. When this freak of nature fell forward, I tried to grab him in a headlock, but his head was as big as a basketball.

As Goliath started to stand up, I whipped around behind him and got him in a chokehold, which was probably not my best option. But I wasn't hired to beat people up; I was hired to keep them from hurting each other, and possibly restraining someone. But when push comes to shove, you have to revert back to Rule Number One: don't let anyone hurt you.

This guy stood up like I was a gnat on his ass. With absolutely no effort, he was back on his feet with me still hanging from around his neck; mine were a foot and a half off the ground.

Right then the poolroom emptied to help Louis. It took six men to push this guy to the front door, with me still swinging around his neck. I'm in his ear yelling, "What the hell's wrong with you?" and he's screaming at me, "Outside!"

Just as they were pushing Paul Bunyan out the front door, this gnat bailed. Okay—I let go and he dropped, with the thud of a sack of potatoes. I immediately jumped up and just as I did, Goliath spun around, reached in and, with his left hand, grabbed me by the shirt dead in the center of my chest, and then launched a right hand towards my head, stepping forward with a stomp that shook the earth.

Just before this howitzer landed, I dropped down to duck. His fist collided with the wall behind me, punching a hole in it the size of a one-gallon milk jug. Then he tried to jerk me out of the club with his left hand, but I wasn't going anywhere. Instead, he tore a chunk out of the chest of my shirt the size of a volleyball. As my shirt tore away, he stumbled backwards, so we slammed the door shut and locked it.

Now this nightclub was located on a plaza, the end of which was recessed. There was a concrete patio leading up to the parking lot in front of the club. As you stepped out the front door of the nightclub, off to your left, a couple of yards away, was a big square brick planter with a palm tree growing out of the middle of it.

The front door of the nightclub was steel-framed with some heavy filler inside it. Just beyond the front door, on both sides of its frame, was a steel pipe, six inches in diameter, filled with concrete and buried into the patio. Each pipe rose up to chest height, for good reason. Just before I had accepted employment at this fine establishment, they had tossed out some buffoon who promptly started his car, drove over the curb, barreled across the patio, and then rammed the front door with his car, causing, as you may have guessed, severe damage to the front of the building as well as the nightclub door. I don't think it did his car any good, either.

After that episode, George called the owner of the building and decided to avoid the annual buffoon demolition derby. He drilled two holes three feet deep and buried those two six-inch diameter steel, galvanized pipes into the patio on either side of the door. His thinking? This should bring all stupidity to an abrupt halt.

Nevertheless, thank God for that steel framed door with its heavy-reinforced center, because after Goliath physically charged the door two or three times like an African rhino, this peanut brain came to the conclusion that this approach wasn't going to work.

So he walked straight over to the planter and pulled up the metal pipes that were the watering system for the palm tree. Now armed with a six foot long steel pipe that he had ripped out of the ground, he was doing his best re-enactment of the Arnold classic: Conan the Barbarian. Using this galvanized steel pipe as a sword, he was doing his best to try to chop his way back in through the front door. There were ten or twelve of us, huddled near the entrance of the nightclub, and we could hear the animal outside howling and growling. And with every blow that sounded, a new dimple appeared on our side of the door. It was like living through a terrifying horror movie!

After a long ten minutes it sounded like the carnage outside had finally ceased, but nobody was in a hurry to step outside that front door, including me. Then it dawned on me. Andy, who was a part-time doorman and full-time Teamster, had been in the storage room stacking cases of beer when all this insanity broke out. So I decided to arm Andy with a ball bat and send him out for a little reconnaissance. Since Goliath hadn't seen him, I sent Andy out the back door with a Louisville slugger, instructing him to walk around to the front of the building to see if Goliath was playing dead.

A few tense, suspenseful moments passed before we heard a knock on the door. *Can you say Alfred Hitchcock?* Then we heard, "I'll huff, and I'll puff, and I'll blow the door down!" *Funny Andy!* We all looked at each other and then burst into nervous laughter. Once we opened the front door, there was Andy with his ballbat in hand, grinning and practicing his new stand-up routine. Meanwhile, about ten to fifteen people were standing behind him, waiting to enter the nightclub and have a night of fun. Apparently it was just another weekend night to them. And oh yeah, over in the planter where that palm tree once stood, now flowed a fountain with a 20-foot geyser.

Once the LAPD had arrived, I was busy explaining to one officer all the havoc and chaos that had ensued, when he received a call on his radio. There was what could only be described as a seven foot, 400 pound wild man running down Balboa Boulevard armed with a six-foot long galvanized steel pipe, randomly breaking the windows of people's automobiles. The officer snapped a startled look at me and I quipped, "I think he went thataway…"

Now it's Monday. Jam night. I arrive early to stock the beer coolers, and you can't imagine the shock and surprise on my face when I walk through the front door, and there sits Goliath, of all people, accompanied by his father, no less. It turned out I recognized his dad, as he habitually stopped in a couple of days a week for happy hour.

Sitting on the bar stool, Goliath was still taller than me standing up! It turns out that Goliath had a construction job and had never had a drink in his life. Come Friday, some of the guys in his crew thought it would be funny to take him out and get him drunk. But with them pouring tequila down his palate, this had the makings of a bad science experiment. At this point, it's more than obvious that not one of the mental midgets had ever read the fable of Frankenstein, nor heeded the lesson; you shouldn't create what you can't control. Not one of the junior scientists took into consideration what happens when the test tube boils over.

But reality has a way of bitch-slapping you sober. After drinking a tequila bottle or two, someone must have said or done something to piss Goliath off. Well, Doctor Frankenstein, Igor, Egad and Idork had to pay for the consequences of their actions. And they had to pay with their own pork. That's right; Goliath started his evening off beating up the four mad scientists, better known as his construction buddies.

After trashing up the place they were in, Goliath decided to wander up the street to find the tavern where his father was drinking. So *here I am*, facing Goliath again, staring at the big red welt on the side of his face that I had administered with my right hand.

And strangely enough, he had no animosity. He turned out to be a very shy and humble man, who came in with his father to apologize, and offer to pay for any damages he may have caused.

Chapter Twenty-seven
Kickstand Cowboys, Murders and a New Arrival

Now it's the summer of 1984. Los Angeles is hosting the Olympics, and I was determined to go. Back in 1976, when I was living in Florida, I was convinced that the '76 Montreal Olympic Games were as close as I'd ever get to that world event. Even though I grew up blue-collar poor, with Montreal a great distance from Palm Beach County, Florida, in an optimistic 19-year-old's mind it still felt like it was within striking distance.

But *here I am* to tell you; this universe works in strange and mysterious ways, because sometimes you're so close to the forest you truly can't see the trees. But as the years ticked forward and I have looked back, I've realized that anywhere I wanted to go, anything I wanted to do, and most things I wanted to see have materialized.

I told Mike my roommate—and anyone who would listen—that I was going to attend the Olympics. And even though I didn't have a pass, a ticket, or a hope and a prayer, when Sunday morning came, the last day of the Olympics, I got up early.

As I backed out of the driveway, Mike and his girl came running out of the house with money. They wanted me to buy them some souvenirs. Mike, and everybody else, thought I was crazy, until they realized I was actually gonna do it.

So *here I am*, standing somewhere on a corner below Downtown LA, witnessing one of the greatest goodwill gatherings in the world. I notice a frenzy across the street, so I stroll over to see what's going on.

And who is it? None other than Olympic medalist American volleyball player Karch Kiraly, who's signing jerseys and selling them to fans.

The next thing I know I'm shaking his hand. And I have no illusions that Karch would remember me; I was just another guy on the street that day. But meeting him sure made my day. As I strolled away, I remember thinking, Karch's gotta sell t-shirts to stay in the game? If you ask me, there's gotta be something dreadfully wrong with the way we fund and support our Olympic athletes. I'm sure he's doing fine now, but I think people would be shocked and amazed at how humble the struggle is—as well as all the hard work it take—to become an Olympian or World Champion.

Buses filled with athletes traveled down the road, displaying their country's flag, all waving at the crowd who would in turn cheer them on, no matter what country they were from. Speaking of Mankind, this was one of the most amazing things you could ever witness.

But *here I am*, standing in front of the Los Angeles Coliseum with the sun going down. I run through the festival in the streets, I witness the closing ceremonies, I had shaken an Olympian's hand, and I watched the fireworks. I had been to the Olympics, although next time I vowed to do more than just the poor boy Olympics or watch them on TV.

My plan is to attend the athletic events, and watch them up close and personal. Going into the second half of 1985, the armpit of rock and roll nightclubs in Los Angeles, better known as Stage West, was wearing a little thin. Recognizing the vast amount of wealth in LA county in the entertainment industry, I decided to put together a resume for personal security. You know, bodyguard work?

Call me naïve—okay, call me stupid—but I placed an ad in the Los Angeles Times. After a couple of days, the phone wouldn't stop ringing, but it was always the same story. How did I feel about homosexuality, and would I be interested in trading off some of my salary for free room and board down in Boy's Town, better known as West Hollywood?

I didn't need to turn on the lights to see who's hiring here. I have nothing against gay people; it's just a lifestyle I choose not to be involved in. When I pulled the ad the following week, I decided I needed a better way to network. And as luck would have it, life once again presented opportunities.

My bouncing bar room buddy, Louis, introduced me to his mom

Joyce. It turns out Joyce just signed a deal with musician Billy Preston to start a record company, Preston Productions. Joyce had done well in the mortgage and real estate industry, and was now looking to branch out into the entertainment world. Additionally, Joyce was looking to impress upon her son Lou that she needed someone streetwise, loyal and fearless to run security for her. Lou, after witnessing me in action more than a couple of dozen times, sold his mother on me in just one word… "Balls."

So *here I am*, sitting in a mortgage broker's office, staring across the desk of the President of Preston Productions, Joyce, who had just offered me employment as chief of security, which sounded a lot more impressive than it was. I *am* the security. My days working as a doorman at Stage West were numbered, although for a while I held on to both jobs and worked a record seventeen weeks without a day off. (For me!)

But then one Friday night, my time at Stage West rock club came to a climactic end. I had consistent problems with one group of biker barroom buffoons who just couldn't get with the program of treating your fellow citizens with a little respect and dignity. As the year passed by, I would find myself barring, one by one, the majority of these biker bozos. The Friday night in question, these buffoons drove their motorcycles over the curb, up over the patio, to the front of Stage West, put their kickstands down, and approached the front door.

Of course, when I denied them entry, they proceeded to tell me what they were going to do to me. Evidently they saw some amusement in lighting me on fire and then dragging me around the parking lot behind one of their motorcycles. While I stood in the doorway blocking their entrance, and they insisted on inviting me out to my own barbecue, one of our customers slipped around them and came inside. As he walked around me he whispered, "Don't go out there." And although I appreciated his concern, what kind of reform-school reject did he take me for?

I assured him, as well as these buffoons, my job description did not include the parking lot. My job was to ensure the safety of the people inside the nightclub. As they taunted me, and called me names, which included parts of a woman's anatomy, I politely pointed out they showed up to storm the Alamo. So who would be the first one to step inside? There were no takers. So they continued to swear and degrade me, hoping that would agitate me enough to step outside.

When this tactic didn't work, they elevated their verbal assault to the point of insulting my mother, which only made me laugh. I responded, "You know Mom?" Now with a look of frustration on their faces, they cranked up their Harleys, and rode up and down the sidewalk and across the patio, with some of them swinging chains around over their heads like lassos. As they rode off, my concerned customer expressed why he didn't think it was a good idea for me to step outside. Although I could think of a dozen of them, our Good Samaritan here came up with the number one reason. As he slid around the collected group of bozos, he couldn't help but notice one standing behind the door with his hand in a paper bag. Inside the bag, a gun.

After the bikers rode off, some clown, who came into the club almost daily, came up to me and blustered how he wouldn't put up with such degradation. Always a critic... I should have 86'd him on principle, but instead I let it go. I was thinking how pathetic they all were. It had taken six or seven of them with weapons to have the courage to face me.

At the end of the evening, I told my friend Sam Skinner I was gonna have to be paid a whole lot more money if I was going to consistently contend with these kickstand cowboys. He agreed, and told me to take it up with George the owner, and he would back me up 100%.

So *here it is*, Saturday night, and here I am, standing in front of George, trying to explain what had taken place the evening before, and why the door crews should be paid more money for the risks they were taking. Something must have broken down in the translation, because George, although hardheaded and stubborn, just didn't get it. He couldn't follow the scenario I had just explained.

I pointed out that Sam and I were the last two people to leave the club, and even a buffoon would find no effort in waiting to see what car I got in so they could follow me home. And if the possibility of me being shot at or run off the road wasn't enough, my concern was, if they found out where I lived they might do something stupid, like try to burn my roommate Mike's house down. But all this fell on deaf ears, so I gave George my week's notice, and gave my door crew the bad news. They would have to find someone else to contend with those cowards.

But working for Joyce turned out to be a blast. I spent my days chauffeuring her around in a brand new Nissan 300ZX with a T-top that never seemed to be on the car. And she always seemed to have the same request. If it took more than twenty minutes to get from point A to point B under normal circumstances (if you can consider dodging traffic in L.A. normal), she'd request that I get her there in twelve. Then one morning she asked me to pick her up a little earlier than usual. Our first stop; the courthouse.

As we went inside and were seated, she began explaining what was taking place. She had mentioned the issue before but never in detail. The short story was, Joyce had been convicted of smuggling cocaine into the country from Mexico. *Praise the pagan gods!* Why did I keep finding myself in the midst of drug dealers? What does one have to do to get *away* from this shit?! But on this particular morning, she was here to receive her sentencing. Which she would receive! So with a gift from her county, Joyce was off with her new silver bracelets to a state funded retreat.

And *BAM!* Jeff was out of a job. A few years earlier, if I recall correctly, Joyce was semi-retired in Puerto Vallarta, Mexico, when she was stricken with cancer. Needing money for treatment, someone approached her with a flaky idea. And in all fairness, once your back is pushed against a wall, you're likely to try it all.

It's a decision you hope you never have to make. On one hand it's the slow death of cancer, and on the other, the slow isolation of prison time. So she rolled the dice, and it didn't come out nice. *Snake eyes.*

I felt horrible. I liked Joyce. Thank God the judge was lenient; he understood her plight. But by locking her up, there was a lot of collateral damage. She had a crew of people working for her at her mortgage company, including daughter. She was also the fireball on the team that generated revenue for Preston Productions.

And like I said, that was the end of my gravy train. So *here I am*, once again unemployed, at the gym doing what I know best, when I look over, and see a guy I know of, but don't really know: Frank Giardina. Frank was the manager of one of the more popular nightclubs in L.A. County: Sash located in the San Fernando Valley in Studio City. The word was it was a hot spot. Rock royalty, as well as young Hollywood, would frequent the place. Working there would put me closer to the clientele I was seeking employment from. I approached Frank, and then I introduced myself. I mentioned that I did security work, but being as I was at the gym, I didn't have a resume with me. Frank blew me off.

Looking to generate some revenue, and half out of desperation, I took a job at a local night spot that was attached to a bowling alley,

333

up in the Santa Clarita Valley, which is where Valencia is located. After a couple of weeks of working at this fine establishment, lo and behold Frank Giardina stopped in. So I introduced myself a second time. Frank vaguely remembered me. When he went to leave, I stepped out the door behind him and offered him my resume. A week later, he called.

As it turns out, Frank had to fill a spot that was vacated by one of his doormen, who was busted for selling Quaaludes to an undercover cop. Finally it seemed as if I was making a move in the right direction. Now I was working in a more suitable environment, meeting a variety of entertainment people to network with, and looking sharp. My working attire consisted of sports coats, ties, and slacks. When Frank hired me, he warned me it might be temporary. He had promised his dope-dealing door man, out of some sense of loyalty, that he would hold on to his job for a week, which should have gave him enough time to make bail.

After a week had passed, Frank approached me, and told me that if I wanted the position permanently, it was mine. In just a few short days, I had the non-pleasure of meeting this dope-dealing dipstick of a human being. After the introduction, Double D, (Dopey Dipstick), announces, "So you're the guy that took my job."

If there's one thing I've noticed that runs consistent with these dope-dealing derelicts, it's a lack of responsibility for their actions and the choices they make in this life. I grinned and told him I was just a guy applying for a job, and I had no idea I'd be replacing him. Looking him in the eyes, which never lie, I can tell what lay inside. Somehow, in his mind, it was all my fault.

Over the next six to eight weeks, I would see Dipstick in the nightclub a handful of times. We never spoke, nor did we acknowledge each other, though I did catch him staring at me more than once. Then one night I was stationed just inside the front door of the nightclub, right at the ticket counter. Frank had stepped outside for a few moments, and when he returned, he walked up to me and stopped. He pointed out that Double D had just shown up at the nightclub, and was standing out front speaking with some of the other doormen.

Frank, being a meticulous manager, had a routine of checking the guest list at the beginning of each night. Working for the club, you had guest privileges. Rule number one: you had to have your guest's name on the list by 8:30 p.m. If their name did not appear on that roster, they paid full cover. Frank had already checked the night's list, and Dopey Dipstick's name was nowhere to be seen on it. Frank, with a twinkle in his eye, reminded me of the rule, and I knew exactly what he meant.

There's something about one man being able to knock another man to his knees that's intriguing among men. Frank had gone back to his office; I'm sure to watch the main event from his security camera monitors. It would turn out Dipstick, being Italian, was a little hotheaded. And from what I understood, the nightclub was dealing with a couple of lawsuits because of it.

It was rumored that Dopey Dipstick had done some boxing, and won a Golden Gloves tournament, but I had serious doubts. But here he comes through the front door with his 'too cool for school' shuffle, and makes a stop at the ticket window to say hello to Laurie, the doll who works the window. He does a jitterbug slide past her, and confronts me. I ask him for his ticket, he says he doesn't need one, so I ask him to go back and sign the guest roster, which I know full well he can't do, because his name's not on it. But hell, I'm here all night, so I'm willing to play this game of charades as long as he is. He stands there glaring at me. I tell him, "Come on, you know the rules better than me. Go back and sign the guest register, or pay full cover and hand me a ticket."

With that he took a hard left, trying to take another route into the club past the band. I cut him off at the pass, and warned him, "Stop pulling this crap because you're not gonna walk over me." That's when I noticed his jaw getting tight, and then Double D did something really dopey: he clenched his fists. Leaving home at fifteen after being in a fistfight with my stepfather… Well, let's just say this wasn't my first rodeo. With a click counter in one hand, and tickets in the other, I did what any red-blooded American black belt would do. When I saw his jaw tighten, I shifted my weight back ever so slightly. When I saw his fist clench, I dropped my weight on my forward leg, hitting him with a head butt that caught him in the bridge of the nose.

He went ass over teacups, falling on the table we had set up for people to leave their drinks on as they left the club. I reached down and grabbed him by his shirt to pull him up to his feet. With the table wiped out and the floor full of drinks, as I jerked him upright my feet slipped out from under me, causing me to fall backwards on a railing with him on top of me, and hyper-extending my back.

I wrestled him over to the gate, and that's when the doormen rushed in from outside and escorted him out the front door. Dipstick suffered a broken nose so he was good looking no more, but I sensed I had done some major damage to my back.

Dipstick would go on to serve prison time for drug-related charges. It was rumored his dad was related to the mob, so he kept trying to get his father's respect with his criminal behavior.

After he had served his time, my good friend Stuart Wilson, Dick Wilson's son, better known as Mr. Whipple, told me that Dopey here had gone on to graduate to contract killing, and now was serving a prison term for murder. *Ah, sweet success.*

This wasn't the first time I had come to a face-off with a murderer. Years earlier, about the time I took up boxing, I had agreed to referee a kickboxing event for my good friend Steve Shepherd. After refereeing the main event, I stepped down out of the ring only to be confronted by a man named Steve Beatty, a black belt in Karate who I knew and who had a chain of health clubs and Karate studios in the Miami Beach area.

He approached me, harshly criticizing how I'd refereed the main event. I simply explained my actions as to how I saw things inside the ring, but he didn't wanna hear any of it, and his already-aggravated state escalated. With him persisting with his point of view, I was beginning to feel like I need to square off.

Beatty, who was also into bodybuilding, outweighed me by forty pounds, all muscled up and tipping the scale at 230, 235 pounds. When I finally had enough, I looked him dead in his eyes and told him I didn't care what he thought. I was the referee in the ring that night, and only my call counted.

Even though Beatty was bigger, he'd seen me come up through the ranks and make black belt and then enter the world of kickboxing. So he not only knew that I could fight, but that I would fight. Eventually he wandered off mumbling, and I wandered off to attend the after fight celebration, only to find out later that week that earlier that night, he had killed his business partner. In the middle of the carnage, the cleaning lady walked in. And what did Beady-eyed Beatty do? He murdered and raped her, then gets cleaned up and dressed up, and drives up to West Palm Beach to witness the very kickboxing event I'm to referee. It's the law of the jungle. When a predator runs up against an animal as dangerous or more than them, they avoid conflict and walk around.

There's no doubt in my mind, had I been smaller in stature, and

336

hadn't possessed my fighting skills, Beatty might have gone for the trifecta, three for three.

But back at Sash, Tommy Chin, the nightclub owner, was nice enough to bring in an acupuncturist to try and treat my back. I started seeing Doctor Stephen Tai, whose father was the equivalent of the U.S. Surgeon General back in Taiwan. Stephen would turn out to be a brilliant man. He had degrees in Western medicine, was a Board Certified Surgeon, and I think also a Neurologist and Gynecologist.

Two or three times a week, Stephen would come all the way down to the nightclub to treat me before I went on duty. I have to say, while I was lying there being treated, it seemed to work, but when I stood upright, the pain was back in its full intensity. So eventually the club had to let me go, and put me on worker's compensation.

Like most people, I wasn't too keen on the idea of having surgery on my lower back, so for the next nine months I tried every alternative medicine I could find, and struggled with the prospect of having surgery. And for a year I lived on $520 a month in Los Angeles, which in this high-end city was little better than being gum on someone's shoe.

In the meantime, I was miserable. After enjoying a gifted athletic life, I was now all but a cripple. There was no position I could obtain to get away from the pain. Standing, sitting, lying down—nothing could relieve the agony I was enduring. The right cheek of my buttocks had flattened out, and I had lost close to three inches in diameter on my right thigh, and a little more than an inch and a half in diameter on my right calf. I went from being able to do the splits to barely being capable of lifting my right foot three inches off the ground. And oh yeah, I was constipated.

Up until this happened I had great constitution. When something went in, something came out. Every girl I ever dated, and every close friend I ever had would tease me about it. You could find me on the throne four to six times per day. With my ancestral background, I would joke and say I was determined to be the king of something. But this was no joke. I went from being able to throw kicks well over my head to barely being able to walk. A friend of mine from the Gym, Greg Garrett, introduced me to a chiropractor, which barely kept me moving. Greg, being a tremendous athlete in his own right, was a collegiate badminton and swim champion, who went on to play professional baseball, and pitch for the Cincinnati Reds, back when they were the Big Red Machine, with Johnny Bench and Pete Rose.

After retiring from baseball, Greg became the World Heavyweight Powerlifting Champion in the Master's division, which was 40 and above. At 325lbs, Greg was in the top 10% of the world's strongest men, and my good friend. After months of exhausting alternative medicine avenues, I found myself on a suicidal path, so I made a decision. I started interviewing a list of orthopedic surgeons that the workman's compensation insurance agent had given me. But my senses were telling me my issue was not skeletal; it was nerve damage. So I decided against an orthopedic doctor, and began looking for a neurosurgeon. And I found, in my opinion, one of the best: Doctor Jeffrey Rush, located at the Culver Medical Center in Culver City.

The problem? Damage to the lumbar discs L4 L5 S1, which is the Achilles heel for anyone over six feet tall. So *here I am*, going in for back surgery number one (of which there will be two) making a promise to myself that if the second surgery didn't work out, I was through. As in, I was going to check myself out. *Adios!* There was no way I was gonna continue my life crippled and in that amount of pain.

The cost of the second surgery was six grand. But prior to the insurance company coming in and picking up the tab, my friend Skip came to my rescue. Anyone who's ever been on workman's comp knows the slow grinding wheel of the insurance company. No caseworker is concerned with your best interest. Their priority is to save the company money. As I said before, the company Skip worked for was based in Burbank. He had just got back into town, and he called me to get together. When he saw that I was fifteen pounds lighter, with a bloated belly and barely able to walk, and my biceps had shrunk down to the size of my wrists, his reaction was instant. What the hell happened, and what the hell could he do?

I filled him in, and told him the insurance company was vacillating on whether they wanted to pay for the surgery or not. Skip assured me that he had the money in the bank, and if I needed it, it was mine. After enduring one more week of agony, I called him on his offer. I scheduled the surgery. A few days before I went into the hospital, I had a consultation with Doctor Rush. While I was sitting in his office, I was informed the insurance company was gonna come through. And boy, what a relief!

When I got home, I picked up the phone to call Skip, but he had already left town to go back to Dallas to build a department store. And then it hit me; I was barely getting by. I was dating a young lady named

Joanne who was a waitress, and if she hadn't been able to bring me food from the restaurant, I might have starved.

So I put the phone down. I made the decision to keep the money that Skip had given me, so I could survive until I got back in the game. Coming out of the second surgery, shaking off the effects of the anesthesia, my instincts instantly told me my problem had been almost entirely solved. Of course, you're never 100% after back surgery…

Now the rest was up to me. My first step: rehab. On day six when they took the stitches out of my back, I went straight home. Mike had a beautiful rectangular pool that was perfect for swimming. It turns out that swimming is one of the best rehab exercises after lower back surgery. With your body buoyant, it takes pressure off your spine while granting you enough fluid resistance to build up strength. Mike's pool would turn out to be a lifesaver. I drove straight home from the doctor's office and jumped in it. I floundered around for about ten laps, which is all I had in me that first day.

In a few short weeks, I was swimming five days a week, completing a hundred laps three days a week, and fifty laps on alternate days. After six weeks, I felt confident enough to go back to the gym and start exercising with light weights. After two months of that, I drove down to Granada Hills in the San Fernando Valley, to a former Chuck Norris Karate Studio. Granada Hills Karate was now owned by Bill Parent, one of Chuck Norris' chief instructors. Bill would turn out to be a great Karate man, as well as a great friend. Back before my surgery, Doctor Rush warned me I probably wouldn't be able to practice the art of Karate any longer, but I just figured that like everyone else, he underestimated me.

Contrary to popular belief, I never considered myself hardheaded or stubborn. I looked at my attitude as being determined. So *here I am*, standing in the middle of the mat, at Granada Hills Karate, slowly walking through my moves. It was a short, 45-minute workout. But when I left, I felt the sensation of seeing an old friend that I hadn't seen in over a year.

Driving on the way home back to Valencia, I was singing at the top of my lungs and pounding on my steering wheel with joy. I knew the Karate that I had eaten, breathed, and slept for, and that I had given up so many things to do, was still within reach.

In the week prior to my second surgery, I had stopped in at Stage West to see my old friend Sam Skinner. While I was there, lo and behold I ran into one of the wannabe bikers I had thrown out of the club. The short story is, we ended up squaring off on the concrete patio in front of the nightclub.

Now I don't know if I wasn't taking the guy too seriously, or if it was because I had enough pain medication in me to sedate a buffalo, but I flipped a left-legged roundhouse kick at him right in front of the planter Goliath had pulled the sprinkler system out of. But as soon as I did, my right foot came out from under me, and I went down.

Bozo the biker was a lot smarter than he looked. He seized the opportunity and jumped on top of me. When we got to our feet, I was bent over at the waist with him facing me. He had me in a frontal headlock. We wrestled for a moment, and then we spun around and went right up against the picture window that belonged to the trophy shop next door to the nightclub. With my back to the glass, I could feel it bow; I knew it was gonna go. When it did, sheets of glass flew down like a guillotine. How it didn't maim or kill one of us is one of those freak happenstances. Looking back, knowing that one of us should have been cut in half, I know it was one of those angelic moments.

So *here I am*, lying on my back in a bed of glass, with my legs hung up on the two foot wall the glass was set in. I've got Bozo by the hair, holding his head down close to that jagged glass frame, trying to saw his head off with the glass that remained in it. That's when biker boys start yelling, "He's cut!" Then I heard someone say, "That's enough" and they grabbed him from behind at the waist and pulled him out of my hands. I scampered to my feet. When I stepped out of the trophy shop and out of the glass, I looked around.

Quite a crowd had gathered. I looked down at my shirt and it was shredded. Then the realization hit me: the cops are on the way. I glanced over and saw Bozo standing with some of his biker buffoons. I told him I would catch him another day, because the way I looked, I thought it better that I fade away. As I drove off, I could hear the alarm at the trophy shop fading away, as well as hear the distant sirens of the police on the way.

Several weeks later, and quite a few after my back surgery, after attacking the pool with my best Michael Phelps impersonation, and with a half a dozen trips down to the Karate school underneath my belt, I was feeling pretty optimistic about the future. So once again, and don't ask me why, I stopped in to see my old friend Sam Skinner at Stage West. *All right, why? Well, it was the only place in town my broke ass*

340

could to afford to hang out in! But this time, unlike other times, I was in the right place at the right time to avert total disaster. And although I know I've had angels watching over me my entire life, they have let me wander into some precarious situations from time to time.

I remember checking in through the front door at Stage West, greeting the door crew as well as some people I knew. Hell, everyone I knew in L.A. hung out there. When I'd come to town, I only knew Mike. Now I had a barful of friends, not to mention a handful of enemies… I followed the front bar all the way to the end, where the waitress station was located. I couldn't have been standing there for more than five minutes when I noticed a disagreement between the barmaid and a customer. When suddenly, without warning he grabbed a beer bottle off the bar and flung it up into the air like he was tossing dice. And what goes up must come down. It landed in the whiskey bottles behind the bar, better known as the top shelf, which is where they keep all the high-end liquor. With the band behind me raging, I couldn't hear a word he was saying. But with the veins in his neck bulging, I could read his lips: "Fuck you, I'll go to the back bar!" and then he turned around and disappeared into the crowd.

My pal Louis was working the door that night and came running in when he heard the crash of the bottles. Louis leaned over the bar and asked what happened. I flagged him down, gesturing to where I was standing. I had red-flagged this guy in my brain. My street senses were telling me there was something about this guy that wasn't right. By the time Louis had worked through the crowd to get to me, my mind was made up. I was gonna keep a handle on this situation. I told Lou I'd witnessed what happened, and I'd be happy to point the guy out, but I warned him: approach this guy with caution. My suggestion: ask him to step out front so you can talk to him.

So we made our way through the crowd to the back bar, where our friend Kelly was serving. Just as we approached, the beer bottle juggler was ordering another beer from Kelly, and I stayed back. The juggler's belly was pressed to the bar, Louis swung around to his left, tapped him on the shoulder, and asked if he could speak with him outside.

I was standing about eight to ten feet away, next to the dance floor, and even with the band raging behind me, I could read his lips as if I could hear what he was saying. The veins were bulging in his neck as he retorted, "Fuck you, I'm not going outside!" And with that, the juggler turned his attention back to Kelly our bartender.

341

Lou tapped him on the shoulder once more, and told him he needed to speak with him out front. The juggler turned his attention towards Louis, with those veins still visible in his neck. He slapped the left side of his coat about chest height, and once again I could read his lips just as if I could hear him, "Fuck you! I'll blow your fucking head off!" All of a sudden there was a new player. Our beer-juggling joker had a friend, who stood between Louis and the juggler. What this friend said to Lou I haven't a clue, but with him standing between the two, Louis lost sight of what was to ensue. Right then this joker reached into his sport coat, and although I somewhat expected it, it still chilled me to the bone. I saw the handle of a revolver, but as his hand went to reach inside his sports coat, I had already covered enough real estate to be within striking distance. When I'd seen the handle of that pistol, I made my play, and the joker must have sensed me moving in. By the time he snapped his attention my way, I had already launched a right hand punch that caught him square on the side of the head. He didn't even have time to put his finger squarely on the trigger. He must have thought my right hand ripped a hole in the fabric from another dimension. The gun went up in the air and, just as our bartender Kelly had turned around to face us, the gun flew over his head, and landed somewhere behind the bar.

This all happened so fast that Kelly never witnessed the gun. As the right side of the juggler's head slammed down on the bar, I grabbed him. At the same time, the juggler's friend spun around to his left. No one saw the knife, but unfortunately, Louis caught it, right in his abdomen. By this time I had jerked the juggler away from the bar, we had spun out onto the dance floor. The next thing that fled through my mind was, I didn't wanna be on my feet wrestling with this guy after just having back surgery, so I kicked his feet out from under him.

Just as I swept him, and we started to go down, I stuck my left thumb deep inside his eye socket. I had positioned myself for him to be between the ground and me when I came down on this joker. By the time we hit the floor, I was twisting my thumb deep inside his eye socket like I was trying to clean the seeds out of a cantaloupe. This tactic had taken all the fight out of him. By the time the door crew had gotten to him, he was like a limp dishrag. All of a sudden he wasn't so tough. He wasn't looking to blow anything off anybody. When I got to my feet, Kelly pushed by me pissed off. He barked Louis had been stabbed. I stepped over to the bar and there was blood all over the floor. Now *here*

I am, frantically fighting my way through the crowd trying to get to the front door. By the time I got outside, the door crew, unaware of the gun and not knowing Louis had been stabbed, had just let this joker and his murderous pal go.

Kelly, totally unaware of the severity of what had just taken place, looked me dead in the eye, pissed off, and asked, "Why the hell did you hit the guy? I had it under control." Then he spun around and went back inside the nightclub. I was in shock, but I followed him anyway, and I caught up with him right in front of the DJ booth. I snapped back, "Kelly! He had a gun!" But I don't think he believed me 'till he got back behind his bar. And lo and behold, lying right on top of the tray of the cash register was a pistol.

Now with the LAPD on site investigating the crime, I find myself on the way to Granada Hills Hospital, which thank God is less than half a mile away, and where I've sent many victims myself in this saga called Bar Wars. Louis had to have exploratory surgery to make sure his bowel hadn't been punctured. He'd be all right, but he ended up with a nasty scar and one hell of a story. And oh, by the way Lou you're welcome, but don't worry about it, I owed you one.

At this point Greg Garrett from the gym had called me to check on my work status. Greg was a supervisor for a HUD funded project in construction for seniors and disabled people. The big man had been holding a job for me, waiting for me to get well enough to go back to work full time. And this was a job opportunity sent from heaven. I was more than ready to get back into the full swing of things.

Greg's office, as well as the place we would meet every morning, was at the community service center in Newhall. Perfect! It was less than two miles from where I lived. It would seem as though I could leave for work by 7:01 a.m., and still get there on time by 6:59. This was as close to a perfect job as you could get.

I spent all day every day working with close friends: Greg Garrett, Al Santos, and later on, Jeff Augustine. All three were terrific guys; we were all jocks and all pranksters. There always seemed to be a trick being played on one or the other of us at any one time.

Although enjoyable, the job was still hard work. Sometimes we'd re-roof a senior's entire home in 100+ degree heat, but more often than not it was interior work. We would do light plumbing and electrical, rebuild kitchens and bathrooms, hang interior doors and replace windows, as well as install safety railing and build wheelchair ramps

343

for the handicapped. And although there wasn't a lot of money to be made, at the end of the day it felt great because you'd helped somebody.

It also afforded me close to a three-hour window where I could go to the gym and work out with any one of these three friends. And then it was off to Granada Hills Karate, where I'd work with yet another good friend, because after all the rehab, I was now back up to speed. Bill Parent offered me a job because he liked what he saw. And I'd still occasionally do security work when I got the call from people who knew my qualifications.

Close to six hours of sleep at night, with a twenty-minute nap later in the day, seemed to suit me, because if I got eight then I wanted ten, if I got ten then I wanted twelve. If I got twelve… Is there really ever enough sleep in this life? Financially, I was climbing back out of the hole, and I had so much going on I was far from bored.

Just to add to all this, and in the middle of my back problems, Dana had called me. She had an appointment in L.A. and wanted to know if I could pick her up at LAX. She wanted to talk to me about something and ask me a question. My friend Skip had leased a place right on PCH, a mile north of Topanga Canyon, right on the beach. As luck would have it, Skip was on the road in Texas, building some department store. I had the keys to his place so I could send him his mail. And before he left, he told me to go ahead and use his beachfront property, because he wouldn't be able to.

Dana and I had a great weekend. After dinner on Saturday night, we went back to the beach cottage, and then she dropped the bomb on me. She explained to me she was helping her father start a new business (that would become a video giant) and that she had given it a lot of thought, and that by the time she turned thirty she wanted to have a little boy. I smiled and said, "What does that have to do with me?" As it turns out, she didn't just want to have a son, she wanted to have *my* son. I was baffled. When I first met Dana, one of the many things that was so attractive about her was that, like me, she never wanted to have kids.

And now, this beautiful woman, who'd never asked me for so much as a glass of water, was asking me for far more than I had bargained for. She went on to explain, she wasn't interested in getting married. She wasn't looking for financial support because she had her own money, and she didn't want anyone interfering with her life and telling her how to raise her child. She knew me well enough to trust me in those areas.

I told her I'd think about it.

Then she assured me that, at 27, this was still a few years away, which would give me plenty of time to contemplate it. Well, by the end of 1988, I had a son with her; Justin Jason. Dana, while she was pregnant, opened the first of many video stores, which would eventually merge into the video giant, Blockbuster. With her help Hank Cartwright, her father, would go on to open a chain of video stores called Major Video, which had almost twice as many stores and locations as Blockbuster before the merger. After some major negotiations, Mr. Eisinger had convinced Hank they shouldn't compete against each other. When Hank agreed, he changed all of his Major Video stores into Blockbusters, and when he sold his shares in the company in the mid-90s, it was for well over 100 million dollars.

Now these are all loose details because obviously I wasn't in on the deal. But this is what a Southern boy would call cutting a fat hog in the ass. If that's not enough 'F-you' money, then you need to check your spending habits.

By 1990, Dana had packed up her stuff in Palmdale California, where she had opened the first store, and moved back to Las Vegas. And who could blame her? She had always professed her love for Las Vegas, she had basically grown up there, and I wasn't helping matters any.

I was basically pursuing a double life: rushing out to Palmdale three or four nights a week to see Justin and Dana. Then on weekends, I was full speed ahead with my foot to the floor enjoying a single L.A. lifestyle. By this point, I was teaching Karate privately to some prominent entertainment people, two of which I liked as good friends. One was singer Joey Gian who in the late 80s all but won Star Search, hosted by Ed McMahon, by competing in the vocal competition.

Joey, being extremely talented, would go on to star in two hit television series, "Hooperman," with Jon Ritter, where he was the starring cast member, and later on, as a leading man on "Knot's Landing," as detective Tom Ryan, (Nicolette Sheridan's love interest).

Another client I had become friends with was arguably the best drummer in the world, period: Bobby Colomby. In today's synthesized and computerized music, Bobby's name might not raise an eyebrow, but there's no denying the greatness of the band Bobby founded. The first Jazz-fusion rock band in America; the immortal Blood, Sweat, and Tears. Bobby would go on to become a record mogul before his retirement with Columbia Records (CBS Records).

So *here I am*, going in to the early 90s, working a construction job during the day, lifting weights in the afternoon, teaching Karate at Granada Hills in the evening, trying to juggle four or five private Karate lessons during the week, and picking up security work when I can. Not to mention heading out to Palmdale/Lancaster area to see Dana and my son.

My time was booked solid. But it wasn't the long hours and work that chased Dana off, it was the womanizing. What she was able to tolerate when she was younger she now had no patience for. I was more than honest and upfront with her, telling her I wasn't going to stop living a single man's life just because I had agreed to father a son with her. Although now that I can look back with the clarity of 20/20 vision, I do believe that she hoped that once we brought a son into the world, I might change my behavior and settle down.

But I found it next to impossible for this old dog to change his spots. Especially the dating pool I was swimming in. Many times my friends would look over and say, "How do you do it?" I'd just grin and shrug, I was as baffled as they were. Here I was, a former professional athlete who'd crashed and burned. I had no money, I had no formal education. I came from blue-collar roots where everyone in my family was a laborer. I didn't want to get married, nor did I wanna have children, and my future wasn't looking too promising.

But what I did posses was a devilish grin with dimples, and a male swagger that my confidence would back up. When people would question me and find me borderline cocky, I'd just shrug and tell them if I didn't believe in me, who would? (Just a little lesson I picked up way back in grade school.) But the truth is, it starts with you. You have to believe in yourself before you can expect others to. Period.

After instructing Joey Gian in Karate for a few months, he called me one evening and asked me if I'd be interested in participating in a charity event. It was a spring carnival being put on at Maclaren Hall, a juvenile detention center, which was sponsored by Henry Winkler and the athletic shoe company, Adidas. Joe, not having had a lot of interaction with kids, thought I'd be the perfect wingman for a hall full of troubled youth.

Joey, out of instinct and recognition, knew that I would be good around kids and adolescents, something that came natural to me from teaching them Karate for over a decade. And he was right. We had a ball.

My approach to working with kids was to treat each one like an individual. Look them dead in the eye and treat them with respect, therefore commanding respect. And then disarm them by acting like a big kid (which comes easy to me because I am juvenile). And I'd like to say something here. We can all learn something from Henry Winkler. He was one of the kindest, most generous and sincere people I've ever witnessed. He truly loved children, and he saw the enormity of their potential.

Let me tell you, "The Fonz" knows how to put on a spread. It seemed like a hundred people would meet at Henry's house, where he had breakfast waiting. And as soon as we were fed, we marched out across his front lawn, where waiting curbside was a fleet of tour buses waiting to take us out to Maclaren Hall.

Once we arrived at the facility, we were introduced to the powers that be, and then we were set free to mingle with the kids. It was up to the children to pick out a celebrity they wanted to hang out with for the day. The whole facility was surrounded by a concrete wall, and although it was painted with cartoons, you still had the sense you were inside a prison. It's not just the criminal and delinquent kids that were locked up here. A lot of these kids had been physically and emotionally abused, so they had to be taken away from their families. And with nowhere else to put them, they were brought here.

The little girl that I bonded with was about ten years old, and I couldn't help but notice the severe scarring on the webbing between her thumb and index finger. When I asked her about it, she tried to hide her hand. As it turns out, her mother used to use her hand as an ashtray, stubbing her lit cigarettes out on this beautiful little girl's hand. If it were up to me, you'd have to apply for a license before you could be blessed with any children.

But the day went great. We played carnival games as a team and won prizes. No matter what direction you looked, there seemed to be enough motion picture and television stars to equal the Milky Way. But the one celebrity that stands out in my mind and takes the cake hands down was MC Hammer. This was way back in his record-selling heyday with "Don't Hurt 'Em Hammer." After we all witnessed the concert by Milli Vanilli (they won a Grammy that year) Hammer marched out onto the lawn with boys aged 14 and above to play a game of flag football.

You can ask any testosterone-filled teenager who's ever played the game what happened to that flag. You might as well wipe your ass on it, because within three plays guys were doing full on hits and tackles, and Hammer was in the middle of all of it. I started laughing my ass off I looked over at Joey and asked him, "Can you believe this?" Hammer was truly inspirational. But so was Henry Winkler. By the end of the day, none of us wanted to leave. All of us wanted to take a kid home, but of course none of us could.

We shared our borderline tearful goodbyes, hopped on the bus, and took what seemed to be a longer ride back to The Fonz's place. You would hope this was a reality check for everyone on the buses. We should all see how bad it can get, so we could appreciate how good we've got it.

Although I'm sure his involvement is constant, Henry Winkler sponsors two major events per year: one at Christmas, and then the spring carnival which I attended, which caused me to do a little net-working on my own.

I met a beautiful little LAPD officer named Merissa, who had actually been a graduate of Maclaren Hall. Merissa was kind enough to introduce me to the people who were in charge of the guest speaker program.

So *here I am*, every third Thursday heading south out of Newhall, in my Jeep Sahara with the top off, and Bruce Hornsby blaring out of the stereo. I'll merge onto the 210 south to the 605, and get off in El Monte where Maclaren Hall was located. And you ask why? Because they thought my story was compelling, and might be inspirational to a bunch of confused kids caught in the riptide of life, being pulled in the wrong direction.

Chapter Twenty-eight

At this point, in the early 90s, my life was good. I had a great network of friends on the East and West coast. I was dating possibly one of the most beautiful women in the world, and although I was working my ass off with never a dull moment, I was making a decent buck, which would afford me more adventures than one man deserves.

Back in 1988, Skip and I, along with another guy, took off on motorcycles down to the Baja Peninsula on the Fourth of July. This four-day adventure would spark off the Annual Fourth of July Baja Ride. What started off as a party of three of us drew as many as ten in our largest group, until the last year we did it.

Prior to that, we'd only been going as far south as Ensenada, having a great time in Tijuana, Rosarito, Puerto Nuevo, and of course topping it off and staying in Ensenada. It could only be described as a fun-filled frat house beer bash on motorcycles. Then, on our last day in Ensenada, I came up with what I thought was a great idea. Why not ride along the whole Baja Peninsula the following year, and park in Cabo San Lucas? Only four of us went…

But in the meantime, Skip and I, along with a couple of friends from Texas and a couple from California, rafted through the Royal Gorge on the Arkansas River in Colorado. And you can believe this; you can randomly pick any one of these life adventures, and it would easily rival if not surpass any offbeat, slapstick comedy Hollywood has ever thought up.

At this point, my oldest friend and cornerman in life George McClease had gotten involved in the Special Olympics. So *here I am*, on a jet airliner headed to South Florida, one year shy of a decade since the last time I was there. I've got my good friend Greg Garrett sitting next to me, who happens to be the World Heavyweight Powerlifting Champion, donating his time so we can stir up interest for the Special Olympics.

No small thanks to George for reaching out with sponsorship and helping us on our way to Florida. And as always, my good friend and other cornerman in life, Skip Walls, was happy to donate some of his time and money as well. He was now going by the name his mother had chosen to give him: Clayton Lee Walls.

We were enjoying motorcycle trips to the Grand Canyon, Big Surf, California, and Telluride and Colorado, and fitting in skiing adventures to Park City, Utah and Lake Tahoe. Not to mention our annual two-week extravaganza, rolling to our turnaround at Cabo San Lucas, where we spent a week over the Fourth of July and didn't head back until we drank the town dry. Life was good. But as always in this life, it was about to change.

At the end of every fiscal year in June, the project we headed up for HUD was up for bid. The newly formed city of Santa Clarita, which includes Newhall, Saugus, Valencia, and Canyon Country, all wanted their piece of the Federal pie. They wanted some control over the Federal money coming into their community. Prior to this turn of events, the money had been controlled by the County, making us, in essence, County employees. The money delegated to us had to come through a non-profit organization, such as our figurehead, the Canyon Country Chamber of Commerce. *Confusing? Of course!* Because everything in government has to be complicated, right? Whatever… The bottom line was that we were more than likely headed for the breadline.

Speaking for myself, I had put in more than five years helping the seniors and disabled people in the Santa Clarita Valley with their construction problems. We had developed a personal relationship with a lot of them, and they knew they could count on us to come back, year after year. The person I really felt for was Greg Garrett. Greg had logged more than a decade working in the Santa Clarita Area, helping the seniors and disabled. Hell, Greg had grown up in Newhall, and had graduated from Hart High. He'd played baseball, gained a scholarship, and then went on to pitch with the pros, where he played for the Angels, and the Big Red Machine, the Cincinnati Reds. And as I said, he was the world-reigning Heavyweight Powerlifting Champion.

In such a small community, Greg was a local hero for Christ's sake. A lot of the people we serviced knew Greg personally, and if not, they followed his career through the paper and cheered him on through high school, college, and then into the pros. Now, tipping the scales at 325lbs, they couldn't miss him walking up to their homes or stepping up on the porch of their mobile home. "Big Greg," as he was affectionately called, was looked upon with loving eyes. Once Greg got the paperwork in order, it was a few short days before we got the job done.

Every year at this time, Greg would go in and renegotiate our contract. He'd try to hammer out a cost of living raise, as well as convince the county to ask the Feds for more money. The more money we got, the more people we could help. While Greg met with county officials and took care of business, this worked out perfectly for me. We had a week to ten-day hiatus right at the Fourth of July, which meant I could take my Annual Fourth of July Motorcycle Trip. But come the summer of '93, I was on the fence about going anywhere.

The trip was a knockout, and had been planned for months. We had an eclectic group of guys coming in from Texas, Florida, and California, all of us meeting in Fort Collins, Colorado, where we had sent our bikes via trailer in advance. We planned on riding from there all the way to Yellowstone National Park, where a couple of cabins had been reserved for the night, before dropping down to Jackson Hole for a few days.

After catching our breath, our plan was to circle back to Steamboat Springs to catch the Fourth of July Rodeo. And what a great trip it was! But my gut feeling was right, and when I got back, I had been hijacked. The city of Santa Clarita had fought and won the money we were once employed with. And like always, it couldn't have happened at a worse time.

Now, with no daytime employment, and my hours of teaching at Granada Hills Karate having been cut back due to a stressed relationship with Bill, believe me this wasn't the only detriment to my income. My private Karate instruction had all but dried up due to people working on their own projects and leaving town.

It was the trifecta in the worst degree. Then, to compound money matters, I had grown tired of roommates and rented a place of my own, which meant that my expenses had gone up.

It would seem as though I had shot myself in both feet. And oh yeah, having a girlfriend who had grown accustomed to living beyond her means with me feeding her the past couple of years. It was a love story of Titanic proportions, with me stepping in for Leonardo as the character of Jack, and we all know how that ended.

But I'm not fooling myself, nor am I whining. For the most part any girl I was attracted to and deeply involved with was as beautiful spiritually as she was aesthetically. Not to mention that they all had a sense of humor... They had to put up with me!

Somewhere within this timeframe, I hooked up with my two buddies, Pete and Andy Steinfeld at the TGI Fridays in Canoga Park for dinner. Pete and Andy were the two younger twin brothers of Jake

351

Steinfeld, better known as "Body by Jake."

I had met the brothers through a mutual friend, Joey Gian, and we hit it off immediately. You couldn't really meet two more decent guys with a tremendous sense of humor. With them being in the private fitness business with their brother, and me teaching Karate privately, we found we had a lot in common.

After dinner, Pete, Andy, and myself were standing in the Friday's restaurant parking lot telling stories and laughing, when a group of college kids, about six or seven of them, passed by having their own party. Petey, as he would so often do, reverted back to his New York accent, and started popping off wisecracks just to have fun.

With his sarcasm not directed at anyone specifically, and the college kids totally unaware that we were there, the whole point to his effort was to make Andy and I laugh. All of a sudden a guy in front of us off to our left pops up from behind a car and screams out, "You think it's funny motherfuckers? We'll see how funny it is when I blow your fucking heads off!"

The three of us look at each other stunned, where did this guy come from? He rushed over to his car and pulled out a .410 shotgun. Now we see that he's got a buddy with him, who's saying, "Put the gun up." Too late. The guy's marching our way, towards Petey and me, with the gun up to his shoulder saying, "Pop off again motherfucker and I'm gonna blow your head off!" Petey went to duck out of the way, and I stepped between my friend and the guy with the shotgun. Or more specifically, I called his attention my way. As soon as the gun first appeared, as in times of jeopardy in the past, a strange wave of calmness washed over me as if an angel had placed a hand on my shoulder to reassure me everything would be all right.

So *here I am*, once again staring death in the face, in a TGI Friday's parking lot in Canoga Park. I've got Johnny Shotgun less than fifteen feet away with his .410 cocked and pointed at my head, and I'm thinking, *when does this shit ever end?* After close to fifteen minutes of dialogue between Johnny Shotgun, his buddy, and myself, we finally convinced this NRA enthusiast to put the gun away.

As it would turn out, Johnny Boy had been on the other side of the car, bent over out of sight throwing up. When he heard us laughing, he thought we were making fun of him. Now for the bizarre part—as if this whole instance was not the least bit unique. Johnny Shotgun all but apologizes by dropping onto his right knee, and throwing his right arm at a 45 degree angle across his chest with his fist clenched at his heart, and stating that it was his honor to walk among men, meaning us. I think he was claiming that we were some sort of Roman Gladiator or Centurion Warriors.

Pete and Andy looked at me. I glanced and them and said, "Well, I think I'll call it a night." When I got home, there were four or five messages on my answering machine, the last one was from Petey, He apologized. I called him back and replied, "Welcome to my world." Then I said I'd see him and Andy Sunday morning in Simi Valley for our Sunday motorcycle ride.

Chapter Twenty-nine
Lost Love, Nightmare Disaster and the Movie Biz

By the end of the summer of '93, I had all but exhausted my bank account. After paying my rent for September, I was down to $126. But once again fate would step in. My friend Elsie Mendoza got me an interview with a subcontractor for the Metrolink, the commuter train system for Los Angeles, which presented itself none too soon.

I had lived with roommates since I had moved to Los Angeles, so I had acquired no furniture other than what was in my bedroom, which wasn't much. Since my back surgery, I had found it more comfortable to sleep with my mattress on the floor. I did have a dresser with some drawers, and my own stereo for my personal listening pleasure. But that was it.

So *here I am*, living in a one-bedroom guest cottage in a Granada Hills neighborhood with a styrofoam cooler as a refrigerator. At the moment, the future looked bright. For anyone who wanted a career in the railroad, this would be a great stepping stone. Once I passed railroad safety school, I would be making twenty bucks an hour, with the potential of making $25, and all the overtime I cared to book.

I could see the wedding bells in my significant other's eyes, but this was never my plan. The great thing about having multiple jobs and various sources of income is, you're your own entity. If one dries up, you have various avenues to travel for income. But this life is not for the faint of heart.

I, for one, had never functioned well within the boundaries of conventional thinking America. My grandfather's teachings struck a chord in my mind: be your own man. I realized early on as a teenager hanging drywall: you weren't going to get rich by working for someone else.

The whole point to being financially fit was to be happy, and I already knew how to do that. I'd watched too many people get bogged down in what they considered the American Dream but I call the American Nightmare. The majority of America is stuck in jobs that they don't care for, but the pay is too much for them to leave. After buying homes they can't really afford, and buying cars that are way too expensive, they find themselves in a prison of their own making. And only some realize, and usually way too late, that this is a situation where less is truly more.

There is nothing in this life—and I mean nothing—that makes a human being happier than freedom. But please don't fool yourself; freedom is not cheap. And as for the lady in my life, she couldn't be more ecstatic about my new job working for the railway. Now with me having a steady job and a place to report to every morning, it was the first step towards domestic bliss. She was all but salivating, waiting for me to ask her for her hand in marriage so I could father her children, put her in a four-bedroom, two-car garage home with a pool in the backyard.

Now that we know what she wants, let's hear from the Polish kid with dimples, who's expected to support this Nightmare on Elm Street. I wasn't having any of it. In my life I had always been honest with the women in my life. I didn't want to get married, nor was I interested in starting a family.

After growing up in a two-bedroom house with eight people, and being forced to clean out shitty diapers over the toilet for most of my single-digit years, I had served my time. (Note to the world: this was before disposable diapers.) After witnessing first hand what the lack of money plus alcoholism can do to a family (and let's face it, alcohol is the poor man's vacation), one thing my brother Frank and I were acutely aware of at a very young age—if you can't afford to have children, then maybe you shouldn't.

Let's be honest, my lifestyle was not conducive to raising a family. So as you might imagine, it was the furthest thing from my mind to view this Rocky Horror Picture Show rerun. I didn't NEED to buy that ticket, thank you!

The one thing that most of the women in my life didn't understand was the reality of the working man. Sure, it's all so exiting when you first meet someone you're attracted to. In the beginning it's candlelit wining and dining, catching a movie premier, or going to a play. And then it's a spontaneous trip to Lake Tahoe, spending the weekend in Santa Barbara, La Jolla, or Monterey. But all this costs money... And with my limited education, that meant I had to work my ass off to make enough money so I could pursue life, and enjoy it the way it was meant to be. The very minute you have children, the romance all but stops. Are we gonna run up to Santa Barbara for the weekend? Or buy little Johnny a mouthful of braces?

Many times I've been accused of being selfish, but in my view it's just the opposite. Why bring children into this life if you're not sure you can provide for them? Well, I guess you can guess what happened next. She wouldn't be the first to leave me, and far from the last... In retrospect, I find it interesting to assess the cards that this life has dealt me. Like very few others I have had great runs of fortune, followed by hands of misfortune. But it would seem as though in my case the pendulum would swing a little more severely in each direction than the average person.

Right after my birthday, in November of '93, misfortune seemed to find me again. During the holiday season between Christmas, Thanksgiving, and New Years, fate would deal from the bottom of the deck. *Aces and eights, yet again.*

The Metro line had to lay me off. The company was gaining its legs and had run out of money for my job description; 'maintenance of way,' which consisted of moving fire hazards and debris, not to mention homeless people, away from the tracks. My relationship with Bill had deteriorated to the point where he no longer welcomed me at Granada Hills Karate. My lady had left me in the first week of December, and my grandmother had called to inform me that my first love, Claire Wulf, had died in a car accident. And then, after the first of the year, I was involved in an accident and wrecked my brand new truck.

So *here I am,* in the middle of the night, sitting cross-legged in the middle of the living room of my unfurnished one bedroom guesthouse, almost in tears, wondering what the hell else can happen. Some questions are better off left unasked (as I've stated before). I've always been fairly even-tempered about things that happen in this world. Like I've said before, I'm kind of a counter-puncher. I've always maintained the disposition, whatever's gonna happen will, so why worry about it?

356

Besides, like most of us, we're all gonna be served up our fair amount of chicken shit, the trick is to turn it into a plate of chicken salad.

Sitting home alone every evening in the dark, listening to the radio, thinking of the love that just left me, and the one I had just lost, left my stomach in knots, only to be interrupted with thoughts of unemployment and survival.

Around this time I began passing blood, so with limited funds I went to go see a doctor who performed a simple blood test and physical. When my blood test came back, my white counts and platelets were off the charts. I mean, literally off the charts. They barely registered.

Now the doctor suggests I see a blood specialist, a hematologist, which meant ringing up Neiman's—and I couldn't afford Kmart. I told him I'd try to get back to him on that. But in my mind I was thinking, I don't need anything else to worry about. So I said to the doc, "As you can see, I'm upright and breathing, so now I must be leaving." It took me over a year before I could afford to see that blood specialist. I found out I had more white blood cells than red, but I wasn't diagnosed with leukemia. I came to find out that a small percentage of the population has this deficiency, but we function well enough, even though it's the red blood cells that transport oxygen throughout your system. Lack of oxygen is somewhat detrimental to an endurance athlete. *Bad for boxing—ya think?!* My daunting question had been answered!

But then a little thing happened that jolted everything back into perspective. And I mean *jolted*.

Speaking of perspective… You can forget the fact that you're unemployed and you have commitments that you can't meet, forget the fact that your friends have let you down and kind of screwed you around. You can forget the fact that the woman who has professed her undying love for you for the past five years has dumped you like last season's fashion. You can forget the fact that you spent the holiday season home and alone in the dark watching the stereo. You can forget the fact that you can't stop reminiscing about a first love and the girl that you will always be missing. You can forget the fact that the concerned look on your doctor's face seems to suggest you have contracted some type of fatal blood disease, you can forget that fact that you wrecked a brand new vehicle that was less than two month's old…

Just after the New Year '94, there was a glimmer of hope. The subcontractors that had previously employed me called me back to work

357

on the rail system. So when the alarm goes off at a pre-dawn hour, you place your feet on the floor and begin to rub the sleep out of your eyes.

And then it happens, the unthinkable, the unimaginable, the impossible—*the ground starts moving.*

Yes folks, it's January 17, 1994, a date marked and forever known in Los Angeles as the day of the Northridge Earthquake. Never in this Universe will you live through a longer 58 seconds of sheer terror. Anyone who was there for Nature's roller coaster ride will be more than happy to testify.

I remember consciously thinking, "This is it. We've screwed up the environment and the world is never gonna stop shaking." But fortunately for most of us, it did. And the aftermath was like Armageddon. Freeways were down, buildings collapsed, and swimming pools buckled out of the ground. And oh yeah, that famous CNN news footage of a gas main busted off Balboa Avenue, shooting flames over 100 feet up in the air? I could watch that every evening for almost a week by simply stepping out on the front porch of my guest cottage.

Things just weren't looking good. But it's funny how when things go from bad to worse, your instincts can snap you back into action. All of a sudden I had a crystal clear vision of what I needed to do. All of my problems and self-pity, my wallowing in misery were a distant memory now.

The first thing I did was check on my neighbors and the people I was renting from to make sure everyone was all right. Then I ran back to my guesthouse, stumbling through the aftershocks, and threw on some jeans. Next I headed to my loaner truck, so I could go to the Metrolink office where I worked, only to realize I was blocked in my driveway. The alley entrance to my guest cottage was crowded with debris, fallen cinder blocks, and telephone poles.

Now all but trapped, that day I sat through what felt like fifty aftershocks. Somehow, and don't ask me how, sometime in the mid morning my old friend Mike Brucker showed up at my guesthouse. The two of us jumped in his vehicle, and we wove our way through debris all the way down to Orange County. The San Fernando Valley was all but wiped out, but this was where we were able to find a market open and buy some bottled water.

By the next morning the city had cleared my alley just enough that I could drive through it. The first thing I did was drive straight to the office of Walter Prince, the subcontractor for the Metrolink. My thinking was, no one would be able to show up for work. At least, no one with priorities like a family and home to worry about.

However I was a free agent. Having no family on the West Coast, and owning no property, it was time for me to step up to the plate, roll up my sleeves, and try to get something positive done. I was just stepping out of my truck when I saw Walter pull into the lot. He looked at me, grinned, and nodded.

Note to the World—folks, there's nothing quite like putting the needs of others before your own to pull you out of self pity. That first week was brutal. Every filing cabinet in that office was turned over. Now we have every folder with a contract mixed up with every contract in a folder.

By the end of the first week, we regained radio service and reconnected our phones, which would enable me to be redirected to every hot spot on the Metrolink rail system. When the smoke and dust cleared, I still had a job, but it would be short lived.

With freeways down, they pulled money from my program to build Metrolink substations to bring people in from the Antelope Valley into Los Angeles. But the one thing that stuck in my mind, and I will never forget, on the daily drive up Zelzah Avenue, past Cal State Northridge, better known as C-Sun, I'd see they had a tent city set up on the university lawn. All the homes and apartment buildings had collapsed around the college, just like an accordion. Structures that had once been three to five stories had collapsed and now they were one or two. All the residents in the surrounding area had been displaced. So now they were sleeping on the university lawn in camps.

And as if that wasn't bad enough, one afternoon driving home I found myself behind two trucks. One Arrowhead and the other a Sparkletts—both water trucks. They pulled over at the University so they could dispense water, and that's when I first witnessed how human beings can devolve to the point of animals.

We all think it can't happen to us, but if you were to go without water for a couple of days, you're liable to kill the human being that stands in your way of getting some. So *here I am*, gingerly trying to weave through what is rapidly becoming a riot. After seeing people crawl over top of each other, viciously punching each other over an individual bottle of water, and witnessing a head being bashed into a curb, I decided to find another route home.

By March, I was unemployed again. No one had anticipated an

earthquake, so there was no excess buffer of money when the contract was originally bid. My job description was eliminated, but I was actually getting pretty good at budgeting on this roller coaster ride.

Oh sure, I still had no furniture, but what the hell? You can't eat furniture. By the end of summer, in September, I was down to eating one slice of Amici Pizza a day. At a buck 25, it was a pretty good deal. You could have tomato and sausage one day, and hamburger and mushroom the next.

Since the used refrigerator I had obtained from Elsie was totaled during the earthquake, I was back to using a styrofoam cooler with ice to keep things fresh. And then miraculously, once again, fate stepped in to lend a helping hand. But before I go on, a few words about the angel I knew as Claire Wulf.

I had met Claire at the last school I had attended, Jefferson Davis Junior High. She was roughly thirteen or fourteen years old. Claire and her friend Pat basically used the same route to go home as my friend Kenny Duncan and I did. Kenny, better known as Bubba.

Bubba and I would basically tease and torture these two girls right to their front door, where we would break off and head home. Whether it was cutting through the tomato fields, starting a tomato fight and pelting them with fruit, or shaking the girls off a branch until they fell into a canal, we were *brutal*, but it was all in fun.

After not seeing them for three months over the summer, when we started back to school that fall, Claire had developed and blossomed into what can only be described as a swan. With blue eyes, straight blonde hair, a button nose and dimples—she was a vision to behold.

I ran into Claire a year after leaving school, at the Palm Beach County Fair, where we started our on and off courtship from our mid teens to our early twenties. The responsibility of being caretaker for her family rested upon her shoulders at a very early age. Watching out for her little sister Suzy, taking care of her alcoholic mother, and worried constantly for her father Herb, who'd already had one heart attack. Herb was a stand up and great guy from Germany, with those old world values.

Claire was much more than my first love affair. We were great friends. And had we not been battling hormones throughout our teens, things might have turned out different. I was dating Claire when I took the beating in Orlando. When I told her I signed up for school, she got overly excited. She thought I meant I was going back to high school. (I didn't have the heart to tell her I'd signed up for the *Karate* school until a month later.)

When I moved to Las Vegas, Claire showed up some months later in Sin City with her father Herb, who had owned restaurants in New York City and had connections. She had told me she was looking for new opportunities, though I sensed she was following me. But I was already seeing Dana...

She didn't once try to interfere with that relationship. The last time I had seen her, she told me she was dating David Brenner, the stand up comedian. And then, not long after that, Claire called me to tell me she was packing it in and heading back to Florida. I never spoke to her again.

Claire was the only girl I ever dated throughout my youth that my Grandmother liked. Gram wouldn't love another woman in my life until she met Dana and, of course, by then she was my son's mother.

Claire had put up with so much of me as a young man running wild. And though I'm sure she knows, God do I wish I had one more time to squeeze her and let her know how much she meant to me. Every time I hear the song "Ventura Highway" by America, I have a flashback of us driving up I-95 with the windows down and her silky blonde hair blowing all around. She was gazing into my eyes and I'm telling you it was a magical moment. And years later, as I was describing her to friends, somehow that song would make the airwaves right then. Folks, I'm telling you something bigger is going on here. In my world, Claire is the poster child for the notion that you truly don't know what you have until it's gone. And please believe me when I tell you this, this world is not as good with her no longer in it...

But right now, I'm down to my last hundred dollars when I bump into my friend Randy Peters, a Chuck Norris black belt I had met through Bill. Randy is a transportation coordinator in the film business, and a part-time stuntman. Randy was a talented black belt who once taught Steve McQueen Karate privately.

He was setting up his office on the Warner Bros. studio lot to start a new movie. Randy told me he had something that I might be interested in and had invited me down. When I got to the Warner lot, Randy marched me over to a building, and I found myself in a room with four other men. As I would find out, we were waiting on Steven Seagal to come in and look us over. Why? Because he needed a new stunt double for the movie he was about to start. "Under Siege."

This would turn out to be the first and most brief of many meetings I would have with Steven. Randy called the following day and asked if I would stop by the Warner lot and have lunch. When I showed up at noon, we rushed over to a Thai restaurant in Toluca Lake.

When we sat down, he told me his friend Gary Hymes, a stunt co-ordinator, had called him. He needed a guy over six feet tall who knew Karate. He emphasized he needed someone strong and fit enough to double as an actor, because they were going to put him in a mascot outfit.

Randy, as it turns out, was too busy. And now, living at the beach, he was doing more surfing than practicing Karate. So Randy had suggested me to Gary. I was stunned. Randy had mentioned to me a couple of times in the past that he would try and get me into the movie business. And although we had a great friendship, I thought it was just idle talk.

Randy had gotten into the film business through Steve McQueen. McQueen, although a big star, would turn out to be a regular guy. After taking private Karate lessons with Randy for quite some time, suggested that Randy get involved in the movie business himself.

Randy, a little over six feet tall with sandy hair and crystal blue eyes, could have been a model, and a poster child for movie stardom. But Steve McQueen was pretty down to earth. He downplayed Randy's good looks, and told him if he wanted to make a good living, he needed to get a trade in the film business.

Randy, being a sensible and logical guy, could see that every Karate jock in southern California was trying to be the next Bruce Lee, so Randy, being Polish *(did I mention Randy was Polish?)* zigged instead of zagged. He followed Steve's advice, and he's done quite well.

Randy has overseen some of the biggest blockbusters in film, going all the way back to "Top Gun" and "Speed" and everything in between all the way up to "Transformers." With Randy giving me his stamp of approval, Gary Hymes decided to hire me, sight unseen, and gave me one of the biggest breaks in my life.

Oh, I had dabbled in a couple of non-union films early on, made with World Light Heavyweight Kickboxing Champion Don "The Dragon" Wilson, who I knew from Cocoa Beach, Florida. Don and I had met somewhere around 1974 when we were both coming up through the ranks, fighting in Karate tournaments back in Florida.

Don had made his way out to California and started making films. When he had heard that I was in Los Angeles, he had his managers track me down, because he was determined to use real fighters in his combat scenes.

But as I said, these were non-union films, and at $150 for a fourteen-hour day, I was hardly making bank. So I go down and help Don out, doing some fight scenes on the rooftops in Venice, California for a few days, and it was more than fun, and I appreciated it, but as soon as it was done, I went back to my real life.

And as it turns out, I was 'Taft-Hartley' eligible for SAG membership—the Screen Actor's Guild—although I had never joined. All of a sudden *here I am*, on the phone with Brian Smrz—one of the best guy's in movies and Gary Hymes' right hand man at the time—setting up my flight reservations to go to Pittsburgh, Pennsylvania.

Now, sitting in first class to fly to Pittsburgh, across the aisle, one seat in front of me I see someone I recognize, one of America's greatest actors; Powers Boothe. Powers had starred in one of my favorite movies, "The Emerald Forest." And if that's not familiar, maybe you would know him from "24" or "Deadwood," or possibly the greatest western ever filmed: "Tombstone," with Kurt Russell and Val Kilmer.

Gary had Brian bring me in to do a big martial arts fight scene with Jean Claude Van Damme in his film "Sudden Death." As I said, they needed someone who was six feet tall, and was strong enough and had the stamina to put on a Pittsburgh Penguin mascot outfit and do seven days of well-choreographed fight sequences with Jean Claude, of which I found out was the equivalent of wearing seventy pounds of carpet, and being expected to do jump spinning back kicks.

But this was a job that had to be done, and it was such a great opportunity. At the time, Gary Hymes was one of the biggest stunt coordinators. With films like "Speed" and "Jurassic Park" under his belt, I couldn't ask for a bigger coordinator to display my skills.

I wasn't about to let him down. Midway through the first week, Gary approached me and asked me how I was with heights. Not having any idea of what was planned, of course I lied and said I was fine. Then I asked how high. He looked out of the corner of his eye, grinned and said, "Pretty high."

As it turns out, Gary was looking at me to double for Powers Boothe. Powers and I could be mistaken for brothers, but of course, he's better looking… With the fight sequence filmed and in the can, *here I am* at the Civic Arena, where the Pittsburgh Penguins play ice hockey.

I find myself in the crow's nest of the arena, over 200 feet above the ground, doubling for Powers, whose character is a Secret Service agent who's turned terrorist. I hear the roar of the crowd. I look down from the crow's nest and see an arena full of people. They are watching a mock game of hockey between the Pittsburgh Penguins and some of my fellow stuntmen. This game is supposed to simulate the final game in the Stanley Cup Finals.

I hear the thundering of a helicopter. I look up, and the roof of the arena has retracted open by one third and now the helicopter is hovering above me. It's dropping a 50-foot rope ladder down to me. For a moment I lose my focus. My life races in front of me, and I wonder how in the hell did this happen. *How in the hell did I get here?*

I snag the rope ladder, and *here I am* ready to step off like a trapeze artist, 200 feet above the ground. It's 37 degrees outside and raining ice, and I'm dressed as Powers Boothe's character. Any moment now I'll be stepping off the crow's nest platform and begin climbing the 50 foot rope ladder up to the relative safety of the helicopter, as the helicopter ascends to 300 feet above the city—a feat I'll have to repeat three more times before they can get the shot that they want. But I don't know this yet.

I'm thinking back to my earliest memories, and how they've prepared me for everything in my life, and everything I've gone through. How the beatings from my mother and fistfights with schoolyard kids had heightened my threshold for pain. How my stepfather's constant relocating and uprooting us prepared me to be on my own at such an early age, as well as giving me the ability to read new places and new situations. How it instilled in me the capability to read people quickly, and how it taught me to be fearless of being broke, because I was born broke, and if you know you're broke, that means you're still alive, that means you can still make something happen.

I'm thinking back to my Grandfather's teachings about being your own man. If your position cannot be swayed by material loss or gain, it makes people nervous because you are your own man. A dangerous man. That the beating I took from hoodlums would turn out to be one of the most positive things in my life. That one act of violence forced me to walk into a Karate school and embark upon a new path. *Man, what a journey it's been.* From starting my own Karate school, to serving as bodyguard to a US Senator, to rising to the top ten status in two different sports, and then traveling across the continent of North America, where I'd call Las Vegas, Nevada; Dallas, Texas; and later Los

Angeles, California home.

When you can look back with the gratification you can only get with self-pride, you find yourself happy for the friends that made it, and sad for the ones that didn't…

This much we know: Jorge flew under the radar down to Columbia in a small plane. It was rumored that on the way back he was shot down over the Islands by smugglers. The plane was stripped, and no one has heard from Jorge since.

Our friend Keith Pender was arrested and served jail time for drug charges, only to be let out and suffer a fatal heart attack that took his life while he was in the Bahamas.

Mark Herman, after spending almost two decades in prison for a murder he didn't commit, would finally be set free, and go on to live his life in Phoenix.

Carl Stone would go on to open another Karate school on the west coast of Florida, and the last I heard, he was doing fine.

My buddy Steve Shepherd would go on to retire from kickboxing after holding a handful of title belts in different weight divisions, only to become a successful entrepreneur in West Palm Beach.

Greg Garrett, a world champion power-lifter and pro baseball player, barely made it into his fifties then suddenly died of liver cancer.

My mother and I had started a friendship by the time I had moved to Las Vegas, only to be strengthened when she finally kicked alcoholism during the late 80s. I finally got to see what a warm and beautiful human being she truly was.

My number one cornerman in life, George McClease, would go on to run a successful air conditioning business in Lake Park Florida.

My brother from another mother, Clayton Walls—better known as Skip when we were kids—would go on to build a successful business and sell it for millions of dollars. Now he bounces between his resort properties, from his ranch in Texas, to his beachfront resort in Puerto Vallarta, and up to his 4700-foot townhouse in Big Sky Montana on Moonlight Basin.

And who knows what the future holds for me? In 1997 I was inducted into the Martial Arts Hall of Fame. And in case you haven't noticed how strange my life can be, after my introduction, I found myself speaking to well over 1000 people, at Universal Studios in Orlando, Florida, the very city I almost lost my life in, 25 years to the week.

Yes it's the second week in September, and my two closest friends,

George McClease and Skip (Clayton) Walls, have taken time out of their lives to travel to Orlando so they can attend the function. As I spoke to the crowd, it was surreal. With both of my Karate instructors on hand, Mark Herman and Carl Stone, you can't imagine the party afterwards.

But this next step in life will afford me the ability to travel the world. From racing motorcycles in Barcelona, Spain at Kenny Robert's Racing Ranch, to going on a safari in South Africa, and Diving with the great white sharks.

I can't help but be humbled by all the friends I've made along the way, and how many of them have helped me on my way. It was once said, you can't judge a man by the worth of his dollars, but you can judge him on the wealth of his friends, and boy, do I feel rich and blessed.

When I was a young man, from my early twenties onwards, people would often mistake my confidence for a cocky attitude. But when you've experienced, and lived through, some of the things that I have, you have two paths you can follow… And I'm not one to quit. The mark of the true champion is the one who can get up when he's been knocked down.

If you've tried your hardest and you haven't succeeded, you're not a loser; you've gained knowledge. So just get up and try again. My confidence is not based in ego; it's based in humility. From standing in septic tanks with human waste up to my scrotum, and knowing what the butt of a shotgun tastes like. Then teaching Karate for up to three classes a night with fifteen to twenty people in each class, with a smile like a jack-o'-lantern, only to be stopped in the first round in my own hometown—these are the things that will temper you and make you stronger if they don't kill you.

But my reminiscing thoughts are abruptly interrupted by Gary Hymes' bullhorn, and only now do I realize I'm shaking and shivering, partly because it's under 40 degrees and raining ice, and partly because of what I'm about to do.

Gary asks me if I'm ready. I give him the thumbs up and he begins the count.

So *here I am…*

3… 2… 1…

And *here I go!* **Action!**

Me, wearing
Muhammad
Ali's boxing
boots. 5th
Street Gym,
Miami, FL.

Me at Johnny Taco's Gym.
Las Vegas, NV.

"Beefcake for the ladies!",
my publicity body shot.
Los Angeles, CA 1979.

Me, publicity head shot.
Los Angeles, CA 1984.

The Angel I knew as Claire Wulf.

Me, Skip Walls and Ken Shot at "The Alamo". San Antonio, TX.

Me and Skip Walls, 'Bull riding.' San Antonio, TX.

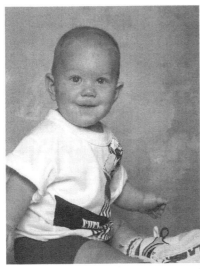

*Justin Jason Cartwright
(my son). Palmdale, CA
1989.*

*Dana and Justin Jason
Cartwright. Palmdale, CA
1989.*

Me and Bill Parent,
Granada Hills Karate,
CA 1988.

Teaching Karate to kids,
Granada Hills Karate Stu-
dio, CA 1989.

Southern California Ka-
rate League patch.

*p. 31 Sports Illustrated,
1980.*

*Special Olympics thank you
letter. Palm Beach County, FL.*

*Letter of thanks from the Fulfillment
Fund, re Maclaren Hall juvenile detention center. P.351. Los Angeles, CA.*

Yellow shirt, on the left is Frank Giardina, manager of Sash Nightclub. James G, Sherry, Skip, Barbara Giardina and me. Las Vegas, NV 1987.

George Mc-Clease and me on George's bass fishing boat. Lake Okeechobee, FL 1990.

George McClease, Greg Garrett and Skip Walls. North Palm Beach, FL 1989.

Me, Bobby Huey and Greg Garrett.
Sagebrush Cantina, Calabasas, CA.

Pete Steinfeld, Joey Gian (lower) Bobby Huey,
Greg Garrett and me. Sagebrush Cantina.

Clockwise from center – Skip, Jamie, Nigel,
Kenny (upside down), Jeff (at 12 o'clock)
Bobby and Scott. Tore up in Telluride. Tel-
luride, CO.

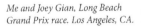

Me and Joey Gian, Long Beach
Grand Prix race. Los Angeles, CA.

Jeff Augustine. Sagebrush Cantina, Calabasas, CA.

Me and Skip Walls, Balloon Festival. Albuquerque, NM.

Keith with me (I'm wearing a mask and snorkel) – ready for diving. Cabo St Lucas.

Skip and me, hitching a ride.
Ensenada, Mexico.

Hombres at the border. Tijuana,
Mexico.

Lazing in the Kern River at McNal-
lys Fairview Lodge. From left: James G,
Pete Steinfeld, me, Andy Steinfeld, Dave
Blevins and Joey Gian. Kernville, CA.

Jumpin' off at the Kern River
with the crew. Kernville, CA.

Beach fun. Cabo St Lucas.

Jamie, Skip and Bobby - lost in Utah, en route to Telluride. UT.

*Me, Skip and Bobby –
"crashed and burned,"
on the road trip back
from Cabo St Lucas.
Baja Peninsular.*

*Clayton, Joey, me
(highest one, of
course) and Bill.
Park City, UT.*

*Bobby, Jeff, Skip and
Dave – 4th July road
trip – surrounded by
a protective aura of
angels. Somewhere
on the Baja Penin-
sular.*

Working through the fight sequence with "Sudden Death" star, Jean Claude Van Damme, Pittsburgh, PA.

In costume as Pittsburgh mascot, for "Sudden Death" movie. Pittsburgh, PA.

Mark Stefanich, me with one of the best guys in the movie business, Brian Smrz. Pittsburgh, PA.

Me with George Foreman, at a benefit dinner. Anaheim, CA.

Me in a classic boxing stance.

Letter of acceptance into the Martial Arts Hall of Fame.

At Bobby Huey's house, on the IntraCoastal. Jupiter, FL.

Me enjoying a pensive moment above the Kern River, on my Harley FXR. Kernville, CA.

For more photographs, visit Jeff's flickr gallery.

http://www.flickr.com/photos/here_i_am_by_jeff_podgurski/sets/

Thanks

I just want to express thanks to all the people who have helped me shape my life and career:

Mark Herman and Carl Stone—two of the best Karate instructors on the planet.
Six of the best black belts that walked the face of the planet —
Tommy Fafarco, Mark's first student who had all the crafty moves. (Karate is more than punches and kicks.)
Jimmy Stewart, the best drill sergeant in the martial arts world.
Rufus Burns, a quiet and genteel man whose talent rivaled his humility.
Steve Shepherd, what can you say? He was a five-time World Champion in five different weight divisions.
Alonso Hall, a quiet and decent man who was as fast as lightning.
And yours truly. I'm still here.

Oh, and thanks, Pop for the moral compass.

15755169R00215

Made in the USA
Middletown, DE
19 November 2014